LANGUAGE
DEVELOPMENT
Structure and
Function

LANGUAGE DEVELOPMENT

Structure and Function

SECOND EDITION

PHILIP S. DALE
University of Washington, Seattle

HOLT RINEHART AND WINSTON   New York   Chicago   San Francisco
Atlanta   Dallas   Montreal
Toronto   London   Sydney

Library of Congress Cataloging in Publication Data

Dale, Philip S.
    Language development.

    Includes bibliographies and index.
        1. Children—Language.   I.   Title.
P118.D3   1976   401   75–43640
ISBN 0–03–089705–X

Preface to the Second Edition

The five years since the completion of the first edition of this book have seen a continuing increase in interest in child language development, an increase that has led to some fundamental changes in our view of the process. Most important has been the accumulation of more data: evidence from more children, evidence from more languages, and evidence concerning more aspects of language. This research has been motivated by the search for broader and deeper generalizations, though in the short run the effect has been to make generalization harder: There is more diversity than we had thought. In the 1960s most child-language research focused on syntax. This was a natural response to the discovery of syntactic patterning in the very early language of children and to the revolutionary changes in linguistics stemming from the work of Noam Chomsky. The 1970s have restored something of a balance; work in phonological development and in semantic development proceeds at a high level in both quantity and quality. There is increasing interest in pragmatics and in the relation of language development to cognitive development. If something of the unity of the field has been lost, we have gained a richer appreciation of the abilities of the child.

The present revision reflects some of these changes. There is a more extensive discussion of semantic development, particularly the development of the word meanings, in Chapters 1 and 7. Early grammatical speech is viewed from the more semantic viewpoint first developed by Bloom and Schlesinger. Case grammar, an augmented form of transformational grammar, is described and examined as a possible model for early grammatical structure, and is contrasted with a more traditional transformational grammar model. The very special case of the sign language of the deaf provides an additional perspective on language development. The relationship of language development to the child's cognitive development, on the one hand, and the nature of the speech the child hears, on the other, is proposed as a fundamental theoretical problem for the study of language development. Although this book focuses almost entirely on language development in normal children, the implications of this research for developing tests of language development are significant, and merit a chapter.

I am grateful to Paul Ammon, Melissa Bowerman, Sidney Culbert, Rebecca Eilers, Dedre Gentner, Michael Maratsos, and D. K. Oller for their very helpful suggestions for various chapters. And my thanks to June Hull for her preparation of the manuscript.

P. S. D.

Contents

Introduction

Some sciences are based on the discovery of new and surprising facts. Nuclear physics began with the discovery that certain substances can fog photographic plates through opaque barriers, genetics with Mendel's discovery of regular patterns in the inheritance of pea characteristics. The study of language development is different. It is based on a very common, unsurprising fact: Children—most children—learn how to talk without any difficulty at all. In a sense, we are never going to discover any astonishing *new* facts; *this* is the fact that we are trying to explain. And the more we examine the process, the more astonishing it becomes.

The process of learning to talk has fascinated parents and other observers of children for centuries. In the reading at the end of this introduction, Herodotus, writing in the fifth century B.C.E., reports on some "research" carried out by the Egyptian king Psammetichus I sometime before 610 B.C.E. Although the methodology of this experiment is dubious both scientifically and ethically, the experiment itself illustrates the hold of this question and the belief that understanding the origin of language would illuminate the nature of man. Saint Augustine "recalled" his own acquisition of language (Book I of *The Confessions*); the nature of the acquisition and use of language were also at the heart of the great philosophic debate between rationalism and empiricism that took place in the seventeenth and eighteenth centuries (Chomsky 1966). But empirical studies of children acquiring language did not begin until the very end of the eighteenth century, when children and childhood came to be regarded as proper subjects for study. A long series of "baby biographies" focusing on language began with Dietrich Tiedemann's diary of infant behavior, which appeared in 1787 (Bar-Adon and Leopold 1971). Educators, philosophers, and others all began to observe carefully young children, usually their own. The most famous of these parent-biographers was Charles Darwin (1877). These diary studies still contain much valuable information. Excerpts from a number of them have been reprinted in Bar-Adon and Leopold (1971).

In recent years there has been an enormous increase in interest in this question. As Roger Brown, a pioneer in the field, has written:

> All over the world the first sentences of small children are being as pains-takingly taped, transcribed, and analyzed as if they were the last sayings of great sages. Which is a surprising fate for the likes of "That doggie," "No more milk," and "Hit ball" (Brown 1973:97).

We realize even more than before the magnitude of the child's accomplishment. And we realize that language development, because of its complexity, is a crucial case for the study of human development, that theories of development must succeed or fail on the basis of how well they explain this achievement.

Two fundamental insights underlie most recent research on language development. The first is the realization that the child does not merely speak a garbled version of the adult language around him, handicapped by limited attention, memory span, and other psychological deficits. Rather, he speaks his own language, with its own characteristic patterns. Thus it is appropriate to study a child as the speaker of an exotic language, to describe its structure by means of a *grammar*—that is, an explicit statement of the patterns, or rules, of the language—and to observe the sequence of changes in the child's language as he brings it into closer approximation to the surrounding adult language.

The second insight is that the child himself must act as a linguist: He is faced with a finite set of utterances, many of them ungrammatical (owing to slips of the tongue, false starts, memory lapses, and so on), from which he must extract the underlying rules in order to be able to use the language creatively for the remainder of his life. Therefore, it becomes fruitful to look for analogies between the child's performance on this task and the linguist's performance. Two striking analogies have been suggested. The first is that language learning, both for the child and for the linguist, is a matter of **hypothesis formation** and **hypothesis testing.** In other words, it is an active process. The child continually formulates hypotheses about underlying rules of the language that he hears and tests them by attempting to use them to understand speech and also to construct his own utterances. Such hypothesis formulation is shown most vividly in what appear to be grammatical mistakes, for example, a child's utterances of *comed* or *doed*. Because such utterances cannot be the result of imitation, their production demonstrates that the child has arrived at an hypothesis: Past tense forms are produced by adding *ed*.

A second analogy is even more far-reaching (as well as somewhat controversial). Although the languages of the world appear to be highly diverse on the surface, recent linguistic research has demonstrated remarkable similarities. And, in fact, whether consciously formulated or not, such similarities are in the mind of the linguist when he approaches a new language, and they guide his analysis. For example, in analyzing a new language a linguist knows that certain aspects of speech-sound production are likely to be important (where the tongue is, whether or not the passage to the nasal cavity is open, and so on); that there will be subjects and predicates; that it will be possible to ask questions, give commands, deny statements, and more. Similarly, the child may already "know" about certain universal aspects of language; this knowledge may be innate or at least present by the time the child approaches the task of language acquisition. Indeed, the assumption of such prior knowledge may offer an explanation for the presence of language universals in adult languages.

Linguistics thus plays a doubly important role in the study of child language; first, in the empirical study of the language of children and, second, in the task of constructing theoretical explanations of language acquisition. For this reason, Chapter 4 includes a brief introduction to linguistics.

In this book we are concerned almost entirely with language development in normal children. For some children, learning language is difficult or impossible. The most important value of research with normal children for clinicians and educators working with these children is the thorough description of the normal course (or courses) of language development. "Deviant" language development can only be defined with respect to normative descriptions. Any young child's language will be different from the language of adults; the diagnostician's job is to separate normal developmental differences from differences that signal an underlying difficulty in language acquisition.

On Studying Child Language

The best way to begin studying child language is to find a young child and listen. All the child's utterances for a given period of time should be recorded, in order that the sample (often called a *corpus*) may be analyzed for underlying patterns. But it is necessary to record more than just the words uttered; something of the context, verbal and nonverbal, must also be recorded. The complexity of child language can be seriously underestimated if the analysis is based only on the words and their combinations. For example, the utterance *baby blanket* contains two nouns, but the nature of their relationship may be clarified only by the setting. The utterance could be a possessive ('baby's blanket'), a subject-object construction ('baby is pulling the blanket'), or a locative ('baby is under the blanket'). An adequate description of the child's language must include the range of such relationships that the child is expressing, and often only the context may make a particular utterance clear.

In the next few chapters we describe some of the results of this approach to child language. But some of the serious methodological problems should be kept in mind. Viewing a child in exactly the way in which a linguist views the speaker of an unknown language is not fully possible.

A linguist has several techniques available to him. First, he can learn the language himself. Once he is a fluent speaker, he is better able to understand and analyze the language. This approach, of course, cannot be used with a child. It is not possible to unlearn all you know of your language. Furthermore, the child's language is changing too rapidly for an adult learner to keep up with him.

Once the linguist has acquired some knowledge of an unknown language, he can ask native speakers of the language questions such as *Does x mean the same thing as y?* or *Can I say x?* This is often called "appealing directly to the linguistic intuition of the speaker." It does not work so well with the typical two-year-old:

> INTERVIEWER: *Adam, which is right, "two shoes" or "two shoe"?*
> ADAM: *Pop goes the weasel* (Brown and Bellugi 1964:135).

For these reasons we are limited, for the most part, to observed speech. In addition, we know that the speech of adults does not reflect their knowledge of the language perfectly. There are mistakes, slips of the tongue, memory lapses, and the like. Presumably similar processes occur in children's speech also. Young children have a very restricted short-term memory capacity, which in turn probably constrains sentence production. "Unimportant" words —auxiliaries, prepositions, conjunctions, and so on—may simply be left out, though the child may be aware of their presence in adult speech and may understand some aspects of their meaning. More than simple memory span for distinct items is relevant here; often a child will expand a complete sentence of an adult into a longer but simpler one. There is a complex interaction between memory and linguistic structure. Because of this possibility, it is difficult to decide whether an observed difference between a child's speech and adult language is owing to different linguistic systems or to the child's difficulty in fully using his knowledge of the adult language.

Sampling problems are also difficult. Does the absence of an item from a child's speech mean that he cannot produce it or merely that in the given situation he has not found it necessary? One implication of this dilemma is that rather sizable corpora are necessary for analysis; samples of 50 or even 100 utterances, though widely used for certain purposes, are inadequate.

Even the production by a child of a construction identical to the adult form is not always easy to interpret. For a period of time, Adam, a boy studied by Roger Brown and his coworkers, often used the expression *just checking*. In adult grammar, the word *checking* is a combination of two elements, *check* and *-ing*. The *-ing* ending may be added to almost any verb. However, Adam never used *-ing* except in the compound *checking*, and it would be entirely unjustified to claim that he had acquired the *-ing* ending. This particular instance is not difficult to interpret: Adam undoubtedly picked up *checking* (and probably the entire phrase *just checking*) from his parents as a single unit, through imitation. But how often must a child use a morpheme or construction, and in how many different contexts, before it is safe to assume that he has acquired a new rule? The problem is aggravated by the fact that we have only a modest amount of data to work with. We cannot return for more data as required, as the linguist does when analyzing an unknown language, because a child's language is constantly changing, often with surprising rapidity.

Because our major source of data is the child's own productions, we often do not know what a word or grammatical construction *means* to the child when he uses it. That words mean different things to children from what they mean to adults is not surprising to anyone who has had much conversation with a young child. But the point is equally valid for constructions which express relationships between objects or events. For example, the conjunction *because* is often used by children in a complex sentence with a meaning of 'Event-1 and then Event-2,' rather than 'Event-2 caused Event-1': *I fell off the bicycle because I hurt my knee.* A related problem concerns the meaning the child assigns to someone else's use of a word or construction, that is, his comprehension. There is a very general belief that children comprehend more than they can produce at any point in development. This issue will be discussed further in Chapter 5. But clearly, if the child's knowledge of the language extends beyond the forms he actually produces, we must include this knowledge in our description of his language. But we should also ask whether the child really understands a sentence or is simply reacting to a few salient words. If a parent at home says *Would you like some ice cream?* the child may walk, or run, to the refrigerator that contains the ice cream. And a proud parent may point to the child's understanding. But the child might have done the same thing if the parent had said *I don't want any ice cream, There isn't any ice cream in the refrigerator,* or even *Colorless green ice cream sleeps furiously.* "Ice cream" is, of course, the salient phrase. In natural settings we do not produce such sentences to test the child's comprehension, but there are some obvious experiments that can be done. This problem also suggests that such experiments may play a more important role in the study of children's language than they do for that of adults.

I. THE NATURAL LANGUAGE OF MAN*

The Egyptians before the reign of Psammetichus used to think that of all races in the world they were the most ancient; Psammetichus, however, when he came to the throne, took it into his head to settle this question of priority, and ever since his time the Egyptians have believed that the Phrygians surpass them in antiquity and that they themselves come second. Psammetichus, finding that mere inquiry failed to reveal which was the original race of mankind, devised an ingenious method of determining the matter. He took at random, from an ordinary family, two newly born infants and gave them to a shepherd to be brought up among his flocks, under strict orders that no one should utter a word in their presence. They were to be kept by themselves in a lonely cottage, and the shepherd was to bring in goats from time to time, to see that the babies had enough milk to drink, and to look after them in any other way that was necessary. All these arrangements were made by Psammetichus because he wished to find out what word the children would first utter, once they had grown out of their meaningless baby-talk. The plan succeeded; two years later the shepherd, who during that time had done everything he had been told to do, happened one day to open the door of the cottage and go in, when both children running up to him with hands outstretched, pronounced the word "becos." The first time this occurred the shepherd made no mention of it; but later, when he found that every time he visited the children to attend to their needs the same word was constantly repeated by them, he informed his master. Psammetichus ordered the children to be brought to him, and when he himself heard them say "becos" he determined to find out to what language the word belonged. His inquiries revealed that it was the Phrygian word for "bread," and in consideration of this the Egyptians yielded their claims and admitted the superior antiquity of the Phrygians.

---

* From *Herodotus, The Histories*, trans. by Aubrey de Sélincourt (Penguin Classics), pp. 102–103. Copyright © the Estate of Aubrey de Sélincourt, 1954. (By permission of Penguin Books Ltd.)

1

The First Words

Sometime around a child's first birthday, his first truly linguistic utterances, the first words, appear. Just when the child achieves this milestone is not easy to determine. It is an event so eagerly anticipated by parents that they often read meaning into the child's babbling. It is difficult to set up firm criteria for true linguistic use of a word, but some that have been proposed are: evidence of understanding (the least stringent criterion), consistent and spontaneous use (not just imitation of adult speech), and occasionally the more stringent requirement that the word be a word of the adult language. Depending on the criteria established, different ages will be noted for the appearance of the first word, but the range ten to thirteen months includes most of the observations recorded (McCarthy 1954). Nelson (1973) has suggested that the age at which the vocabulary reaches ten words is a more stable indicator of true language development; in her sample this occurred at a mean age of fifteen months. For the next few months, language occurs, in Bloom's phrase, "one word at a time" (Bloom 1973).

The first words are distinctive in at least three respects: their pronunciations, or phonetic forms; their meanings; and the ways in which they are used. Phonetically they are quite regular. Typically they consist of one or two syllables, each syllable most often of the form consonant-vowel. Consonant clusters (the *st* of *stop*) and diphthongs (for example, the word *you*) are almost never observed. The consonants are especially likely to be drawn from the set of sounds produced near the front of the mouth (p, b, d, t, m, and n); among the vowels, those found in *stop* and *meet* are very much predominant. If the word is an approximation to an adult word, certain sounds may be changed to make them similar to other sounds, for example, "gog" for *dog* and "nam" for *lamb* (the *l* is replaced by a nasal, like *m*, but one that is still produced at the same point in the mouth as *l*). A very common extreme version of this process is reduplication, for example, "baba" for *bottle*, in which one syllable simply duplicates another. The great restriction on the elements used for the first words contrasts with the immediately preceding stage of babbling, in which a wide range of sounds may be observed. The nature of the transition from babbling to the first words and the later development of the pronunciation of words will be discussed in Chapter 8. In the remainder of this chapter we shall refer to children's productions by the corresponding adult forms.

The First Words and Their Meanings

Nelson (1973) studied the first fifty words acquired by eighteen children. Most children acquire at least fifty words before beginning to put two or more words together. She found considerable uniformity in these early vocabularies. Using a six-part classification, she found that the most common category (51 percent) was that of general nominals: *ball, doggie, snow,* and so on. Next most common (14 percent) was the category of specific nominals: *mommy,* pet names, and the like. Nearly as common was the category of action words, describing or demanding actions: *give, byebye, up.* Less common (9 percent) were modifiers: *red, dirty, outside, mine,* and so on. Personal-social words, such as *no, yes,* and *please,* made up 8 percent of the vocabularies. Function words, such as *what* and *for* made up only 4 percent of the vocabularies. It should be noted that Nelson's figures reflect the number of terms in each category, not necessarily the frequency of use of those terms. Probably some terms, such as action terms, are used over and over again, whereas some of the nominals are more specialized. Clearly these early vocabularies are highly selective. The important individuals in the child's life and certain kinds of objects are particularly likely to be incorporated in the linguistic system. Among the general nominal words, the most common are *juice, milk, cookie, dog, cat, shoes, ball,* and *car.* There is nothing very surprising about the presence of food, clothing, animal, toy, and vehicle names here.

As Nelson points out, it is interesting to look at the omissions from this list, as well as the inclusions. Although *shoes* and *socks* are common, *pants, sweaters, mittens,* and *diapers* are missing. The words learned are the names of articles that the child can act on easily. Among the words for furniture, words for tables, stoves, televisions, or windows did not occur, but *clock, blanket,* and *key* were reasonably common. Again, a crucial factor seems to be the possibility that the child can act on the object. Large objects that are simply "there"—trees, sofas, parks—are not named. The world of the child is a small one. Change is important; objects that move and change themselves—cars, clocks, and animals—are likely to be named. But change induced by the child is most important of all.

So far, we have been talking as if a given word meant the same thing for the child as for an adult. This is far from the truth. Words do not mean the same things to children. Discovery of the meaning of a word for a child is exceptionally difficult, and it is not surprising that most of the information available comes from careful observation by linguists and psychologists of their own children, rather than from carefully controlled experimental studies.

The words *mama* and *papa* (or their equivalents) are often among the very first words to be acquired. How many parents have been chagrined when their year-old child cheerfully called every adult male *daddy*! Although *mama* is often the first word, it is not unusual for it to follow *papa* or *daddy.* Furthermore, the distinction between the two parental names may not be based on sex (or physical appearance). Jakobson (1962; reprinted in Bar-Adon and Leopold 1971) discusses one division of meaning in which *papa* refers to a parent who is present, whereas *mama* is used to request fulfillment of a need or to request the presence of a parent who can fulfill the need. Jakobson quotes Grégoire's observation: "Edm. appeared to call back his mother, absent for the day, by saying 'mam-am-am'; but it is 'papa' which he declared when he saw her return. . . . Edm. saw me prepare a slice of bread for him; he said 'mama,' and not 'papa.' "[1] Other divisions of meaning also occur.

Eve Clark has carefully reviewed a large number of diary studies that offer evidence on the meanings of the first words. A phenomenon that is widespread in every language is that of overextension of the use of a word to refer to a broader category than is appropriate in the corresponding adult language. For example, the word *ball* may be used for round stones, radishes, and other round objects. As the example indicates, the basis of the overextension often appears to be shape, or perhaps size combined with shape: Small, round objects are often grouped together. Clark calls attention to the large number of overextensions that are based on static perceptual attributes or movement and has classified them in six categories. Examples are shown in Table 1.1. Overextension of concrete nouns appears to be most common between the ages of thirteen months (1;1) and thirty months (2;6). Curiously, overextensions based on color are almost nonexistent. In addition, young children seem to be aware very early of the special status of proper names, in that they are hardly ever overextended

[1] Translated from the French by the author.

TABLE 1.1   Some Perceptually Based Overextensions

Source and Language	Lexical Item	First Referent	Extensions in order of Occurrence
Shape			
Lewis (1951) English	tee (from name of cat)	cat	dogs; cows and sheep; horse
Pavlovitch (1920) French	bébé	reflection of self in mirror	photograph of self; all photographs; all pictures; all books with pictures; all books
Imedadze (1960) Russian	buti	ball	toy; radish; stone spheres at park entrance
Size			
Moore (1896) English	fly	fly	specks of dirt; dust; all small insects; his own toes; crumbs of bread; a toad
Taine (1877) French	bebe	baby	other babies; all small statues; figures in small pictures and prints
Sound			
Shvachkin (1948) Russian	dany	sound of bell	clock; telephone; doorbells
Leopold (1949) German-English	sch	noise of train	music; noise of movement; wheels; balls
Movement			
Moore (1896) English	bird	sparrows	cows and dogs; cats; any animal moving
Taste			
Leopold (1949) English	candy	candy	cherries; anything sweet
Texture			
Shvachkin (1948) Russian	kiki	cat	cotton; any soft material
Idelberger (1903) German	bow-wow	dog	toy dog; fur piece with animal head; fur piece without head

SOURCE: Adapted from E. V. Clark, What's in a word? On the child's acquisition of semantics in his first language. In T. E. Moore (Ed.), *Cognitive development and the acquisition of language.* New York: Academic Press, 1973.

to other individuals, with the possible exception of *mommy* and *daddy* very early in development. There is some evidence that the end of this period (which is well beyond the stage of one-word utterances) coincides with a period of rapid vocabulary growth, sparked by the child's intensive questions of the *What's that?* variety. This shift may reflect the acquisition by the child of the basic "mental building blocks" for the meanings of words of this type and thus the ability to learn new meanings very efficiently. What the nature of the basic "mental building blocks" for meaning may be will be considered in Chapter 7.

Static perceptual attributes, like size and shape, are not the only bases for early word meanings. As we have seen in describing the nature of early vocabularies, aspects of change and action are also potent. The word *allgone* may refer to people leaving, to the opening and closing of doors, or to any disappearance from sight. Some of Clark's examples of shape- or size-based overextension might be interpreted as action-based: Small round objects are to play with in characteristic ways. Other words have meanings that are more abstract than can be captured in perceptual or action terms. For example, as Bloom (in press) points out, a child may call for a second cookie by saying *more* after eating the first one, and he may also say *more* when he sees a second horse go by. No particular event or object is common to these uses of *more*; only the repetition, either desired or actual. The meaning of *more* is inherently relational and is independent of particular perceptions or actions. The current conflict over the relative importance of *static perceptual attributes* (argued by Clark 1973) and *function* (Nelson 1973) in defining early words is one which can only be resolved by additional evidence on the actual meanings of words as used by young children. It is certainly possible that individual children vary in their reliance on these two aspects of meaning.

Eventually the child must narrow the meanings of overextended terms. There are very few fairly complete observations of the ways in which particular words change their meanings after the initial overextensions. But the few examples we have suggest that an important role is played by the acquisition of new words that take over parts of the meanings. For example, Pavlovitch (1920; cited in Clark 1973) describes the later development of the meaning of *bébé* (see Table 1.1). The first step was the acquisition of *deda* ('grandfather'), which was used for all photographs. The word *bébé* still referred to a reflection in a mirror, photographs of self, pictures, and books with pictures. Next the word *kata* ('card') was acquired and used for pictures of landscapes. Other pictures were still referred to as *bébé*. Then the word *kiga* ('book') was acquired and used for books. Finally, the word *slika* ('reflection') was used for reflections in a mirror, and the world *duda* (from 'Douchau,' the child's name) was used for photographs of self. By that time, *bébé* was restricted to the self and to small children in pictures.

An interesting question, which cannot be resolved with the present evidence, is whether or not a new word is used, however briefly, for correct instances before it is overextended. That is, does the overextension represent an initial misunderstanding or a developmental phenomenon that appears after the initial acquisition? In the example of *bébé* just discussed the new words that restricted the meaning of the overextended form appear to have been acquired with approximately their correct meanings. But we might expect to see that when the word *horse* is acquired, restricting the meaning of *dog* (which initially included all four-legged animals), *horse* might refer to cows as well, on the basis of size. These questions can be answered only through very detailed and complete observations of the use of words in the first few days or weeks (Clark 1973). Overextension is not the only way in which child meaning differs from adult meaning. The opposite process, overrestriction, in which the word is used for a narrower range of objects or events, also occurs.

Overextensions, in which a label is used for something inappropriate (*bird* for cow moving) are more striking, and hence more likely to be recorded, than overrestrictions, in which a label is not applied where it would be appropriate (failing to label certain books as *book*). A systematic sampling of children's vocabularies, paying careful attention to both overextension and overrestriction, is necessary to evaluate the relative frequency of these two types of errors. In still other cases, child meanings and adult meanings overlap, with both overextension and overrestriction occurring. For example, my daughter (age 2;0) used *muffin* to refer to both blueberries and blueberry muffins, but not other muffins or cupcakes. The term is used both more broadly and more narrowly than in the adult sense.

We do not know what factors are necessary for a word to be acquired or for its meaning to be changed. For example, how many instances are necessary? Experiments that introduce new words to the child in controlled fashion may answer some of these questions. Vincent-Smith, Bricker, and Bricker (1974), working with somewhat older children (twenty to thirty-one months), found that, when a new object, such as a paddle, was presented along with a familiar object, such as a truck, and the child was asked to "take the paddle," fewer than five trials were necessary for the child to learn the new word receptively. Although this experimental setting was much more structured than the child's everyday environment, situations like this undoubtedly do occur. Nelson and Bonvillian (1973) have also attempted to introduce new words to young children (at eighteen months) in a controlled, but somewhat more natural, fashion. Within a dozen or so presentations, some of their subjects had acquired new words (like *canteen* and *sifter*) and were correctly generalizing these words to new instances of the objects. They also found considerable variation from child to child in the rate of acquisition and the kinds of generalization that occurred.

Words or Sentences?

Children use their first words in several ways. They are seldom used simply as names, though this does occur when the object named evokes strong feelings, for example when the child sees a familiar ball and says *ball!* More typical is the child who sees his father's slippers and says *daddy*. He is making a comment about the slippers, that they are daddy's. Often the first words are used to comment on objects or events in the environment. A child may respond to some food by saying *hot*.

Words are especially likely to occur at transition points in the child's activity, for example, when he first notices something new in the environment. In the film *Early Words*,[2] Mathew sees an airplane, points to it, and says *airplane*; he tracks the plane across the sky visually, pointing, and when it disappears he says *byebye*. This behavior again points up the importance of change in the child's early word usage.

Many of the child's expressions at this stage concern location and especially changes of location. For example, when an object is discovered at a certain location or moves to a new location, a comment such as *down* may result.

The first words are used for more than description. Often the child will command, using a word as an imperative, for example, *open* meaning 'open the jar.' Or the child may command the self, saying *blow* as she blows her nose. It is difficult to tell with these latter commands if the utterance is a self-imperative or a running description of what is going on, which children also produce. Commands often arise when the child has begun some activity or attempted to reach some goal but has run into an obstacle: needing to have a jar opened or a piece of candy moved nearer. Such commands are usually accompanied by appropriate gestures. Learning to ask for food without reaching across the table takes a long time.

Negatives are also common. The child may reject a proffered object or an attempted action (like face washing) by an adult. Not only the simple negative *no* is used but also more complex kinds of negation. A child may reject a parent's attempt to help in a task by saying *self* and pushing the adult away (presumably derived from the adult's use of the phrase "Want to do it yourself?")

In all these ways, the first words seem to be more than single words. They appear to be attempts to express complex ideas, ideas that would be expressed in sentences by an adult. The term "holophrastic speech" is often used to capture this idea of "words that are sentences." It is very difficult

---

[2] J. Bruner, A. May and P. Greenfield. *Early words: Action and the structure of language.* New York: Wiley, 1973.

to be more precise about this notion, however. A strong version of the words-as-sentences hypothesis would claim that the child has something like a full sentence in mind but can emit only one word because of limitations on attention and memory. One argument for such an hypothesis is based on the ability of children to understand simple sentences at this stage, though better evidence on the comprehension skills of children at this level is needed. If the hypothesis were valid, however, it would change our interpretation of the onset of multiword sentences. That development would then represent a maturational development in attention and memory, rather than a basically linguistic development. McNeill (1970) discusses a version of this hypothesis.

Another hypothesis is that children have relatively complete ideas in mind, ideas that would require full sentences, but lack the linguistic expertise to translate these ideas into sentences. A child may understand the meanings expressed by the word *give*, the fact that it involves a relationship among three entities—the person giving, the recipient, and the object given—yet he may express only one of them in any utterance. But a different selection may be made on different occasions. Antinucci and Parisi (1973) and Ingram (1971) discuss versions of this hypothesis.

Another possibility is that children fail to produce more than one word at a time because they fail to realize that one word alone does not convey accurately their meaning to the listener. We shall return to this possibility in the next chapter.

Bloom (1973) argues for a more skeptical interpretation of one-word utterances. She believes that there is no evidence that the child really understands anything about syntax:

> Although she [Allison Bloom] evidently knew something about the meanings of words, that is, something about lexical meaning, there was no evidence that she knew about the meaning relations between words or the possible changes in meaning that were possible for words in relation to one another, that is, grammatical meaning. (Bloom, in press).

Our problem in evaluating these hypotheses is that we are attempting to "read the mind" of the child, who is providing us with only the barest of clues, a single word. Nevertheless, it is an important question because it is relevant to understanding the relationship between the child's ideas and his language and also to understanding the transition to multiword utterances.

Some Differences among Children

In general the similarities among children in their pattern of language development are quite striking. As we shall see later, children acquiring English (Chapter 2) and even other languages (Chapter 3) show many of the same processes at work. Nevertheless, we should not ignore the existence of differences among children. Different children may use somewhat different processes: not just differences in rate, which are common and well established, but also differences in the nature of early language. Not much attention has been paid to this question in recent years, although thirty or forty years ago more attention was paid to differences than to similarities—which says something about the social and scientific *Zeitgeist*. To identify significant differences will require looking at more children than have been observed in most recent studies. Nelson's study (1973) revealed one interesting difference at the early one-word stage. Although all children showed a large proportion of general nominal words in their early vocabularies and a smaller proportion of personal-social words, the balance between the two types varied. Nelson divided her sample into two groups: In the first group, general nominals made up 62 percent and personal-social words 5 percent of the vocabularies; in the second group, general nominals made up 38 percent and personal-social words 11 percent. To a certain extent, children in the first group (referential, or R) were talking more about things, whereas children in the second group (expressive, or E) were talking about self and other people. It is possible to make certain predictions on the basis of the child's category. For example, although there was no difference in the ages at which the first fifty words were acquired, the R group then learned words more rapidly and consequently had larger vocabularies at two years (though not at two and a half years). In addition, there was a small but significant difference in favor of the R group in the age at which two-word utterances appeared.

Nelson related each child's classification to birth order and education of the parents. Although neither variable predicted the age at which the first fifty words were acquired, they did predict something of the nature of those fifty words (see Table 1.2). Notice that *all* of the first-born children of parents with high educational achievement fell in the R group. As Nelson points out, this group is the one most often studied; though the numbers

TABLE 1.2   Distribution of Groups by Birth Order and Education of Parents

Birth Order	Education	Referential	Expressive
first	high	5	0
later	high	2	2
first	low	3	3
later	low	0	3
		10	8

SOURCE: K. Nelson, Pre-syntactic strategies for learning to talk. Paper delivered to the Society for Research in Child Development, Minneapolis, March 1971.

are small, they suggest that "characteristics thought to be general—even universal—may be confined to a group that differs . . . from other groups within the general population" (Nelson 1973:61).

To examine the adult-child interaction directly, Nelson watched the mothers as they showed their children some familiar and some unfamiliar toys and allowed them to become familiar with the latter. She found that though mothers of children in the R group did not name objects significantly more frequently than did mothers of children in the E group, they did talk *about* the objects more. Conversely, mothers of children in the E group talked more about their children. The ratio of object-centered to child-centered remarks was 1.33 for the R group, .93 for the E group. This difference was observed when the children were eleven to fifteen months of age, that is, several months before differences among the children were determined.

It is important to realize that the differences here are not enormous; all the children acquired both general nominal and personal-social words, and all the mothers talked about both objects and their children. The differences are statistical, and their significance for later development is unclear. Nevertheless, this paradigm is valuable for studying language development.

The End of the One-Word Stage

Often a transitional stage occurs between that of "one word at a time" and that of true multiword utterances. Sequences of two or three words are produced but with distinct intonation contours, that is, with pauses between them. Bloom's daughter Allison (Bloom 1973) said *door, open* as she passed a door being opened, *daddy, door* when daddy came home, and both *daddy, car* and *car, daddy* when daddy left to take the car. As the examples demonstrate, there are no constraints on the order of combination of words. This contrasts with the next stage of development and, along with the distinct intonation contours, provides the justification for not viewing these sequences as single sentences.

Summary

From the very beginning of language development, a process of selection is at work. From the enormous number of words encountered, the child focuses his linguistic attention on a subset, guided by factors that are only partially understood, though such features as size, shape, change, and the possibility of self-induced change play an important role. One major question is whether the selection of words to be acquired and the selection of aspects of their meaning to be used at first are governed entirely by conceptual factors broader than language or whether specifically linguistic factors play a role. Another major question concerns the relationship between these early one word utterances and the multiword sentences that the child is hearing and that he will himself be producing in a few months. Are one-word utterances to be viewed as words or as sentences?

The challenge of studying the first words is that this stage of language development exemplifies best the dilemma of psycholinguist and parent alike: trying to understand what a person means on the basis of what he has said.

further reading

Bloom, L. *One word at a time*. The Hague: Mouton, 1973.

Clark, E. What's in a word? On the child's acquisition of semantics in his first language. In T. E. Moore (Ed.), *Cognitive development and the acquisition of language*. New York: Academic Press, 1973.

Nelson, K. E., and J. D. Bonvillian. Concepts and words in the 18-month-old: Acquiring concept names under controlled conditions. *Cognition*, 1973, **2**, 435–450.

The Course of
Syntactic Development: I

From One Word to Two

Around eighteen or twenty months of age children begin to put words together. In the sense that language is essentially a systematic means for expressing and understanding an unlimited number of ideas, this point is the true beginning of language. Although child language at this stage is simple, it is particularly interesting because it reflects the child's initial organizing strategies. And, as we shall see, it is not an easy stage to understand.

Age is not a good indicator of language development. Children vary greatly in their rates of development. Just why this is so—what variables are correlated with rate—is not at all understood, but we shall return to the question in the last chapter of this book. However, many regularities in development reveal themselves when children are compared on the basis of a better index of development. Mean length of utterance (MLU) is often used for this purpose. Although MLU has often been based on the number of words, in recent work the number of meaningful elements has been found more useful. These meaningful elements may be words, such as *see*, but they are often smaller than words. The word *cats*, for example, consists of two such elements, *cat* and the plural indicator *s*. Although the plural cannot stand by itself, it is an independent unit in that it can combine with many other words. These smallest meaningful elements, such as *cat* and *s*, are called **morphemes.** MLU is defined as the average length of the child's utterance in morphemes. It is important to realize, though, that the length of a particular sentence is not the same as the sentence's complexity. Complexity is not easy to define (Chapter 4 will consider some of the issues), but it should be clear that *Can't he do that again?*, which involves question-formation, pronominalization, and the use of *do* to refer back to a previously mentioned verb, is more complex than *I want a big red apple*, a declarative, subject-verb-object sentence of the same length. A child might be able to produce or imitate the former but not the latter sentence. Empirically, however, as children's MLU increases, their language includes more complex constructions. Table 2.1 presents some general rules for calculating MLU.

TABLE 2.1 Rules for Calculating Mean Length of Utterance (MLU)

The following rules are reasonable for MLU up to about 4.0; by this time many of the assumptions underlying the rules are no longer valid.

1. Start with the second page of the transcription unless that page involves a recitation of some kind. In this latter case start with the first recitation-free stretch. Count the first 100 utterances satisfying the following rules. (A 50-utterance sample may be used for preliminary estimate.)
2. Only fully transcribed utterances are used. Portions of utterances, entered in parentheses to indicate doubtful transcription, are used.
3. Include all exact utterance repetitions (marked with a plus sign in records). Stuttering is marked as repeated efforts at a single word; count the word once in the most complete form produced. In the few instances in which a word is produced for emphasis or the like ("no, no, no") count each occurrence.
4. Do not count such fillers as "um" and "oh," but do count "no," "yeah," and "hi."
5. All compound words (two or more free morphemes), proper names, and ritualized reduplications count as single morphemes. Examples: "birthday," "rackety-boom," "choo-choo," "quack-quack," "night-night," "pocketbook," "see-saw."
6. Count as one morpheme all irregular pasts of the verb ("got," "did," "want," "saw"). Justification is that there is no evidence that the child relates these to present forms.
7. Count as one morpheme all diminutives ("doggie," "mommy") because these children at least do not seem to use the suffix productively. Dimunitives are the standard forms used by the child.
8. Count as separate morphemes all auxiliaries ("is," "have," "will," "can," "must," "would"). Also all catenatives: "gonna," "wanna," "hafta." The latter are counted as single morphemes rather than as "going to" or "want to" because the evidence is that they function so for children. Count as separate morphemes all inflections, for example, possessive "s," plural "s," third person singular "s," regular past tense "d," progressive "ing."

SOURCE: Adapted from Table 7 of R. Brown, *A first language: The early stages.* Cambridge, Mass.: Harvard University Press, 1973, p. 54. © 1973 by the President and Fellows of Harvard College.

The rules are not always straightforward in application; both the division of conversation into utterances and the division of utterances into morphemes can be difficult (Crystal 1974). As a result, calculated MLU for a sample should be thought of as an estimate, which may be off by .10 or more in either direction (see Chapter 11 for other considerations).

Brown has proposed the term "stage I" for the period beginning with the emergence of the first multiword utterances and continuing until MLU reaches 2.0. Stages II, III, IV, and V are defined by increments of .5 to the MLU. It should be kept in mind that there is a great deal of variation in length of utterance at any point. A child with MLU of 2.0 may produce utterances from one to six morphemes in length. Nevertheless, children of comparable MLU are generally as similar in language as is possible to find.

Stage I Speech

In this chapter we shall look at the ways in which children combine morphemes in the first two stages, that is, during early syntactic development. A crucial question is how best to describe this simple language. It is important to understand the role of these possible linguistic descriptions of child language. They are not explanations; rather, they are the data to be explained by theories of language development.

Several descriptions have been proposed for early child language. All of them rest on two basic observations about child language (although they vary in relative weight). First, child language is simpler than adult language, simpler in a regular way; some kinds of words are present (typically nouns, verbs, and adjectives and the like), whereas others are generally missing (articles, conjunctions, prepositions, and endings such as the plural). (Because endings are not yet present, most words consist of a single morpheme. An MLU computed on the basis of words will be nearly identical to an MLU based on morphemes during stage I. In later stages the two measures will increasingly diverge.) Second is the fact that early child language is genuinely creative; not only are many child utterances not identical to adult utterances the child may have heard, but they are also not even simplifications. A child who watches a door being closed and says *allgone outside* has constructed a novel utterance.

Telegraphic Speech

One characterization of early child language is the term **telegraphic speech.** Children's sentences generally omit just those words—prepositions, auxiliary verbs, articles, and so on—that we leave out of telegrams, for which the cost is figured by the word. In Reading 2.1 Roger Brown and

Ursula Bellugi discuss the telegraphic nature of child language and consider its origin. The term describes children's imitations, as well as their spontaneous speech. A two-year-old, asked to say *I can see the truck*, is likely to say *I see truck*. The concept of telegraphic speech emphasizes the first of the two properties, the simplicity of child speech. The creativity is presumably the result of the child's using a system that is similar to the creative system of the adult, except for the omission of certain elements. Nevertheless, this concept is not a very satisfactory one, as it is mainly negative; it focuses on what is missing from child language.

Pivot Grammars

During the decade of the 1960s, **pivot-open grammars** were widely used by researchers. They are based on the observation that children's language does have its own structure; it is not just adult language with things missing. As we shall see, pivot-open grammars (or simply pivot grammars) are also ultimately inadequate, but they merit examination, both because they do capture certain important aspects of child language and because their rejection is a good example of how new evidence can lead to changes in theory.

Certain words in the child's vocabulary in stage I are used especially heavily and in very specific ways, whereas other words are used less frequently and more flexibly. These two classes can be labeled in various ways (Braine 1963; McNeill 1970; Slobin 1968) but most commonly are called the "pivot class" and the "open class." The pivot class is small, and each word in it is used with many different words from the much larger open class. For example, a child might say *bandage on, blanket on, fix on*, and other similar utterances. For this child, *on* is a pivot word. It is always used in the second position, and many other words can occur with it. Or a child might say *allgone shoe, allgone lettuce, allgone outside,* and others. Here *allgone* is a pivot that always occurs in the first position. A pivot word may be the first or the second element in two-word utterances, but *each pivot word has its own fixed position.*

The pivot class is generally small and contains words of high frequency in the child's speech. The words are called "pivots" because the child seems to be attaching other words to them. Membership of the pivot class expands slowly; only a few new words enter it each month. In contrast, the open class is large and contains all the words in the child's vocabulary that are not in the pivot class. Most early growth in vocabulary occurs in the open class. Words from the open class can combine with either type of pivot word or with one another. All the open-class words can occur as single-word utterances, but pivot words seldom, if ever, do (McNeill 1970).

We can summarize these observations by saying that two-word utterances are formed in the following patterns:

1. $P_1 + O$ $\Bigg\}$ (different pivots are used in first and second position)
2. $O + P_2$
3. $O + O$

The important aspect of these patterns is their generality. They provide productive means for combining words, and they capture the creativity of early child speech. Some examples from Braine (1963) are *allgone sticky*, said after washing hands; *more page*, a request to continue reading; and *allgone outside*, after the door was closed. It is highly unlikely that the child had ever heard sentences quite like these three. They must represent his attempts to express himself in his own way, through his own linguistic system.

Semantic Relationships

Pivot grammars have been extensively used to describe the early language of children acquiring English and also children acquiring other languages. Nevertheless, they are inadequate. There are two serious difficulties, each revealing something about the ways in which new evidence can change interpretations. First, the speech of some (perhaps most) children cannot be described accurately by a pivot grammar (Bowerman 1973), and, second, even when such a grammar is appropriate, it fails to capture the richness of the linguistic system (Bloom 1970).

The core of the pivot grammar is the pivot class. Pivot words are defined as

a. Occurring in fixed positions
b. Never occurring alone
c. Never occurring with other pivot words
d. Able to combine with all open words.

In fact, as Bowerman (1973) has shown, children may have words that satisfy one or two of these criteria but hardly ever all of them. *No* often occurs in first position in many two-word utterances (a and d), but it also occurs alone (violating b). Christy Bowerman (Bowerman personal communication) produced many *name + byebye* combinations but also *byebye again* and *byebye cat* (violating a). She produced a number of *name + off* combinations but also *awant off; awant* ('I want') was perhaps the best example of a pivot word in her language (violating c). Many more counterexamples have been obtained as more children have been studied. In short, the pivot grammar is too restrictive; children's language is hardly ever as simple as that. Thus, the accumulation of evidence from more children has weighed against pivot grammars.

Even when a pivot grammar does describe child language, it says very little about the relation among the words in the sentence. The meaning of any sentence is a function not only of the meanings of the words, but also of their relationship. *John loves Mary* does not mean the same thing as *Mary loves John.* A description of child language should indicate something of how word combinations express meanings. Bloom (1970) and Schlesinger (1971) first proposed describing sentences not only in terms of word classes and their combinations but also in terms of the functions that the words serve in the sentences. Here the context of the child's utterance is invaluable. If we look only at the words and their order (as pivot grammars do), we are using a restricted kind of evidence.

Bloom (1970) kept very complete records of the context of each utterance and was able in many cases to formulate a more precise hypothesis about the meaning intended. One of the children she studied, Kathryn, provided a particularly striking example of the value of context. Kathryn said *mommy sock* twice in one day, once when she picked up her mother's sock and again when her mother put Kathryn's own sock on her. Clearly the relationship between *mommy* and *sock* differs in these two utterances; in the first, *mommy* is a **possessive** modifier of sock, whereas in the second, *mommy* is the **agent** of the sentence and *sock* is the **object**. A pivot grammar assigns both sentences identical structures, because they consist of the same words in identical order. Other relationships were also common. In the sentence *sweater chair,* the second word indicates the location of the object named first; thus the sentence is an **object-location** construction. When Kathryn picked up a hat for a party, she said *party hat,* an instance of an **attribute-object** construction. All of these sentences are noun-noun sequences, but the use of that description by itself would obscure important semantic distinctions.

The classification scheme just introduced is based more on the meaning of each sentence than on the details of its structure. The concept of agent reflects this point. Agents are, by definition, active instigators of actions. Hence *John* is an agent in *John ran* but not in *John died,* despite the formal similarity of the two sentences. Objects are entities that are affected by the actions of agents or whose properties, possessors, or locations are being specified. The word *sock* is an object in *Put on my sock* and *The sock got put on already,* despite the differences in form between the two sentences.

Kathryn also produced constructions in which the meanings were primarily determined by a key word (rather like a pivot word); for example, *more X* asked for the recurrence of an object or event. *Hi* indicated notice or attention: *hi spoon.* A sentence type such as possessive-object embodies a relationship that can occur between many different word pairs: *mommy sock, daddy chair, baby lunch.* In contrast, relations such as recurrence and attention center around single words; for example, recurrence is expressed in *more shoe, more read,* and *more up* through the word *more.* Both types of relationship occur in stage I speech.

Brown has examined records from a number of children acquiring English and other languages and has concluded that the most common relationships are the eleven listed in Table 2.2. They appear to account for

TABLE 2.2   Semantic Relations in Two-Word Sentences

Semantic Relation	Form	Example
1. Nomination	that + N	*that book*
2. Notice	hi + N	*hi belt*
3. Recurrence	more + N, 'nother + N	*more milk*
4. Nonexistence	allgone + N, no more + N	*allgone rattle*
5. Attributive	Adj + N	*big train*
6. Possessive	N + N	*mommy lunch*
7. Locative	N + N	*sweater chair*
8. Locative	V + N	*walk street*
9. Agent-Action	N + V	*Eve read*
10. Agent-Object	N + N	*mommy sock*
11. Action-Object	V + N	*put book*

SOURCE: Adapted from R. Brown, *Psycholinguistics*, p. 220. New York: Free Press, 1970.

about 75 percent of stage I utterances. Some infrequent, but occurring, relationships are action-indirect object (*give mommy*), instrumentals (*sweep broom*, meaning 'sweep with a broom,' comitatives (*walk mommy*, meaning 'walk with mommy'), and conjunctions (*umbrella boot*).

Even in stage I, several different types of sentences are common. In addition to describing objects and events, children ask questions and command others. But the questions and imperatives are of simple form. Questions are likely to be identical to statements, except for a rising intonation, for example, *mommie hat?* The characteristic order auxiliary verb-subject, as in *Did he leave?* and *What can you see?* does not appear until later. Locations seem to be especially interesting to young children, as the examples given illustrate, and questions about location (*Where doggie go?*) are among the earliest questions. Questions about names (*What's that?*) are also common. Like questions, imperatives have a characteristic intonation. In adult language, the omission of a subject, as in *Go home now*, signals an imperative. But children leave subjects out of nonimperative sentences too: for example, *See doggie* meaning 'I see the doggie.' But the child's nonverbal behavior generally communicates the intent to command.

The relations shown in Table 2.2 are propositons about the sensorimotor world of the toddler emerging from infancy. As the work of the great Swiss developmental psychologist Jean Piaget has shown, the great achievement of infancy is the establishment of a world of stable, enduring objects, distinct from one another and from the observer; attributes of the objects; and actions upon them. Many observers (for example Bloom, 1970; Brown 1973) have proposed that the relations of Table 2.2 be viewed as the linguistic expression of sensorimotor intelligence. However, this proposal should not be taken to mean either that all the child's concepts immediately find expression in language or that absence of a feature in language means that the corresponding concept is missing from the cognition of the child. In addition to the underlying concept, the child must master the linguistic means of expression of that concept, and there will be many instances of lag between the concept and its linguistic expression. We shall return to this question in Chapter 6.

Changes During Stage I

At the beginning of stage I, only one- and two-word sentences are produced. Gradually the mean length of utterance increases. Typically, around MLU 1.5 (which results from approximately equal numbers of one- and two-word sentences) longer sentences appear. Three-word sentences are constructed out of the two-term relations shown in Table 2.1. No new relations appear. The constructions seem to be of two types. Sentences of the general form agent-action-object (*I see doggie*) and agent-action-location seem to represent conjoining of previously produced two-term relations: for example, agent-action and action-object, "summing" to agent-action-object. A second kind of advance comes from retaining a basic two-term relation like action-location and expanding one term by using one of the relations. For example, *sit daddy chair* ('sit in daddy's chair') is still basically an action-location, but the location (*daddy chair*) has been expanded as a possessive. The expansion is almost always one of possession, recurrence, or attribution (Brown 1973).

Not much later, four-word utterances appear, for example, *I take truck home*, which is of the form agent-action-object-location. Even these four-term relations are constructed from the same basic set of relations present since the beginning of stage I speech. As Brown points out, this pattern of development has a biological flavor, reminiscent of cells dividing and subdividing.

A comparison of the four-word sentences often observed toward the end of stage I with the two-word sentences typical of the beginning raises an interesting question about the nature of development. Notice that, even early in stage I, the child can produce a sentence consisting of any two of the terms in the string agent-action-object-location. Furthermore, the two terms produced will generally be in the order given in the general pattern. In a sense, the child at the beginning of the stage demonstrates that he knows the ordering agent-action-object-location. Yet he never produces the full string. So the transition from two- to three- and four-word sentences may represent, not the acquisition of new information about the language, but rather the lifting of some kind of constraint, from memory or otherwise.

Word Order and Stress

One reason why children's utterances in stage I are often difficult to interpret is that they are missing many of the cues present in adult speech. Locatives in adult speech are often signaled by prepositions such as *on* and *in*; possessives are signaled by the possessive inflection -*s*; actions are marked by various verb endings such as -*ing*; the objects of actions are sometimes marked by inflections (*I pushed him*, not *I pushed he*). The inflections and so-called function words are omitted. This observation gave rise to the descriptive term "telegraphic speech." Instead, relations are signaled primarily by word order. It is important to realize that it is the order of terms in relationships, and not particular words, that is ordered. The particular word *sweater* may be first in *sweater chair*, an object-locative sentence, but second in *mommy sweater*, a possessive-object sentence, but both sentences follow the general order for their types.

Among children acquiring English, violations of normal word order occur only rarely. If the child is talking about, or requesting, book reading, *read book* is far more likely than *book read*. This fact plays a dual role in understanding child language. On the one hand, this consistent order is really a major piece of evidence that the child "intends" specific relations (Brown 1973). For example, the fact that nouns come before verbs in sentences that express agent-action relationships but that verbs come before nouns in sentences that express action-object relationships is evidence that the two relationships are genuinely distinct for the child. On the other hand, the very fact that this is possible confirms the fact that children use word order for expressing semantic relationships and not such other plausible means as inflections and function words.

Although order is generally fixed, there are a few exceptions. Braine (1971) reported that at twenty-four to twenty-five months, his subject Gregory passed through a phase in which the order of major constituents appeared to be free. Braine could not observe any semantic contrast between *truck fix it* and *fix it truck* or between locative sentences of the form *inside + N* and *N + inside*. In a more recent study, Braine (in press) has found evidence for a fairly frequent, but generally brief, period of variable word order when new relations are being expressed. Braine views these as "groping patterns" associated with new rules for sentence construction which are not yet well established, since they are generally followed by the establishment of a clear-cut order preference.

The general trend to follow a fixed word order is not too surprising for children acquiring English, which is a relatively fixed-order language (compare *Dog bites man* with *Man bites dog*). A particularly interesting question, to be considered in Chapter 3, is what happens to children acquiring other languages in which order is more variable.

Another signal that can mark relationships is stress, that is, accent. Miller and Ervin-Tripp (1964) reported that a child whom they studied used the expression *Christy room* sometimes as a possessive ("Christy's room") and sometimes as a locative ("Christy is in the room"). The first was pronounced with stress on the first word, *Chrísty room*, and the second with stress on the second word, *Christy róom*. Wieman (1974) studied the two-word utterances of five children with MLU between 1.4 and 2.3. She found that children are highly consistent in stress patterns. For example, every one of the twenty-three action-location sentences had heavier stress on the locations. All but four of the thirty-two possessive-object sentences had stress on the possessives. Other typical patterns were: agent-action'; action-object', if the object was a noun (*get cár*); action'-object, if the object was a pronoun (*gét it*); attribute-object; and object-locative' (this last was not as clear a trend, however). On the basis of these findings, she proposed a hierarchy of stress assignment:

locative
possessive
noun object
action   increasing stress ↑
pronoun object
agent

If a sentence consists of two elements from this list, the higher one will receive heavier stress.

The apparent exceptions to these generalizations were almost always of a special sort. One child produced the locative sentence *firetruck street* with stress on the object, not the locative. However, this sentence was a response to the mother's question *What's in the street?* Another child produced an agent-action sentence *Mómmy turn it* with stress on the agent, rather than on the action. This sentence was in response to an inquiry from an interviewer as to whether she should turn the watch. In both instances, the child was stressing the *new* element of the sentence, new either in the sense of providing new information or in the sense of contrasting with something said by another person. The distinction between new and old information explains the different treatment accorded noun and pronoun objects: The former are stressed, whereas the latter are not. Pronouns are inherently old information; they refer back to entities previously discussed. Wieman argues, on the basis of work in linguistics by Chafe and others, that this distinction between new and old really underlies the entire hierarchy. Normally, agents are old information, locatives are new, and so on. *Jim is playing in the corner* is probably a statement about a person who has already been introduced; the new information is his location, and stress will probably be on *corner*. But in particular situations, any element may be the new one. Notice that *Jim is playing in the corner* sounds like a reply to the question *Who is that playing in the corner?* Wieman revised the hierarchy to read:

new or contrasting information

locative

possessive

noun object   increasing stress

action

pronoun object

agent

The distinctive use of stress is further evidence for the semantic relations listed in Table 2.2. Furthermore, Wieman's findings demonstrate that, even early in language development, children are sensitive to the distinction between new and old information, a distinction at the heart of conversational communication.

A Look Back at Single-Word Utterances

It is interesting to look back at single-word utterances from the perspective of the next stage. Just as we can try to use the context of the child's two-word sentence to determine its interpretation—the method of "rich interpretation," as Brown has dubbed it—we can try to determine the ways in which the single words are used. If we do so, it looks as if most of the basic meanings of stage I, as listed in Table 2.2, are present at the one-word stage. There is especially good evidence for the meanings of recurrence, nonexistence, locative, attribution, agent, object, and possessive. In this sense, stage I builds on the earlier period. However, a stronger proposal has been made. Just as we can use the method of "rich interpretation" to establish sentence meanings for two-word utterances, we can use the same method to establish sentence meanings for single-word utterances. If *mommy pigtail* means 'mommy make me a pigtail' on the basis of context, then the occurrence of just *mommy* or just *pigtail* in the same context could be taken to mean that the child has the full sentence meaning in mind—*mommy* as agent, *make* as action, *pigtail* as object—but is prevented by limitations of linguistic knowledge (perhaps of particular words) and memory from uttering the entire sentence. This would be a solution to the question raised in Chapter 1: In what sense are these single-word utterances really expressing sentence meanings?

However, Bloom (1970) and Brown (1973) argue against this interpretation. Bloom points out that contextual information is not the only source of evidence for the semantic relations expressed in two-word utterances. One important source of evidence is the consistent use of word order, as already discussed. This evidence is missing for the single-word utterance stage. Another kind of evidence comes from other utterances of the child. The interpretation of *mommy pigtail* as an agent-object construction, despite the missing verb that links them, gains strength from the fact that verbs do appear in other sentences: *mommy kiss* (agent-action) and *hit ball* (action-object). If these other sentence types were not observed, most investigators, including Bloom, would not postulate the missing verb. This kind of evidence, too, is missing from single-word utterances. Finally, a third aspect of the data is the relatively small set of relationships being expressed in two-word utterances. Not every possible relationship is expressed, not even every relationship expressed simply in adult speech. A problem with single-word utterances is that too *many* interpretations are possible. As Bloom puts it,

> the less a child says, the more his utterance is open to alternative interpreta-
> tion . . . given the single word *nana* in reference to the top of the refrigerator,
> where there are no bananas but where bananas are usually stored, there are
> at least two alternative interpretations: "I want bananas" or "there are no
> bananas" in addition to the one offered by McNeill (location of bananas).
> (Bloom 1973:137)

Although it is difficult to achieve a balance between giving the child credit for knowledge, however it is expressed, and skepticism about attributing too much linguistic knowledge to him, that balance must be our goal.

Stage II and the Development of Inflections

Although the absence of inflections virtually defines stage I language, the first inflections appear as MLU approaches 2.0. The inflections begin to be mastered in what Brown calls stage II: MLU between 2.0 and 2.5. But, in fact, the process of development is a long one; even the set of inflections discussed in this section is not fully mastered until MLU is beyond 4.0.

Two aspects of development of these items are especially interesting. One is the order of acquisition; as we shall see, these inflections are acquired in a remarkably consistent order by children acquiring English. Second is the process by which each inflection is acquired, including the characteristic kinds of mistakes children make.

Brown (1973) has studied fourteen of the "grammatical morphemes" of English. He uses the term to refer to morphemes whose primary purpose is either to modify the meaning of the major content words—nouns and verbs, especially—by adding such notions as plurality or to indicate more precisely the relations of the content words, as in the possessive inflection of *John's book*. The fourteen include the present progressive *-ing* of *He is running*, the third-person singular in both its regular form (the *-s* of *She* *walks*) and its irregular form (the *has* of *She has the light*), the past tense in both its regular (*walked*) and irregular (*went*) forms, the plural -*s*, the prepositions *on* and *in*, the possessive -*s*, the articles *the* and *a* (not a single morpheme, of course, but treated as equivalent), *be* as an auxiliary verb (the *is* of *He is running* and the *were* of *They were watching*), and *be* as a copula verb (the *is* of *He is tired* and the *are* of *You are left fielder*). These last two are further divided according to use in contractible and uncontractible positions. These terms refer not to actual contraction, which is extremely rare in early child language, but rather to positions that would permit or not permit contraction. The copula *is* of *He is tired* is contractible; *He's tired* is fully acceptable. But the copula of *Yes, he is* is not; even in response to the question *Is he tired?* one would not reply *Yes, he's*. The distinction is an important one, because the two types of copula and the two types of auxiliary appear at different points in development.

How do we decide when a child has mastered one of these morphemes? It is not enough to observe just one occurrence. A child may use a morpheme occasionally, in just a few contexts, for a long period of time. Gradually or suddenly, production of the morpheme increases; eventually the child provides it wherever it is called for. The notion "wherever it is called for" provides the basis for the decision. Obligatory contexts can be defined for each of the morphemes. For example, the plural morpheme is required in the contexts *two book . . .* and *They are the book . . .*, on purely linguistic grounds. The present progressive is required in *I am run. . . .* The nonlinguistic context may also define an obligatory context: Pointing to several books and saying *book . . .* calls for the plural. Brown (1973) suggests crediting the child with productive control over the morpheme when he provides it in at least 90 percent of the obligatory contexts. (Dialects of English vary in their specification of obligatory contexts; see Chapter 10. Obviously the appropriate dialect must be used in scoring obligatory contexts for each child.)

According to this definition of acquisition, the order of development is remarkably regular. Brown studied three children longitudinally; de Villiers and de Villiers (1973a) studied another twenty-one children in a cross-sectional experiment. Brown's order is shown in Table 2.3. Although the order is not always identical, if two children are selected at random, the rank-order correlation between the orders of acquisition for the two will be between .80 and .90. The correlation between age and order is .68, but between MLU and order it is .92, illustrating the value of MLU as an overall index of development.

Why should it be this way? What determines the order? Brown has considered three possibilities in detail. First is frequency in parental speech: Perhaps children acquire first the morphemes that they hear most often. However, there is virtually no correlation between frequency in parental speech and order of acquisition.

More interesting possibilities are grammatical complexity and semantic complexity. Some of the morphemes are more complex in their grammar; for example, auxiliaries are more complex than the past tense. Perhaps the simpler ones are required earlier. Similarly, some of the morphemes are complex semantically; for example, auxiliaries are more complex than the plural. If we knew which aspect of complexity contributed more to the actual order of acquisition, we would know something more about the child's processes of acquisition. Brown worked through a particular grammar of English (Jacobs and Rosenbaum 1968), in order to analyze the morphemes grammatically and also semantically. The grammatical analysis was based on the transformations—a particular kind of linguistic rule, to be discussed further in Chapter 4—required for each morpheme. The fourth column of Table 2.3 orders the morphemes by the number of transformations involved. The correlation between grammatical complexity in this sense and order of acquisition is about .80. It is not really appropriate, however, to use number of transformations as an index, because such a procedure assumes that all transformations are equal in adding complexity, which is not a justifiable assumption (Fodor and Garret 1966). Brown has proposed a more conservative strategy, based on what he calls the **law of cumulative complexity:** If one morpheme involves everything involved in another morpheme and more, then the first is more complex than the second. This principle is safer but weaker; not as many predictions can be made. Those that can be made are shown at the bottom of the third column of Table 2.3. For example, the present progressive requires only the progressive-affix transformation. The contractible auxiliary requires this transformation, as well as three others. The prediction that the present progressive precedes the contractible auxiliary follows from this fact. But no prediction can be made about the contractible auxiliary and the past irregular, even though the former involves four transformations and the latter only one, because the verb-agreement transformation required for the past irregular is not required for the contractible auxiliary. All predictions based on the law of cumulative complexity are confirmed. Clearly grammatical complexity is a partial, but not complete, predictor of the observed order.

A similar analysis for elements of meaning is shown in the fifth and sixth columns of Table 2.3. Again, one possibility is to correlate the number of meaning elements (semantic dimensions) with the order of acquisition. The correlation is again about .80. This correlation is open to the objection already raised: It hardly seems valid to equate the concept of possession with that of containment (*in*). If the law of cumulative complexity is used for semantic dimensions, the number of predictions is smaller. And again all are confirmed. Semantic complexity, like grammatical complexity, is a partial, but not complete, predictor.

The two factors appear to be about equally important. One problem with this interpretation is that the two are not independent; they are

TABLE 2.3　The Acquisition of 14 Grammatical Morphemes of English

Morpheme	Order of Acquisition	Transformations	Ordering by Grammatical Complexity[a]	Semantic Dimensions	Ordering by Semantic Complexity[b]
present progressive	1	progressive affix	3	temporary duration	4
on	2.5	preposition segment	3	support	4
in	2.5	preposition segment	3	containment	4
plural	4	noun suffix, nominal agreement, article	7[c]	number	4
past irregular	5	verb agreement	3	earlierness	4
possessive	6	(not given in source)		possession	4
uncontractible copula	7	copula, auxiliary agreement, auxiliary incorporation	10	number, earlierness	8.5
articles	8	article	3	specific-nonspecific	4
past regular	9	verb agreement, verb suffix	7	earlierness	4
third-person singular regular	10	auxiliary agreement, verb agreement, verb suffix	10	number, earlierness	8.5
third-person singular irregular	11	auxiliary agreement, verb agreement	7	number, earlierness	8.5
uncontractible auxiliary	12	auxiliary incorporation, progressive affix, progressive segment, auxiliary agreement	12.5	temporary duration, number, earlierness	10

contractible copula	13	copula, auxiliary agreement, auxiliary incorporation	10	number, earlierness	8.5
contractible auxiliary	14	progressive affix, progressive segment, auxiliary incorporation, auxiliary agreement	12.5	temporary duration, number, earlierness	10

predictions according to the law of cumulative complexity

present progressive → contractible auxiliary

present progressive → uncontractible auxiliary

past irregular → past regular

past irregular → third-person singular regular

past irregular → third-person singular irregular

third-person singular irregular → third-person singular regular

plural → copula
plural → third-person singular
plural → auxiliary
past → auxiliary
progressive → auxiliary
past singular → third-person
past → copula
third-person singular → auxiliary
copula → auxiliary

[a] Ordering includes thirteen items only, as possessive is not analyzed in source.

[b] Ordering includes ten items; it is assumed that regular-irregular and contractible-uncontractible contrasts are irrelevant to mastery of semantic content.

[c] The second and third transformations are not involved in all instances of the plural; for this reason Brown bases the ordering on an average of two transformations for the plural.

SOURCE: A construction based on Tables 32, 45, 60, 61, and 67 of R. Brown, *A first language.* Cambridge, Mass.: Harvard University Press, 1973. © 1973 by the President and fellows of Harvard College.

highly correlated with each other and thus tend to make the same predictions. Either factor alone might be the primary influence. Brown suggests that, by making comparisons across languages, we may eventually be able to disentangle these factors. Two other factors that are probably important are the perceptual salience of the morpheme and the amount of new information conveyed by it. As many contractible auxiliaries and copulas are indeed contracted in the adult speech heard by the child, contractible forms are probably less salient than uncontractible ones. And, indeed, the uncontractible versions of the auxiliary and the copula are acquired before the respective contractible ones. Some morphemes are basically redundant. For example, the third-person singular morpheme is completely redundant as far as number is concerned; the morpheme simply duplicates the information available in most instances in the subject of the sentence (*The boy walks*).

In any case, the *fact* of the invariance of order remains, and it is striking. Furthermore, this approach allows us to formulate questions about the relative importance of perceptual salience, grammatical complexity, and semantic complexity in a very precise way.

In addition to order of acquisition, the actual process of acquiring each morpheme is interesting. Cazden (1968) reports a very careful study of five inflections; Brown (1973) has information on the remaining nine. Typically, the early use of a particular grammatical morpheme is entirely correct, though it may be present in only 10 percent of the obligatory contexts. Then there is a rise to approximately a 90 percent criterion level. Performance stays between 90 percent and 100 percent for some time.

Syntactically, the acquisition of inflections reflects one of the most interesting and widespread phenomena of language acquisition: **overregularization.** Children learning English produce *comed, doed, breaked*, and similar forms. That is, the irregular (or strong) verbs of English are inflected for the past tense in the same manner as the regular (or weak) verbs, like *walked* and *hugged*. We might expect that children would begin by using some regular forms correctly, for example, *walked* or *helped*, and then would extend the rule to the irregular verbs, producing the incorrect forms *comed, doed*, and so on. But this is not what happens. The first past-tense forms used are the correct forms of the irregular verbs—*came, did, broke*, and so on. This is, perhaps, not so surprising, for irregular forms are four times as common in parental speech to children as are regular forms (Slobin 1971). After a few weeks or months, the regular past-tense morpheme *-ed* suddenly appears with all verbs, regular and irregular alike: *comed, breaked, walked* (Ervin 1964). The correct irregular past-tense forms are simply abandoned (Cazden 1968 points out that overregularized and correct irregular forms may coexist for a period).

The crucial point here is that the irregular verbs, even though they are the most frequent verbs in English, do not follow a pattern; we can only conclude that the child is fundamentally a pattern learner. Once a pattern is acquired, it will be applied as broadly as possible, even if this results in the production of words the child has never heard. Cazden's finding that regular endings, like other grammatical morphemes, are used at first in just a few contexts suggests that at first a few regular endings are memorized by rote, as are the irregulars, and then the generality of the pattern is seen, resulting in a rapid rise to the 90 percent level and overregularization. Ervin (1964) observed a similar process in the development of plurals.

Many adult language learners have discovered to their dismay that it is usually the most common words of a language that are irregular. The exceptions cannot be put off until later. In English, for example, the irregular verbs *be, come, go,* and *do* are among the most frequent verbs. The phenomenon of overregularization suggests an explanation for this fact. Children have a strong tendency to regularize all verbs. In the case of infrequent verbs, they hear the correct form very few times or not at all, and there is little to prevent them from regularization. But they have heard the common irregular verbs often and are thus reminded of their irregularity. Furthermore, adults are more likely to correct children when they produce such forms as *doed* than when they produce regularized forms of infrequent verbs. Even adults are unsure about the few infrequent irregular verbs of English, such as *thrive*—is the past tense *thrived* or *throve*? Thus children may be responsible for the regularization of infrequent items. Schleicher (1971, but written in 1861) was the first to hypothesize a connection between language change and language acquisition by children. More recently, Kiparsky (1968) and others have explored this possibility.

Though overregularization is the most frequent type of error, other types do occur. *Going to put some sugars* reflects a failure to distinguish between count nouns, such as *rock* and *shoes*, which can be pluralized and counted, and mass nouns, such as *sand, milk,* and *sugar,* which are not pluralized. Another type of error is shown in *I didn't spilled it.* In simple sentences the past tense is indicated on the verb. But, if there is an auxiliary verb such as *do,* the past tense is indicated on it, giving *did.* Often children successfully mark the past tense on the auxiliary but fail to remove it from the verb. The same error may be made with the third-person singular morpheme: *Does the kitty stands up?* All these errors show the independence of the child's grammar from rote reproduction; the child has acquired something of the adult language around him, but it is filtered through his own emerging grammatical system.

The return of the irregular past-tense forms has not been studied in any detail. Why do the overregularized forms go away at all? Presumably during the period of overregularization, the child is comprehending adults' use of the irregular past tense. Are *comed* and *came* simply viewed as equally satisfactory alternatives? It would be interesting to know whether or not certain irregulars consistently reappear before others; this might make it possible to form hypotheses about the factors that lead to the termination of overregularization.

Summary

It is striking how little difficulty the child has with any of the general mechanisms of language: the notion of a sentence, rules for combining various classes of words, the expression of a wide variety of meanings, the concept of inflections, and more. All are present from a very early age. Particular rules, meanings, and inflections may, however, require time for mastery.

The early appearance of many semantic relationships, together with the striking differences between many child utterances and the adult speech around the child, strongly suggests that the child is attempting above all to express his own ideas, emotions, and actions through whatever system he has so far constructed.

The regular sequence of acquisition of the grammatical morphemes of English is determined in part by grammatical complexity and in part by semantic complexity, though other factors undoubtedly are also important. Widespread overregularization of inflections shows a search for patterns on the part of the child, a search that can even override his desire to match the patterns of the language around him.

2.1   TELEGRAPHIC SPEECH*

We adults sometimes operate under a constraint on length and the curious fact is that the English we produce in these circumstances bears a formal resemblance to the English produced by two year old children. When words cost money there is a premium on brevity or to put it otherwise, a constraint on length. The result is "telegraphic" English, and telegraphic English is an English of nouns, verbs, and adjectives. One does not send a cable reading: "My car has broken down and I have lost my wallet; send money to me at the American Express in Paris" but rather "Car broken down; wallet lost, send money American Express Paris." The telegram omits *my, has, and, I, have, my, to, me, at, the, in.* All of these are functors. We make the

---

* From R. Brown and U. Bellugi, Three processes in the child's acquisition of syntax. *Harvard Educational Review*, Spring 1964, 34, 138–139. Copyright © 1964 by President and Fellows of Harvard College.

same kind of telegraphic reduction when time or fatigue constrains us to be brief, as witness any set of notes taken at a fast-moving lecture.

A telegraphic transformation of English generally communicates very well. It does so because it retains the high-information words and drops the low-information words. We are here using "information" in the sense of the mathematical theory of communication. The information carried by a word is inversely related to the chances of guessing it from context. From a given string of content words, missing functors can often be guessed but the message "my has and I have my to me at the in" will not serve to get money to Paris. Perhaps children are able to make a communication analysis of adult speech and so adapt in an optimal way to their limitation of span. There is, however, another way in which the adaptive outcome might be achieved.

If you say aloud sentences you will find that you place the heavier stresses, the primary and secondary stresses in the sentences, on contentives rather than on functors. In fact the heavier stresses fall, for the most part, on the words the child retains. We first realized that this was the case when we found that in transcribing tapes, the words of the mother that we could hear most clearly were usually the words that the child reproduced. We had trouble hearing the weakly stressed functors and, of course, the child usually failed to reproduce them. Differential stress may then be the cause of the child's differential retention. The outcome is a maximally informative reduction, but the cause of this outcome need not be the making of an information analysis. The outcome may be an incidental consequence of the fact that English is a well-designed language that places its heavier stresses where they are needed, on contentives that cannot easily be guessed from context.

We are fairly sure that differential stress is one of the determinants of the child's telegraphic productions. For one thing, stress will also account for the way in which children reproduce polysyllabic words when the total is too much for them. Adam, for instance, gave us *'pression* for *expression* and Eve gave us *'raff* for *giraffe*; the more heavily-stressed syllables were the ones retained.

further reading

Bloom, L. Why not pivot grammar? *Journal of Speech and Hearing Disorders,* 1971, **36**, 40–50.

Brown, R. The development of the human child's native language. In A. Silverstein (Ed.), *Human communication: Theoretical explorations.* Hillsdale, N.J.: Lawrence Erlbaum Associates, 1974.

Brown, R. *A first language: The early stages.* Cambridge, Mass.: Harvard University Press, 1973.

The Evidence from Other Languages

In seeking an understanding of how children acquire language, we can obtain a biased view if we limit ourselves to children acquiring English. The nature of early language discussed in the previous chapter is determined both by the nature of English and by the nature of children as language learners. We need to look at the acquisition of other languages in order to distinguish the two factors.

In this chapter we shall consider the acquisition of certain languages other than English by monolingual children. Space does not permit us to examine still other very interesting cases. Simultaneous bilingual development (Leopold 1939, 1947, 1949a, 1949b) is a particularly impressive feat, yet it appears to be easy for young children. True second-language learning by children (after, say, age four years) is particularly intriguing, for it offers a test case midway between second-language learning by adults, which is notoriously difficult, and first-language learning by children, which is virtually effortless. The relative importance of difference in age and the knowledge of a first language in these two instances may be estimated from second-language learning by children. Lambert and Tucker (1962), Oller and Richards (1973), and the series *Working Papers in Bilingualism* (published by the Ontario Institute for Studies in Education) are good sources for work on this question. A recent provocative development is the attempt to teach chimpanzees language-like systems (Gardner and Gardner 1969, 1975; Brown 1970, 1973b; Fleming 1974), which illuminates both the nature of language and man's evolutionary specialization for language. Also relevant for understanding the relationship between age and language-learning abilities are studies of children acquiring their first language after the usual age period: the so-called "wolf children" (Itard 1962; Curtiss *et al.* 1974).

Stage I Speech in Cross-Linguistic Perspective

Slobin (1973) has provided a bibliography of available studies on the acquisition of about forty native languages. However, only about fifteen or so have been studied in detail, that is, on the basis of reasonably complete longitudinal records. Even then, some have been studied only with one or two children. Prucha (1974) has also reviewed contemporary research in eastern European countries. Interestingly, we have more evidence about the acquisition of Russian than about any other language. This evidence ranges from the monumental diary study by Gvozdev of his son Zhenya (discussed in Slobin 1966a) to surveys of hundreds of preschool children (for example, Zakharova 1973). This interest in child language has arisen from two sources. First is a great appreciation on the part of Russian psychologists and linguists of the creative nature of language and of the importance of language development for cognitive development (to be discussed later in this chapter); second is the very practical task of raising infants and very young children in day nurseries and boarding institutions, a major aspect of Soviet policy since the 1930s. Russian is a good contrast to English, as it is a highly inflected language and freer in word order. An even better contrast is Finnish, which is not, like English and Russian, an Indo-European language. Bowerman (1973) reports a study of two children in stage I of the acquisition of Finnish, as well as a comparison of these children with children acquiring English, Samoan, and Luo. An even greater contrast is provided by sign language, which is often acquired as a native language by young deaf children.

Stage I language is very much the same all over the world. As Slobin wrote, "If you ignore word order and read through transcriptions of two word utterances in the various languages we have studied, the utterances read like direct translations of one another" (1970:177). Table 3.1, adapted from Slobin (1970), illustrates some of the semantic relations in a few of the languages that have been studied. The similarity of children's earliest language is remarkable.

In early stage I (MLU from 1.0 to 1.5), utterances are almost always one or two words long. The two-word utterances are drawn from the basic set of semantic relations shown in Table 2.2 plus a few rarer types. Not every child produces every type, nor has every type been observed in child language in every linguistic community, but all are very common. The fifteen or eighteen semantic relations appear to be a stock of universally available

TABLE 3.1 Some Semantic Relations in Stage I Speech from Several Languages

Relation	English	German	Russian	Finnish	Luo	Samoan
Recurrence	more milk	mehr Milch (more milk)	yesche moloka (more milk)	lisäiä kakkua (more cake)		
Attributive	big boat	Milch heiss (milk hot)	papa bol-shoy (papa big)	rikki auto (broken car)	piypiy kech (pepper hot)	fa'alii pepe (headstrong baby)
Possessive	mama dress	Mamas Hut mama's hat)	mami chashka (mama's cup)	täti auto (aunt car)	kom baba (chair father)	paluni mama (balloon mama)
Action-Locative	walk street	Sofa sitzen (sofa sit)		viediäin kauppa (take store)	odhi skul (he-went school)	tu'u lala (put down)
Agent-Action	Bambi go	Puppe kommt (doll comes)	mama prua (mama walk)	Seppo putoo (Seppo fall)	chungu biro (European comes)	pa'u pepe (fall doll)
Action-Object	hit ball		nasbla yaechko (found egg)	ajaa bmbm (drives car)	omoyo oduma (she dries maize)	
Question	where ball	wo Ball (where ball)	gdu papa (where papa)	missa pallo (where ball)		fea pupafu (where Punafu)

SOURCE: Adapted from Table 1 of D. I. Slobin, Universals of grammatical development in children. In G. B. Flores d'Arcais and W. J. M. Levelt (Eds.), *Advances in psycholinguistics*, pp. 178–179. Amsterdam: North-Holland Publishing Company, 1970.

means for combining word meanings. A distinction between animate and inanimate nouns is very common: Typically agents are animate and objects inanimate. Very simple negative constructions are common, but yes/no questions are *not* universal, as will be discussed later. Copulas, articles, auxiliaries, prepositions, and catenatives (*wanna* in *I wanna go*) are absent, as are most inflections. All these elements may occur as part of unanalyzed routines, as in *drink of water* and *"What's that?"* (which contain a preposition and a copula, respectively), but not as productive elements of stage I language. Interestingly, the one class of inflections which has been observed in stage I language are those which mark a major semantic role, such as agent or object. English does not mark these elements inflectionally, but many languages do. Some of these inflections are acquired in stage I by children learning such languages (Bowerman 1973).

Late stage I speech (MLU between 1.5 and 2.0) appears to differ from early stage I speech in the same ways in a variety of languages. Three-word utterances begin to appear as MLU passes 1.5. This development is not necessary; arithmetically the child could continue to increase his MLU up to 2.0 by simply increasing the proportion of two-word utterances, but they do not do so. Even a few four-word utterances are observed. More of the basic stock of semantic relations are observed in late stage I than in early stage I, but they are still drawn from the basic list. Modified objects, for example, possessive-object and attribute-object, continue to occur as independent utterances, but they also begin to occur as constituents of longer utterances, such as *push daddy chair* ('push daddy's chair'), which is an action-object construction in which the object is itself a two-term possessive-object construction. We might symbolize it as action-(possessive-object) object. Just as in early stage I speech, in which a child may produce agent-action, action-object, and agent-object constructions but not yet full agent-action-object sequences, in late stage I speech a child may produce strings of any three or four of the following list but not yet all of them at once:

agent-action-modifier-indirect object-locative
(possessive or attributive).

In both instances the child appears to be prevented from producing an utterance that would incorporate all he knows of the language. Toward the end of this period, the first few inflections, prepositions, and the like may appear. The direction of development after the beginning of stage I is thus nearly as uniform as that at the beginning (Bowerman 1973).

Although yes/no questions seem simple, they are not universal in stage I. Young Finnish children do *not* produce them in stage I (Bowerman 1973), and the explanation is enlightening. In English and many other languages, one way to form a yes/no question is simply to add a rising intonation to an otherwise normal declarative sentence. For example, *You see the dog* with a falling intonation is a declarative; *You see the dog?* with a rising intonation is a question. Although this form is not the most common for a question in English (*Do you see the dog?* is more typical), American children produce their first questions in this way. They do not yet know about the importance of auxiliary placement in questions (the defining characteristic of questions in English is that an auxiliary verb precedes the subject in almost all instances); in fact, they do not know about auxiliaries at all. But in Finnish it is not possible to form a question in this way; the simplest means available is the use of an interrogative inflection, and no intonation change is necessary. Children in stage I, however, do not master inflections, so they cannot ask questions in this way. The Finnish children do ask very simple *wh* questions, such as *Where ball?* and *Where sit?* These questions are very like the simple *wh* questions asked by American children at this stage. Each question is marked by a distinct word, not by an inflection.

Word Order

Children acquiring English seem to use word order as their basic device for indicating structure. This observation is not surprising, for the English that these children hear relies heavily on order. Languages differ, however, in the extent to which they rely on order. Some languages use inflections to a much greater extent and thus permit freer order. The words of a Latin sentence may be placed in almost any order. *Vir mordet canem, Mordet canem vir, Canem mordet vir, Vir canem mordet, Canem vir mordet,* and *Mordet vir canem* all mean, approximately 'Man bites dog.' What makes the sentences intelligible are the inflections, in this instance, suffixes at the ends of words. The subject is marked by the nominative case ending (in the example, no suffix at all), the object by the accusative case ending (in the example, *-em*), and the verb by suffixes that convey tense, number, and other information. Thus the order of words is not necessary for determination of the structure; instead it serves purposes of emphasis. English is close to the opposite extreme: Compare *Man bites dog* with *Dog bites man.* The change in order reverses the meaning. English has very few case inflections; among them are the pronoun inflections, for example, nominative *he* versus accusative *him.*

The imitations of adult speech produced by American children are as free of inflections and as respectful of order as are their spontaneous utterances. When Eve and Adam (two of the children studied by Brown and his associates) were asked to imitate the sentence *I showed you the book*, both produced *I show book.* Adam imitated *I am drawing a dog* with *I draw dog* (Brown and Fraser 1964).

Russian has a rich noun-inflectional system and no articles. For simple sentences all six orderings of subject (S), verb (V), and object (O) are possible—SVO (probably the most frequent), SOV, VSO, VOS, OSV and OVS—and are stylistic variants.[1] Gvozdev reported that his son Zhenya began with SOV order and later changed to SVO; he was highly consistent in each stage. Similarly, Park (cited in Brown 1973) observed a Korean girl who heard SOV, OSV, OVS, and SVO in her parents' speech but consistently produced only the SVO order. These and other findings suggest that children's tendency to use fixed word order is stronger than their dependence on the language they have heard.

However, additional evidence has made it clear that no such generalization can be made. In Finnish, adult order is relatively free, though SVO is the most frequent. Bowerman's two subjects differed (1973). Rina used SVO order predominantly, but Seppo produced SOV orders almost as frequently as SVO. Other combinations were also produced in various orders, for example, SVL (L:locative), SLV, LSV, and LVS. Seppo even reordered strings when he imitated adult speech, for example, when his mother said *vetää auto, niin* ('pulls car, indeed'); with *auto* as the subject, Seppo said *auto vetää* ('car pulls'). Seppo's orders were, however, closely tailored to those of the input. In virtually every instance, his most favored order was the most frequent in his mother's speech, and his most frequent alternative orders were his mother's most frequent alternatives. Rina, who followed a more rigid order, had a mother who generally favored one order for each possible sentence type (though not exclusively). This correlation between maternal and child language is striking, but like all correlations it must be approached with caution. Is the child modeling his speech on that of the parent? Or is the parent responding to the language of the child? Or are both influenced by some third factor? We shall return to these questions in Chapter 6.

Restriction to a single order (Zhenya) and use of the orders heard (Seppo) do not exhaust the possibilities. Three children acquiring German, studied by Park (cited in Brown 1973b), actually produced a *wider* range of orders than is acceptable for German simple sentences.

Clearly fixed word order is *not* a universal of early child language. About all that can be said is that, if the model language is consistent with respect to order, as English is, most children will use order to express semantic relations. If there is more freedom in the model language, children will continue to omit inflections, but their use of order will vary. Some will select one order from those heard, others will produce variations corresponding to the range of variations heard, and still others will go beyond

---

[1] Note that we have changed terminology from "agent-action-object" to "subject-verb-object," following the terminology of Slobin, Bowerman, and others. For the present discussion, the two sets of terms may be considered equivalent, as subjects are agents in early child language (though not always in adult language; recall *John died*) and verbs describe actions.

the variations heard. What leads a particular child to follow one path rather than another is a mystery.

Flexibility of word order raises a methodological problem. Recall from Chapter 2 that consistent word order is a major piece of evidence for distinguishing among various semantic relationships in child language. For example, the fact that agents precede actions, as in *mommy push*, whereas actions precede objects, as in *push chair*, is evidence for the distinction between the two relations. For children with flexible word order, this evidence is missing. What evidence do we have for the postulation of relations in these instances? One is the semantic similarity among early child languages. As children acquiring Russian, Finnish, and so on seem to be saying the same things as children acquiring English and as we have the evidence of word order in the instance of English, we can infer similar linguistic systems for Russian, Finnish, and other languages. But this reasoning by analogy is not very satisfactory. A more promising approach would be to study patterns of stress in two-word utterances, as Wieman (1974) has begun to do for English. Wieman found, for example, that agents were stressed in agent-action constructions, objects in action-object constructions (if the objects were nouns). This evidence of distinctive treatment of semantic relations may be found for languages in which word order varies.

Stage II and the Development of Inflections in Other Languages

In Chapter 2 both the order of development of inflections and the processes by which each is developed were discussed. Few conclusions are possible about the order of development in other languages. As Brown has pointed out, an explicit criterion of mastery is needed, something like his definition based on appearance in 90 percent of the obligatory contexts. This precise a definition has not been used in studies of other languages, although much work is now in progress. It is difficult to know, in reading studies on other languages, whether the author is talking about first appearance, full mastery, or something in between. This lack of data is unfortunate, as evidence on order would be invaluable for evaluating the relative role of perceptual, syntactic, semantic, and other factors influencing language development. The past tense in English has a certain syntax and a certain meaning. A comparison with the development of the past tense in another language in which it has similar meaning but different syntactic properties would be illuminating.

Soviet psycholinguists usually argue (or assume) that order of acquisition is determined mainly by semantic complexity. Gvozdev wrote, "semantics is the primordial nucleus which further directs the acquisition of all grammatical means of expression . . ." (Slobin 1966a). The available evidence does support the notion of a development from the most concrete to the most abstract inflections. Plurals are learned very early, cases and persons of the verb somewhat later, the possessive and progressive later still, and gender latest of all. Grammatical gender has virtually no systematic semantic reference in Russian: *stol* ('table') is masculine, *kniga* ('book') is feminine, and *piero* ('pen') is neuter. Classification is on the basis of the final sound of the word in the nominative case. Mastering the gender system—adjectives and other modifiers must agree with the noun in gender— is the most drawn-out learning process for the Russian child.

Gvozdev also wrote, "the acquisition of a given grammatical meaning precedes acquisition of its external expression" (Slobin 1966a). Slobin (1973) has translated this notion into a general principle: *New forms express old ideas.* When a child masters a new technique—suffixes, prepositions, or whatever—it will be used first to express something he already knows but does not explicitly mark. For example, children clearly express locatives in stage I speech, as in *sweater chair*, though the function of *chair* as a location for *sweater* must be inferred from the context, rather than from anything in the sentence. When prepositions first appear in the development of English, usually *on* and *in*, they are used to mark locatives. Only later will prepositions be used to express new meanings, such as the use of *for* to mark the beneficiary of an action (*I made it for you*). This is the converse of the principle stated: *New ideas are expressed with old forms.*

Slobin has pointed out an especially interesting test case for evaluating the role of syntactic complexity in determining difficulty of acquisition. It involves children bilingual in Hungarian and Serbo-Croatian in northern Yugoslavia. Hungarian and Serbo-Croatian express locatives differently. In Hungarian noun inflections indicate position and direction: *hajo* 'boat,' *hajoban* 'in the boat,' *hajotal* 'moving away from next to the boat,' and so on. In Serbo-Croatian, location is encoded by prepositions, essentially equivalent to *on, in, from,* and the like. Certain additional information is encoded by an inflection on the noun, in particular directional information. The distinction between *in the house* (as a location) and *into the house* (as a direction) is thus encoded by inflections on the noun. The case of the noun inflection is also determined by the preposition; Serbo-Croatian is like Latin in that certain prepositions call for specific case suffixes on their objects in a relatively arbitrary way. The two major differences between the languages are thus that the main portion of the locative meaning is expressed by a suffix in Hungarian and a preposition in Serbo-Croatian and that the suffix in Serbo-Croatian does not have a clear, concrete meaning.

Before the age of two years these children use a number of the Hungarian suffixes to express location. But when they speak Serbo-Croatian the locative is not marked with either the preposition or the suffix, though it is often clear on other grounds that a locative is intended, for example, a child putting a doll into a drawer and saying in Serbo-Croatian *doll drawer*. Obviously the child has the same locative intention as when he describes the situation in Hungarian with an utterance of the form *drawer-into*. But he has not yet mastered the linguistic means of expressing this intention in Serbo-Croatian. In addition to having the concept to be expressed, the child must do something more, something purely linguistic, and this extra task may be more or less difficult. Slobin argues that, by making a number of cross-linguistic comparisons, we can become more precise about what it means to be linguistically more complex. A generalization suggested by this example, and supported by evidence from other languages, is that suffixes are acquired earlier than prefixes or prepositions, for comparable meanings.

A great deal of information about the pattern of development of particular inflections in Russian is available. Overregularizations are extremely common in the acquisition of Russian. One of the Russian cases is the instrumental. In the Russian equivalent of *He hit the block with a hammer*, the word for 'hammer' has an instrumental case ending, because 'hammer' is the instrument of hitting. The exact form of the instrumental case suffix depends on the gender of the noun and on its number, singular or plural. Masculine and neuter singular nouns require *-om*, whereas feminine singular nouns require *-oy*. Zhenya first used the suffix *-om* for all instrumental singular nouns, even though it was correct only for masculine and neuter singular nouns (Slobin 1966a). This is surprising, for feminine nouns are more frequent in Russian child speech. However, the suffix *-om* has only one other function—as the masculine and neuter prepositional case ending for adjectives. In contrast, the suffix *-oy* serves a variety of other functions, being an adjectival suffix for four cases in the feminine and one in the masculine. Zhenya selected the suffix with fewer meanings for use in all instances of the singular instrumental case.

This *-om* ending was dominant in Zhenya's language from 2;1 to 2;4. But, as soon as he began using the feminine singular instrumental ending *-oy*, he completely abandoned *-om* and used *-oy* universally. This phase lasted from 2;5 to 3;0, after which he mastered the conventional usage. Table 3.2 summarizes this development and compares it with the develop-

---

TABLE 3.2   The Development of Two Inflections

Phase	English	Russian
i.	came, did	*-om* for masculine, neuter, feminine
ii.	comed, doed, helped	*-oy* for masculine, neuter, feminine
iii.	came, did, helped	*-om* for masculine, neuter
		-oy for feminine

ment of the past tense by English-speaking children. Here again, a well-practiced form, which was in many instances correct, has been abandoned and an overregularization made. In one sense, this phenomenon is even more striking than that observed in the development of the past tense in English. In the latter instance, a pattern drove out the use of certain special cases. With Zhenya one pattern replaces another pattern. This development appears to be quite general among Russian children (Zakharova 1973).

The singular accusative case for nouns also is overregularized. There are actually four accusative forms in adult Russian: the zero ending (no suffix at all), *-u*, *-a*, and *-o*. As we would expect, Zhenya used one form for all nouns. But which form was it? The zero ending is the most frequent form in adult speech, followed by *-u*. But it is *-u* that enters child language first, and it is used for all singular accusative nouns. This example suggests that children prefer marked forms to unmarked forms, probably for reasons of distinctiveness; unmarked forms are highly ambiguous.

Notice that the dominant inflections, which Slobin has called "imperialistic inflections," are not simply chosen from one particular paradigm. The predominant instrumental singular suffix *-om* is masculine and neuter, whereas the predominant accusative singular suffix *-u* is feminine. The choice is made separately in each instance, presumably on the basis of distinctiveness and lack of ambiguity.

Like English, Russian has both count nouns and mass nouns. Count nouns can be pluralized and counted: *brick, two bricks*. Mass nouns cannot: *some sugar* but not *two sugars*. It is quite common in Russian that, when noun plurals first appear, any noun may be pluralized or counted. Children count mass nouns, for example, *odna sakhara* ('one sugar'), and pluralize them, *bumagi* ('papers'). They also invent singulars for plural nouns that have no singular forms in Russian: *lyut*, a singular for *lyudi* ('people'). Only later is the class of nouns divided into count and mass nouns. At first, the children treat all nouns as the same, capable of having singular and plural forms, an overgeneralization from the count nouns. Bogoyavlenskiy (1973) studied the development of certain suffixes that are not actually inflectional, in the sense of signaling the structure of the sentence, but rather change the meaning of the word somewhat. These suffixes included the diminutive *-enok* (comparable to the *-y* of *doggy* and *mommy* but used more generally in Russian than in English), the augmentative *-ishche* (the opposite of the diminutive), and the agentive suffixes *-nits* and *-shchik* (which convert other words to nouns that signify agents responsible for actions or products, something like the *-er* of *baker*). New words were introduced to the child: *lar* (an animal), *lafit* (a sweet drink), and *kashemir* (a fabric). Then the children, aged five and six years, were asked questions to test their understanding of the suffixes: for example, *Who is a lar? Who is larishche? What is the difference between them?* and *What is kashemirshchik?* A correct response to the third question would indicate smallness. One correct response to the fourth question was *He turns a handle and gets kashemir*. The children generally succeeded with the diminutive and augmentative suffixes but were not as successful with the agentive suffixes. Bogoyavlenskiy's discussion of the results highlights many recurring themes in Soviet psychology: the importance of meaning, the tendency to regularity and overregularizations, and the fundamental creativity of language.

   Popova (1973) explored the development of gender suffixes on past-tense verbs, which must match the genders of the subject nouns. The basic sequence of development is similar to that of case endings, such as the instrumental singular discussed. The child first does not mark the past tense at all. Then a single form, here the feminine, is used for all genders (I). Next the masculine form is overgeneralized for all genders (II). A period of confusion follows (III), and then correct agreement for all genders is observed (IV). The feminine is probably selected first because it is the most clearly marked, having only two forms -*a* and -*ya*, whereas the masculine has a variety of forms. Popova then proceeded to attempt to teach children the correct forms, in order to determine what conditions lead to development. Two methods were used with the children, who were two and three years old. In the first, the teacher demonstrated the various forms in talking about toys and pictures and asked the children questions like *What was the bird doing in the hunter's room?* If a child gave a wrong answer, he was immediately corrected and told the correct form. Despite training sessions four times a week for two months, the procedure was not very successful. In general, the children advanced only one step in the sequence outlined. In the second teaching method, the teacher and child played with a tower and toy animals. The teacher asked *Who went into the tower?* If the child's answer included correct past-tense agreement, the tower doors opened, and the animals could enter. If not, the mistake was pointed out to the child. If he then corrected himself, the doors opened. If not, the teacher proceeded to the next toy. Popova does not report how long this procedure was followed, but the children seem to have advanced very rapidly, even omitting some stages, so that all of them reached stage IV. Popova concludes, concerning the role of repetition and correction in learning:

> Correcting mistakes in a child's pronunciation is not the same as correcting expressions which do not correspond to reality . . . when the experimenter gives the child a ready-made correct agreement to repeat (first method), the child is not faced with the necessity of manipulating linguistic material; what takes place is a simple juxtaposition of phrases . . . to find correct endings the child must actively approach the word structure. (1973:276, 279)

It is interesting to compare these results with some similar experiments performed with American children learning English, which will be reviewed in Chapter 6.

Russian Views of Language Acquisition

Despite the fact that American behaviorism looks to Ivan Pavlov as its intellectual father and despite the great veneration Soviet psychologists feel for Pavlov, Soviet psychology has never adopted the mechanistic, rather passive, models of learning and experience characteristic of the behavioristic tradition of psychological theorizing. Late in his life Pavlov himself came to the conclusion that, although fundamental reflex principles of the kind he had studied in dogs and other species apply to all species, the presence in humans of a complex and organized system of linguistic signals leads to a new dimension of behavior. He carefully distinguished "first signals" (all the individual physical stimuli to which animals and humans alike can respond) from "second signals" (primarily words). Although some second-order signals are observable in other animals, in man the second signal system is large and organized, with its own structures and functions. Slobin quotes Pavlov:

> The word created a second system of signals of reality which is peculiarly ours, being a signal of signals. On the one hand, numerous speech stimuli have removed us from reality. . . . On the other hand, it is precisely speech which has made us human (1966c:112).

There are many reasons for this conclusion by Soviet psychologists. Pavlov himself felt that virtually all the laws he had discovered concerning classical conditioning did not hold for the second signal system. For example, words can affect behavior immediately, without the gradual process of conditioning. But one of the most important reasons, especially for Soviet theories of language and language behavior, comes from the extensive and productive morphology—the means of constructing words out of morphemes —of the Russian language, which children use so creatively.

The most charming and enlightening record of such creativity is Kornei Chukovsky's *From Two to Five* (1968). Chukovsky was a famous Soviet writer and translater of children's stories who, over many years, collected hundreds of child-language anecdotes and analyzed them. Chukovsky writes: "It seems to me that, beginning with the age of two, every child becomes for a short period of time a linguistic genius. Later, beginning with the age of five or six, this talent begins to fade" (1968:7).

Some of the examples tell us about the child's conceptual powers and imagination: "Can't you see? I'm barefoot all over! I'll get up so early that it will still be late. Isn't there something to eat in the cupboard? There's only a small piece of cake, but it's middle-aged" (1968:3).

Other examples illustrate the child's manipulation of Russian morphology and syntax: "Another child, whose exact age I did not know, created the words 'shoeware' (*obutki*) and 'clothesware' (*odetki*) . . . these were formulated by a small child from the household words for footwear and clothes heard from adults" (1968:4–5). Interestingly enough, Chukovsky discovered that in another section of Russia, far from the area in which this child lived, these words had been part of the Russian language, in precisely the same forms and with the same meanings, several centuries ago.

> A two-year-old girl was taking a bath and making her doll "dive" into the water and "dive out" of it, commenting: "There, she drowns-in—now, she drowns-out!" *Vot pritonula, vot vytonula* . . . "Drowns-in" is not the same thing as drowns—it is to drown only temporarily with a definite expectation implied that the doll would be "drowning-out" again. . . . (1968:7).

In another example, a child refers to the husband of a grasshopper as a *daddy-hopper*. Children also enjoy making up verse, either intentionally or accidentally. A mother asks her son *Where did you put the broom?* He replies *Over there—on the stair*, then realizes the rhyme and begins to chant *Over there—on the stair, over there on the stair.*

   One kind of verse that Chukovsky believes is especially interesting is nonsense verse. Of course, much of children's poetry is nonsense, but there is one kind that is especially nonsensical. Chukovsky calls these verses "topsy-turvies." They are common in Russian folk tales and nursery rhymes. "An old woman mounted a sheep/And rode up the mountain steep." "The village rode/Past the peasant." "He sat with his back to the front/As he rode off to the hunt." We have these in English as well. There are nursery rhymes about going to sea in a bowl, a washtub, or even a sieve.

   Children often make up topsy-turvies. Chukovsky tells the story about how he finally came to understand why such topsy-turvies had such fascination for young children. His two-year-old daughter taught him. She had just been learning, with great delight, that cats meow, dogs bark, and so on. She would show anyone exactly what sound each animal made. Then, one day at age twenty-three months, she came up to her father and said *Daddy, 'oggie meow!* telling him that a dog meows. And she burst into laughter, but somewhat tentatively, as if waiting to see what her father would do. He said, "No, the doggie bow-wows"; *'oggie meow!* she repeated, laughing and watching. This time her father decided to join in the game and said, "And the rooster meows!" Then she laughed and laughed.

   Topsy-turvies are fun, then, because they turn the world upside-down at your own whim, yet the world has not really changed. The combination of the truth and the nonsense is funny—it is the basic discovery of comedy. Topsy-turvies are a special kind of play. When a child learns something, he wants to play with it. And what better way to play than to turn it upside down?

   Chukovsky also illustrates children's activity as critics of adult speech. Despite their own highly creative use of language, often including metaphor and simile, children are essentially nonmetaphorical and almost completely literal in their interpretation of other people's speech. Here are two examples (Chukovsky 1968:12):

> "Why do you say penknife? It should be pencil-knife," a little boy objected.
>
> A woman . . . asked her four-year-old Natasha: "Tell me, what does it mean to say that a person is trying to drown another in a spoonful of water (a Russian expression)?"
>
> "What did you say? In what kind of spoon? Say that again."
>
> The mother repeated the adage.
>
> "That's impossible" Natasha said categorically. "It can never happen!"
>
> Right then and there she (Natasha) demonstrated the physical impossibility of such an act; she grabbed a spoon and quickly placed it on the floor.
>
> "Look, here am I," and she stood on the spoon. "All right, drown me. There isn't enough room for a whole person—all of him will remain on top. . . . Look for yourself . . . the foot is much larger than spoon!"
>
> And Natasha expressed scorn for such an absurd idea conceived by grown-ups, saying: "Let's not talk about it any more—it's such nonsense."

The more we study child language, the more we come to share Chukovsky's view of the child as a "linguistic genius."

Sign Language and Its Development

Childhood deafness is a tragedy of development. The deaf form one of the most highly segregated minorities in our society; there is little contact with the hearing population after leaving school. In this section we shall provide some perspective before turning to the acquisition of sign language as a native language.

About half of all deaf individuals are genetically deaf, deaf from birth. Deafness is carried by a recessive gene, so that hearing parents may have a deaf child, though of course genetically deaf children are more frequently born to deaf parents. In many ways, genetically deaf children are the most fortunate, for they are least likely to have other medical problems. Children may also be born deaf when rubella, often called German measles, has been contracted during the first three months of the mother's pregnancy. Although rubella is not serious for the mother, it can be disastrous for the developing fetus, and deafness is only one possible result of it. Rubella is gradually being reduced (about 10 percent of deaf individuals are deaf for this reason), but an epidemic in 1963–1965 produced large numbers of deaf children.

Deafness may also be acquired after birth from diseases such as meningitis and encephalitis, which attack the nervous system. These diseases, like rubella, are likely to produce other problems. An important point is that, historically, acquired deafness has been very common. However, in recent years, with the development of antibiotics and other medical techniques, it has become rarer, so that at the present time the majority of deaf children are congenitally (from birth) deaf. This change has important implications for the education of the deaf, as there is clearly a difference between a child who has never heard and a child who has at least briefly heard language. Incidentally, Helen Keller, who triumphed over the twin handicaps of deafness and blindness, had acquired deafness at about one year of age.

The term "hearing impairment" is often used to indicate that the hearing loss may not be complete. Of course, if the impairment is severe, the child is little better off than a profoundly deaf child. But even moderate amounts of impairment will seriously affect language acquisition.

We tend to think of deafness—whether complete or partial—as a matter of turning down the volume. We may think that the sound is essentially the same but weaker. However, many kinds of deafness also distort the signal seriously. This is one reason why hearing aids are not a panacea and in fact are often rejected by children.

What is the prognosis for deaf children? Not very encouraging, on the average. Reading and writing are key skills for educational achievement and job success. The average deaf adult has a reading ability at about the fourth-grade level. There are similar lags for writing. Yet reading and writing would seem to be independent of the hearing difficulty. Deaf children are also given training in speaking and speech reading (popularly called "lip reading"). Speech reading is extremely difficult, because very little information is actually given in the visual signal. No visual cue is available to distinguish p from b, b from m, u from o, t from s, and many other contrasts. One study found that trained deaf individuals could not do as well as completely untrained hearing persons! This is because the only way speech reading can be done is for the "listener" to pick up the little information available visually and to piece it together, using everything he knows about the language, the topic of conversation, and so on. It is rather like listening to someone on a noisy telephone line; it can be done if you know the speaker and the topic. And English. But it is not possible to learn the system of language in this way. Similarly, deaf individuals are seldom able to communicate effectively with hearing persons who do not have special experience with the deaf, using speech.

The outlook is equally discouraging for educational achievement and job success. But none of this is for reasons of intelligence. Tested properly, that is, with nonverbal tests, many deaf children do very well.

There is one very significant exception to this gloomy picture: deaf children of deaf parents. It is paradoxical, as we would expect that having deaf parents would be an extra handicap. But on virtually every measure, these children do better than other deaf children.

There are several possible explanations. One is that deaf children of deaf parents are more likely to be genetically deaf and hence free of other handicaps. Another concerns parental acceptance of deafness. Many hearing parents find it difficult to accept that they have handicapped children, and the difficulty is compounded by the very real practical problems of living with a child with whom communication is often impossible. But the most important reason is that deaf children of deaf parents are usually exposed to sign language at an early age. In contrast, hearing parents seldom know sign language.

This brings us to the major controversy in the area of education for the deaf—the comparative merits of sign language and a speech-oriented approach. For a number of years, the leading educational method has been the oralist approach, which emphasizes training in speech production and speech reading. The use of signs—manual communication—is strongly discouraged and sometimes punished. Some such programs have refused to take children of deaf parents or other children who have been exposed to signing for fear of contaminating the school. The contrasting position is sometimes called the "total-communication method;" that is, it favors signing plus speech training.

At the present time, a major shift away from purely oralist approaches is taking place, and it is interesting to consider the reasons. Oral programs begin either in kindergarten or in preschools for three- to four-year-olds. To the extent that early childhood is a time of special ease for language learning (Lenneberg 1967), it would seem crucial to expose the child to language as early as possible. In fact, many programs do eventually give the children signing opportunities if they "fail" the oral approach, as part of vocational training in early adolescence. But the force of this argument for signing really depends on whether or not it is accepted as a language, and this is part of the controversy. Another objection to the oral approach is that it simply does not work for the majority of deaf children, as already discussed.

One defense of oralism against such criticisms is that every child must have a chance to learn to speak and that to allow him to use manual communication would destroy his motivation or ability to learn speech. There is an interesting unspoken assumption here: that allowing use of one system early in development will lower the chance of another system's being mastered later. This assumption is similar to an assumption about the language of many black children: It is assumed that to allow children to use Black English (to be discussed further in Chapter 10) will lower the chances of their eventually mastering Standard White English. In both instances the assumptions are just that, assumptions. The converse may be more nearly correct: Having an initial success in communication or reading is most important, and this success will provide a basis for later learning.

It should be pointed out that there is a reason for the preeminence of the oralist approach. Remember that historically there have been more children with acquired deafness than with congenital deafness. For these children, the oralist approach has a chance of success, building on whatever experience the child has had before deafness. But the situation is different now, when a large proportion of the deaf population has congenital handicaps.

Over the last few years, a number of studies have been conducted to evaluate the outcomes of oralist and manual-communication programs for young children. Stuckless and Birch (1966), Meadow (1968), and Vernon and Koh (1970; 1971) have compared children who have had early exposure to manual communication with children who have not had this early exposure. The results consistently show that on measures of reading, writing, school achievement, and social adjustment the manual groups are superior. Despite extensive training in speech and speech reading for the oral group, there are either no differences on these measures, or the manual group is slightly superior. In these studies, the manual group consists primarily of children of deaf parents and the oral group of children of hearing parents. This fact results in some confounding of educational method with cause of deafness, for the children of deaf parents are more likely to be genetically deaf. Vernon and Koh (1970) compared manual and oral children who were known to be genetically deaf, in order to eliminate this confounding. The results showed the same differences in favor of the manual group. Despite the fact that the parents of the oral group had more education than the parents of the manual group and despite the fact that the oral group had been to a preschool, the ability of the parents of the manual group to communicate with their children made all the difference.

In short, it is clear that teaching a young child sign language will not be detrimental to later attempts to teach him English and in many ways will increase his chances of success.

Sign Language

The most commonly used sign language in the United States is American Sign Language (ASL). American Sign Language was originally created by a French priest, l'Épée, in the mid-eighteenth century. He opened the first public school for the deaf in Paris in 1755. This sign language was in some ways similar to French, and to this day ASL retains some features in common with French. However, it has evolved in many ways, as we would expect of any living language over two centuries. The sign language used in Great Britain is quite different, and American and English signers may have some initial difficulty in communication.

It is important to realize that finger spelling is not sign language. It is simply spelling out English words. Deaf persons find it helpful for new or unusual words and for names, but it is too slow to be satisfactory as a communication system. In contrast, true sign language is as rapid as oral language in expressing sentence meanings (Bellugi and Fischer 1973).

Essentially, sign language has one sign for each morpheme of the language. A sign consists of a particular configuration of the hand, made at a particular position in space, and usually associated with a particular motion. For example, a particular hand configuration called the "tapered O," made on the cheek with movement up and away from the mouth, is *home*. A different hand configuration, made at the same place and with the same movement, signifies *yesterday*. A change in location, for example, placing the tapered O on both sides of the nose, signifies *flower*. Often signs with related meanings have one aspect in common. For example, many male/female pairs—father/mother, brother/sister, and so on—are identical except that the male item is made near the forehead, whereas the female item is made on the lower cheek. Figure 3.1 illustrates a few signs of American Sign Language.

Movement is very important in signing. A change in direction may reverse the meaning. For example, reversal of direction turns *join* into *disconnect* and *with* to *without*. Negation may be added by means of movement away from the face and downward: *Want* to *don't want*. Similarly for tense: Signs for future activity generally move forward from the signer at face level; signs for the past generally move toward the signer or back over the shoulder.

Movement also signals subject and object pronouns. The signed sentences for *I inform you, You inform me, You inform him* and so on are identical except for the direction of movement: to or from the signer, addressee, or a third person. The same process occurs with *teach, look at,* and certain other verbs. But not all signs can be used this way (all languages have exceptions!). *Chase, follow, lead,* and other verbs do not change in this way. Separate signs for subject and object are added, or they may be omitted if clear from context.

The effect of movement in signifying negation, tense, and subject and object pronouns is to make possible the encoding of two or more morphemes at once. In other instances the two hands or the hands and the face can encode two morphemes. This flexibility makes possible the rapidity of communication in sign language.

Sometimes it is said that signs are just gestures or pictures. But in fact it is easy to see the meaning only after one knows the sign. The sign

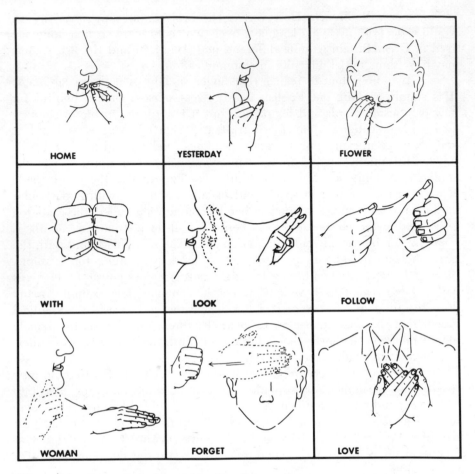

Figure 3.1   Some signs of American Sign Language.

SOURCE: Lottie Riekehof, *Talk to the deaf*. Springfield, Mo.: Gospel Publishing House, 1963. Reprinted by permission.

for *girl*, with the thumb moving along the lower check, originally symbolized the strings of women's bonnets; it is hardly a meaningful picture today. Similarly, the fact that the sign for *milk* resembles a milking motion is not very helpful for the average urban child, who knows little about milking cows. Like Chinese characters, *some* signs have some relation to the meanings signified, but the relations are seldom obvious to the learner.

ASL has been analyzed by linguists (Stokoe 1960), who have concluded that, although there are certain differences arising from the difference in modality, it is very much like oral languages: ASL has relatively few inflections, and it has dialects, ranging from a rather formal dialect, often used in formal settings or in communication with hearing individuals who know signing, to dialects used in informal settings, which are most different from spoken English. Most deaf individuals switch among these dialects according to the setting. In recent years, new sign languages that more closely resemble spoken English have been introduced (Bornstein 1973). They may have signs for the progressive *-ing*, the past tense *-ed*, auxiliaries, and so on. These sign languages are, of course, easier for hearing individuals who know English to learn. And it is thought that learning such sign language will make it easier for deaf children to learn to read and write English. However, they are necessarily much slower than ASL, which remains the primary language for most deaf people. Like oral language, ASL permits slips of the tongue (hand?), spoonerisms, puns, and poetry (Bellugi & Klima 1972).

Acquisition of Sign Language

Is the acquisition of sign language like the acquisition of oral language? Is it harder or easier?

Until recently, very little information has been available on the acquisition of signing, as hearing linguists and psychologists have had little contact with parents of children learning signing, who are typically deaf. Some anecdotal information is suggestive, however. Meadow (1968) reports interviewing two mothers of deaf children who were included in her study. One reported that both her deaf children signed well before one year of age. Another reported that her doctor was amazed to find that her deaf child knew almost 100 signs at one year of age. Larry Peterson (personal communication) has informed us that his deaf child produced her first sign at eight months, her first sign combinations at twelve months, and three sign combinations at eighteen months.

Two more formal studies are being conducted. A major research project on signing as a language and its acquisition is being conducted by Ursula Bellugi and others at the Salk Institute. Bellugi and Klima (1972) have presented some preliminary impressions. They believe that the similarities between deaf and hearing children are overwhelming. The same set of semantic relations appears in the first two-sign strings as in the first two-word utterances of hearing children. There is a steady increase in mean length of strings, paralleling the steady increase in MLU. Overgeneralizations similar to those in oral language occur. We have mentioned that movement often modifies the meanings of verbs. Verbs like *see* and *give* have characteristic motions, but the direction of motion varies. If the hand configuration is moved outward from signer to receiver, it signifies *I see you*; if the direction is reversed, it signifies *You see me*. However, this is only true for certain verbs. Pola, the child studied by Bellugi's group, requested her mother to finger-spell to her, that is, *You spell me*, by turning her hand with the fingers wiggling in toward herself. This sign is usually made with the palm facing out from the signer with fingers wiggling; it is not reversed by adult signers. Here Pola was using creatively the morphological structure of ASL, a move not unlike some of the examples in Chukovsky.

Another project has been conducted by Schlesinger and Meadow and reported in their book *Sound and Sign* (1972), a particularly good source on deaf children and signing. They studied the acquisition of signing in four children. Two of the children had deaf parents; two had hearing parents.

The first child, Ann, was a deaf child of deaf parents. Her first clear signs, as opposed to "babbling," which does occur in sign, were *pretty* and *wrong*, at twelve months. She seemed to understand many more. Vocabulary growth was rapid: she had 106 words at eighteen months. These words were not just the more pictographic signs. Most of the signs she had acquired were far from obvious: *milk* and *girl*, for example. Single signs were used for a range of meanings, as one-word utterances. Signs had broad meanings. For example, at fifteen months *smell* meant 'want to go to bathroom,' 'soiled, please change me,' and 'I want that pretty flower.' Signs were first produced in the presence of the object and later were produced spontaneously, even when the object was not present.

Just as the first words are not pronounced exactly like those of adults, the first signs are not perfect reproductions of adult models. Often two of the three key features are reasonably accurate, but the third is off. Signs made at the mouth by adults may be made at the chin; the location is incorrect. Hand configuration may be inaccurate, though this seems less common. *Girl* was made with the thumb stroking the cheek but with a hand configuration from another sign. Less common still is altered movement. *Kitty* was given a downward stroke, rather than a horizontal one. Children seem to be especially sensitive to movement, probably because it is the most perceptually salient.

Sign language appeared to play the same role in Ann's life as it does in the hearing toddler's life. At fourteen-and-a-half months Ann went upstairs; her mother asked in sign *sleep you?*; Ann nodded, waved byebye, and went upstairs. Another time her mother was leaving Ann with a hearing babysitter. She became upset; her mother signed *Don't cry; mommy daddy going out; will come back.* Ann appeared to understand and did not cry. These incidents seem ordinary, but many parents of four- and five-year-old deaf children report that they cannot understand what their children want, whether it is food, drink, the toilet, or whatever. Clearly the emotional bond between parent and child requires communication for its full development.

A second child, Karen, was studied between 2;10 and 3;6, so that the beginning of syntax could be observed. Schlesinger and Meadow do not report MLU, but they looked primarily at two-sign strings. They found basically the same set of semantic relations as are observed in hearing children: *daddy work*, a locative ('daddy is at work'); *Barry train*, a possessive (her brother's train); *bed shoes*, an attributive (referring to slippers); and *daddy shoe*, an agent-object string (trying to persuade daddy to take off his shoe and get into the sandbox with her). Negatives are also common.

The third child, Ruth, was born to hearing parents. When she was one-and-a-half years old they decided to learn signing and to teach it to Ruth. At three years, her vocabulary included 348 signs; four months later it included 604. This explosion of vocabulary resembles that of hearing children. Ruth's language was grammatically more advanced than that of Karen. She produced strings like *Come out rabbit* and *Mark in picture.* Like hearing children, she was very good at picking up nursery rhymes. At one point she signed *All the king's horses and all the king's men.*

The fourth child, Marie, was somewhat older. Her mother used a great deal of finger spelling with her, in addition to signs. She attempted to add the basic inflections of English to her signing. By age three-and-a-half years, Marie was consistently using the past-tense, plural, and present-progressive endings appropriately. At age four-and-a-half years, when Marie began to learn to read, she could transfer these finger-spelling skills to reading.

Studies of the latter two children, who were living in a hearing (and hence speaking) environment, have shown that sign-language acquisition did not interfere with speech acquisition. These two children learned to read speech and to produce words better than do most deaf children who are not exposed to signing.

Still more striking are the findings of Goldin-Meadow and Feldman (1975), who studied four deaf children of hearing parents. Since the parents of these children did not know sign language, and the children's deafness precluded auditory input, the children essentially received no language input. Each child responded to his situation by *creating* a sign language, devising signs to specify objects and actions, and in two cases, going beyond this to specify relations between objects and actions by combining gestures in rule-governed ways similar to the very early oral language of hearing children and the early sign language of deaf children. Without the benefit of input, these children took the first steps in language development on their own.

What conclusion can we draw from this admittedly small body of evidence? The really important aspects of language and the really important abilities the child brings to the problem of language learning are independent of the modality in which the linguistic system operates. Language is a central process, not a peripheral one. The abilities that children have are so general, and so powerful, that they proceed through the same milestones of development as do hearing children.

Summary

Regardless of the linguistic community into which they are born, children approach the problem of language learning in very similar ways. The first stage of language learning consists primarily of expressions of a basic set of semantic relationships. Inflections and grammatical morphemes are omitted. The process of development within stage I, the progressive elaboration of longer sequences, is also cross-linguistically validated. One point on which children differ is their use of word order. Most children hearing a word-order language will produce sentences with fixed orders, but children who hear a relatively free language may produce sentences with fixed orders, with the range of orders they hear, or with a range of orders even broader than those they hear.

In the next stage of development, many of the most important inflections and other grammatical morphemes are acquired. Both syntactic complexity and semantic complexity determine the sequence of acquisition. Not only the concept underlying a grammatical morpheme must be mastered but also its linguistic means of expression. Phenomena like overgeneralization and overregularization are universal in child language.

Even when the linguistic system being acquired operates in a completely different modality—sign language—the milestones of development are similar, illustrating the generality and power of the language-learning ability of the child.

further reading

Bowerman, M. *Early syntactic development: A cross-linguistic study with special reference to Finnish*. Cambridge: Cambridge University Press, 1973.

Ferguson, C. A., and D. I. Slobin. *Studies of child language development*. New York: Holt, Rinehart and Winston, 1973.

Schlesinger, H. S., and K. P. Meadow. *Sound and sign*. Berkeley: University of California Press, 1972.

4

Linguistics and Child Language

We have, in the preceding descriptions of early child language, avoided linguistic concepts and terminology for the most part. Instead, we have used verbal descriptions, without attempting to define terms. However, such an approach is eventually inadequate; more precision in concept and in terminology is necessary. In the previous chapters, utterances have been classified on an after-the-fact basis; a list or catalogue of types has been compiled. But we really want to see the underlying system that ties these utterance types together, to specify which kinds of utterances are possible at a given stage and which not. Linguistics provides a way of talking about a language as a system. Furthermore, we have so far ignored detail in child language. For example, not all words can be agents in agent-object sentences, nor is the set of words that can be agents the same as the set of words that can be objects. If our goal is to describe the child's total language system, the total of his knowledge of language at a particular stage, we must specify such details. Linguistics provides a language for talking about language. In addition, we have to understand the end point of language development, that is, adult English. What does the child have to learn, and how does his language at any stage compare to the adult language? Linguistics attempts to provide a characterization of adult English.

As a science, linguistics has two goals. The first is to characterize, or to describe, a particular language. What does a person know when he knows English? The second goal is to characterize *language* as a general phenomenon. What do languages have in common; what are the distinguishing characteristics of language? The first goal is the better known, but the second is equally relevant for understanding child language.

Language as Rule-Governed Behavior

Imagine tying your shoelaces. Now try to explain exactly how you do it. To keep the game honest, clasp your hands together in front of you, so that you cannot simply demonstrate the action. It is all but impossible to explain the process.

Language has this elusive I-can-do-it-but-I-cannot-tell-you-how property. As human beings, we spend a large proportion of our time engaged in speaking or listening, but the process is usually so effortless that we are unaware of how we do it. Our goal now is to stand back and to examine this activity that permeates our lives.

We shall begin with two of the most important facts about language. First, **a language is a productive system.** Using a language is a creative act. The overwhelming majority of all the sentences that a person utters or hears are novel. They have not occurred in his experience. For example, there are more than 5,000 sentences in this book, and no two are identical. This does not mean that sentences are never repeated. Many standard formulas—such as *How are you?*—are repeated thousands of times in a lifetime, but they are clearly exceptional.

Although the set of words of a language, its vocabulary, or lexicon, is finite, the number of possible sentences in a language is unlimited. There are just so many words, and it is possible to construct a list of them. But there is no limit to the number of sentences or to their lengths. From any English declarative sentence, a new and longer sentence may be created by adding *and the moon is not made of green cheese* to the end or *I think that* to the beginning. There are dictionaries of words in English but no dictionaries of sentences. To say that a person knows a language is to say that he is able to understand any sentence of the language (assuming that he knows the meanings of the words used). But he cannot have learned these sentences as a list; he must have mastered some set of principles that specifies how words can be combined to form sentences. In other words, with a finite amount of knowledge, the speaker of a language[1] can understand or produce an unlimited number of sentences if he knows the principles of combining words meaningfully.

This may sound paradoxical, but in fact it is not unusual. For exam-

---

[1] "Speaker of a language" is merely a shorthand term. It does not mean that speaking is the most important language function or that speaking and understanding are completely distinct activities.

ple, to know how to multiply means to know how to obtain the product of any number with any number. One way to multiply would be to refer to a table of the products of all possible pairs of numbers. Such a table would be very easy to use but infinitely long because there is an unlimited number of numbers. It would also be impossible to learn. Instead, we multiply using a short (100-entry) multiplication table.

$$3 \times 4 = 12$$
$$3 \times 5 = 15$$
$$3 \times 6 = 18$$

And we use a relatively short set of rules for using the table:

1. Multiply the right-most digit of one number by the right-most digit of the second.
2. Then multiply the right-most digit of the first number by the next-to-right-most digit of the second, and move the product one place to the left.
3. And so on until each digit of the first number has been multiplied by each digit of the other, moving the product an appropriate number of places to the left.
4. Add all the resulting products.

Once the table and rules have been mastered, we are prepared for any possible multiplication problem, not just the ones that have been practiced.

A second important fact about language is that **many of the utterances encountered in normal conversation are not perfectly grammatical.** There are slips of the tongue, changes of topic in mid-sentence, false starts, forgetting of the subject of the sentence by the time the verb rolls around, and more. In conversational context, fragments may be meaningful that would not be grammatical in isolation, for example, *his* as a response to *Whose hat is this?* The child who is acquiring language, therefore, is not even presented with very high-quality information. To be sure, the speech addressed to children is not identical with speech addressed to other adults, as we will see in Chapter 6, but the point is still valid to a somewhat lesser extent.

These two facts imply that language consists essentially of a set of patterns, or **rules**—rules that can be applied in situations that are not identical to those in which they are learned and rules that can be violated. To put this another way, language is systematic, as well as productive. Despite the unlimited number of sentences that can be created, most word combinations are ungrammatical.

The behavioral sciences, other than linguistics, have not used the concept of rule-governed behavior, and it is easily (and often) misunderstood. The business of linguistics is to *describe* language, not to *prescribe* it. Linguists tell us how we talk, not how we should talk. The phrase "grammatical sentence" occurs often in the literature of linguistics. Linguists do not decide for other people whether sentences are grammatical or not. They want to know which strings of words are grammatical sentences for the speakers of a·language and which are not. Grammatical sentences and ungrammatical ones are the raw data of linguistics, not the result. For example, any speaker of English can recognize that *Wash your hands* is a well-formed sentence in a sense that *°Your wash hands*² is not. *I play the flute* is correct in a sense that *°Flute I the play* is not. There is a large (in fact, unlimited) number of word strings that are well formed, or grammatical, and there is a large (again, unlimited) number of strings that are not. And, of course, there are the inevitable fuzzy cases in between. This is what all linguists mean by "grammatical" and "ungrammatical." Their task is to determine what it is that makes some strings grammatical and some not. Rules are attempts to explain the division.

If it is true, as we claimed at the beginning of this chapter, that not all sentences produced by speakers actually follow the rules, that is, that many of them are ungrammatical, what kind of reality do these rules have? It is easier to answer this question for the example of multiplication. Although a person may know the principles for multiplying two numbers, he will in fact occasionally (or often) make mistakes in multiplying, especially if the numbers are large. Suppose a person can correctly multiply any two two-digit numbers in his head but not any two eight-digit numbers. It would be unreasonable to say that he knows how to multiply only two-digit numbers and not eight-digit numbers. It would be more natural to say that he knows how to multiply any two numbers but that, when the numbers are large and many steps are involved, he is likely to make mistakes. Additional support for this view is the fact that, given enough time, as well as paper and pencil, he can probably multiply two eight-digit numbers accurately.

The same principle holds for language. People make mistakes for a variety of reasons. Perhaps a speaker is tired or distracted. Although the speaker has knowledge of the principles that define grammatical sentences, he may not use this knowledge without error. This is the foundation of the important distinction between linguistic competence and linquistic performance. **Linguistic competence** is the set of learned principles that a person must have in order to be a speaker of a language. **Linguistic performance** is the translation of this knowledge into action. Performance involves many factors, including competence, memory, distraction, perception, and others. Competence at multiplying consists of knowledge of the rules of multiplication; performance is the actual work of multiplying. Obviously the rules for multiplying are involved in the work, but so are many other factors, such as memory, fatigue, and distraction.

---

² By convention, an ungrammatical sequence of words is marked by an asterisk.

There is one very important difference between competence at multiplying and linguistic competence. Anyone who can multiply can state the rules explicitly. They are part of conscious knowledge. This is not so with language. In general, speakers of a language cannot state the rules of their language. It is the goal of linguistics to formulate these rules. Linguistic competence is an example of *tacit knowledge*.

Grammars

A grammar is essentially a theory. Like any other scientific theory, it is an attempt to explain some domain of natural phenomena. In the theory called "a grammar," the natural phenomenon is *the knowledge of a language that is possessed by every native speaker of that language*. This knowledge includes knowledge about which utterances are grammatical sentences and which are not (*His authority persuaded John* or *°John persuaded his authority*), which sentences are ambiguous (*Visiting relatives can be a nuisance*), which sentences have the same meanings as other sentences (*Silas Marner counted the gold* and *The gold was counted by Silas Marner*), and more. Furthermore, like any scientific theory, it must be *explicit*: It must clearly and unambiguously lead to testable predictions. In a grammar, the predictions include, among others, statements about which strings of words are grammatical sentences and which are not. It is the requirement of explicitness that leads, in linguistics as in many other sciences, to the expression of theories in symbolic form.

Grammars are theories of language in a dual sense. In the first sense, a grammar represents a linguist's (that is, an outside observer's) best attempt to summarize and characterize the language of a speaker or group of speakers. In the second, far stronger sense, it is an attempt to describe the organization of language in the mind of the speaker. The first we can do with some confidence; the second requires far greater use of inference. Nevertheless, it is the ultimate goal of our descriptions.

Sentence Structure

Constituent Structure

What is it that makes some utterances grammatical sentences of English and some ungrammatical? Sentences are composed of smaller units, of words. For example, *I see her* is composed of the three words *I*, *see*, and *her*. However, many words themselves consist of two or more smaller units, each making a contribution to the meaning of the sentence. The word *walked*, for example, consists of two units: *walk*, which is a word referring to a particular kind of action, and the ending *-ed*, which indicates that the action took place in the past. Although the *-ed* ending cannot stand by itself, it is a distinct unit, or element, and can be combined with almost any verb. Similarly, *troubleshooter* consists of three distinct elements, *trouble, shoot,* and *-er,* and the meaning of the word is a composite of the meanings of its three basic elements. These basic elements of meaning are called **morphemes.**

A sentence, then, is a collection of morphemes. Some collections are acceptable (that is, they are grammatical sentences), whereas others are not (ungrammatical sentences). However, there is more to the sentence than the morphemes that compose it. Compare *John loves Mary* with *Mary loves John.* The two sentences contain the same morphemes, yet their meanings are different. The difference in meaning is signaled by order. In general, we can think of the meaning of a sentence as consisting of the meanings of the morphemes plus the meaning contributed by the way they are joined, that is, by the **structure** of the sentence.

Ordering is not the only aspect of structure that contributes to meaning. One of the most important aspects of a sentence is the way in which it seems to break up into subunits, or **clusters.** Often a single sentence, a string of morphemes in a particular order, is **ambiguous;** that is, it corresponds to two meanings. For example, *We fed her dog bones* is ambiguous. In one interpretation, the sentence reports feeding a dog; in the other, a female human being. The two meanings appear to correspond to two ways of breaking up the sentence. In the first, *her* and *dog* form one unit, and *bones* comprises another; in the second, *dog* and *bones* form one unit, and *her* comprises another.

Let us look more closely at this process of dividing sentences. Consider the sentence *The old woman saw a small boy.* (We shall return to *We fed her dog bones* shortly.) The sentence consists of a string of seven words, arranged in a particular order. In addition, the words of the sentence fall into groups, or clusters, which speakers of English have little difficulty in recognizing. Suppose you were asked to divide this sentence into two parts in the way that seemed most natural to you. Which of these two alternatives would you produce?

The   old woman saw a small boy.

The old woman saw a small   boy.

Probably neither; instead you would divide the string this way:

The old woman   saw a small boy.

There is something in this string of words that enables you to make this division. If, instead, you were given the string

brick dog ham cloud girl tree water

which is also an ordered string of seven items, and were asked to divide it naturally, you would have no idea of how to do it. Probably everyone would divide it differently. The difference between *The old woman saw a small boy* and *brick dog ham cloud girl tree water* is that the former has structure: natural subunits in the sentence, clusters of words that go together.

One way of indicating how words are clustered in a sentence is to diagram them:

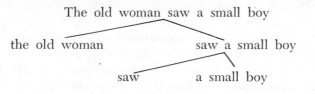

Going farther, suppose you were asked to divide the string *saw a small boy* into two clusters. The most likely answer would be *saw* and *a small boy*. The diagram would then look like this:

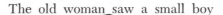

Because diagrams like this begin to look like upside-down trees, minus trunks, they are called **tree diagrams.**

The clusters of words into which a sentence can be divided in this way are called the **constituents** of the sentence. We have found four constituents so far: *the old woman, saw a small boy, saw,* and *a small boy.* The example can be continued by dividing *the old woman* into two parts, *the* and *old woman. Old woman* can be divided into *old* and *woman.* A *small boy* can be divided into *a* and *small boy.* Finally, *small boy* yields *small* and *boy.* Keeping track of all these divisions in a tree diagram produces:

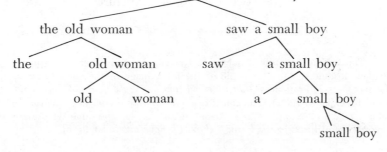

For the sake of completeness, the entire sentence is also considered a constituent. Counting it, we have a total of thirteen constituents. Notice that many of the constituents are made up of smaller constituents and themselves are parts of larger constituents. *A small boy*, for example, is made up of *a* and *small boy* and is part of *saw a small boy*. This kind of structure is called **hierarchical structure.** The fact that language has hierarchical structure is one of its most important properties, for it allows unlimited elaboration of detail to be combined into a coherent structure.

Looking over the thirteen constituents of our sentence, we see some similarities and some differences among them. The constituent *the old woman* seems to be similar to the constituent *a small boy*, and *the* seems to be similar to *a* in a way that is not true of *the* and *small boy*. One way to check whether or not two constituents are of the same general type is to try substitution. Replace each constituent with the other, and see if the resulting string of words is a grammatical sentence. For example, switching *the* and *small boy*, we have *small boy old woman saw a the*, which is not a grammatical sentence. But, if we switch *the old woman* and *a small boy*, we have *A small boy saw the old woman*, which is grammatical. In this way we can determine the basic types of constituents.[3]

We have just analyzed the **constituent structure,** that is, the set of constituents of one sentence and how they are combined.

If we were to analyze the constituent structures of *My new radio makes an unpleasant noise* and *I bought a radio at the store*, we would find that the first sentence has the same constituent structure as *The old woman saw a small boy* and that the second sentence has a different constituent structure. Try it. These observations suggest part of the answer to our question What makes a string of words a grammatical sentence? *If the string has a correct English constituent structure, it is a grammatical sentence.* If it violates English constituent structure, it is ungrammatical.

Knowing the constituent structure of a sentence is necessary in order to determine the meaning of the sentence, as well as whether or not it is grammatical. Recall that one aspect of the meaning of a sentence concerns the way in which the individual words are joined in the sentence. This point can be seen most clearly in ambiguous sentences like *We fed her dog bones.* The two meanings, one about dinner for a dog and one about dinner for a person, correspond to the two constituent structures this sentence can have:

---

[3] The substitution test is not perfectly reliable, and other techniques must be used in many instances. As an example of the inadequacy of the substitution test, consider the sentences *Falstaff drank hot buttered rum* and *Falstaff drank incessantly* (from Jacobs and Rosenbaum 1968). The constituents *hot buttered rum* and *incessantly* can be substituted for each other in these sentences, but they are not the same type of constituent and cannot be substituted in the frame *I think I'll have another mug of . . . .*

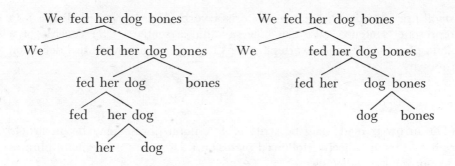

The ambiguity does not arise from a difference in words or in the order of words but, rather, from a difference in constituent structure. Another example is the phrase *little girl's bike*. If it is divided

little girl's   bike

it refers to a bike that belongs to a little girl. If it is divided

little   girl's bike

it refers to a girl's bike that is little.

Phrase-Structure Grammar

We have been examining a few English sentences and their properties. But looking at individual sentences will not lead us to a complete theory of English because there is an unlimited number of sentences in English. We want to describe the knowledge that speakers of English must have in order to create and understand these sentences.

One characteristic that seems to distinguish sentences from non-sentences involves the constituent structure of the sentence, that is, the way the words are grouped together. How can we represent this characteristic in a grammar? Remember that the goal is to have a theory that explicitly indicates, among other things, which strings of words are grammatical English sentences and which are not.

When we considered the constituent structure of sentences, we saw that there are characteristic ways in which the various kinds of constituents can be further divided. And this is the basic principle we shall use.

Each type of constituent in a sentence has a characteristic name, which is usually represented symbolically. Constituents like *the old woman* and *a small boy* are called **noun phrases** (NP). Constituents like *saw a small boy* are called **verb phrases** (VP). Individual words, which are themselves constituents, are also labeled: *the* and *a* are **articles** (Art), *old* and *small* are **adjectives** (Adj), and *saw* is a verb (V). And we shall use S to represent "sentence." We can now say that a sentence (S) consists of a noun phrase (NP) and a verb phrase (VP), and we can write this definition this way:

PS1[4]   S → NP + VP

(The arrow is read "may be written.") A noun phrase may be an article followed by an adjective followed by a noun. Of course, some noun phrases do not contain adjectives:

PS2   NP → Art + (Adj) + N

(Parentheses mean "optional.") Note that in the formulation of this rule, which has three terms on the right side, we have abandoned the assumption of division into two parts only, which we followed in the tree diagrams on the previous pages. Restriction to two terms per division is not necessary and seems artificial in many instances.

A verb phrase is a verb followed by a noun phrase:

PS3   VP → V + NP

Some possible nouns are *man, woman,* and *boy*:

PS4   N → $\left\{ \begin{array}{c} man \\ woman \\ boy \end{array} \right\}$

(Braces mean "any one of these.") Some possible verbs are *saw* and *heard*:

PS5   V → $\left\{ \begin{array}{c} saw \\ heard \end{array} \right\}$

Some possible adjectives are *young* and *old*:

PS6   Adj → $\left\{ \begin{array}{c} young \\ old \end{array} \right\}$

And some possible articles are *the* and *a*:

PS7   Art → $\left\{ \begin{array}{c} the \\ a \end{array} \right\}$

---

[4] PS is an abbreviation for **phrase structure**. When it appears in front of a rule, it designates a phrase-structure rule. "Phrase" here means about the same thing as "constituent."

This set of seven statements is a phrase-structure grammar. It indicates that certain strings of words are sentences. It does this by

1. Starting with S (sentence)
2. Interpreting the arrows as instructions to rewrite; that is, S may be rewritten as NP + VP
3. And continuing in this way until the string of symbols has been replaced by a string of words.

For example:

S	
NP + VP	PS1
NP + V + NP	PS3
Art + Adj + N + V + NP	PS2 (with option)
Art + Adj + N + V + Art + Adj + N	PS2 (with option)
The + Adj + N + V + Art + Adj + N	PS7
The + old + N + V + Art + Adj + N	PS6
The + old + woman + V + Art + Adj + N	PS4
The + old + woman + saw + Art + Adj + N	PS5
The + old + woman + saw + a + Adj + N	PS7
The + old + woman + saw + a + small + N	PS6
The + old + woman + saw + a + small + boy	PS4

The record of the steps involved in this process is called a **derivation.** From the derivation, the proper tree diagram can be produced.

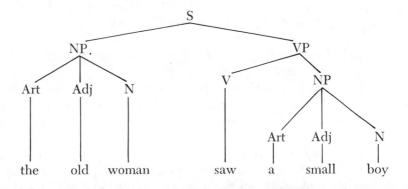

The phrase-structure grammar we have just constructed is a theory of English. It indicates which strings of words are English sentences: those that can be produced by the mechanical procedure we used to derive *The old woman saw a young boy.* There are, in all, 648 sentences that can be derived using this set of seven rules, including *The boy saw a dog, The young boy heard a dog,* and others. Furthermore, this grammar indicates the constituent structure of the sentences that it generates. Of course, it is a rather trivial theory of English. It produces only very simple sentences with a limited vocabulary. But the grammar can be expanded to produce more sentences, of more varied structure, by means of additional rules and modifications to existing ones. The most obvious one would be the addition of vocabulary items. Simply adding one adjective to PS6 would result in the production of 504 additional sentences.

Adding new vocabulary items will not lead to the derivation of other kinds of sentences, such as those without objects (for example, *The man fell*). Simply adding *fell* to the list of verbs in PS3 is not adequate, because it would lead to the production of *°The man fell a young boy.* Instead, we must distinguish between two kinds of verbs, those that take objects, usually called **transitive verbs** (VT), and those that do not, the **intransitive verbs** (VI). They determine two distinct types of verb phrases. One way to distinguish the two would be to replace PS3 with a new rule:

$$\text{PS8} \qquad \text{VP} \rightarrow \begin{Bmatrix} \text{VI} \\ \text{VT} + \text{NP} \end{Bmatrix}$$

A related type of sentence is exemplified by *I gave the boy a book.* This sentence contains two objects: an object that is given and an object (usually a person) to whom the first object is given. The former is usually called the **direct object** and the latter the **indirect object.** Verbs that take indirect objects form a special subset of transitive verbs. To generate sentences of this type, PS8 might in turn be replaced by:

$$\text{PS9} \qquad \text{VP} \rightarrow \begin{Bmatrix} \text{VI} \\ \text{VT1} + \text{NP} \\ \text{VT2} + (\text{NP}) + \text{NP} \end{Bmatrix}$$

The parentheses in the third line of PS9 reflect the fact that indirect objects may be omitted, as in *I gave the book.*

In this way, by adding to the number and complexity of rules and by carefully distinguishing classes of words that are used differently, we can extend phrase-structure grammars to account for more and more English sentences.

Phrase-structure grammars can account for certain types of ambiguity, which we have seen to be an aspect of the knowledge of a language possessed by speakers. Recall the sentence *We fed her dog bones.* Several additions to the grammar would be necessary in order to generate this sentence: pronouns as noun phrases and as modifiers (like adjectives) and the possibility of plural nouns. However, the basic form of the sentence is captured by the rules already established. Both interpretations of the sentence are based on the use of the third option in PS9. But in the first instance (concerning the feeding of a dog), the first NP is expanded to *her dog* (by a modified version of PS2) and the second NP is limited to *bones*. In the second interpretation, the first NP is rewritten as *her* and the second to *dog bones*. That is, the grammar generates the sentence *We fed her dog bones* in two distinct ways, which result in two distinct tree diagrams, corresponding to the two meanings:

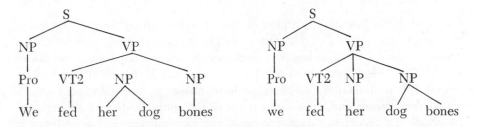

Transformational Grammar

Deep Structures

During most of this century linguists have written their theories of particular languages in the form of phrase-structure grammars. Although not always formalized in quite the way illustrated in the previous section, they have been essentially the same kinds of grammar (Postal 1964). Phrase-structure grammars do account for our intuitions about how the words of a sentence are grouped together, the constituent structure of a sentence, and they also account for certain kinds of ambiguity, like that of *We fed her dog bones*. Despite these qualities, such grammars are now considered to be inadequate for the description of language. Instead linguists, beginning with Noam Chomsky (1957), have turned to **transformational grammar.** The major advantage of transformational grammar is that, in addition to the constituent structure of a sentence as just described, which is called the **surface structure,** there is another level of constituent structure, called the **deep structure** (or **base structure** or **underlying structure**). In both instances "structure" refers to the relations among the morphemes of a sentence.

This claim amounts to a complication in our theories of language. Why is it necessary? For just the usual reasons leading to the rejection of one scientific theory in favor of another one: The new theory is more powerful, is more efficient, captures more generalizations, and so on. We shall examine several specific aspects of English that can be best explained by distinguishing between deep and surface structure. But first we shall look at a general motivation for this innovation.

Consider these two ambiguous sentences:

1. We fed her dog bones.
2. Visiting relatives can be a nuisance.

The two meanings of sentence 1 correspond to two different surface structures, which can be indicated in shorthand form with parentheses:

1a. (We)   (fed   (her dog)·   bones)
1b. (We)   ((fed her)   (dog bones))

One cue to the intended meaning of this sentence migıt be the placement of pauses: *we—fed—her dog—bones* is clearly a statement about feeding a dog; *we fed her—dog bones* is a statement about giving someone bones to eat. The difference in meaning between 1a and 1b can also be cued by stress. When spoken, 1a is likely to have stress on both *dog* and *bones*, 1b on *dog*. Pauses and stress are aspects of the sound system of a language, its **phonology.** As the examples suggest, the pronunciation of a sentence is largely determined by its surface structure.

Sentence 2 also has two meanings: one about relatives who visit (2a), the other about going to visit relatives (2b). But the two meanings cannot be distinguished by means of pauses, for the most natural place for a pause in either instance is *Visiting relatives—can be a nuisance.* Stress is placed on the first syllables of both *visiting* and *relatives* for both meanings. In fact, the surface structure is identical for the two meanings:

2a and 2b. (Visiting relatives)   ((can be)   (a nuisance))

Nevertheless, the relations among the words of the sentence are different for each interpretation. If we transform, or **paraphrase,** the sentence, attempting to preserve the meaning, we can produce for 2a *Relatives who visit can be a nuisance* and for 2b *It can be a nuisance to visit relatives.* The difference between 2a and 2b corresponds to the different relationship between *relatives* and *visit* in these two paraphrases. The surface structure does not reflect this difference; the ambiguity arises from the presence of two deep structures corresponding to the single surface structure. As the example suggests, the meaning of a sentence is primarily determined by its deep structure.

The theory of transformational grammar claims that every sentence has a deep structure and a surface structure and that the two are by no means necessarily identical. How the deep and surface structures are related is specified by the rules of transformation or, simply, by transformations.

In sentence 2, the two interpretations seem to hinge on whether *relatives* is the subject or the object of the verb *visit.* The concepts of subject, predicate, and object are different from those of noun phrase and verb phrase. In the simple sentence *The dog bit the timid mailman, the dog* is an NP, and it is also the subject of the sentence. But being the subject is not the same thing as being an NP. *The timid mailman* is also an NP, but it is the object of the verb and not the subject. Saying that a constituent is an NP is a statement about how the constituent is constructed, that it has a certain kind of internal structure—article + adjective + noun and so on. In contrast, to say that an NP is a subject, predicate, or object is to make a statement about the function of the constituent in the sentence, that is, to make a statement about how it relates to the other parts of the sentence.

The sentence *The dog bit the timid mailman* suggests that the subject of a sentence might be defined as the first NP. Such a definition is adequate only for very simple sentences. Consider the pair of sentences:

   3. John is easy to please.
   4. John is eager to please.

Any definition of subject and object, if it applies to the surface structure, will imply that the relation between *John* and *please* is the same for the two sentences, because the surface structures of the two sentences are identical. But clearly the relation is not the same. *John* is the object of *please* in sentence 3, which might be paraphrased *It is easy to please John.* In sentence 4, *John* is the subject of *please*, which might be paraphrased *John is eager that he please.* The distinction is clearly represented in the deep structures of the two sentences. Both sentences contain two simple sentences in their deep structures:

   3a. (Someone pleases John)   (is easy)
   4a. (John is eager)   (John pleases someone)

Consistent and reasonable definitions of subject, object, and other related terms can be given for the deep structures of sentences. There are six basic grammatical relations in all:

  I. If a sentence consists (in the deep structure) of an NP and a VP, the NP is the **subject** of the sentence, and the VP is the **predicate.**
 II. If a VP consists of a V and an NP, the V is the **main verb** of the verb phrase, and the NP is the **object.**
III. If an NP consists of an N and something else, the N is the head of a noun phrase (or **head noun**), and the "something else" (usually called a **determiner**) is the **modifier.**

The definitions are easily applied to simple sentences. The sentence *I dropped the cookies* consists of a noun phrase (the pronoun *I*), a verb, and another noun phrase consisting of an article and a noun. The subject is *I*, the predicate *dropped the cookies*; the predicate consists of a main verb (*dropped*) and an object (*the cookies*). The object is a noun phrase consisting of a modifier (*the*) and a head noun (*cookies*).

But in sentence 3 the subject of *please* is not present in the surface structure at all; similarly, in sentence 4 the object of *please* is not present. Elements of deep structure are often not present in the surface structure. A particularly good example is the imperative. *Sit down!* has no subject in the surface structure, but the subject is clearly understood to be *you*. The imperative transformation removes (or deletes) the subject of an imperative sentence in most instances.

One defect of surface-structure analysis of sentences is that it fails to clarify the relations among sentences of different forms. Speakers of English feel intuitively that sentences are related, even though they have distinct surface structures. Perhaps the clearest example in English is that of active and passive sentences. The sentences *The dog bites the man* and *The man is bitten by the dog* have the same meaning, even though the elements of the sentence are arranged quite differently. According to a surface-structure analysis, they are simply two different sentence types with entirely distinct structures.[5]

(the dog)   ((bites)   (the man))
(the man)   ((is bitten)   (by the dog))

Although there is nothing essentially incorrect about such an analysis, it misses many important facts about English; that is, it does not provide generalizations that hold true for active, passive, and other types of sentences. Not only can active and passive sentences have the same meanings (although they may have different emphases), but they can also have many aspects of structure in common. Consider the following sentences:

5. John prefers steak.
6. Steak is preferred by John.
7. *Steak prefers John.
8. *John is preferred by steak.

Sentences 5 and 6 are grammatical, whereas 7 and 8 are ungrammatical. What is needed is a rule, or **restriction,** on possible combinations of words to prevent the occurrence of ungrammatical sentences. In this instance, verbs such as *prefer, admire,* and so on must be used with human nouns as "actors," that is, with **animate subjects.** Sentences 7 and 8 violate this restriction and are therefore ungrammatical. Now, if we limit ourselves to surface structure, we find that we have to state the restriction twice: once for the relationship between the subjects and the verbs of active sentences (*animate noun prefers X*) and again for the verbs and the NPs after *by* in passive

---

[5] Although a structure can be represented fully only with a tree diagram, to save space we shall often use only the bottom line of the diagram, which indicates the elements and their order and grouping by means of parentheses.

sentences (*X is preferred by animate noun*). Such an account seems redundant. The relationship between the verb and the noun phrase is the same,
whether the noun phrase comes before the verb in an active sentence or
after *by* in a passive sentence. A simpler description would result from
viewing actives and passives as essentially the same at the level of deep
structure. A transformation will convert the deep structure of an active sentence into a passive sentence. The transformation is called a **passive transformation.** Thus sentences 5 and 6 have the same deep structure:

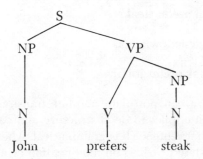

This deep structure may be converted into the sentence *Steak is preferred
by John* by means of the passive transformation, which inverts the two noun
phrases *steak* and *John*, changes the form of the verb, and supplies *by*. Or
it may be left essentially as is, which results in the sentence *John prefers
steak.*

Similarly, sentences 7 and 8 have the same deep structure:

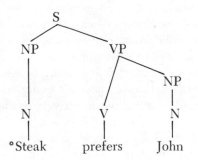

Depending on whether or not the passive transformation is applied, this
deep structure corresponds to the sentence **John is preferred by steak* or
Steak is preferred by John.

Now we can state the restriction just once: *Prefer* must have an
animate subject *in the deep structure.* This rules out the deep structure for
7 and 8 and therefore those sentences themselves. But the deep structure
for 5 and 6 is admissible, and the passive transformation can be applied to
produce the passive sentence 6.

In this way, we can use the distinction between deep and surface structure to make an important linguistic generalization (here a statement about a class of English verbs, but there are many other, similar restrictions), ignoring the distinction between active and passive sentences, which is irrelevant to this generalization. The fact that sentences 5 and 6 have the same meaning follows from the claim that *it is the deep structure that primarily determines the meaning of a sentence.*

With this framework, many other related facts about English can be explained. For example,

9. Does John prefer steak?

is a grammatical sentence, whereas

10. *Does steak prefer John?

is ungrammatical. We can postulate another transformation, the question transformation, which applies to deep structure and converts sentences into questions. The fact that sentence 9 is grammatical, whereas 10 is not, follows from the restriction stated earlier; no modification or addition to the theory is necessary.

Is steak preferred by John? and **Is John preferred by steak?* illustrate the application of both the passive and question transformations. Assuming the deep structure postulated earlier, the restriction already stated explains why the first sentence, but not the second, is grammatical. And by now it should be obvious how negative sentences—*John does not prefer steak* and **Steak does not prefer John*—may be described.

In this way, many important generalizations that are independent of the surface forms of the sentences can be made. This is probably what underlies our intuitive feeling that actives, passives, questions, and negatives are related forms. The passive exemplifies the two major justifications for transformational grammar: first, that it is more economical (one restriction, not two) and, second, that it makes possible generalizations across sentence types that are superficially distinct but intuitively similar.

It is important to realize that it is not the active sentences themselves that are transformed into passive sentences, questions, and so on; rather, it is the deep structures. Is the introduction of such an abstract entity as deep structure an unnecessary complication? Perhaps we could simply postulate that active sentences are directly transformed into passive ones. The passive transformation could be stated quite simply: Invert the first and second noun phrases, place *is* before the verb and *-en* after it,[6] and supply *by* before the (new) second noun phrase. Or, symbolically,

---

[6] Some verbs add an *-en* in the passive (*eat, is eaten by*), whereas others add *-ed* (*prefer, is preferred by*). The transformation is stated here with *-en* to emphasize that it is not the past-tense ending that is used (*eat* has the past *ate*, not *eaten*, and so on).

T passive: $NP_1 + V + s + NP_2 => NP_2 + is + V + en + by + NP_1$

This transformation will convert *John prefers steak* into *Steak is preferred by John*. However, the active sentence *The boy drops the cookies* would be converted by this transformation into *The cookies is dropped by the boy, which is ungrammatical. The correct version of the sentence is *The cookies are dropped by the boy*. The number of the verb has changed; that is, *boy* is singular and takes one form of the verb, and *cookies* is plural and takes another form. The number of the verb is determined by the first noun phrase in the sentence, and this phrase itself is not determined until after the passive transformation has or has not been applied. It is not possible to state a *single* passive transformation that can be applied to active sentences directly to produce correct passives, though separate transformations for the singular and plural are possible. However, a single passive transformation that correctly produces passives can be stated, if it applies to a deep structure that does not have the verb marked for number. This is one difference between the structure to which the passive transformation applies and the active sentence itself; there are many others.

The Form of a Transformational Grammar

Considerations like those just discussed lead to the construction of a transformational grammar consisting of three parts: a deep (or underlying or base)-structure component, which produces the set of deep structures (essentially a phrase-structure grammar); a set of transformations that operate on the deep structures; and the set of surface structures that result from the transformations. Diagrammed it looks like this:

Transformational Grammar

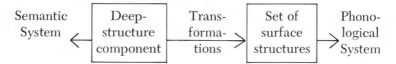

Each sentence has a deep structure, which is produced by the deep-structure component, and each also has a surface structure, which is the result of the transformations acting on the deep structure. The deep structure of the sentence is one essential factor in determining the meaning of the sentence. The other essential factor is the set of meanings for the individual words in the sentence. The diagram indicates that the deep-structure component is attached to the **semantic system** of the language: the specific rules by which individual word meanings are combined to form the meaning of the sentence. Similarly, the surface structure of the sentence is an essential factor in determining the actual sounds of the sentence, along with the sounds of the individual words. The diagram indicates that it is the surface structures that are important for the **phonological system:** the specific rules by which the pronunciation of the sentence, including stress and intonation, are determined.[7]

The difference, then, between a phrase-structure grammar and a transformational grammar is that a phrase-structure grammar *directly* generates the surface structure of sentences

Phrase-Structure Grammar

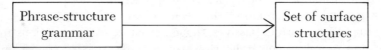

whereas the transformational grammar generates surface structures in more than one step.

It is rare for only a single transformation to be required to change a deep structure into a surface structure; it is more common for several transformations to be applied. When a number of transformations are required, the structures formed between the deep structure and the surface structure are called **intermediate structures.**

A passive question, such as *Is steak preferred by John?*, is an example of multiple transformations applied in a single sentence. Here the deep structure is essentially the same as for the active declarative sentence *John prefers steak*, but at least two transformations have been applied, the passive transformation and the question transformation. Which one of these two transformations is applied first? Or does it matter?

Let's look at the two transformations in more detail. Both transformations involve the use and placement of auxiliary, or "helping," verbs. Auxiliary verbs play a central role in English grammar; they convey information about future tense (*I shall go*), completion versus continuation of activity (*I have walked* versus *I am walking*), ability (*He can drive*), and other aspects of meaning, individually and in combination (compare *I walk* with *I shall have been walking for ten hours*).

The declarative sentence *John can swim* has as its corresponding question *Can John swim?* The sentence *Mary will peel the potatoes* has as its corresponding question *Will Mary peel the potatoes?* In general, the question transformation changes the order of (inverts) the subject of the sentence and the auxiliary verb. But what if there is no auxiliary verb in the sentence? The sentence *Columbus discovered America* has a correspond-

---

[7] Although the deep structure of a sentence is the primary determinant of meaning, under certain conditions aspects of the surface structure, such as stress, can affect meaning (Chomsky 1971).

ing question *Did Columbus discover America?* When there is no auxiliary verb, the dummy auxiliary *do* is inserted and inverted with the subject. (There are only two exceptions to this rule in modern American English: The verbs *be* and *have*, even when used as main verbs, are inverted with the subject, as in *Is he happy?* and *Have you any milk?*)

The passive transformation also inserts an auxiliary verb, *is. The man bites the dog* has as its passive counterpart *The dog is bitten by the man.*

Now consider passive questions. *The man bites the dog* has as its passive-question counterpart *Is the dog bitten by the man?* Suppose the question transformation is applied first to the deep structure (*the man bites the dog*), and is followed by the passive transformation. The question transformation converts the deep structure of the sentence into the intermediate structure underlying *Does the man bite the dog?* And then the passive transformation is applied, producing *Does the dog is bitten by the man?* which is incorrect.

But if the order is reversed so that first the passive transformation and then the question transformation are applied, the sentence is successfully generated. The passive transformation converts the deep structure for *The man bites the dog* into the structure underlying *The dog is bitten by the man.* Then the question transformation does not have to insert *do;* it merely inverts the subject and auxiliary verb producing *Is the dog bitten by the man?* This example illustrates a very general point about language: **Transformations may be ordered.**

Subcategorization Rules

Phrase-structure rules specify the general possibilities for sentence structure, for example NP + V + NP. But not all verbs can occur in the same contexts or all nouns in all contexts. A grammar requires further specification of the possible uses of each word. Consider the distinction between intransitive verbs, transitive verbs that take direct objects, and transitive verbs that take both direct and indirect objects. Phrase-structure rule PS9 is an attempt to capture this distinction, but it is an awkward solution to the problem because the class of verbs cannot be divided into these three classes so simply. Some verbs can be used only intransitively (*fall*), some both transitively and intransitively (*saw, heard*). Verbs that can take both direct and indirect objects generally require only the former (*I gave her the book, I gave the book*). Indirect objects for some verbs can be expressed with the preposition *to* (*I gave the book to her*); others use the preposition *for* (*I built the table for her*). As verbs are so individual in their patterns of use at this level of detail, it is simpler to assume that part of knowing a verb (or, in fact, any word) is knowing the contexts in which it may be used. That is, part of a vocabulary entry for any word, along with pronunciation and meaning, is a specification of possible environments for that word.

A slightly different kind of restriction on possible combinations of words is exemplified by the contrast between *John prefers steak* and *°Steak prefers John*. The ungrammatical nature of the latter sentence does not arise from incorrect use of the verb *prefer* in a subject-verb-object sentence. What is unacceptable is the combination of the verb *prefer* with the particular subject *steak*. In particular, verbs like *prefer* require subjects that are animate. Thus nouns must be classified as animate or inanimate and verbs classified according to which types of nouns they can occur with. Another division of nouns is between count and mass nouns; the former can be pluralized and counted (*two dogs*), the latter cannot (*some water, much sand*, but *°two sands*). The vocabulary entry for mass nouns must include information that prohibits combination with the plural morpheme. Many other classifications and restrictions on combinations must be explicitly stated if we wish to describe a language fully.

Various formal methods for expressing this information have been proposed (Chomsky 1965 has provided two), but for our purposes a verbal statement is sufficient. The important thing is to capture any valid generalizations about the language of a child. Sometimes these generalizations do not correspond to restrictions in adult speech. For example, it is often the case in Stage I speech (though not universal) that adjectives are used only with inanimate nouns, not with animate ones. That is, the child does not produce phrases like *red pony*, though he may produce *red ball*. This generalization is just one kind of evidence for the claim that animate/inanimate is one of the first distinctions drawn in child language.

Complex Sentences

The creativity and flexibility of any language are largely owing to the fact that we are not limited to simple sentences like the ones discussed but can combine them in complex sentences to express complex meanings. Two important processes of combination are **conjunction** and **embedding**.

When two simple sentences are conjoined, they are simply combined as equals: *Tom plays the flute, and Alice plays the piano*. Conjunction is most useful when the two simple sentences share part of their content. When *I went to the store* and *I bought some milk* are combined, the resulting sentence is *I went to the store, and I bought some milk*. But it is possible to abbreviate it to *I went to the store and bought some milk*, using a transformation. Similarly, the conjoined sentence *Tom can drive, and John can drive* may be abbreviated to *Tom and John can drive*. Whenever two **conjuncts,** corresponding elements of two conjoined simple sentences, are identical, one may be deleted. Actually, the two conjuncts must be not only identical in form but also in reference. *John ate* and *John drank* can be transformed into *John ate and drank* only if the two occurrences of *John* refer to the same individual. If John Smith ate and John Jones drank, this deletion cannot occur. One way to characterize conjoined sentences is to posit a rule of the form

$$PS10 \qquad S \rightarrow S + and + S$$

and a transformation that deletes any unit that is repeated in both simple sentences.

The complex sentence *Now where's a pencil I can use?* is also a combination of two simple sentences, *Now where's a pencil?* and *I can use a pencil.* However, these two simple sentences are not simply conjoined. Instead, the first is inserted, or **embedded,** in the second as a **relative clause** in order to identify more precisely the pencil referred to. The embedding occurs through a rule of the form

$$PS11 \qquad NP \rightarrow NP + S$$

S is now the origin of a derivation of a new sentence, *I can use a pencil.* The deep structure of the complex sentence is approximately

now   (where)   (is   (a pencil)   (I can use a pencil))

One kind of evidence for the claim that relative clauses are identical with sentences at the deep-structure level is historical. Two centuries ago, the sentence *Now where's a pencil, which pencil I can use?* would have been fully grammatical.

A sentence may be embedded as a relative clause only if it contains an NP identical to the NP it modifies. Several transformations (relativization transformations) then move the second occurrence of the NP to the beginning of the embedded sentence and replace it by a relative pronoun (*that* or *which* for most nonhuman entities, *who* or *whom* for humans and pets), producing *Now where's a pencil that I can use?* There is another optional transformation that deletes the relative pronoun, producing *Now where's a pencil I can use?*

In addition to relative clauses, there are several other important kinds of embeddings. A very common one is shown in *I think it's the wrong way.* The difference between this sentence and *I think nice things* is that in the former an intact simple sentence occupies the same position as the simple object noun phrase in the latter. Another example of this structure, called **object complementation,** is *I hope I don't hurt it.*

A third type of embedding is the embedded question. It need not be a question at all, but typically contains a question word like *what, when,* or *whoever*. Two examples are *Know where my games are?* and *When I get big I can lift you up*. The embedded sentences *where my games are* and *when I get big* serve the same function as single words specifying location or time but are full sentences. (Incidentally, all the examples of embedding in this section were produced by children below the age of five years; Brown 1973).

These and other mechanisms for combining simple sentences are all powerful tools for the precise expression of complex messages.

Case Grammar

One of the primary arguments for introducing the level of deep structure is that sentences that appear to be very different on the surface can be similar in structure and meaning, for example, actives and passives. Conversely, sentences with similar surface structures can be in fact quite different: *John is easy/eager to please*. The search for generalizations independent of surface structure led to the postulation of deep structure.

Many linguists believe that this process can be carried farther, that levels of representation even more distinct from surface structure are necessary to describe language. One that is especially interesting for child language is **case grammar,** as formulated by the linguist Charles Fillmore (1968). (It should be pointed out that Fillmore's proposals were based entirely on studies of adult language.) Consider the sentences

11. John opened the door.
12. The key opened the door.
13. John opened the door with a key.

Sentences 11 and 12 have similar deep and surface structures. The only difference is that *John* is the subject of 11 and *key* of 12. Nevertheless, there seems to be a real difference between them. Sentence 11 might answer the question *Who opened the door?* and sentence 12 *What did you use to open the door?* Sentences 12 and 13 have different deep structures, though in fact their meanings are quite similar. The relation of *key* to *opened* is the same in both sentences, though *key* is the subject in 12 and the object of a preposition in 13.

The problem seems to be that the concept of "subject," even as a deep-structural concept, is too broad. Subjects can express several roles in the sentence: the agent or person who performs an action or an instrument used for the action. Other roles are also possible. The same is true for objects.

The basic contribution of case grammar is to specify more precisely the relations of noun phrases to verbs. It provides an additional level of structure "below" deep structure. Deep structure and the concepts of subject and object are still necessary. Many aspects of grammatical structure must still be defined in terms of subject and object, for example, the passive transformation, which applies to all subjects, regardless of their semantic role, as discussed (*The door was opened by John, The door was opened by the key*).

These distinct semantic roles for noun phrases are **cases**. Particular verbs call for different sets of cases. For example, the verb *open* requires the object affected (the objective case) to be specified, whereas the instigator of the action (the agentive case) and the instrument used (the instrumental case) are optional—compare sentences 11, 12, and 13. The verb *give* can take almost any subset of the following three cases: agent (the person who does the giving), objective (the object given), and dative (the recipient of the giving). The verbs *own* and *have* require the dative (the person who possesses) and the objective (the thing possessed). And so on. Table 4.1 defines and exemplifies some of the major cases (adapted from Fillmore, 1968; 1971). Clearly Fillmore's proposals relate grammatical structure more closely to meaning.[8] The experiencer case requires some comment. Many linguists distinguish such verbs as *see, hear,* and *know* from verbs like *look, listen,* and *learn.* Whereas the latter set takes the agentive case for subjects, as does *open,* the former takes the experiencer case. There are several justifications for this distinction. The first is that intuitively the former verbs seem passive (the subject is being affected by some external event), whereas the latter are more active (the subject is actually doing something). Grammatically, the former, unlike the latter, does not usually take the progressive ending *-ing* (compare *°I am seeing him* with *I am looking at him*). The latter are preferred for imperatives (compare *°Know calculus* with *Learn calculus*).

Case grammar is still very much in a state of development, and a definitive list of cases has not yet been established. One issue that has not been settled is the relative importance of semantic and syntactic criteria for defining cases. Nevertheless, the cases listed in Table 4.1 are fairly well agreed upon.

Cases, as semantic relationships, are distinct from any particular means of expressing them. In some languages (Russian and Latin) the par-

---

[8] Other linguists, such as James McCawley (1968), have carried this process still farther, attempting to make generalizations across sentences that are still more distinct on the surface. Note that even a framework of case grammar as presented here does not allow us to express the fact that *John sold a book to Bill* means the same as *Bill bought a book from John.* If we wish to postulate that at some level the two sentences are identical, at this level the verb must be more abstract than either *buy* or *sell.* Similarly, for *John reminded Bill* and *John caused Bill to remember.* This attempt to go beyond the morphemes actually present in the sentence is one of the foundations of the generative-semantics school of linguistics.

TABLE 4.1   Definitions and Examples of Case Concepts

Case Name	Definition	Example (italicized noun is in designated case)
Agentive (A)	The typically animate, perceived instigator of action	*John* opened the door. The door was opened by *John*.
Instrumental (I)	The inanimate force or object causally involved in the state or action named by the verb	The *key* opened the door. John opened the door with the *key*.
Dative (D)	The animate being affected by the action named by the verb (includes possession)	John gave the book to *Bill*. *Daddy* has a study.
Experiencer (E)	The animate being having a given experience or mental disposition	*Tom* wanted a drink. *Adam* saw Eve.
Factitive (F)	The object or being resulting from the state or action named by the verb	God created *woman*. John built a *table*.
Locative (L)	The location or spatial orientation of the state or action named by the verb	The sweater is on the *chair*. *Chicago* is windy. John walked to *school*.
Objective (O)	The semantically most neutral case; anything representable by a noun whose role in the state or action named by the verb depends on the meaning of the verb itself	Adam sees *Eve*. The *sweater* is on the chair. John opened the *door*.

ticular semantic role served by a particular noun phrase may be indicated by inflections; in others (English) a combination of word order, prepositions, and the particular verb serves the same purpose. In English, noun phrases serving as subjects are not marked, regardless of their cases. Noun phrases in other positions are often identified by prepositions. For example, the agent is typically marked with *by* (*The door was opened by John*), the dative with *to* (*He gave the present to Mary*), the objective with no preposition, the instrumental with *by* or *with* (depending on whether or not there is an agent specified in the sentence: *John opened the door with a key* or *The car was hit by a stone*), and the locative with a special set of prepositions that also add meaning (*in, on, under,* and so on).

Fillmore captures this flexibility of means by positing a case rule that expands every case as a case marker (K) plus a noun phrase (NP):

$$\text{PS12} \quad \left. \begin{array}{l} \text{A} \\ \text{I} \\ \text{D} \\ \text{E} \\ \text{F} \\ \text{L} \\ \text{O} \end{array} \right\} \rightarrow \text{K} + \text{NP}$$

The verb and the set of noun phrases that relate to it form the "proposition" of the sentence. Other aspects of the sentence, like tense, negativity, and so on, are considered the modality of the sentence; they are tied together by the most general rules:

PS13   sentence → modality + proposition

PS14   modality → (tense) + (negativity) + (interrogative) and so on

PS15   proposition → V + (A) + (I) + (D) + (F) + (L) + (O)

Particular verbs, of course, can occur only with certain subsets of cases. The verb *open* must occur with an objective-case noun and may occur with an instrumental- or an agentive-case noun or both. These restrictions may be expressed similarly to that for transformational grammar. The verb *open* is marked in the lexicon (that is, knowing the proper use of the verb means to know that it can be used) with a required O and an optional I and A. There are also restrictions on nouns that can serve in various cases. For example, agentive and dative cases require animate nouns.

Rule PS15 is not meant to imply any particular order of cases in sentences. Languages have a variety of means of arranging cases for purposes of emphasis and otherwise. Additional rules, basically transformations, are therefore needed to express the possible orders. For example, in English, if an agentive-case noun is present in the sentence, it will become the subject in the deep structure. In general, datives occur before objectives, which in turn occur before locatives, if present.

Applying Grammatical Models to Children's Speech

Some of the problems of attempting to write grammars for individual children were described in the *Introduction*. Others are encountered when models developed for adult language are applied to that of children. Transformational grammar, for example, posits the basic scheme for a sentence as NP + VP. Children produce VPs without NPs as subjects, for example, *cook eggs*; NPs without VPs, as in *party hat*; and even NP + NP constructions without the verb that ties subject and object together, as in *daddy ball*, meaning 'daddy throw ball.' We can either modify the grammar to describe the child's language directly, or we can preserve the adult model by assuming that the child can form NP + V + NP sequences at an underlying level but that he leaves out (deletes) the V or other element. The objection that this approach involves reading more into the child's utterances than is actually there can be countered by the fact that NP + V, V + NP, and NP + NP strings all do occur, demonstrating an implicit knowledge of the order NP + V + NP.

Modifier-noun combinations are also problematical. In many grammars of adult language, they are derived from embedded sentences. For example, *little fish* is a transformed version of *fish* (*fish be little*). The embedded sentence is relativized to *fish that is little*, which is in turn simplified and reordered to *little fish*. The argument for this analysis in adult language is based on the fact that the relationship between modifier and noun is the same in these three structures. Similarly, possessives such as *John's book* are transformed versions of structures such as *book* (*John has book*). This structure is an implausible description for child languages since the simple forms (*little fish, John's book*) are produced long before the embedded structures (*the fish that is little*) from which the former are supposed to be derived. Here it seems best to modify the grammar for child language.

Bloom (1970) was the first to use transformational grammars which distinguished deep and surface structure for child language, and they have been used widely since her work. Generally there is little in the way of transformations in stage I, except for optional reorderings (which account for variable word order) and perhaps some deletions, as we shall see. The grammars are transformational grammars in that they are syntactically based; that is, the basic units of description are elements such as NP and VP. The goal in writing such a grammar is to distinguish sentences that have distinct semantic relationships. For example, the two versions of *mommy sock* should have distinct structures; otherwise the grammar fails to capture the distinction between the two meanings.

Table 4.2 presents a simplified version of a grammar written by Bloom for one of the children she studied, Kathryn, during early stage I. The phrase-structure rules specify the basic forms of sentences at this stage, the lexicon-feature rules specify which kinds of words can occur in the sentences and where, and the transformations rearrange the elements and delete certain elements. The rules bear some resemblance to rules for adult language but differ in significant ways. A grammar is a compromise between two goals: first, not generating sentences that are clearly different from those produced by the child and, second, not postulating any rules or distinctions that are not justified by the child's language, even if they are part of adult grammar. For example, *this* and *that*, two demonstratives, are derived from the Nom(inal) category, because they occur in exactly the

---

TABLE 4.2   A Grammar for Kathryn at MLU 1.32

Phrase Structure

1. $S_1 \rightarrow$ Nom $+$ (Ng) $+ \begin{Bmatrix} NP \\ VP \end{Bmatrix}$

2. $S_2 \rightarrow$ Pivot $+$ N

3. VP $\rightarrow$ V $+ \left(\begin{Bmatrix} NP \\ Part \end{Bmatrix} \right)$

4. NP $\rightarrow$ (ADJ) $+$ N

5. Nom $\rightarrow \begin{Bmatrix} N \\ Dem \end{Bmatrix}$

Lexicon Feature Rules

  i. Only animate nouns occur before verbs
  ii. Animate nouns never occur after Nom or after adjectives
  iii. Any noun can occur after a preposition (*on, off, up*)
  iv. Pivots include *Hi, Oh, thank you, O.K.*

Transformations

(1) ^{T} placement $\begin{Bmatrix} ADJ \\ Prep \end{Bmatrix} + N => N + \begin{Bmatrix} ADJ \\ Prep \end{Bmatrix}$
    (optional)

(2) ^{T} reduction
    (obligatory)
    (a) $X + Ng + Y => Ng + Y$
    (b) $X_1 + X_2 + X_3 => X_i + X_j$, where $1 \leq i < j \leq 3$

SOURCE: Adapted from L. Bloom, *Language development: Form and function in emerging grammars*, pp. 68–69. Cambridge, Mass.: M.I.T. Press, 1970.

same contexts as subject nouns in Kathryn's language. In adult language, these demonstratives have quite a distinct pattern of use.

    The two interpretations of *mommy sock* illustrate the operation of the grammar. Consider first the agent-object interpretation ('mommy put on my sock'):

Nom $+$ VP	Rule 1
N $+$ VP	5
N $+$ V $+$ NP	3
N $+$ V $+$ N	4
N $+$ N	^{T} reduction[b]
mommy sock	permitted by lexicon-feature rules

Second is the possessive interpretation ('mommy's sock'):

Nom $+$ NP	Rule 1 (second option)
N $+$ NP	5
N $+$ N	4
mommy sock	permitted by lexicon-feature rules

Thus, the difference in meaning between the two interpretations is represented by the existence of a VB constituent in the underlying structure of the first, but not the second, interpretation.

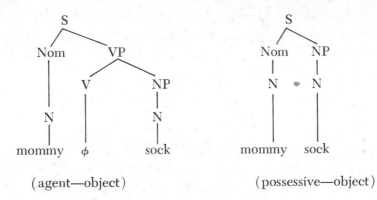

    (agent—object)   (possessive—object)

A particularly interesting and controversial aspect of Bloom's approach is the reduction transformation. Elements are assumed to be in the underlying structure but to be deleted by the reduction transformation (especially part b; see Table 4.2). Bloom argues that a child actually knows the three-term ordering subject-verb-object, if he produces all sets of two elements from this set, as many, but not all, children do. An alternative approach would be to say that all three elements are optional, something like (NP) + (V) + (NP). However, as Bloom points out, this approach is unsatisfactory, for, if each element were considered optional in the grammar, the grammar would generate a string with all *three* elements, and such strings are not produced at this stage. Furthermore, without some representation of the verb element, the concepts of subject and object are difficult to explain. Subject and object are linked and mutually defined by the verb.

Part a of the reduction transformation (see Table 4.2) applies specifically to negative sentences. Bloom noticed that if the sentence is negative, the subject is very likely to be omitted. It is as if there were a limit to what the child can produce; if the sentence is negative, something must be left out. This is not so for adult language, of course; we can negate any sentence without deleting any element. But it seems to be a general phenomenon of early child language.

An alternative approach to describing early child language is case grammar. This alternative has been explored by Bowerman (1973) and Brown (1973). The concepts we have used to describe early sentences in Chapters 2 and 3—agent, actions, object, locative, and so on—sound very much like the concepts proposed by Fillmore for an underlying level in adult language. In part this reflects the interest of developmental psycholinguists in recent work in linguistic theory; but in part it represents a genuine convergence of ideas. Fillmore argues that categories more specific than subject and object are needed, categories such as agent, instrument, and so on. And, in fact, these more specific categories are more appropriate for child language. Subjects of sentences, which in adult language can be agentives, instruments, objectives, and others, are always agentives in child language. "Agent" is therefore a better label than "subject."

The most common cases in stage I speech are the agentive, objective,[9] locative, dative, experiencer, and essive. The essive case (Es) has an uncertain status in adult language, but it seems appropriate for child language; the term refers to predicate nominals like *doggie* in *that doggie* ('that is a doggie'). Other cases, like the instrumental and factitive, are absent or rare in stage I, though common in adult language.

Brown (1973) has attempted to write a case grammar that will account for the general characteristics of stage I speech. A somewhat modified version of the grammar is summarized in Table 4.3. The "case-frame rules" provide the same sort of information that lexicon-feature rules provide in a transformational grammar: the details of possible uses for each verb. Note that unlike adult language, child language has no required cases for any verb; all cases are optional.

Case grammar has several advantages as a framework for characterizing early child language. It is intuitively reasonable and simple; the concepts seem appropriate for child language. It makes particularly clear the relationship between child and adult language: Child language has many of the cases but not the means for marking them explicitly. Compare rule 4 of Table 4.3 with rule PS12 stated earlier in this chapter. In adult language, each case is marked by K, which is typically a preposition (*by*, *with*, *to*) or an inflection (as for the possessive).[10] Children acquire these aspects of language later. Nevertheless, in certain ways case grammar as formulated for adult language does not seem to be a perfect fit for child language. Rule PS15 specifies the verb as obligatory and the other cases as optional; verbs have a central role in case grammar. Yet young children produce a considerable number of verbless sentences. The verb is as optional as is any other element. To be sure, these verbless sentences are at least as serious a problem for transformational grammars, and perhaps more so. Verbs are necessary for the definition of concepts such as subject and object in a transformational grammar, and, more important, they are necessary for the determination of the semantic relation between the subject noun phrase and the object noun phrase. The fact that a noun phrase is a subject does not specify the semantic role; recall the comparison of *John ran* with *John*

[9] Unfortunately, the term "object" (or "objective") is used to name both a grammatical relation and a semantic relation, though the concepts are quite distinct. For clarity, the term "objective" should be used for the semantic relation.

[10] In appropriate contexts, any case may occur without explicit marking: for example, the locative *home* in *he's home now*, which is related to *he's at home now*.

TABLE 4.3   A Case Grammar for Late Stage I English

Phrase-Structure Rules

1. Sentence → modality + proposition
2. Modality →
$$\left\{\begin{array}{l}\text{question}\\\text{imperative}\\\text{negative}\\\phi\end{array}\right\}$$
3. Proposition →
$$\left\{\begin{array}{l}(V) + (A) + (D) + (E) + (L) + (O)\\(V) + Es + (O)\\V + (L) + (O)\end{array}\right\}$$
4. A or D or E or Es or L or O → NP
5. NP → N + (S)

Case Frames for Verbs

fix	(A)	(O)	
put	(A)	(L)	(O)
see	(E)	(O)	
big	(O)		
want	(E)	(O)	
ϕ^a	(L)	(O)	
	Es	(O)	
	(D)	(O)	

Transformations

1. Subjectivization; determines which NP will be subject of sentence.
   a. M-V-A-X => A-M-V-X
   b. M-want-E(O) => E-M-want-O
   c. M-ϕ-L-O => O-M-ϕ-L
   d. M-ϕ-E-O => O-M-ϕ-O
   e. M-ϕ-D-O => D-M-ϕ-O
2. Sequential ordering; determines ordering of remainder of sentence.
   X-V-(D)-(L)-(O) => X-V-(D)-(O)-(L)

SOURCE: Adapted from Table 32 of R. Brown, *A first language: The early stages*. Cambridge, Mass.: Harvard University Press, 1973, pp. 219–220. © 1973 by the President and Fellows of Harvard College.

mommy fix?
(agent—action)

T_{1a} yields *mommy fix?*

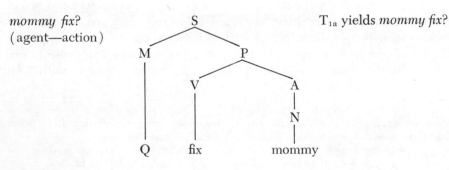

I want grape juice
(experiencer—verb—object)

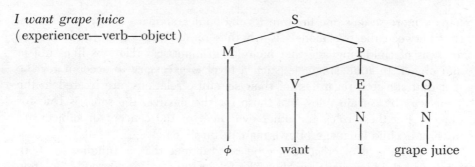

ᵀ1b yields *I want grape juice*

Sit Adam chair
(action—locative [possessor-possessed])

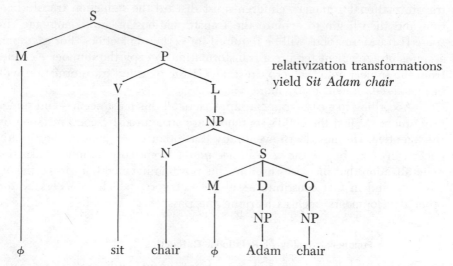

relativization transformations
yield *Sit Adam chair*

died. The verb is necessary, and its absence in early child language weakens the value of transformational grammar.

Negative sentences also pose a difficulty for case grammar. Rule PS13 seems to claim that the modality of the sentence (which may include negativity) and the proposition are completely independent. Yet the presence of a negative element constrains the elaboration of the proposition. A reduction transformation, referring to both modality and proposition, would be necessary to account for this phenomenon.

Both transformational grammar and case grammar can capture most of the important characteristics of early child language, though neither model, developed for adult language, fits child language perfectly. The production of verbless sentences is a problem for both models, though perhaps a more serious one for transformational grammar. The major distinction between the two models is whether or not there is a valid level of analysis of child language that includes grammatical relations like subject and object. In adult language, such a level is necessary to account for the fact that subjects, regardless of their semantic relations, are treated in the same way by certain rules, like those for the passive; the same is true for objects. But these rules and other evidence for the concept of subject are missing in child language (Bowerman 1973: ch. 6).

The goal of creating a type of grammar that is suitable for both adult and child language remains. The two cannot be considered in isolation from each other, for eventually the child's language becomes that of the adult.

The two grammatical models describe development after this early stage in similar, though not identical, terms. From the point of view of transformational grammar, children must discard the reduction transformation and then begin to acquire the transformations of adult language. In stage II transformations will be required for certain inflections. For example, systems of agreement require a transformation to copy the number element from the subject onto the verb. In stage III the question transformation will be mastered, as will many more.

According to a case-grammar approach, all this must occur—and something more. At first the child's sentences are structured by concepts such as the agentive. He must learn eventually that other cases such as the experiencer can occur before the verb (*I see you*). Eventually he must make the generalization that the cases used in this position have certain properties in common and in fact constitute a subject category, which is necessary for other developments, such as learning the passive.

The Functional Reality of Relational Categories

Relational concepts such as subject, agent, and location are categories of linguistic structures. They are useful to us as investigators for describing the data of child language. But what reality do they have for the child? Do these concepts correspond to anything in the child's mind? Brown (1973) has pointed out that we begin by imposing our own classification system on the data from children; it remains to be proven whether the classifications are "psychologically functional." The use of these categories for adult language is justified in two years, first, by a judgment of semantic similarity. We classify many verbs together because they all seem to share the concept of action instigated by a particular animate entity; this animate entity we call the agent. A second justification for the category of agent relies on shared syntactic properties, such as the relatively uniform treatment of agents by certain transformations. Neither source of evidence is available during the early stages of language acquisition. Young children cannot make judgments of semantic similarity; there is every reason to believe that if they could do so, their judgments would differ from those of adults. Their language does not yet contain the transformations relevant to the second justification.

Schlesinger (1974), Bowerman (in press), and Braine (in press) have discussed this difficult question. It is very possible that children initially work with quite different concepts than those of adults. Verbs of action are generally combined in a single category in adult language. But a child might group *touch*, *hit*, and *poke* together as verbs of surface contact; *walk*, *run*, and *fly* as descriptions of animate beings moving; *carry*, *put*, and *throw* as descriptions of relocation of objects; and so on. Or the division might be finer still. The category of possessives includes body parts of animate beings (*dog's nose*), customary territory of human beings (*mommy's chair*), and own possessions (*my book*, *my shoe*). These three categories might be functionally distinct for a child at an early stage of development. On the other hand, the concept of possession and that of location might be grouped together into a still larger category, since they share certain major aspects of meaning; the major difference is that a possessor is usually animate, a location, inanimate.

Thus, like the development of word meaning, the relational categories that underly sentence construction may begin very broadly, later to be refined, or they may begin narrowly, later to be extended (Schlesinger 1974). These questions are, in principle, empirical ones; they are questions about child language and not simply about the categories investigators use. A child's grammar allows him to combine members of various categories according to specific rules of combination. ". . . the breadth and makeup of the categories upon which rules for word combination operate determine what kinds of novel utterances the child can produce" (Bowerman, in press). Broader or narrower categories have different implications for the generation of new sentences.

Schlesinger (1974) has suggested one criterion for establishing categories: If two relations emerge simultaneously in children's speech, expressed in the same way, there is good reason to believe that they constitute a single concept for the child. Conversely, if a proposed relation emerges gradually, one subclass early and other subclasses later, there is reason to believe that this relation is not, in fact, a unitary one for the child.

Braine (in press) has used a similar approach in analyzing at a very fine level of detail the stage I language of children acquiring English, Finnish, Samoan, Hebrew, and Swedish. His evidence has led him to conclude that, although there is a considerable amount of variation among children in the exact specification of the early relational concepts used, at first children develop very limited categories. For example, sentences expressing size modification, such as *big house* or *little dog*, are distinct from those expressing other attributes, such as *wet* + *X*. For many children, locative actions and locations of objects (items 7 and 8 in Table 2.2) are distinct, though for others they emerge simultaneously. Bowerman (in press) reports that one of her daughters appeared to treat each word as semantically unique, with its own developmental history of possible combinations. For example, though Eva had several adjectival noun modifiers in her vocabulary, for a time only *more* was combined with other words. In contrast, Christy refrained from producing modifier-modified constructions for two months after other kinds of two-word combinations appeared, but then appeared to combine modifiers with nouns quite generally.

Eventually, this kind of "microanalysis" of the earliest stages of language acquisition should help to provide descriptive systems—grammars—for a child language that are more appropriate than the models for adult language which have been stretched, trimmed, and squeezed for children.

Universals, Strategies, and the Innateness Hypothesis

One of the goals of linguistics is to understand the nature of language as a general phenomenon, not just particular languages. Language is often viewed as the characteristic that defines human beings. The very great similarity of early child language around the world suggests that all children come to the problem of learning language with similar, and very strong, capacities. In this section we shall consider the question Is language transmitted entirely culturally from one generation to the next, or do children possess an innate biological capacity for language? The very earliest stages of language development, as described in Chapters 2 and 3, are especially important with respect to this question, because there we can see most clearly the strategies that children use in their initial organization of language.

Traditionally there have been two divergent positions on the question of man's language ability. At one extreme it has been claimed that no linguistic structure is innate, that language is learned entirely through experience. In John Locke's vivid phrase, children begin as *tabulae rasae* ('blank slates'). They learn language through general learning principles, which are usually assumed to be the same in many species of organisms. This is the **empiricist** position.

At the opposite extreme is the **rationalist** (or **nativist**) position. The structure of language is believed to be to a considerable degree specified biologically. The function of experience is not so much to teach directly as to activate the innate capacity, to turn it into linguistic competence (Chomsky 1968).

There are two important differences between these positions. The empiricist view holds that very little psychological structure is innately specified, whereas the rationalist view claims that a great deal is specified.

This is a difference of degree, but of a very large degree. The empiricist admits that there are certain innate abilities but insists that they are relatively simple, like the ability to form associations. The rationalist does not deny that experience has a function, for children must hear language in order to learn to speak and, indeed, eventually do speak the language spoken in their communities.

The second difference between these positions is absolute. In the empiricist view, the human child has no special ability for language, only general abilities to learn. Language is induced from experience by means of the same processes that are responsible for other aspects of mental development. In the rationalist view, there is a specific, and strong, capacity for language.

Undoubtedly the original stimulus for the formulation of the rationalist position was the observation that man is alone in possessing language. But equally important is the observation that language is the common possession of nearly all human beings. That is, language is **species specific** and **species uniform.** Descartes was aware of both these points in the seventeenth century when he wrote:

> . . . it is a very remarkable fact that there are none so depraved and stupid, without even excepting idiots, that they cannot arrange different words together, forming of them a statement by which they make known their thoughts; while, on the other hand, there is no other animal, however perfect and fortunately circumstanced it may be, which can do the same. (Descartes 1955:116)

Both species specificity and species uniformity are suggestive of the innateness hypothesis. First, species specificity: Chimpanzees are intelligent animals. They can learn to use tools and solve problems that are not trivial for human beings, yet they do not ordinarily develop a complex symbolic communication system like language. To be sure, we may have to modify this conclusion, given the recent success of Gardner and Gardner (1969) in teaching a form of American Sign Language to Washoe, a chimpanzee. Washoe has acquired a productive communication system that has striking similarities and dissimilarities to human language. For comparisons between Washoe and human children, see Bronowski and Bellugi (1970), Brown (1970), and Brown (1973). Brown concludes that Washoe has demonstrated stage I language and that future experiments (a number of which are already in progress) may raise our estimate of the abilities of chimpanzees even farther.

Premack (1972) has taken a rather different approach to teaching a chimpanzee aspects of language. Fleming (1974) reviews a number of such projects. In any case, these projects clearly involve an extraordinary kind of language development, requiring the intervention of another species (humans).

Species uniformity is also consistent with the innateness hypothesis. If language is the result of general learning abilities, the empiricist position, linguistic competence should be a function of learning ability, that is, of intelligence. Intelligence is highly variable, and some children should therefore do far better in language than others, and some should fail altogether, just as some children fail to learn how to take square roots or play the piano. But this is not the case. Over a wide range of intelligence, down to IQ levels of about 50 (Lenneberg 1967), bright, average, and less intelligent children learn how to talk. They differ greatly in their inclination to talk, in their vocabulary, and in what they have to say, but the mastery of the linguistic system does not vary greatly. The variation that does occur is far less than that in the mastery of, for example, arithmetic, which is much less complex than language. This finding is consistent with the rationalist position, which claims that language is part of the specific biological endowment of man.

The nature of child language should provide evidence on this question. McNeill (1970) has argued for the essential identity of the task faced by a child, a linguist in the field, a computer, and any "language acquisition device." He hypothesizes that in each instance an important role is played by knowledge of linguistic universals: the features common to all the languages of the world. These universal properties are the subject of **linguistic theory,** the goal of the science of human language, in contrast to the study of individual languages. Language universals exist because all languages are acquired by children. Each generation creates language anew, and in the process children impose features corresponding to their innate capacities.

This emphasis on similarities among languages seems surprising. When we first compare languages—when learning a foreign language, for example—we are usually struck by the differences. Languages do differ greatly in their superficial details, but the underlying principles are far more uniform. Two types of universal properties of language are possible (Chomsky 1965). A particular element, or rule, (a shared element) may appear in all languages. It appears that nouns and verbs are found in all languages, although the concepts encoded by them vary. The deep structure rule for negative sentences may be universal. These are examples of **substantive universals.** In addition to actual shared elements, languages may have strong similarities in form, that is, constraints on the possible form of a language. Such constraints are **formal universals.** A grammar is a system for combining morphemes to express meanings. Similarities among languages imply that the existing language systems are a highly restricted subset of the systems that are logically possible. The general form of a transformational grammar is universal; it is necessary to draw a distinction between the surface structure and a more abstract deep structure for every language. Even if there were no other similarities among languages, this would be one formal universal. Furthermore, the deep structure is hierarchical in nature and generated by phrase-structure rules, although the precise nature of the rules may vary.

The study of language universals is in its infancy, but the research that has been done indicates that most universal features are properties of the deep structure: the existence of a hierarchical deep structure; grammatical relations between subject and predicate and other elements; the possibility of posing questions, giving commands, and expressing negations; and more. Whether or not the entire deep structure is universal is still a controversial question. The basic relationships at the heart of case grammar are even more clearly universal. In Reading 4.1, Chomsky argues that the existence of abstract (in the sense of underlying, not directly observable) universal properties of language is itself an argument for a rationalist theory of language.

The transformations of a particular language are generally unique to that language. Yet there are similarities in transformations as well (Bach 1974: ch. 11). Questions provide a good example. In English, the question transformation inverts the auxiliary verb and the subject noun phrase. This is one of just three methods used for creating questions: use of a special question word or morpheme, use of a special intonation, or a shift of the normal order from subject first to verb first. Other plausible, equally simple manipulations, such as inverting all the words in the sentence, or inverting just the verb and object, do not occur. In general, the operations performed by transformations—the ways in which transformations change deep structure by adding, deleting, substituting, or permuting constituents—are remarkably similar from language to language.

If the argument in the preceding paragraphs is correct, the innateness hypothesis can be rephrased more precisely: *The features of language that children must acquire from the speech around them are the unique features of their language, and they include the actual transformations of that language. Children do not have to learn those features of the deep structure that are universal, nor do they have to eliminate those possibilities that are ruled out by the formal universals.*

Two major predictions follow from this hypothesis. Because the child has not yet had time to learn much about the unique features of the language about him, early child language should be free of transformations. The structure of the child's sentence should be similar to the deep structure of adult sentences and not necessarily similar to the surface structure that he actually hears.

The second prediction is a corollary of the first. The early speech of all children should be very similar, regardless of the form of linguistic input. The universals of child language should be even more apparent than the universals of adult language, which are more abstract. The language of children exposed to English or Russian or Japanese should be essentially the same, even though the adult languages around them are highly diverse in surface structure.

To evaluate this sweeping hypothesis by testing the two predictions requires a substantial amount of evidence from children acquiring a wide variety of languages. There is not nearly enough information of this kind available, although an increasing amount of cross-linguistic research is in progress.

To an extent, the available evidence on early child language, described in Chapters 2 and 3, is in accordance with these predictions. Whether the language is described by means of a transformational grammar or a case grammar, the basic properties of language in stages I and II are remarkably uniform. A small number of structures is used at the beginning, and a regular pattern of elaboration follows. Inflections and function words are generally absent. Transformations are generally absent, with two exceptions, which are not strictly comparable to transformations in adult language. The first consists of deletion rules, which leave out elements required in adult languages. The second comprises rearrangement rules necessary for the free word order produced by some children; these transformations are not comparable to the subject-auxiliary inversion of the question transformation, for example.

Slobin (1966b) and others have suggested that a more useful concept than innate knowledge of universals is that of universal strategies for language learning. Such a concept emphasizes that the nature of child language is determined by the learning strategy used by the child. Highly specific strategies of learning lead to relatively uniform languages. It is not clear, however, what differences there are between the concepts of innate universals and universal strategies, for the strategies must be defined in terms of linguistic constructs. One possible advantage of the concept of strategies may be to explain trends in order of acquisition, as well as universals. All children are capable of learning both prefixes and suffixes, yet there is good evidence (recall Chapter 3) that suffixes are acquired earlier than prefixes. A strategy of "looking at the ends of words first" seems to underlie this fact. The concept of strategies might link together universal aspects of language and the process of learning a particular language.

Even if we take certain aspects of language, such as the basic semantic relationships, to be innate, the question remains of whether these aspects are reflections of general cognitive development, or whether they are due to a specifically linguistic endowment. This question is the second half of the rationalist-empiricist debate discussed earlier. A number of investigators have considered the possibility that many of the universal aspects of language can be accounted for by the nature of the human cognitive capacity, and do not require a separate and purely linguistic explanation. For example, the concepts that appear most useful for describing stage I language, such as agent, objective, location, animacy, action, and so on, seem equally useful in describing the cognitive development of the first two years (Schlesinger 1971). Both Sinclair-de Zwart (1973) and Bever (1970) have argued that the way in which very young children interpret sentences is best explained by a comparison with their nonverbal cognitive development. For the most part, these arguments have rested on a perceived similarity between some aspect of early language and some aspect of cognitive development, which is suggestive but not conclusive. What is needed are longitudinal studies comparing linguistic and cognitive development in the same children. Another useful approach might be to attempt to accelerate some aspect of either linguistic or cognitive development and observe whether other aspects of development are facilitated. The question of the relationship between language development and cognitive development is a difficult and multifaceted one; we will return to it again in Chapters 6, 7, and 9.

Summary

In this chapter we have examined the end product of language acquisition, adult linguistic competence. Language acquisition is, in a sense, just the opposite of linguistic performance. Speaking and listening require a conversion of knowledge into action, whereas in language acquisition, action—the sentences the child hears and produces—must be converted into knowledge.

The description of language provided by linguistics demonstrates just how impressive the achievement of language learning is. We have looked at a few transformations of English; they are part of a large and interlocking network of hundreds of transformations. Language is also highly abstract, in the sense that many of the relations that exist in language are not directly presented in speech. NPs and VPs do not occur in the stream of speech; they are at least one step removed from what the hearer perceives. Deep structures are even more abstract, yet knowledge of the deep structure is necessary in order to understand a sentence. All of these and more must be mastered by the child.

Two grammatical models developed for adult language—transformational grammar and case grammar—have also been proposed for child language. Each captures much of the important structure of early child language, though neither model fits child language perfectly. The two differ primarily in that transformational grammar provides a basically grammatical level of representation (subject and predicate), whereas case grammar provides a fundamentally more semantic level of analysis (agentive, locative, and so on).

The striking similarities among child languages, despite the superficial differences among the adult languages heard, suggests that children bring to the problem of language acquisition, as part of their biological endowment as human beings, a universal and relatively structured learning ability. Whether this ability is to be viewed as primarily grammatical, semantic, or cognitive is an issue that can be resolved only through further understanding of adult language, child language, and cognitive development in children.

4.1 CHOMSKY ON LANGUAGE ACQUISITION*

Assuming the rough accuracy of conclusions that seem tenable today, it is reasonable to suppose that a generative grammar is a system of many hundreds of rules of several different types organized in accordance with certain fixed principles of ordering and applicability and containing a certain fixed substructure, which, along with the general principles of organization, is common to all languages. There is no apriori "naturalness" to such a system, any more than there is to the detailed structure of the visual cortex. . . .

Suppose that we assign to the mind, as an innate property, the general theory of language that we have called "universal grammar" (language universals, both substantive and formal). . . . The theory of universal grammar . . . provides a schema to which any particular grammar must conform. Suppose, furthermore, that we can make this schema sufficiently restrictive so that very few possible grammars conforming to the schema will be consistent with the meager and degenerate data actually available to the language learner. His task, then, is to search among the possible grammars and select one that is not definitely rejected by the data available to him. What faces the language learner, under these assumptions, is not the impossible task of inventing a highly abstract and intricately structured theory on the basis of degenerate data, but rather the much more manageable task of determining whether these data belong to one or another of a fairly restricted set of potential languages.

The tasks of the psychologists, then, divide into several subtasks. The first is to discover the innate schema that characterizes the class of potential languages—that defines the "essence" of human language. This subtask falls to that branch of human psychology known as linguistics; it is the problem of traditional universal grammar, of contemporary linguistic theory. The second subtask is the detailed study of the actual character of the stimulation and the organism-environment interaction that sets the innate cognitive mechanisms into operation. This is a study now being undertaken by a few psychologists. . . . It has already led to interesting and suggestive conclusions. One might hope that such study will reveal a succession of maturational stages leading finally to a full generative grammar.

* From *Language and mind*, pp. 75–77, by Noam Chomsky. © 1968 by Harcourt Brace Jovanovich, Inc., and reprinted with their permission.

A third task is that of determining just what it means for a hypothesis about the generative grammar of a language to be "consistent" with the data of sense. Notice that it is a great oversimplification to suppose that a child must discover a generative grammar that accounts for all the linguistic data that have been presented to him and that "projects" such data to an infinite range of potential sound-meaning relations. In addition to achieving this, he must also differentiate the data of sense into those utterances that give direct evidence as to the character of the underlying grammar and those that must be rejected by the hypothesis he selects as ill-formed, deviant, fragmentary, and so on. Clearly, everyone succeeds in carrying out this task of differentiation—we all know, within tolerable limits of consistency, which sentences are well-formed and literally interpretable, and which must be interpreted as metaphorical, fragmentary and deviant along many possible dimensions. I doubt that it has been fully appreciated to what extent this complicates the problem of accounting for language acquisition. Formally speaking, the learner must select a hypothesis regarding the language to which he is exposed that rejects a good part of the data on which this hypothesis must rest. Again, it is reasonable to suppose this is possible only if the range of tenable hypotheses is quite limited—if the innate schema of universal grammar is highly restrictive. The third subtask, then, is to study what we might think of as the problem of "confirmation"—in this context, the problem of what relation must hold between a potential grammar and a set of data for this grammar to be confirmed as the actual theory of the language in question.

I have been describing the problem of acquisition of knowledge of language in terms that are more familiar in an epistemological than a psychological context, but I think that this is quite appropriate. Formally speaking, acquistion of "common sense knowledge"—knowledge of a language, for example—is not unlike theory construction of the most abstract sort. Speculating about the future development of the subject, it seems to me not unlikely, for the reasons I have mentioned, that learning theory will progress by establishing the innately determined set of possible hypotheses, determining the conditions of interaction that lead the mind to put forth hypotheses from this set, and fixing the conditions under which such a hypothesis is confirmed—and perhaps, under which much of the data are rejected as irrelevant for one reason or another.

further reading

Bach, E. *Syntactic theory*. New York: Holt, Rinehart and Winston, 1974.

Bowerman, M. *Early syntactic development: A cross-linguistic study with special reference to Finnish*. New York: Cambridge, 1973.

Chomsky, N. *Language and mind*. (2nd ed.) New York: Harcourt Brace Jovanovich, 1972.

Fillmore, C. J. The case for case. In E. Bach and R. T. Harms (Eds.), *Universals in linguistic theory*. New York: Holt, Rinehart and Winston, 1968.

The Course of
Syntactic Development: II

To a large extent, the course of syntactic development after Stage II is a matter of learning the major transformations of English. The full range of English sentence types—declaratives, negatives, yes/no question, *wh* questions, and imperatives—is produced in the early stages of development, but their forms are quite different from the adult forms. As MLU rises above 2.5, the transformations necessary for the adult forms are learned in a step-by-step fashion. The development of questions, to be discussed in the next section, illustrates many of the general aspects of this development. The discussion here is based on that of Bellugi (1965) and Brown, Cazden, and Bellugi (1969); further information on the development of questions can be found in Klima and Bellugi-Klima (1966), Brown (1968), and Ervin-Tripp (1970). The development of negative sentences has been traced by Klima and Bellugi-Klima (1966), Bloom (1970), and McNeill (1970). Menyuk (1969) has investigated a variety of related constructions.

The Development of Questions

English, like all languages, has two kinds of questions. For almost any declarative sentence we can form a question, asking if the declarative is true or false. For example, we can ask whether or not *John can swim* with *Can John swim?* In contrast to these **yes/no questions**, **wh questions** ask for specific information. They are called *wh* questions because in English they almost always begin with one of the so-called *wh* words: *who, what, when, where, which,* and *how.*

The transformations involved in yes/no questions in English can be seen by comparing declaratives with their corresponding interrogatives:

John can swim.	Can John swim?
She was looking.	Was she looking?
You had been running.	Had you been running?
They will have been driving all day.	Will they have been driving all day?

The distinguishing characteristic of all the questions is that an auxiliary verb precedes the subject noun phrase. If more than one auxiliary is present in the corresponding declarative, only the first is inverted with the subject. Notice that it is always the first auxiliary that carries any marking for tense and number. This inversion of the first auxiliary (which may be a form of *be, have,* or a modal verb like *can* and *will*) and the subject is the basic **question transformation.** In sentences without an auxiliary a different process occurs:

He knows how to swim.	Does he know how to swim?
They danced all night.	Did they dance all night?

The verb *do* is provided before the subject. In addition, any marking for number and tense is moved to the initial position and attached to *do* (compare *knows* with *Does he know?, danced* with *Did they dance?*). In a question that has an auxiliary, this marking for number and tense would be moved with the first auxiliary, to which it would be attached. However, in these sentences, number and tense are marked on the main verb, which is not moved. The **do-insertion transformation** provides an auxiliary verb as a "hook" for number and tense, moved by the question transformation. Interestingly, at an earlier stage in the historical development of English, this transformation was not always required, as main verbs could be inverted just as are auxiliaries. Many examples can be found in Shakespeare, for example, *heard you that, Gonzalo?*

The do-insertion transformation has wider importance in English than as a simple question formation. In forming negative sentences, the negative element is attached to just that element that is inverted with the subject in questions: Compare *John can swim* with *John can't swim* and *He knows how to swim* with *He doesn't know how to swim.* In either question or negative, there is an element—either the marking for number and tense or the negative morpheme—that must be attached to the first auxiliary; when there is none, *do* is provided.

The second type of question, the *wh* question, is similar to a "fill in the blank" test question. Asking *What can she see?* is very much like asking *She can see . . .?* Although the *wh* word is always at the beginning of the sentence, it is clear just what kind of information is being requested. It is clear even in questions with nonsense words. Consider *What can the wug sporn?* The auxiliary before the subject *wug* signals that the sentence is a question. The question transformation applies to *wh* questions as well as to yes/no questions. In fact, the do-insertion transformation also applies when needed, as in *What did the wug sporn?* The presence of a *wh* word like *what* signals that the answer desired is more than a yes or no; it is a noun phrase. It is also clear that the answer is to be the object of *sporn*, despite the fact that the *wh* word occurs at the beginning of the question and not after the verb. It is the fact that there is an object missing from the remainder of the question that conveys this information. *Wh* questions have essentially the same deep structures as their corresponding declaratives; the item questioned is labeled with a *wh* word, and this word is moved to the beginning of the question by the *wh* transformation.

In the example question, it is the object of the verb that is questioned, but almost any constituent of the sentence may be questioned:

subject	Who will call?[1]
object	Whom will you call?
predicate	What are you doing?
determiner	Which boy did it?
locative	Where did he leave it?
time	When can you leave?
manner	How will you go?

Questions in Child Language

Bellugi (1965) has traced the development of questions in the group of children studied at Harvard University: Adam, Eve, and Sarah. She arbitrarily selected three points in development, as measured by MLU. Table 5.1, derived from Bellugi's work, summarizes the course of development.

In the first stage questions differ from corresponding declaratives only in the presence of the question intonation, a rising intonation at the end of the sentence (symbolized by ? in the table). The *wh* questions have very little internal structure; they are basically frames such as *Where . . . going?* into which almost any NP may be inserted. At this point in development,

[1] Superficially, questions that ask for a subject constituent do not appear to involve the question transformation, since the auxiliary follows the subject. However, if we assume that the question transformation applies before the *wh* transformation, the two cancel each other out as far as order is concerned.

TABLE 5.1   Three Points in the Development of Questions

Mean Length of Utterance (Morphemes)	Age (months)	Examples	Structures
1.8–2.0	Adam 28 Eve 18 Sarah 27	a. No ear? See hole? Mommy eggnog?	S^a + ?
		b. What's that? Where Daddy going?	What NP (doing)[b] Where NP (going)[b]
2.3–2.9	Adam 32 Eve 22 Sarah 32	a. You can't fix it? See my doggie? Mom pinch finger?	S + ?
		b. Who is it? What book name? Why not he eat? Why you smiling? Why not cracker can't talk?	*wh* + S
3.4–3.6	Adam 38 Eve 25 Sarah 38	a. Do I look like a little baby? Can't you get it? Can't it be a bigger truck? Am I silly? Does turtles crawl? Did you broke that part? Does the kitty stands up?	Aux + (n't) + NP + VP (result of question and do-insertion transformations)
		b. Why you caught it? What we saw? What did you doed? What he can ride in? What you have in you mouth? Why the kitty can't stand up?	*wh* + NP + VP (result of *wh* transformation; question and do-insertion transformations usually omitted)
		c. Who took this off? What lives in that house?	*wh* + VP (*wh* subject question)

[a] S is the origin of a derivation of a new sentence (see Chapter 4).
[b] Optional; may be omitted.

the children are also producing very simple negatives such as *No want soup*, in which a negative is added to a predicate, without a subject. Negative questions are produced by simply adding the question intonation to negative sentences: *No ear?*, *No more milk?*

At this age, children not only fail to pronounce *wh* questions; they also appear to fail to understand them:

Mother	Child
What did you hit?	hit
What did you do?	head
What are you writing?	arm

This stage is clearly pretransformational.

At the second developmental point, the children's grammars have become considerably more advanced. Articles and modifiers are used, some inflections appear, and occasionally a prepositional phrase may be observed. But there are still no auxiliary verbs. As there are no auxiliaries, there can be no inversion of auxiliary and subject. The yes/no questions are still constructed according to the same schema as at the earlier point: adding a rising intonation.

In addition to this simple form, one of the children (Adam) also produced a number of yes/no questions that began with *D'you want: D'you want its turn? D'you want me get it?* The introductory phrase always appeared in just that form and was pronounced as if it were a single word. Certainly it was not the result of the do-insertion transformation and the question transformation, for these operations were not observed anywhere else in his language. It may have been an effort to produce such adult forms as *do you want . . .* by means of phrase-structure rules. Adam may have enriched his grammar by adding a rule of the form $Q \rightarrow d'you\ want$, which operated after the rule $S \rightarrow (Q) + NP + VP$.

The words *can't* and *don't* present a similar phenomenon. At first children never use *can* and *do* without the negative element, and they are used in only one position: just before the verb. They are, it appears, single negative elements. In adult English, *can't* is the result of the attachment of the negative element to the auxiliary by the negative transformation. But here, as in the *d'you want* questions, the child may be trying to find a phrase-structure solution to what is actually a transformational problem.

The *wh* words are always in the initial position in the sentences at this stage. In adult questions, this positioning is the result of a transformation. But the evidence for this result is not as clear in children's questions. Though some questions, like *What you doing, mommy?* are produced, in which the *wh* word clearly stands for an object constituent, many other questions are produced in which it is hard to distinguish the structure:

What getting? Why need him more? Where put him on a chair? The *wh* words appear to serve primarily as question introducers, rather than as true constituent replacements.

Another piece of evidence for this analysis is the structure of *why not* questions. The child simply adds *why not* to the beginning of a sentence, even if the sentence already contains a negative, thus producing a double negative like *Why not cracker can't talk?* There is still no evidence for auxiliary inversion, and if the *d'you want* questions and *wh* questions are indeed the result of phrase-structure rules, this stage is still pretransformational.

The children can answer many questions appropriately:

Mother	Child
What d'you hear?	Hear a duck
What do you need?	Need some chocolate
Who do you love?	Mommy, you. I love fishie, too.

Adult *wh*-question forms are not being produced yet, but they are understood and answered. However, the converse also occurs. Although children produce many, many *why* and *why not* questions, they are not able to answer such questions appropriately: an example of the ability to produce a construction before the ability to comprehend it, a counterexample to the general belief that comprehension precedes production. Table 5.2 shows that these questions are closely related to the immediately preceding sentences of the mother. As generally occurs when young children imitate adult utterances, they are reduced: Elements like *-ing*, *a*, and auxiliary verbs are dropped. Aside from these minor differences, these questions are a simple function of the mothers' declaratives: *Why* is placed at the beginning of affirmative declaratives, *why not* at the beginning of negative declaratives.

Major advances in syntax have occurred by the third point observed. In particular, the auxiliary system has developed. Auxiliaries are used in

---

TABLE 5.2   "Why" and "Why Not" Questions

Mother	Child
I see a seal.	Why you see seal?
You bent that game.	Why me bent that game?
I guess I'm not looking in the right place.	Why not you looking right place?
You can't dance.	Why not me can't dance?

SOURCE: Roger Brown, Courtney Cazden and Ursula Bellugi, The child's grammar from I to III. In John P. Hill (Ed.), *Minnesota symposium on child psychology*, Vol. II, p. 49. Minneapolis: University of Minnesota Press, 1969.

declaratives, negatives, and questions. More complex sentence forms have appeared, including relative clauses and conjunctions: *You have two things that turn around, Let's go upstairs and take it from him because it's mine.*

In the yes/no questions, the auxiliary is placed correctly before the NP, and *do* is provided if necessary. Two of the transformations of adult English, then, are present. Sometimes tense and number are marked on both the auxiliary and the main verb, as in *Did you broke that part?* and *Does the kitty stands up?* Negative yes/no questions have the negative elements properly attached to the auxiliary verbs.

The *wh* questions are rather different. When there are auxiliary verbs present, they are not usually inverted with the subjects, as they should be. There are questions without auxiliaries, in which *do* should be supplied. Such questions as *What you have in you mouth?* are missing both *do* and inversion. If inversion had been performed, the question would be *What have you in you mouth?* If both the *do* and question transformations had been performed, the question would be *What do you have in you mouth?* Two transformations that are present in yes/no questions at this time are frequently not performed in *wh* questions.

What about the third transformation, which moves the *wh* word to the initial position? Up to this point, the *wh* questions have appeared to be of the form *wh* + S; that is, if the *wh* were removed, the remainder would be very much like any other sentence of the child's language at that stage. This is no longer true. If we remove the *wh* word from some of the questions, we have *We saw*, which is obviously missing the object of *saw; He can ride in*, which is obviously missing the object of *in; Lost it*, which is obviously missing the subject of *lost*. At this stage, the *wh* words do stand for particular constituents, and they are moved to the beginnings of the questions by the *wh* transformation.

Negative questions show the same principles: Negative yes/no questions like *Can't it be a bigger truck?* are inverted, whereas negative *wh* questions like *Why the kitty can't stand up?* are not.

At this point, then, children appear to have developed all the transformations, but there is a limit to how many of them can be applied to a single sentence. Inversion (the question transformation) and the *do*-insertion transformation are found in yes/no questions but not in *wh* questions. Perhaps transformations of this type really are mental operations of some kind. Young children have severely limited cognitive capacities, which can easily be overloaded. As a result, operations that are within a child's competence may be omitted for performance reasons. Both Bellugi (1967) and Bloom (1970) have observed a tendency at early stages of development for the presence of a negative element in a sentence to be accompanied by decreased complexity of the remainder of the sentence, relative to the child's competence as manifested in affirmative sentences.

However, such an explanation entails at least one important difficulty. Children always eliminate the same transformation. They do not produce such questions as *Can he ride in what?* or *We saw what?*—questions in which subject and auxiliary are inverted but *wh* is not moved. It is the question transformation that is always eliminated. At this stage the question transformation is fully mastered; perhaps the *wh* transformation is the focus of the child's attention because it is now at the boundary of his competence. An alternative explanation is that *wh* words are first learned as question-introducing forms; even when the *wh* transformation is mastered, a strong preference remains for placing *wh* words at the beginning of the sentence.

Children now understand and respond correctly to even more complex questions than at the preceding point:

Mother	Child
What d'you need a rifle for?	I wanna shoot.
Then what will you do for milk?	I gonna buy some more cow.
What d'you think we should do?	I know what I should do; play with some more toys.

The Functions of Questions and Other Sentence Types

Declaratives, questions, and imperatives are well-defined syntactic categories. Informing, interrogation, and direction are well-defined functions of sentences. But the two classifications are not in one-to-one correspondence. Declaratives can be used for informing but also for interrogation (*I wonder what time it is*, as a request for information); questions can request information, but they can also direct (*Would you like to put away your blocks?*); and so on. Almost any syntactic form can be used for any function, though of course some uses are more common than others.

As do most languages, English provides a particularly rich repertoire of ways to direct or command another person, and much of this richness appears even in speech to young children. Some directives are syntactically declarative statements: *The garbage is still here, I told you not to pull on the plants,* and so on (these and other examples are from Ervin-Tripp: 1974). Others are syntactically information-requesting questions: *Is your mother here?* In addition to simple imperatives, there are such embedded imperatives as *Can you open that window?* and *Why don't you sit down over there?* in which the imperative, complete with the second-person pronoun (usually deleted in imperatives), is embedded in a question. Directives vary in their explicitness from mentioning the desired act to mentioning the desired object only to mentioning neither. Compare *Did you finish your homework? Is there any more coffee?* and *Would you like another drink?* (meaning 'go home now').

Why do we have such a variety of forms for direction? In part, there seems to be a system for "softening" requests, for appearing to make compliance a matter not of bowing to the authority of the speaker but of choosing. The particular form of directive used is very much a function of whom it is addressed to, the relationship (in age, rank, familiarity, and so on) of the listener to the speaker.

True imperatives appear early in language development. Ervin-Tripp (1974) has studied the use of other syntactic forms for directive function. Among the first of these are location questions and claims, for example, *Where's my doll?* and *That's mine.* By age three years, questions, embedded imperatives, and declaratives are all used for this purpose, but only when the object or action desired is indicated explicitly in the sentence. Directives that imply, but do not mention explicitly, the goal do not appear until later in the preschool period: *We haven't had any candy in a long time.*

Ervin-Tripp also studied children's understanding of the use of these forms for direction. Three-year-olds have no difficulty in interpreting all the directive forms that explicitly indicate the desired state. They even understand some directives that are only implied, responding to *It's noisy in here* with *Want me to shut the door?* and to *I'm not tall enough* with *Get a chair.* However, even school-age children often fail to understand *Is your mother there?* as a telephone directive. Presumably specific experience with directives is important here.

In addition to having mastered many of the forms to be used for directives, preschoolers have learned something of the conditions for their use. Three- and four-year-olds are more likely to give true imperatives, and negative directives generally, to other children; whereas adults are more likely to be given the polite and respectful declaratives and embedded imperatives.

Complex Sentences

Nearly as important as the joining of two words together for the first time is the first appearance of complex sentences, in which two or more simple sentences are joined together by embedding or conjunction. In general, any sentence with more than one main verb (excluding auxiliaries) represents two or more sentences in deep structure.

The first complex constructions, appearing at approximately MLU 3.5–4.0 (which may occur anywhere between two and three-and-a-half years), are often object noun-phrase complements (Limber 1973; Brown 1973). A full sentence can take the place of the object of a verb, which would be a noun phrase in a simple sentence. Some examples:

I think it's the wrong way
I mean that's a D
I see you sit down
Watch me draw circles
I don't want you read that book

The embedded sentence that is the object of the verb is present in the surface structure in its unembedded form. In adult English, complements may appear quite different from simple sentences: *It annoys the neighbors for John to play the bugle* has as its object complement *John plays the bugle*; this type of transformational process does not appear in child language until much later.

A second type of complex sentence to appear is that containing a *wh* clause. The *wh* clause is a very general mechanism permitting one sentence to serve in virtually any role in another sentence. Some examples in adult English, with the embedded sentences in parentheses:

(Whoever did this) will pay for it	subject
He did (what he could)	object
He solved the problem with (what he found)	instrument
I know (where he is)	locative
(When you leave) the party will be over	time

Although *wh* words are present in these sentences (and they are sometimes called "embedded questions"), they are declaratives. The question transformation does not apply. Some examples from children (Brown 1973; Limber 1973):

> *Know where my games are?*
> *When I get big I can lift you up*
> *I remember where it is*
> *I show you what I got*
> *I don't know who is it*

Clauses referring to location and to time seem to emerge somewhat before other *wh* clauses.

Relative clauses are related to *wh* clauses, though they are distinct structures. In sentences with *wh* clauses, the embedded sentence is the noun phrase in a particular slot. A relative clause, in contrast, is a sentence that modifies a noun phrase; in *The man who came to dinner stayed a week, The man came to dinner* modifies and further specifies the subject of *the man stayed a week*. Relative clauses appear slightly later than the constructions just discussed (Brown 1973; Limber 1973):

> *That a box that they put it in*
> *I show you the place we went*
> *Now where's a pencil I can use?*

Relative clauses are first produced to modify objects and predicate nominals; subjects are modified in this way only later. This progression is similar to that for simple modification by attributive or possessive modifiers in stage I; then, too, objects are modified before subjects. This may reflect a distinction in the child's grammar between noun phrases in subject position and noun phrases in object position. Or it may simply reflect the fact that subjects are often pronouns or proper nouns, which cannot be modified by relative clauses. In contrast, object noun phrases are more often inanimate nouns.

Conjoined sentences also begin to appear at this time, though full mastery of their structure requires much longer. The first conjoined sentences are simply groupings of two sentences without a conjunction: *You lookit that book; I lookit this book.* Shortly afterward the conjunction *and* appears:

> *You snap and he comes*
> *I did this and he did that*
> *He was stuck and I got him out*

In these examples, the two conjoined sentences appear in full; no deletion is possible because the two sentences are different in content. Conjoined sentences with deletion also appear:

> *He still has milk and spaghetti*
> *I went to the aquarium and saw the fish*

The partial identity of content makes possible the abbreviation.

These generalizations about the emergence of complex sentences can only be viewed as tentative, given the limited amount of research in this area. R. Clark (1974) and Ingram (1975) have pointed out that it is often fallacious to posit rules similar to those of adult grammar for sentences produced by children which resemble adult complex sentences. The child's system may be fundamentally simpler. For example, the sentence *Let's go see baby Ivan have a bath* (Clark 1974) is a relatively complex sentence in adult English, with at least three distinct sentences in deep structure, one with the main verb *go,* one with *see,* and one with *have.* However, this sentence was produced by a boy less than three years old. It was produced in the context *Baby Ivan have a bath, let's go see Baby Ivan have a bath.* A more complete examination of this child's language makes it clear that the sentence is simply a juxtaposition of two elements; the first, *let's go see,* essentially functions as a single word which can introduce sentences; the second element is a simple sentence. Similarly, *I want I eat apple* is based on the addition of *I want* to a simple sentence. These sentences, and others like them, are based on fairly simple phrase-structure rules.

Ingram (1975) has proposed that evidence of productive use of a transformational rule, not just the production of a few simple instances of the structure, be required before we credit the child with knowledge of the rule. He concludes that with this more stringent requirement, acquisition of the transformations for embedding sentences does not really begin until after age six. Before this time, sentences are simply juxtaposed by simple phrase structure rules. Resolving the apparent discrepancy between his results and those of Brown and Limber will require more evidence, together with some consensus as to what constitutes "productive use" of a transformational rule.

Imitation

The account of child language presented so far in this book has been based almost entirely on children's spontaneous productions. Productions may lead to underestimation of the child's competence, or to overestimations. The second point (MLU 2.3–2.9) in Bellugi's study of the development of questions contains errors of both kinds: Many *wh* questions are answered appropriately, but they are not formulated correctly. *Why* questions, on the other hand, are asked but apparently not comprehended. In order to have a more complete picture of the child's knowledge of language, we need other kinds of performance, especially imitation and comprehension.

Often a child imitates an utterance of another person, usually a parent, in a **spontaneous imitation.** In contrast, an adult in some way may ask the child to imitate him, in **elicited imitation.** Spontaneous imitation is of interest because of the role it may play in language acquisition. Children may acquire new aspects of language through imitation of sentences containing those features. Elicited imitations are valuable as a research tool for the developmental psycholinguist. Suppose a child has not produced any auxiliary verbs during a conversational session. It is possible that this is the result of sampling error: The child may have the ability to use auxiliary verbs, but no occasion calling for them arises during the interval in which he is observed. Perhaps he can be prompted to produce auxiliaries if he is given sentences to imitate that contain auxiliaries.

When children spontaneously imitate, they typically simplify the sentences. In general, content words, like nouns, verbs, and adjectives, are retained in their proper order, whereas function words, like articles, prepositions, and conjunctions, together with various inflections, are omitted. In short, the imitations look very much like spontaneous (nonimitative) utterances, as if the sentences have been reformulated within the children's own grammar of the moment. Some examples from Brown and Bellugi (1964):

Model Utterance	*Child's Imitation*
Daddy's brief case	Daddy brief case
Fraser will be unhappy	Fraser unhappy
He's going out	He go out
No, you can't write on Mr. Cromer's shoe	Write Cromer shoe

However, a more precise comparison of the spontaneous speech of individual children with their imitations is necessary to evaluate the role of imitations in development. Ervin (1964) studied the spontaneous imitations of five young children between 1;10 and 2;10 and compared them with the free speech of the same children. She found that in every instance the imitations were of essentially the same structure as the free speech or somewhat simpler; she concluded that spontaneous imitations were no more advanced than free speech. Ervin though, considered primarily the child's knowledge of the word-order rules of English, which is only one aspect of language.

Two recent studies provide additional, and complementary, information about spontaneous imitations. Bloom, Hood, and Lightbown (1974) examined spontaneous imitations as part of an extensive longitudinal study of six children in stage I (MLU 1.0–2.0). The samples of free speech and imitations were gathered in the children's homes in natural conversational settings. Kemp and Dale (1973) studied the imitations of thirty children at a somewhat later stage (MLU 1.5–3.5). Kemp talked with each child individually in a laboratory setting, with toys and picture books. In the session he produced (among other sentences) a fixed set of forty "model sentences." These sentences referred to pictures in the books and were introduced at appropriate times. The goal was to present the same input stimuli to all children. A small sample of free speech was also obtained for the children.

It is clear from both studies that children vary enormously in their tendency to imitate. In the study by Bloom and her colleagues, one child (Allison) never produced imitations at a rate greater than 6 percent, whereas for another child (Peter) the imitations made up about a third of the total set of utterances. Of the forty model sentences in Kemp and Dale's study, the number imitated ranged from zero to fourteen. This variability alone suggests that "imitation is not required behavior for learning to talk; two of the children progressed from single-word utterances to MLU of 2.0 without imitating the speech they heard" (Bloom, Hood and Lightbown 1974: 387).

For the children who do a substantial amount of imitation, the important question is the grammatical relationship between the imitations and free speech. Is any *new* structure ever imitated? The analysis by Bloom and her colleagues focused on the basic semantic relationships of stage I: action-object, possession, action-location, nonexistence, and so on. In every instance, imitation did not occur before use in free speech. However, there was a strong tendency for patterns that were well-established in free speech also *not* to be imitated. Patterns that were just beginning to emerge in free speech were the most frequently imitated. This result has a rather Piagetian flavor: A schema is most likely to be "exercised" just after it is acquired. Well-established schemas no longer need this kind of practice. The analysis by Kemp and Dale included such morphological features as the progressive, the plural, and articles and also major transformations such as the question transformation. They too found that, in general, sentences were greatly simplified when imitated. Not only were features omitted that were not produced in free speech, but often features that did occur in free speech were also not reproduced in imitations. One of their analyses suggests that the same process that Bloom observed—the tendency for features acquired earlier *not* to be imitated—occurred in their data. Together the two studies demonstrate that imitation is a selective process that represents the "growing edge" of language; it may serve a useful function in firmly establishing new aspects of language, but it is not the means by which the child picks up new features.

Bloom and her colleagues also observed many instances when children imitated new *words* that had not yet occurred in spontaneous speech. Again, words that were well-established in a child's productive vocabulary were often not imitated. What is not clear is whether or not the children understood the new words they were imitating, whether or not these words were already part of each child's receptive vocabulary.

If the finding that the child can produce in imitation only what he can produce in spontaneous speech holds for elicited imitations, as well as for spontaneous ones, imitation can be used to study children's productive capacities. In fact, the equivalence of production and elicited information is only approximately valid. The sentence offered for imitation must be reasonably long and composed of familiar words. If the sentence is too short and thus does not stretch the child's memory capacity, it may be imitated, even though it contains features that are not in the child's free speech. A more important point has been raised by Bloom (1974). She presented a number of sentences to Peter, who was naturally an imitative child. Following are three examples:

Adult	Peter
I'm trying to get this cow in here	Cow in here
You made him stand up over here	Stand up here
I'm gonna get the cow to drink milk	Get the cow to drink milk

The adult utterances seem clearly beyond Peter; in particular, the main verbs *trying* and *made* in the first two complex sentences and the auxiliary *gonna* in the third were not produced. Yet all three sentences had in fact been produced by him on the preceding day (Bloom 1974:299):

| (Peter trying to get a colt's feet to fit into a barrel) | I'm trying to get this cow in there |
| (Peter, holding the cow, going to the toy bag to get barrels) | I'm gonna get the cow to drink some milk |

(Peter, trying to get investigator to   You made him stand up
spread an animal's legs, so that it   over there
will stand in a spot he had
cleared for it)

The difference between production of the full sentences one day and simplification the next must lie in the fact that on the second day the sentences
were presented completely out of context. The child is generally talking
about the here and now; this contextual support, together with his own
behavior and intentions, plays an important role in the formulation of sentences. Without this support, he cannot produce utterances that he has
produced earlier.

Despite these cautions, elicited imitations can often provide useful
evidence. Slobin and Welsh (1973) have explored this tool with a child
they call Echo. Echo imitated *The pussy eats bread, and the pussy runs fast*
with *Pussy eat bread, and he run fast*, demonstrating mastery of the transformation that pronominalizes a repeated noun phrase. Even if the repeated
noun phrase were deleted in the sentence offered for imitation, Echo would
introduce a pronoun for the noun phrase (which is present in the deep
structure), thus imitating *The owl eats candy and runs fast* with *Owl eat
candy . . . owl eat candy, and . . . he run fast.*

Comprehension

Elicited imitations can be a useful tool for solving the sampling
problem. Other problems remain, however. Suppose a child does not produce
auxiliary verbs in either her free speech or her imitations. Does this omission
necessarily imply that the auxiliary is not part of her language, that is, her
competence, or does it merely mean that auxiliaries are omitted because
the child can only produce very short sentences because of a small memory
span? Such a question can be answered only after examining the child's
comprehension ability.

The development of comprehension of language is as interesting
as the development of production, which has received more attention. In
addition to the intrinsic interest of comprehension, we would like to be able
to compare comprehension and production, in order to evaluate the common
belief that understanding precedes production. Children do seem to comprehend speech somewhat before they produce any true language. However,
the interesting hypothesis is that specific grammatical features are understood before they are produced. Testing this hypothesis has proved exceed-
ingly difficult. The concepts of comprehension and production, apparently
simple, are not easy to define and measure in ways that make the comparison
appropriate.

Consider comprehension first. When a child hears a sentence in his everyday activities, he has several cues to meaning:

a. Knowledge of words and syntactic structure
b. The linguistic context
c. The nonlinguistic context
d. General knowledge of the world

Here are some examples from Adam, a boy studied by Clark, Hutcheson, and van Buren (1974). Adam is picking strawberries out of a bowl and carrying them to his father. His mother asks *Don't you think that's enough?* and Adam offers her a strawberry. The erroneous interpretation is presumably based on the nonlinguistic context, the situation, in which a request for a strawberry is likely. If his mother had said *May I have one?* Adam would probably have given her one and given an observer the impression that he had understood. At age two years, Adam used the words *mummy* and *daddy* more or less interchangeably, and in general he showed little evidence of comprehending the linguistic distinction. However, if his mother said to him either *Give that to mummy* or *Give that to daddy*, he would give it to his father. Similarly, in response to either imperative from his father, he would give it to his mother. This pattern of response is probably based on Adam's knowledge of the social world: that typically one parent asks the child to give an object to the other parent. The importance of gestural cues should not be overlooked. The sentence *It's up there*, spoken without accompanying gesture, failed to elicit a response from Adam, but a "very slight upward twitch of the finger was enough to cause the child to look up immediately" (Clark, Hutcheson and van Buren 1974:46).

We can carefully set up laboratory experiments to rule out all cues except a, by having the child point to pictures or act out sentences with dolls. For example, to test comprehension of the plural, the child could be asked to point to the picture of dogs, where one picture portrays one dog and the second picture two dogs. In the natural setting, if the child is asked to bring books to the table and there are two books on the couch, comprehension of the plural morpheme is not crucial to understanding the request. But, if we remove all "extraneous cues," the comprehension task is no longer comparable to production. That is, whether or not the child uses the plural either in the natural setting or when asked to describe a picture of two dogs depends on aid (or its absence) from the nonlinguistic context of the picture. Recall Bloom's attempt, discussed in the preceding section, to have a child imitate his own utterances of the day before. Without help from the context, imitation was often unsuccessful.

The first systematic attempt to compare comprehension and production was the ICP (imitation, comprehension, production) test, devised by Fraser, Bellugi, and Brown (1963). For each of ten contrasts, for example,

singular-plural subject, a pair of sentences that differed only in that particular feature was constructed. For the example of singular versus plural
subject, Fraser, Bellugi, and Brown used the sentences *The boy draws* and
The boys draw. An appropriate picture was prepared for each of the sentences. In this example, one picture showed one boy drawing, and the other
showed two boys drawing. Another contrast was between subject and object
in the active voice. The sentences were *The train bumps the car* and *The
car bumps the train*. The corresponding pictures showed the train doing the
bumping and the car doing the bumping.

There were three tasks: imitation, comprehension, and production.
In the imitation task, the experimenter simply recited the two sentences and
asked the children to repeat them, one by one. In the comprehension task,
the experimenter first showed the two pictures and recited the two sentences,
without revealing which sentence belonged to which picture. Then the
experimenter recited one of the sentences and asked the child to point to the
picture he had named. Then the other sentence was recited, and the child
was asked to point to the appropriate picture. In the production task the
pictures were again used. First, the child heard the sentences but was not
told which sentence went with which picture. Then the experimenter pointed
to one picture at a time and asked the child to name it. In scoring of the
children's responses on the imitation and production tasks, only the relevant
aspects of the sentences were considered. The subjects for this experiment
were between thirty-seven and forty-three months old.

The findings were remarkably clear-cut (see Table 5.3). Comprehension scores exceeded production scores on all but one of the ten contrasts;
imitation scores exceeded comprehension scores on all ten. Furthermore,
this pattern occurred with nearly all the children considered individually.
This experiment has been repeated by Lovell and Dixon (1967) with children over a wider age range—two years to six years—and with retarded
six- and seven-year-olds. They found the expected differences arising from
age (older children did better overall than younger ones) and from IQ
(normal children did better overall than retarded ones). They also found
the same highly consistent ordering of imitation, comprehension, and production scores for each group of children.

In addition to their quantitative findings, Fraser, Bellugi, and Brown
(1963) observed several interesting errors. Some children, when presented
with the pair of sentences *The girl is pushed by the boy* and *The boy is
pushed by the girl* in the production task, made precisely the opposite
responses to the pictures. That is, when they were shown the picture in
which the girl was doing the pushing, the children said *The girl is pushed
by the boy*, for the picture in which the boy was doing the pushing, they
said *The boy is pushed by the girl*. Five children responded in this way, and
they seemed to be doing so with confidence. This finding suggests that
passive sentences are being processed as if they were active. Thus *The girl*

TABLE 5.3   Example Sentences and Results from the ICP Test

		Number Correct (out of 24 each)			
	Contrasts in Order of Increasing Difficulty	*I*	*C*	*P*	*Total*
I.	Affirmative-Negative The girl is cooking The girl is not cooking	18	17	12	47
II.	Singular-Plural of Third-Person Possessive Pronoun His wagon Their wagon	23	15	8	46
III.	Subject-Object in the Active Voice The train bumps the car The car bumps the train	19	16	11	46
IV.	Present Progressive-Future Tense The girl is drinking The girl will drink	20	16	6	42
V.	Singular-Plural Marked by *Is* and *Are* The deer is running The deer are running	20	12	7	39
VI.	Present Progressive-Past Tense The paint is spilling The paint spilled	17	13	6	36
VII.	Mass Noun-Count Noun Some mog A dap	12	13	1	26
VIII.	Singular-Plural, Marked by Inflections The boy draws The boys draw	14	7	1	22
IX.	Subject-Object in the Passive Voice The car is bumped by the train The train is bumped by the car	12	7	2	21
X.	Indirect Object-Direct Object The girl shows the cat the dog The girl shows the dog the cat	11	5	3	19

SOURCE: Adapted from C. Fraser, U. Bellugi and R. Brown, Control of grammar in imitation, comprehension, and production. *Journal of Verbal Learning and Verbal Behavior*, 1963, **2**, 121–135.

is pushed by the boy is not handled as object-passive verb-subject, but rather as subject-"funny" verb-object.

The fact that imitation performance was superior to production ability apparently contradicts the findings of Ervin, Bloom and her colleagues, and Kemp and Dale, discussed in the previous section. However, the imitations in this experiment were elicited imitations and were probably fairly short for the relatively older children. Children do seem to develop a "tape recorder" type of imitation, without processing for meaning, and these imitations seem to be different from spontaneous imitations and elicited imitations of sentences that exceed the span of immediate memory.

Although the results of this study seem clear, the procedure used by Fraser, Bellugi, and Brown and hence the conclusions drawn from the experiment, are open to question. Baird (1972) and others have pointed to the role of chance factors. In the comprehension task, the child must point to one of two pictures; he has a 50 percent chance of being right even if he guesses. What is the probability of success by chance on the production task? It is not possible to define it precisely, but surely it must be far less than 50 percent. This factor alone might account for the superiority of comprehension. It is possible to lower the chance probability of success by adding more pictures, but this procedure can be adopted only to a limited extent. The pictures added must be plausible alternatives. If the sentences concern one or more boys drawing, a picture of a dog running is not a good alternative, as the child can rule it out on the basis of knowing the words *dog* and *boy*. It is difficult to have more than three or four pictures, which still leaves the chance probability at least 25 percent.

Other problems with the production task have been pointed out by Fernald (1972). If we show a young child a picture of deer jumping and ask the child to describe the picture, he may respond *The grass is green.* Such irrelevant responses are frequent from young children, yet it seems unfair to count them as errors. Fernald has suggested waiting until all test items have been administered, then returning to items that have produced irrelevant responses. If the second response is also irrelevant, he has suggested randomly calling these items correct or incorrect. This approach tends to bring the chance level back toward 50 percent, which is comparable to comprehension. A second objection to the production task is that the scoring is too stringent. For the singular-plural contrast, the child must mark both subject and verb for number. But in the comprehension task the child can respond correctly by attending only to the noun inflection. That is, many grammatical contrasts are redundantly marked. Fernald proposed scoring a production correct if either the noun or verb inflection was included and similarly for other contrasts. A third problem concerns the relation between responses to the two items that are the two sides of the contrast, for example, *The boy draws* and *The boys draw.* These responses are not really independent pieces of evidence. Some children favor an alternation strategy, others consistently point to the same picture for both. Fernald (1972) suggested considering only the response to the first item of the pair. He then replicated the experiment by Fraser, Bellugi, and Brown (1963), using their scoring system; the results clearly showed that comprehension was superior to production. But, when his proposed revisions in scoring were applied, there was no significant difference between comprehension and production. As the modifications seem reasonable ones, doubt is cast on the findings of Fraser, Bellugi, and Brown. Unfortunately, Fernald does not report the exact effect of each of his three modifications, so it is not possible to interpret his results unambiguously. In addition, his procedure is open to the objection, raised at the beginning of this section, about the elimination of nonlinguistic context from comprehension but not from production.

It seems undeniable that in many instances comprehension of a structure, even in the narrow sense of use of linguistic information only, precedes production. For example, passives are hardly ever produced by children, even when they do comprehend them. However, it must be concluded that demonstrating this lag more generally has proved far more difficult than expected.

There appear to be several instances in which an aspect of language is appropriately produced but in which comprehension is not yet mastered. Two particularly interesting ones are word order in simple sentences and subject-verb agreement in number. Even in the earliest multiword sentences, children use appropriate word order for subject and object; that is, subjects precede verbs, and objects follow. De Villiers and de Villiers (1973b) assessed the ability of children to identify the subject and object of a sentence from the information provided by word order. The children were given dolls and asked to act out sentences. (This seems to work better with young children than pointing to pictures.) Both active and passive sentences were used: *Make the dog bite the cat* and *Make the boat be bumped by the train.* All sentences were reversible; that is, either noun could plausibly be taken as the subject. A sample of spontaneous speech from the children revealed that all used appropriate word order at least 95 percent of the time. Comprehension was not nearly as successful; when de Villiers and de Villiers related comprehension to MLU of spontaneous speech, a regular pattern of development emerged:

MLU of Spontaneous Speech	*Comprehension*
1.0–1.5	chance[1] performance on actives (31%) and passives (29%)
1.5–3.0	good performance on actives (70–80%), slowly increasing performance on passives (rising from 29% to 42%)

[1] A frequent response from the youngest children was for the child himself to become the agent of the action; for example, he might respond to *Make the dog bite the cat* by biting (or pretending to bite) the cat. This response occurred about a third of the time; thus, responses that actually involved both entities (dog and cat) occurred about two thirds of the time, so that chance performance with respect to word order corresponds to half these responses, or approximately one third correct overall.

MLU of Spontaneous Speech	Comprehension
3.0–3.5	still better on actives (86%), but performance on passives *declining* to 13%: subject and object reversed in 87% of instances of basic strategy to interpret *all* noun-verb-noun sequences as subject-verb-object, whether active or passive sentence
3.5–4.25	performance on passives beginning to recover (39%)

There are two striking findings from this study. The first is the decline in performance with passives in the third stage. This decline had been noticed before (Bever 1970; Maratsos 1974a), but it seems much sharper when comprehension is related to MLU rather than age. The exact significance of the decline is still controversial (Maratsos 1974a), but it seems to reflect an attempt to use a particular kind of syntactic information, word order, in an oversimplified way: overgeneralization from actives.

The second striking finding is the paradox in the first stage between appropriate use of order in production but not in comprehension. The paradox is not resolved by de Villiers and de Villiers, but some illumination is provided by the findings of Chapman and Miller (1975). They used a comprehension task similar to that of de Villiers and de Villiers with children in the range of MLU 1.8–2.9. The sentences used by de Villiers and de Villiers contained either two animate nouns or two inanimate nouns; Chapman and Miller (1975) systematically varied animate and inanimate subjects and objects, using sentences with animate subject and inanimate object (*The dog is chasing the car*), inanimate subject and animate object (*The boat is hitting the girl*), and so on. In the production task children were asked to describe similar events that the experimenter acted out. Chapman and Miller's solution to the problem of irrelevant responses was to give a second trial later and then to consider only the responses that included at least two elements of subject-verb-object. That is, irrelevant responses were considered neither incorrect nor randomly correct or incorrect. This is probably the most reasonable solution to a difficult problem, when irrelevant responses are frequent. As had de Villiers and de Villiers, Chapman and Miller found comprehension to be greatly inferior to production. But most interesting was the relation of comprehension to the lexical makeup of the sentence, shown here for the youngest group:

Subject	Object	Percentage Correct in Comprehension
animate	inanimate	96
animate	animate	76
inanimate	inanimate	54
inanimate	animate	37

The older groups showed a similar trend but smaller differences among sentence types. These figures reflect a clear reliance on a particular semantic strategy in comprehension: Identify the animate entity as subject, the inanimate entity as object. Some syntactic processing is also occurring, for animate-animate sentences (for which there is no semantic cue) are responded to correctly more than half the time, and inanimate-animate sentences (which violate the semantic strategy) are correctly comprehended at least some of the time. But the semantic factor plays a larger role than the grammatical factor of word order. Why performance on animate-animate sentences is better than on inanimate-inanimate ones is puzzling, however. The most striking finding of the study is that a similar semantic strategy is *not* used in production. If children followed a pattern of ordering animate nouns before inanimate ones, a similar pattern of success should hold for production. Yet it does not. The four types of situation are described in the production task with about equal, and relatively high (80 to 90 percent) success. Thus it appears that use of word order information to identify subject and object in comprehension follows observance of correct subject-object order in production. Chapman and Miller feel that these results show that the competence underlying comprehension may be distinct from that underlying production in the early phases of language acquisition.

Another case of production preceding comprehension is that of subject-verb agreement in number, studied by Keeney and Wolfe (1972). In third-person, present-tense sentences, the verb must be inflected to agree with the subject: *The bird flies, The birds fly, The bird is flying, The birds are flying.* As Brown (1973) discovered, the third person singular ending -*s* and full control of the auxiliary come considerably later than does the plural morpheme for nouns. This is not surprising, for number marking on verbs is usually redundant with marking on subjects. Nouns are almost always marked for number, verbs only in certain kinds of sentences. Furthermore, number is essentially a property of nouns, rather than of verbs. Three-year-old children, however, have mastered subject-verb agreement, as can be shown from an examination of their spontaneous speech. Keeney and Wolfe used several comprehension tasks. If the children were given the full sentence (*The birds fly*), they could point to an appropriate picture, but this would have been possible on the basis of the noun marking alone. If given just the verb, . . . *is flying,* children could not do this task at a level better than chance. Although the task seems a little bizarre—it is unusual to produce just the verb component of a sentence—the finding is probably valid and has interesting theoretical implications. Meaning undoubtedly plays an important role in language learning, as we have established at several points in the preceding chapters. But here is an instance in which an aspect of language is learned quite independently of meaning. The child learns, purely syntactically, the pattern of matching subject and verb for number. Of course, this presupposes mastery of the plural morpheme for nouns, which has a highly concrete meaning.

The problem of devising methods of investigating comprehension remains one of the most challenging problems in the study of language acquisition. Slobin and Welsh (1973) have suggested a technique for using elicited imitations to study comprehension as well as production (discussed earlier). If the model sentences are longer than the immediate memory span of the child, they will be first comprehended and then reformulated. The reformulation is not always identical to the sentence being imitated, but the meaning is approximately the same. This procedure requires the child to have understood the model. If the child has failed to comprehend, then the imitation is most likely to express a different meaning or no meaning at all. Comprehension may then be tested by noting whether the reformulated imitation preserves the meaning of the original:

ADULT: John who cried came to my party.
CHILD: John cried and he came to my party.
ADULT: The boy the book hit was crying.
CHILD: Boy the book was crying.

The child's imitation successfully preserves the meaning of the first model, indicating comprehension of the embedded clause, in particular, that John is the subject of both *cried* and *came*. But the second imitation has hardly any meaning at all, showing failure to comprehend embedded clauses of this more complex type (note that *boy* is the subject of *was crying* and the object of *hit*). Here is another example of successful imitation:

ADULT: The man who I saw yesterday got wet.
CHILD: I saw the man, and he got wet.

The major difficulty with this method is determining whether or not a particular imitation preserves the meaning of the original. Some instances are clear, but others are not. If the method can be demonstrated to work reliably, it will have several important advantages over other means of assessing comprehension. First, it can be used with quite young children, especially if they are familiar with the investigator. And, second, as the investigator can choose any type of sentence to be imitated, it can be a very general technique. Of course, the sentence must not be too short. Echo, for example, at age 2;3 could repeat all possible orders of the three words *John loves company*.

What can be concluded from this confusing array of methodological and theoretical arguments and empirical findings? At the very least, the concepts of comprehension and production are not simple ones. Syntactic, semantic, contextual, and other factors enter intimately into each process and make comparisons between the two difficult, if not impossible. Comprehension probably precedes production in some instances, is simultaneous in others, and follows in yet others. But any particular conclusion must be made relative to the constellation of syntactic, semantic, and contextual factors making up the particular measures used. Comparisons of responses on comprehension tests and spontaneous performances are especially difficult to interpret. When a child produces sentences, he is presumably interested in what he is saying and thus more likely to be paying attention than during a comprehension test, when he may be asked to respond while he is not fully attending. He may have acquired some aspect of language from the relatively few instances of the structure that he has attended to in everyday context and thus be capable of using the structure accurately in his production, though his performance on a structured comprehension task may be disappointing. All these considerations suggest that establishing a single "linguistic competence" for a child in isolation from contextual factors is not only difficult but perhaps impossible in principle. Grammars for children are far more artificial idealizations for children than for adults.

Metalinguistic Awareness

Metalinguistic awareness, the ability to think about language and to comment on it, as well as to produce and comprehend it, is late in developing. The fundamental tool of the linguist of adult language, the ability of speakers to judge sentences as grammatical or ungrammatical and to correct ungrammatical sentences, emerges only about age five years or so.

Gleitman, Gleitman, and Shipley (1972) and de Villiers and de Villiers (1974) have explored this development. Very young children will occasionally comment on the oddity of clearly ungrammatical sentences. In the study by Gleitman and his colleagues, thirty-month-old children judged at least some scrambled imperatives, like *Ball me the bring*, as "silly." However, their corrections generally changed the implicit meaning as well as the word order, for example, correcting *the box open* to *Get in the box*, suggesting that they were responding to the semantic oddity of the sentences, rather than to the scrambled word order specifically.

De Villiers and de Villiers investigated the ability to judge and correct word order in active sentences, particularly verb-object order in imperatives. We have seen that by the time MLU has reached 3.0 children are both producing active sentences with correct order and are comprehending word-order information. The subjects were told that they were helping to teach a puppet how to talk properly. The puppet produced correct imperatives (*Pat the dog*), reversed imperatives (*Cake the eat*), and semantically anomalous imperatives (*Drink the chair*). The child was asked to judge the sentences as "right" or "wrong." He was also asked to tell the experimenter "the right way to say it." Judgment and correction performance were highly related to MLU, as the following summary of de Villiers and de Villiers' findings (1974) shows:

MLU	Judgment	Correction
2.5–3.0	unable to judge reversed word order wrong	no corrections
3.0–3.5	semantic anomaly, but not reversed order, judged wrong	no corrections
3.5–4.0		corrections of semantic anomaly only
4.0–4.5	accurate judgments of both anomaly and reversed order	semantic corrections for reversed-order sentences
above 4.5		direct word-order corrections

Ability to judge sentences on the basis of word order clearly follows by a considerable interval the use of order in comprehension and production, and the ability to correct ungrammatical strings follows somewhat the ability to reject them. Semantic anomaly is easier to judge and to correct than syntactic (order) anomaly. In fact, for a time (around MLU 4.0–4.5) sentences with reversed order are recognized as "wrong," but the corrections generally change the meanings, as in the study by Gleitman, Gleitman, and Shipley (1972). The specific ability to correct reversed order was found, in a second study, to be highly correlated with the ability to comprehend reversible passives, which for a time are interpreted as actives (see table summarizing de Villiers and de Villiers 1974). The correlation is suggestive, for comprehension of reversible passives also seems to require manipulation of word order (the subject is the last word of the sentence).

These results show clearly that a child may "know" a particular linguistic rule, in the sense of following the rule in producing sentences and understanding sentences when the only clue is the structure described by the rule, long before he can consciously state the rule or use it to make judgments of grammatical and ungrammatical sentences.

The process of becoming aware of language is one that continues throughout development. In its highest form, it becomes the basis of aesthetic pleasure in poetry and prose.

Later Syntactic Development

Past the age of five or six years, differences between the child's grammar and adult grammar are not obvious from spontaneous observation of free speech. There are a few characteristic difficulties that remain, including mastery of subject-verb agreement and case endings on personal pronouns (Him and her went), reacquisition of the irregular past tense and perfect forms (went, held, cut), and a few others. However, these are relatively minor features. The basic syntactic structure of most of the child's sentences appears to be that of adult grammar. (But recall the caution concerning interpretation of complex-appearing sentences presented in the section on complex sentences.) Carol Chomsky (1969) has shown how some major syntactic differences may be observed in studies of comprehension. She reasoned that recent studies of the structure of English have increased our awareness of the complexity of a natural language (English) and that the more complex aspects should be the last to be mastered.

Comprehension of a sentence requires understanding of the basic elements, that is, the morphemes, and also of the structure of the sentence, which specifies the relations among the individual morphemes. In particular it is the deep structure that is most important, because it is the deep structure that indicates the basic grammatical relations, especially subject and object. Such comprehension is likely to be especially difficult with complex sentences, each consisting of two or more simple sentences, which must be sorted and related to each other.

Chomsky studied several conditions under which this might be particularly difficult. We shall consider two of her examples. To the extent that the true grammatical relations are not directly expressed in the surface structure, comprehension should be difficult. In *John saw Mary*, the surface structure indicates that *John* is the subject and *Mary* the object; in the passive *Mary was seen by John*, the order in surface structure does not indicate the deep-structure relations. And, in fact, both children and adults find it harder to understand passives than actives (Slobin 1966b).

Recall the sentences discussed in Chapter 4 to illustrate the concept of deep structure:

1. John is easy to please.
2. John is eager to please.

In the first sentence *John* is the object of *please*, whereas in the second sentence *John* is the subject of *please*. In other words, these apparently similar surface structures are composed of two deep-structure simple sentences in quite different ways:

1a. (John pleases someone)   (is easy)
2a. (John is eager)   (Someone pleases John)

The surface structure of sentence 2 indicates the relations among the elements of the sentence more clearly than does the surface structure of sentence 1. In the surface structure of sentence 1 the subject of *please* (the indefinite pronoun *someone*) is not even present. Sentences of the second type should be easier to understand. Perhaps they are acquired earlier. A child who has mastered sentences of the second type may interpret sentences of the first type as if they were of the second type, just as at an earlier stage she may interpret passives as actives.

How might such miscomprehension be observed? Some sentences can be understood without using full knowledge of structure. For example, *The book is hard to read,* a sentence of the first type, is unlikely to be misinterpreted; books do not read. To investigate the child's understanding of the syntactic structure, it is necessary to have sentences that do not provide semantic clues. Chomsky selected *The doll is easy to see,* which can be interpreted correctly to mean that someone else sees the doll or incorrectly to mean that the doll is doing the seeing.

She placed a blindfolded doll in front of each child, who was asked, "Is the doll easy to see or hard to see?" The children generally answered without hesitation and with confidence, but they were often wrong. Mastery of this construction comes quite late; before attaining such mastery, children assign the incorrect interpretation. Here are Chomsky's data on this question:

Age	Correct
5	22%
6	42%
7	86%
8	75%
9	100%

A sample protocol follows (1969:30):

> Lisa V., 6;5
> Q. Is this doll easy to see or hard to see?
> A. Hard to see.
> Q. Will you make her easy to see?
> A. If I can get this untied.
> Q. Will you explain why she was hard to see?
> A. (To doll)   Because you had a blindfold over your eyes.
> Q. And what did you do?
> A. I took it off.

It may seem that there is something of a trick to this procedure. Cromer (1970) and others have pointed to the possibility that poor performance before age seven years arises from nonsyntactic factors. For example, the blindfolding may be misleading. The child may know something about the grammatical structure but may think that the blindfold must be there for some purpose. The young child may believe that it is necessary to see the eyes of another person or doll in order to feel that it is "easy" to see them. Like the proverbial ostrich, the young child may believe that, if his eyes are covered, others cannot see him; as the doll's eyes are blindfolded, others cannot see the doll. Cromer developed a more fully verbal technique. He showed the child a toy wolf and a toy duck, said a sentence of the form

The wolf is happy to bite (first sentence type) or *The duck is fun to bite* (second sentence type). He also included sentences with ambiguous adjectives, like *The wolf is nasty to bite*. The child was then asked who does the biting. Cromer related performance to mental age, as assessed by the Peabody Picture Vocabulary Test (to be discussed in Chapter 11). Below 5;8, the children interpreted all sentences as referring to the named animal as subject, in accordance with the pattern of sentence 1. Between 5;9 and 6;6, most children vacillated between giving the named animal or the other animal as subject. Past 6;8, most children were correct on all types of sentences (for the ambiguous sentences, they gave some examples of both types of interpretation). This is, perhaps, somewhat earlier than Chomsky found, but the difference is not large. The blindfold may mislead a few children in a transitional stage, but the effect is not large.

Cromer also invented new adjectives, to see if children could learn in a single trial how they were used in grammatical structures of this type. Compare "See, someone gave this dog a bone, and so he's feeling very risp. Now show me the wolf is risp to bite" with "Chewing the rose was larsp. Now show me the wolf is larsp to bite." Below 6;6 the named animal was taken as subject, but above 6;8 most children could respond correctly. That is, once the appropriate rules are mastered, a new adjective can be merged into the grammar after only a single exposure.

Kessel (1970) has also analyzed and revised many of Chomsky's procedures. Like Cromer, he has shown that children move through the overall sequence of development reported by Chomsky at a somewhat faster rate than she observed. Cambon and Sinclair (1974) have investigated a similar construction in French.

A second condition that might lead to difficulty in comprehension is the particular structure that is an exception to a general principle describing the relation between deep and surface structure. Consider the following sentences:

3. John persuaded Bill to leave.
4. John told Bill to leave.
5. John permitted Bill to leave.
6. John selected Bill to leave.

There are many other verbs that fit this pattern—*allow, urge, cause,* and so on. Notice that the subject of the second verb, *leave,* is always the second NP, *Bill.* There are other verbs that may or may not have a second NP:

7. John wanted (Bill) to leave.
8. John expected (Bill) to leave.
9. John asked (Bill) to leave.

If there is a second NP, it is the subject of *leave*. If not, the first NP, *John*, is the subject. The general rule in English is the **minimal-distance principle** (MDP): The subject of a complement verb (a verb with *to*) is the NP most immediately preceding it. This principle describes all the examples considered. However, there are exceptions. *Ask* is an exception in sentences with *wh* clauses, though *tell* is *not*: *I asked him what to do* means *I asked him what I should do; I told him what to do* means *I told him what he should do*. In sentences without a *wh* clause, *ask* is not an exception: *Mary asked John to leave* means *Mary asked John if he (John) would leave*. *Promise* is always an exception to the MDP: *John promised Bill to leave* means *John promised Bill that he (John) would leave*.

Chomsky hypothesized that a child may first learn the MDP and only later the exceptions. Sentences that do not follow the principle may be interpreted as if they did. In exploring this possibility with five- and six-year-olds, she discovered another difficulty: In a variety of instances, children use *ask* as if it were *tell* (Chomsky 1969:45):

Q. Ask Joe what to feed the doll.
A. The cucumber.
Q. Now tell Joe what to feed the doll.
A. The tomato.
Q. Now ask Joe which food to put back in the box.
A. The hot dog.
Q. And ask Joe which piece of food to pick up.
A. The watermelon.

That this is not simply a matter of vocabulary learning is shown by the fact that somewhat older children interpret *ask* as *tell* in some syntactic structures and not others. Chomsky discovered a regular sequence of development. Four constructions were used in the experiment. The first was *ask* in the sense of *request*: *Bozo asks to go first in line* or *Bozo asks/tells Michie to go first in line*. This is the simplest use of *ask*. The more important use of *ask* is in the sense of *question*. Here there are three cases.

Case 1. *Ask/tell Laura what color this is* and *Ask/tell Laura how many pencils there are here*. In case 1 sentences, the subject of the *wh* clause is supplied. This means that the child merely has to move the words around:

Q. Ask Laura what color this is.
A. What color is that?

Case 2. *Ask/tell Laura her/your last name* and *Ask/tell Laura the color of this book*. Here the complement clause is abbreviated, and the question word and verb must be supplied by the child.

Q. Ask Laura her last name.
A. What's your last name?

Case 3. *Ask/tell Laura what to feed the doll* and *Ask/tell Laura which food to put back in the box.* Here the subject of the verb is not supplied; the child must supply it.

Q. Ask Laura what to feed the doll.
A. What should I feed the doll?

This is more difficult than case 2 because the child must refer outside the clause to choose between two possible subjects for the verb.

A wide variety of sentences, randomly arranged, were used. Actually, two children were present, the one being questioned and another one, who was to be asked or told.

The subjects, between five and ten years of age, interpreted *ask* in the sense of *request* correctly without any difficulty. But interpretation of *ask* in the question sense proceeded through a sequence of five stages. In the first stage (A), a *tell* interpretation was imposed on *ask* in all three cases:

Stage A: Failure on All Cases.

Christine M., 5;1
Q. Ask Eric his last name.
A. Handel.
Q. Ask Eric this doll's name.
A. I don't know.
Q. Ask Eric what time it is.
A. I don't know how to tell time.
Q. Tell Eric what class is in the library.
A. Kindergarten.
Q. Ask Eric who his teacher is.
A. Miss Turner.
Q. Ask Eric who this is.
A. Bozo

In the second stage (B), *ask* is correctly interpreted in case 1 but not in cases 2 or 3. In the third stage, *ask* is interpreted correctly in both cases 1 and 2 but not yet in case 3:

Stage C: Success on Cases 1 and 2, Failure on Case 3

Laura S., 6;5
Q. Ask Joanne what color this book is.
A. What color's that book?
Q. Ask Joanne her last name.
A. What's your last name?

Q. Tell Joanne what color this tray is.
A. Tan.
Q. Ask Joanne what's in the box.
A. What's in the box?
Q. Ask Joanne what to feed the doll.
A. The hot dog.
Q. Now I want you to *ask* Joanne something. *Ask* her what to feed the doll.
A. The piece of bread.
Q. Ask Joanne what you should feed the doll (Case 1).
A. What should I feed the doll?

The ability to interpret *ask* correctly in the simpler constructions is not enough to enable the child to succeed in the more complex case 3.

In the fourth stage (D), correct interpretation in cases 1 and 2 occurs with partial success in case 3:

Stage D: Success in Cases 1 and 2, Partial Success on Case 3.

Penny O., 7;0
Q. Ask Ann what to feed the doll.
A. What d'you feed the doll?
Q. Ask Ann what to put back in the box.
A. What d'ya put back?

In stage D the child asks a question (not just telling, as in stage C), but it is the wrong question. In particular, she assigns the wrong subject. To the instruction *Ask Lynn what to put back in the box* she answers, *What are you going to put in the box?* This is what Chomsky originally hypothesized: a stage in which *ask* and *tell* are distinguished but in which the exception to the MDP has not been learned. But this stage occurs remarkably late. The children in this group were at an average age of about seven and one half years. They had various ways of coping with the difficulty, and there was a wide variety of responses, but they all failed to assign the correct subject.

In stage E all sentences were correctly interpreted. The stages formed a regular sequence, in that no child succeeded on a later case without also succeeding on all earlier cases. The stages were not strongly correlated with age. One child who was 5;10 succeeded on all constructions; that is, was at stage E. Another child, who was ten years old, was only at stage C. There was a general tendency, of course, for the children at later stages to be older than those at earlier stages, but there was great variation. Furthermore, linguistic development in this sense did not always coincide with the teacher's general assessments of the children. The one second-grade boy who was at stage E was a child who was rated by his teacher as below average.

It should be pointed out that the misinterpretation of case 3 characteristic of stage D is not simply a survival of the tendency to process passives as actives, which occurs much earlier. Instead, it reflects the acquisition, however partial, of new grammatical structures. Maratsos (1974) has pointed out that the minimal-distance principle as stated here is an oversimplification. Compare sentences 10 and 11:

10. John told Bill to leave.
11. Bill was told by John to leave.

In sentence 11, even though *John* is closer to the verb *leave*, *Bill* is understood to be the subject of *leave*, just as it is in sentence 10. That is, the minimal-distance principle cannot be formulated simply on the basis of surface-structure order but must be related to aspects of the transformational character of the sentence. For active sentences of the type discussed earlier in this section, this point is not significant. But for passive sentences like sentence 11, it is crucial to correct interpretation.

Maratsos (1974b) tested comprehension of passive sentences with *ask* and *tell*, for example, *The bear is told by the elephant to get in* and *The daddy is asked by the mommy to get in.* (These sentences are similar to Chomsky's simplest, unnumbered case.) In addition, active sentences with *promise* were tested: for example, *The monkey promises the dog to jump off.* In sentences of this type *promise*, but not *ask*, violates the MDP. Maratsos found that even children who could comprehend such simple passives as *The boy is bumped by the dog* and more complex passives like *The daddy is asked by the mommy to get in* still interpreted sentences with *promise* incorrectly. Despite the fact that these children had advanced past simple use of surface-structure word order to use of more complex rules relating deep and surface structure, they took *dog* to be the subject of *jump off* in the sample sentence with *promise* more than three quarters of the time, in accordance with the MDP.

Summary

The sentences produced by a child at any point in his development are determined by his own grammar, not by the adult grammar that he will eventually master. In the development of questions, as in other areas of language development, children regularly produce forms they have not heard. It is doubtful that any mother has ever said *Why not cracker can't talk?* or *What you have in you mouth?* These questions reflect the child's construction of a grammar a step at a time. Even when the child attempts to imitate an adult utterance, he simplifies it to conform to his own grammar.

The development of the ability to comprehend language also proceeds through a regular pattern, though it has not been studied as much as has production. Part of the problem is that the term "comprehension" really covers a number of distinct concepts, depending on the involvement of linguistic and nonlinguistic contextual factors. For this reason, it is difficult to make any generalizations about whether comprehension precedes, is equal to, or lags behind production. Undoubtedly all these relations occur in different aspects of language development. What is clear is that comprehension is rule-governed, just as production is. Unfortunately for the linguist studying child language, the rules are not the same in the two processes. The discrepancy renders the search for *the* grammar of child language problematic, at best.

Children obviously have preferences for a small number of general rules. Overgeneralizations are as common in syntax as in inflectional development. Just as American and Russian children overgeneralize past-tense, case, and other inflections, the children in Chomsky's experiment overgeneralized rules relating deep and surface structure. Exceptions to rules—sentences in which the objects occur before the subjects, sentences that violate the minimal-distance principle—are mastered only after a considerable interval.

further reading

Bloom, L. Talking, understanding, and thinking. In R. L. Schiefelbusch and L. L. Lloyd (Eds.), *Language perspectives—Acquisition, retardation, and intervention*. Baltimore: University Park Press, 1974. Pp. 285–311.

Brown, R. Derivational complexity and order of acquisition in child speech. In R. Brown, *Psycholinguistics*. New York: Free Press, 1970. Pp. 155–207.

Maratsos, M. P. How preschool children understand missing complement sentences. *Child Development*, 1974, **45**, 700–706.

6

Theories of
Syntactic Development

In the previous four chapters we have provided a description of the course of syntactic development. The child's language gradually unfolds in an ever more elaborate system. How does she do it? We do not have any complete theories that can be seriously considered as explanations for syntactic development *in toto*. Instead, we have a mixed bag of mechanisms, processes, and strategies that may each play a role.

Imitation and Reinforcement

Two processes with a considerable tradition in psychology are imitation and reinforcement. Expressed without jargon, one common-sense theory of language acquisition is that children just imitate what they hear. Parents teach them by telling them when they make mistakes. According to this account, there are three processes: imitation, which is the source of new linguistic forms; practice, that is, repetition by the child in his free speech; and reinforcement, which teaches the child which situations are appropriate for the use of each form. Each of these three must be considered closely.

Imitation

At the end of the process of language development, children generally are talking as their parents do. But to take this as evidence that language development is the result of imitation is to coi fuse the *product* of learning with the *process* of learning that leads to the product. We should also distinguish *motivation* from *mechanism*. Children vant to be like their parents and older siblings, and speech is an obvious cl aracteristic of these significant people. But motivation is not identical with the mechanism of acquisition. A young child whose older brother or sister has a bicycle wants to learn to ride the bicycle as his sibling does, but the learning does not take place by imitation. Instead, a complex kind of sensorimotor learning, based on the child's own active efforts to ride the bicycle, usually including frequent falling, is necessary.

Several kinds of evidence suggest that imitation, in the sense of a child's attempt to reproduce the actual adult utterances he hears, does not play an important role in the acquisition of syntax. Many of the very earliest utterances of children cannot be viewed as imitations or even reduced imitations of adult speech; for example, *Allgone sticky*. Furthermore, even when children do imitate parental speech (which is not uncommon), they reformulate the sentences using their own grammars. Children can hardly acquire new grammatical features through imitation when it is precisely these new features that are omitted in imitations.

Perhaps the most dramatic evidence against imitation is the fact that children who cannot speak at all but who can hear normally acquire normal competence in language comprehension. Eric Lenneberg (1962) has reported the case of a boy who, for unknown neuromuscular reasons, was unable to articulate speech at all. Such a child could never have imitated adult speech. Indeed, he could not have been reinforced for speaking grammatically. Yet he did learn to comprehend language. Such examples are strong evidence against any theory of language acquisition that depends very strongly on the child's productions, for example, the selective-reinforcement theory of the development of speech sounds from babbling.

Although this extreme example is the most striking, something similar occurs for every child. The fact that comprehension can be superior to production in many cases, even when comprehension is partially based on linguistic and nonlinguistic contexts, is virtually impossible to square with the view of learning through imitation.

Ammon and Ammon (1971) used elicited imitation in a training study with disadvantaged black preschool children. One group received vocabulary training; a second group received sentence training. Both groups participated in twice-a-week, twenty-minute training sessions for six weeks. A control group received no special training. Receptive and productive vocabulary and syntactic development, as measured by a sentence-imitation test, were measured before and after the training. The sentence-imitation test and the sentence training focused on features that occur in both Standard English and Black English (to be discussed in Chapter 10): prenominal adjectives, locative prepositional phrases, possessive nouns, relative clauses, and adverbial clauses. Vocabulary training led to increased recognition and production of the words taught, but there was no transfer to sentence imitation. Sentence training had no significant effect on either measure. Ammon and Ammon concluded that "time devoted to early language training . . . is better spent on vocabulary than on sentence construction." Their conclusion is consistent with the findings of Bloom and her colleagues (1974) that at least some children show a consistent tendency to imitate unfamiliar words but that constructions are not imitated until they have occurred in spontaneous speech.

One of the most difficult problems in developmental psychology is the relation between research findings on normal children and therapeutic methods for exceptional children. The fact that imitation may not play a role in the syntactic development of normal children does not imply that it may not be of great value for the speech therapist or other language trainer. Children are referred to the therapist precisely when the normal process of development has failed. The use of imitation must be evaluated in each appropriate context. The negative conclusion for normal children does suggest, however, that the process of imitation ought to be closely examined in the therapeutic setting. Under what conditions do children in the therapy setting successfully imitate? If the child does not match the model sentence, what changes occur? Are there regular patterns of distortion? Particularly worthy of investigation is the tendency to drill language patterns without any supporting context. Normal children first comprehend and produce aspects of syntax with the support of linguistic and nonlinguistic contexts, but too often, in the therapy setting, meaning in this larger sense is missing.

Practice

Practice cannot really help to explain language acquisition, but presumably it is the mechanism by which features are firmly fixed in the child's language. The development of inflections in English and Russian casts doubt on the efficacy of practice, however. English-speaking children have the correct past-tense forms of the irregular verbs and use them correctly, and Zhenya and other Russian children have mastered the correct instrumental singular forms and used them correctly for months; both fit the definition of practice perfectly. But these forms are given up unhesitatingly when the regular endings are learned.

Reinforcement

Parents often approve or disapprove of what their children say, but they do not really carry on intensive teaching programs of the kind necessary for second-language learning after adolescence. And in fact such approval or disapproval does not seem to be necessary, as immigrant children pick up a second language in the streets without any reinforcement of this type.

The claim that it is direct reinforcement that leads to the predominance of grammatically correct sentences assumes that parental approval and disapproval are in fact dependent on grammar. Of course, even if these expressions are appropriately contingent, they may not have an effect. Brown, Cazden, and Bellugi (1969) worked through several samples of data, comparing the correctness of those child utterances that were followed by signs of approval from parents with those child utterances that were followed by signs of disapproval. In the majority of instances the grounds on which an utterance was approved or disapproved were not linguistic at all but, rather, were based on the correspondence between utterance and reality, that is, the truth of the sentence. Reading 6.1 is a summary of Brown's findings.

Furthermore, attempts at direct instruction in language are almost always total failures. Here is a report by a psycholinguist of such an attempt:

> . . . I have occasionally made an extensive effort to change the syntax of my two children through correction. One case was the use by my two-and-a-half-year-old daughter of *other one* as a noun modifier. . . . I repeatedly but fruitlessly tried to persuade her to substitute *other* + N for *other one* + N . . . the interchange went somewhat as follows: "Want other one spoon, Daddy"—"You mean, you want THE OTHER SPOON"—"Yes, I want other one spoon, please, Daddy"—"Can you say 'the other spoon'?"— "other . . . one . . . spoon"—"Say . . . other"—"Other"—"Spoon"— "Spoon"—"Other . . . spoon"—"Other spoon. Now give me other one spoon." Further tuition is ruled out by her protest, vigorously supported by my wife. (Braine 1971:160–161)

Less anecdotally, Nelson (1973) observed that children at the one-word stage—whose mothers engaged in selective reinforcement for good and bad pronunciations and word choice—developed more *slowly*, not more rapidly, than those whose mothers were generally accepting.

Perhaps viewing parental approval and disapproval as positive and negative reinforcers is too literal. Any parental speech to a child is a kind of attention, and children crave such attention. When the child produces his first words, he is likely to receive a great deal of attention, much of it positive. Later, the speech of the child is likely to provoke some response from the parent. However, this attention is largely independent of the form of the child's utterance; that is, attention may motivate a child to talk but not necessarily to speak grammatically.

Another possible reinforcer is satisfaction of the child's wants. This possibility is at the heart of the **communication-pressure hypothesis:** Children learn to talk because they need to communicate their needs to others. Such an hypothesis can be correct only if satisfaction of the child's needs is more likely following a syntactically correct utterance than following a syntactically incorrect one. It would be difficult, for methodological reasons discussed in Brown and Hanlon (1970), to test this hypothesis formally, but the weight of anecdotal evidence is against it. My son Jonathan at age twenty-six months requested the repetition of some favored activity by saying *'gain*, with a characteristic rising intonation; at age thirty-one months he said *Do that again, Dad*. The latter sentence is far more complex linguistically but no more effective. Parents are highly understanding, and communication with them is easy even with primitive linguistic systems. If acquisition of a word or linguistic feature is long overdue, a parent may actively take a hand, but what is striking is how seldom this occurs. The child moves on from *mi* to *milk* to *want milk* to *I want milk* before the parent may begin to disapprove more primitive forms.

Brown and Hanlon evaluated a hypothesis combining attention and communication pressure. The hypothesized contingent event, the proposed reinforcer, was a relevant reply from the addressee. Answers to questions, statements related to the child's utterance, and questions to the child on the same topic all continue the conversation; Brown and Hanlon called them "sequiturs." In contrast, such questions as *What did you say?*, sentences introducing new topics, misunderstandings, and failure to respond constitute "nonsequiturs."

Are sequiturs contingent? That is, do they occur more often in response to well-formed utterances than to those that are not well formed? When Brown and Hanlon examined their records of mother-child conversations, they found that well-formed utterances had a 45 percent probability of eliciting sequiturs from the adults addressed but that more primitive utterances also had a 45 percent probability of eliciting sequiturs. Clearly, sequiturs are not the reinforcers that guide syntactic development. What is happening here is similar to the case of approval/disapproval. Parents fit some meaning to even the most fragmentary utterance and respond as best they can to that meaning.

It seems reasonable to assume that communication is intrinsically satisfying. The ultimate reward of language learning is understanding other people's talking and making oneself understood. Perhaps this experience in communication is the reinforcer that underlies language development. Plausible as this sounds, it robs reinforcement of any explanatory power. How can this reinforcement be contingent unless the child *knows* when he has expressed himself well, when he has been understood, and when he is understanding others accurately? That is, the reinforcement theory *assumes* that the child has learned the language.

The appeal of imitation, practice, and reinforcement as explanatory concepts in large part lies in the fact that they are easily observable and quantifiable. Surely they play some role in language development. Yet they reflect a passive conception of the language learner. The emphasis in the theory is on what the environment does for and to the child. An understanding of language as a creative system, with the consequence that linguistic competence must consist in large part of a set of rules, not a collection of elements, leads to skepticism of such explanations.

On Talking to Children

The problem for the language learner is to work from the data available—the speech heard by the young child and responses to his own speech—to arrive at the rules underlying the data. Most of what the child hears is the speech of his primary caretaker, usually his mother. What kind of linguistic environment do mothers provide for their children?

Although most people who have had experience speaking with children have strong feelings that their speech in such situations is quite different from their other speech, actual studies of maternal speech had not been conducted until quite recently. Two studies of sizable samples of mothers have been conducted by Phillips (1973), who compared speech to a child with speech to an adult interviewer for fifty-seven mothers, and by Snow (1972a), who compared speech to ten-year-olds with speech to two-year-olds for thirty women, some mothers and some not. In addition, a considerable number of studies of particular aspects of maternal speech have been conducted with small numbers (sometimes just one) of mothers (see Vorster 1974 for a review).

Phillips (1973) compared the speech of thirty white, middle-class mothers of first-born boys to their children in a play session with their speech in casual conversation with an adult interviewer. The mothers' speech to their children was significantly different in several respects: Sentences were shorter; fewer verbs, modifiers, and function words (conjunctions, prepositions, and the like) were used; fewer distinct verb forms (such as tenses) were produced; vocabulary was less diverse and generally more concrete. Some of the differences were quite large; for example, the mean lengths of utterance to child and to adult were 3.7 and 8.4 respectively. Others were small, often less than 20 percent in magnitude. The speech of mothers of twenty-eight-month-olds showed these tendencies to a much weaker extent than the speech of mothers of younger boys. A replication study including mothers of boys and mothers of girls revealed no difference with respect to the children's sex; mothers of girls talked to their daughters just as mothers of boys talked to their sons.

Snow (1972a) compared the speech of women to two-year-old children with their speech to ten-year-old children. She, too, found differences; for example, speech to the younger children was shorter, less complex in terms of subordinate clauses, and more repetitious, and it included fewer pronouns. Snow also included a condition in which the adult was asked to speak "into a tape recorder in the absence of the child, but as if she were speaking to a child of the appropriate age group" (Snow 1972a:552). In this condition, differences between speech to the two age groups were considerably smaller. This finding suggests that the process of simplification depends in some sense on the presence of the child and on his providing feedback to the adult. Snow also compared mothers with other women, who presumably had had much less experience with young children; she found only small differences between the two groups. Thus it does not seem to be a cumulative learning process that leads to simplification as much as the actual presence of the child being addressed. We shall return to this point later.

Vorster (1974) has reviewed a number of additional studies and has concluded that among the most reliable differences to be found in maternal speech are shorter length of utterance, slower rate of speech, fewer tenses, a smaller type-token ratio (a measure of vocabulary diversity), and frequency of complex sentences. There is also evidence that, over the course of language acquisition, maternal speech[1] gradually becomes more complex and similar to normal adult-adult speech. However, the correlation is not a close one, in that changes in child language are not immediately and directly reflected in changes in maternal speech.

We probably overestimate the importance of adult speech for the child. Even in our own society, much of the input comes from older children. And, from a global perspective, it is probably the norm for the majority of speech to the young child to come from older children. Shatz and Gelman (1973) have found that four-year-old children, like adults, modify their speech as a function of the age of the listener. In free speech, as well as in descriptions of a new toy, four-year-olds produce fewer, shorter, and in some respects simpler sentences to two-year-olds than to adults. We might suspect that this simplification is owing to imitation of adults' simplifications

---

[1] By now the reader may be wondering about fathers, typically the parents ignored in psychological research. There are no studies of father-child verbal interaction during the language-learning period. However, Rebelsky and Hanks (1971) observed infants during the first three months of age, using a twenty-four-hour recording every two weeks. They found that fathers just do not spend much time talking to their infants. Talking most likely occurs in the morning, before fathers go to work and also in the evening after work. But on the average there were only 2.7 interactions per twenty-four-hour period, totaling an average of thirty-eight seconds! We should probably not leap to any serious conclusions from this study. What happens at three months probably does not predict what will happen at twelve, eighteen, or twenty-four months of age. Furthermore, the relative contributions of quality and quantity are hardly understood.

to younger siblings, but even four-year-olds without younger siblings make this adjustment. Speech to fellow four-year-olds resembles speech to adults. The relative unimportance of actual experience with younger siblings is reminiscent of Snow's finding that experience with young children does not affect speech as much as does the actual presence of the children. In both instances the speakers are responding to some kind of feedback.

What is the significance of this simplification? What difference does it make? It is at least plausible that simplification is an aid to learning. In many instances it is just the difficult constructions that are avoided. The fact that passives are virtually never spoken to young children and complex sentences less frequently means that two kinds of sentence in which the deep structures are quite different from the surface structures are not as frequent. Of course, these sentence types will have to be mastered later, but the immediate problem is simplified. For example, the subject, verb, and object should be easier to identify in maternal speech, for they fall into a more regular order than in the complex constructions of normal adult-adult speech. Repetition, both exact and in paraphrase, is extremely common. Snow gives an example: "Pick up the red one. Find the red one. Not the green one. I want the red one. Can you find the red one?" (Snow 1972a:563). In addition to presenting the basic message several times, this string of sentences illustrates something of the way in which basic units of language can be rearranged.

Nevertheless, arguments of this type are basically *post hoc*. We observe differences and guess how they *might* affect the language-learning process. The real question is whether or not empirical evidence can be found for an effect of simplification in maternal speech. For ethical and practical reasons, the experiment of eliminating simplification in maternal speech cannot be conducted. But some indirect evidence is available.

Talking in baby talk to a child for the first five years of his life would surely hinder his learning, but so would speaking in the language of an encyclopedia or a diplomatic treaty. There must be an optimum level of language complexity, challenging to the child but not impossibly so. Shipley, Smith, and Gleitman (1969) studied the spontaneous responses of young children to commands that varied in structure. They found that children past the one-word stage responded appropriately more often when the command was cast in adult form (*Throw me the ball*) than when it was cast in a simplified form similar to that of the children's own language (*Throw ball*). To the extent that comprehension is in advance of production, this finding is not surprising. But it also suggests the central role of attention as a mediator of language development. Learning cannot take place without attention to the relevant events; attention controls the gates to learning. One experimental test of the importance of maternal speech would show whether or not children prefer to attend to maternal speech.

Spring (1974) and Snow (1972b) have done just such a test. Spring recorded a mother talking to her own twelve-month-old child and to an adult. Each was recorded on one track of a tape recorder. Other twelve-month-olds were offered the choice. That is, they were presented with two plastic panels. When they pushed one, they heard one track for several seconds; when they pushed the other, they heard the other track. Over a twenty-minute session, most (though not all) of the twelve-month-olds showed preference for the maternal speech to infant. In Snow's study (1972b) two- and three-year-old children listened to a taped story while looking at pictures. Half of the story was in normal adult speech; the other half had been "translated" into simplified speech on the basis of the findings of Snow (1972a) just discussed. Every fifteen seconds observers rated the child's attention. The children were significantly more attentive during the simplified portion of the story.

The preference for maternal speech in these two studies probably rests on distinct aspects of language. The twelve-month-olds studied by Spring had relatively little command of vocabulary and syntax, and the crucial factor was probably the greater intonational character of maternal speech. This hypothesis could easily be checked with additional tapes in which content is constant but intonation varies. For the more advanced children studied by Snow, the simplified vocabulary and syntax were probably the determinants of attention.

The claim that children are more attentive to simplified speech, if true, would explain the findings of Snow (1972a) and Phillips (1973) that it is the actual presence of a child that influences simplification. Also relevant is the observation by Ervin-Tripp (1973) that hearing children of deaf parents do not learn language from radio or television. The most important characteristic of such input is that it is in no way dependent on the response of the child.

The extent of simplification in maternal speech should not be over-estimated. Every study that has compared maternal speech with the child's own language at the same time has found that the mother's speech is significantly more complex than the child's speech. Brown and Hanlon (1970) calculated that only 30 percent of the sentences heard by the child are simple, active, affirmative, declarative sentences. The remaining 70 percent are complex, passive, negatives, questions, fragments, and other forms. There is still a considerable variety and richness to maternal speech. The findings of Shipley, Smith, and Gleitman (1969) are relevant here also, as they suggest that children are most attentive to utterances that are somewhat beyond their own productive level.

The concept of attention is also a reminder that it is not parental speech that directs the path of language acquisition but, rather, what the child does with it. Frequency in parental speech seldom predicts order of acquisition; recall Brown's negative finding concerning frequency in parental speech as a predictor of the order of acquisition of fourteen grammatical morphemes of English (see Chapter 2).

Thus children may control the linguistic input available to them by means of their selective attention to the speech of other people. And, as the child's language advances and he attends to more complex speech, the speech addressed to him advances as well.

Expansions and Other Special Interchanges

Probably more important than the absolute quality of the mother's speech is the nature of the linguistic interchange between parent and child. Several intriguing kinds of verbal interchange have been discovered by Brown and his coworkers. In these interchanges, the deep structure of a sentence and its transformed surface structure seem to be presented simultaneously. This would provide just the appropriate information for the child to formulate a transformation.

Prompting

One kind of interchange is called **prompting,** or **constituent prompting.** The parent asks a question, like *What do you want?* The child does not respond, and the parent tries again: *You want what?* The parent may be assuming that the second question, which is a sort of sentence-completion item, is easier to understand. If he is correct and the child does understand the question without *wh* movement to initial position, then he has in mind something closer to the deep structure (*You want what?*) just after being presented with the surface structure (*What do you want?*). He might learn how to ask questions this way, that is, learn to formulate the transformations that invert subject and auxiliary, supply *do* if necessary, and move the *wh* word to the initial position.

Echoing

A different exchange begins when a child utters a sentence that is partly unintelligible, like *I going owa nah* or *I'm gonna splay.* The mother then imitates the child insofar as she can and replaces the unintelligible part with one of the *wh* words of English, producing questions like *You're going where?* and *You're gonna do what?* Such an exchange is called **echo** or **say constituent again.** The mother's question is similar to the deep structure of a well-formed *wh* question. It does not correspond directly with the child's utterance, which is a declarative. The child's sentence is the answer to the question. A proper answer to *You're going where?* might be *I'm going home.* For example.

CHILD: I going owa nah.
MOTHER: You're going where?
CHILD: I going . . .

The mother is asking a question to which what the child has just said and (it is to be hoped) will repeat more clearly is the answer. As Bellugi's study of questions (see Chapter 5) has shown, children cannot answer questions properly early in their development; they must learn. Notice that the answer to a *wh* question is basically identical with the deep structure of the *wh* question, the *wh* word being replaced by the information desired. The question provided by the mother may help the child to learn.

In both these types of exchange, the mother is producing a form of question that Brown calls the **occasional question** because it is occasionally produced by adults in normal discourse. The children in Brown's sample whose grammatical competence advanced more rapidly had mothers who produced such occasional questions more often. Adam's mother produced them at the rate of one in 57 utterances, Eve's mother one in 80, and Sarah's mother only one in 146. Sarah advanced more slowly than the others. However, these children and their environments differed on many other dimensions, so that this difference is hardly proof. It should also be pointed out that the children never used the simplified forms themselves.

Expansion

The most interesting exchange between mother and child is the expansion. Children imitate adults, but adults imitate children more often. And, just as children's imitations generally change the adult model, adults' imitations change the child's model. Something is usually added to the child's utterance. Table 6.1 illustrates some typical expansions.

In general, there are many possible expansions that a parent might provide. Suppose a child says *Mommy soup*. Among the possible expansions are *Mommy is having her soup*, *Mommy had her soup*, and *This is mommy's soup*. The decision among these sentences cannot be made on linguistic

---

TABLE 6.1   Expansions of Child Speech Produced by Mothers

Child	Mother
Baby highchair.	Baby is in the highchair.
Mommy eggnog.	Mommy had her eggnog.
Eve lunch.	Eve is having lunch.
Mommy sandwich.	Mommy'll have a sandwich.
Sat wall.	He sat on the wall.
Throw daddy.	Throw it to daddy.
Pick glove.	Pick the glove up.

SOURCE: R. Brown and U. Bellugi. Three processes in the child's acquisition of syntax. *Harvard Educational Review*, Spring 1964, 34, 141. Copyright © 1964 by President and Fellows of Harvard College.

grounds alone. Similarly, the first four child utterances in Table 6.1 are all of the same linguistic form: proper noun followed by common noun. But they are expanded quite differently. A mother selects an expansion on the basis of various extralinguistic cues; perhaps the first course is just over, in which case the expansion would probably be in the past tense, *Mommy had her soup*. If the mother has read the situation correctly, then the child would have had in mind a meaning, and the mother would have provided the proper surface structure.

Brown's group noticed that the middle-class parents expanded about 30 percent of the children's utterances. The parents of the working-class child, Sarah, did so much less often, and Sarah advanced less rapidly. But Sarah's mother also talked less to her child in general, so that expansion rate and volubility were confounded.

Slobin (1968) observed that children's imitations of their parents' expansions of their own utterances are often grammatically more advanced than their free speech, in contrast to their other imitations, which are not more advanced grammatically. Table 6.2 illustrates such exchanges and their frequency. The mismatch between the child's original utterance and the adult's expanded form may serve as a motivation for imitation of the expansion. Like Brown's observations, these data are only circumstantial evidence for the role of expansions in the learning of syntax.

Cazden was the first to attempt to distinguish the effect of expansions from those of other kinds of verbal experience (Cazden 1965; also discussed

---

TABLE 6.2   Imitations of Expansions

Type of Imitation	Example		Relative Frequency[a]	
			Adam	Eve
a. Unexpanded	CHILD:	Just like cowboy.	45	17
	ADULT:	Oh, just like the cowboy's.		
	CHILD:	Just like cowboy.		
b. Reduced	CHILD:	Play piano.	7	29
	ADULT:	Playing the piano.		
	CHILD:	Piano.		
c. Expanded	CHILD:	Pick-mato.	48	54
	ADULT:	Picking tomatoes up?		
	CHILD:	Pick 'mato up.		

[a] These figures cover Adam from age 2;3 to age 2;10 and Eve from 1;6 to 2;2.
SOURCE: From Dan I. Slobin, Imitation and grammatical development in children. In Norman S. Endler, Lawrence R. Boulter and Harry Osser (Eds.), *Contemporary Issues in Development in Psychology*, New York: Holt, Rinehart and Winston, 1968. Reprinted by permission.

from a different perspective in Cazden 1972). She worked with twelve black children, aged twenty-eight to thirty-eight months, who were attending a day-care center where the child-adult ratio was approximately 30:1. Cazden thought that this situation justified the assumption that the children were sufficiently linguistically deprived so that the modest amount of stimulation provided in the experiment might make a significant difference. The children were grouped into four trios, the children in each trio being approximately equal in chronological age, talkativeness, and initial level of development measured by MLU. Within each trio, the children were randomly assigned to one of three treatment groups: control, expansion, and modeling.

The expansion group received forty minutes a day of deliberate expansions. Everything each child said was expanded. The modeling group received exposure to an equal number of well-formed sentences that were not expansions but were relevant to the child's utterances. For example, if the child said *I got apples*, the experimenter said *Do you like them?* If the child said *We got some more*, the experimenter said *There's a lot in here.* Children in the control group received no special treatment, but they were brought into the treatment rooms every few days, so that they would remain familiar with the materials and the tutors.

Several measures of language development were obtained before and after the twelve-week experimental period, because all the children, even the controls, could be expected to advance over a twelve-week period. The measures included MLU, a copula index (use of copular *be* in sentences like *This is red*), verb complexity, and others. For each group, a change score—"after" minus "before"—was computed. There was no evidence that expansions aided the acquisition of grammar. The trend of the results favored the modeling condition, but even then the differences were not large statistically.[2]

We can, for the time being, assume that the order of the three groups—modeling, expansion, control—is a valid one, and we can speculate on the reasons, though a strict interpretation of the results would insist that no clearly significant differences have been shown. Three explanations have been proposed. McNeill (1970) suggested that the experimenter, just like a parent, might guess wrong and provide the wrong surface structure for an expansion: for example, if the child had the future tense in mind but the parent produced *This is mommy's soup* instead of *Mommy will have her soup.* This error probably does not occur often in natural settings. Parents do not expand more than about 30 percent of their children's utterances;

---

[2] Other authors, including McNeill (1970), Menyuk (1971), and the present author (in the first edition of the present book, Dale, 1972), have emphasized the superiority of the modeling treatment, but Cazden's own interpretation has been more cautious and is followed here.

perhaps that is all that they can expand correctly. But in Cazden's experiment the children were given 100 percent expansions; many of these were probably based on misinterpretations of the children's utterances. Such misleading expansions may have interfered with language learning.

This process may also have been aggravated by dialect differences. As we shall see in Chapter 10, many black Americans speak a dialect that is somewhat different from Standard English. Because the tutors in Cazden's experiment, like most white Americans, were not familiar with the dialect, they may have been even more prone to misinterpretation. A replication of this training program with tutors from the children's own linguistic community might produce very different results.

A second explanation is Cazden's own proposal that richness of verbal stimulation was more important than the grammatical contingency found in expansions. The modeling responses were of wide variety, for they were not connected as closely with what the child had just said. If the process of language acquisition is similar to the construction of a scientific theory, in which hypotheses are formulated and tested against the available data, then, the richer the set of data, the better (but see our earlier comments on simplification).

A third explanation is possible. Imagine what it would be like to be with someone who expanded everything you said. After a while, it would become either boring or annoying or both. Such an artificial elevation of the expansion rate may simply reduce the child's attention. Many studies of children have shown that stimuli of a certain degree of novelty—not too familiar and not too strange—command the greatest attention. Modeling responses may have been more interesting than the expansions for the children.

One way to evaluate the first and second interpretations—incorrect expansions versus richness of stimulation—would be to use a hybrid treatment: Expansion when the experimenter thinks that he has understood the child's sentence, a modeling response otherwise. Feldman (1971) compared such a "contingent expansion" treatment with 100 percent expansions, expatiations (what Cazden called "modeling"), and a control group. She worked with twenty-four black children, thirty to forty-six months, in a day-care facility. The children in the four groups were matched for initial language development, as assessed by a sentence-imitation pretest. Each child participated in half-hour sessions on twelve consecutive school days. As in Cazden's study, all experimenters were white.

The children were given a vocabulary test (the Peabody Picture Vocabulary Test) and a sentence-imitation test to assess syntax. No significant differences were observed between groups on either the vocabulary test or the sentence-imitation test.[3] The actual ranking of average gain from

---

[3] Feldman (1971) rejects as inappropriate the preliminary analysis reported in McNeill (1970).

pretest to posttest was: 100 percent expansions, control, contingent expan.. sions, expatiations (modeling). This pattern is impossible to interpret; it does not even replicate Cazden's findings for the three groups in her original experiment. The differences are inflated by the presence in the 100 percent expansion group and the control group of one child each who made a very large change, with impact on the group mean. If these children are set aside, it is obvious that there are no differences among the groups.

Together, the findings of Cazden and Feldman suggest either that syntactic development cannot be facilitated or that expansions are not the way to facilitate it. A more positive evaluation is suggested by the findings of Nelson, Garskaddon, and Bonvillian (1973). Their experiment differs in several small but important ways from the preceding ones. Their subjects were twenty-seven white, middle-class children, aged thirty-two to forty months. Judged by MLU, these children appeared to be close to age norms before the experiment began; this factor should work against any treatment effect. Nelson and his colleagues used a more adequate set of measures: In addition to a sentence-imitation test, they collected a sample of spontaneous speech and computed several specific measures, including MLU, noun-phrase elaboration (number of elements per noun phrase), verb elaboration (tenses, auxiliaries, and so on), and auxiliaries per verb construction. In addition, their treatment conditions were subtly different from those of Cazden and Feldman. In the "recast sentence" condition, incomplete sentences were expanded; for children's sentences that were complete, "new but related syntactical information can be presented by referring to the same event or basic meaning in a different form, such as a question in response to a child's affirmative statement" (Nelson, Garskaddon and Bonvillian 1973:498). The sentence *The bunny chased fireflies* might receive the reply *The bunny did chase fireflies, didn't he?* Whether the response was an expansion or a recast sentence in this larger sense, the experimenter retained the content words of the child's utterance. In the "new sentence" condition, the experimenter's reply specifically excluded the content words of the child's sentence. (No examples are given by Nelson and his colleagues.) Each child attended eleven weeks of twice-a-week twenty-minute treatment sessions. The control group received no special experience.

On all five measures ranking of groups on the posttest was: recast sentence, new sentence, control. But in no instance was the new-sentence group significantly superior to the control group, whereas on three measures (verb elaboration, auxiliaries, and sentence imitation), the recast-sentence group was significantly superior to the control group. The differences on the other measures were nearly significant. The fact that significant results were obtained for verb elaboration and auxiliaries is particularly interesting, because the experimenters were instructed, whenever possible, to add new information in the predicates of the sentences.

It is hard to decide to what to attribute the success of this experiment, in contrast to the earlier two. The sentences heard by the children

...ice group were probably of greater variety than the
...e previous experiments. The lack of any possible dialect
...tween children and experimenter may have been significant.
...entences produced by the experimenters may have been more
... from the children's sentences than the modeling responses in
pr... ...us experiments, and this difference may actually have been disruptive.

In any case, recast sentences—a broadened category of expansions—have been shown to facilitate syntactic development in at least one instance in the laboratory setting. What are the implications of these studies for understanding the role of parental expansions? Parental responses often combine the categories so carefully distinguished here. A parent might respond to the child's *dog bark* with *Yes, the dog's barking at kitty* (Cazden 1972). The fact that parent's responses do not fit perfectly into the categories used in these experiments makes it difficult to judge the relevance of the experiments. On the other hand, it may be just this fact that makes parental responses helpful in language acquisition. At the present time, the most judicious assessment of the role of expansions is probably the old Scots legal verdict of "not proven." Unlike "guilty" and "not guilty" it conveys no presumption of guilt or innocence; the role of expansions is "not proven."

The Role of the Child

Passive models of syntactic development, like those of imitation and reinforcement, appear to be inadequate. But, in addition, they seem, to almost any observer of a young child who is learning to talk, to miss the sense of activity, of trial and error, of continual creation on the part of the child. Child psychology is increasingly recognizing the functioning of the child as an autonomous investigator of the world, as a "little scientist." The work of Jean Piaget has been a major factor in this trend. In a summary of Piaget's work, Ginsburg and Opper wrote:

> . . . Piaget places major emphasis on the role of activity in intellectual development, especially in the early years of life. In Piaget's view, one of the major sources of learning, if not the most essential one, is the intrinsic activity of the child. The child must act on things to understand them. Almost from birth, he touches objects, manipulates them, turns them around, looks at them, and in these ways he develops an increasing understanding of their properties. It is through manipulation that he develops schemes relating to objects. When new objects are presented, the child may at first try to apply them to already established schemes. If not successful, he attempts, again through manipulation, to develop new schemes; that is, new ways of acting on and thereby comprehending the world. (1969:221)

Piaget has written, with respect to the aims of education, "the principal goal of education is to create men who are capable of doing new things, not simply of repeating what other generations have done—men who are creative, inventive, and discoverers" (Piaget 1964:5). It is difficult to imagine a more apt description of language development. In the remainder of this chapter, we shall consider explanations of syntactic learning that emphasize the role of the child, rather than of external reinforcers—models, expanders, and so on.

Many children go through a sort of linguistic drill before falling asleep at night; a few do the same thing upon waking up. The first systematic study of this process was undertaken by Ruth Weir and reported in her book *Language in the Crib* (1962). She recorded the presleep monologues of her son Anthony when he was about two and a half years old.

Especially fascinating are the sequences of related utterances produced by Anthony. Many of them focused on pronunciation; the child corrected his own pronunciation and drilled himself on consonant clusters. Others appear to have been grammatical exercises, not so different from the exercises in foreign-language textbooks. The most frequent type of sequence Weir recorded is the buildup *block; yellow block; Look at the yellow block.* The breakdown also proceeds in the opposite direction: *another big bottle; big bottle.* Substitutions of nouns in fixed sentence frames occurred: *What color? What color blanket? What color mop? What color glass?* Anthony practiced affirmation and negation: *Not the yellow blanket; The white; It's not black; It's yellow; Not yellow; Red.*

This last example is striking because Anthony was interweaving syntactic negation—*It's yellow; Not yellow*—with a kind of semantic negation—*Not yellow; Red.* Other sequences that occurred included tense practice, pronominal substitution, practice in formulating declaratives and questions, and others.

It is obvious from the transcripts that Anthony enjoyed playing with his language. There were many examples of rhyming and alliteration. In general, the content was subordinate to the linguistic form. These presleep monologues are a kind of practice, not a passive repetition of items, but practice at actively forming new combinations. What role they play in language development is unknown.

Cognitive Development and the Acquisition of Syntax

Over the year and a half that precedes the momentous step of combining two words into a sentence for the first time, children have learned a great deal about the world. This knowledge is not so much a collection of facts as a systematic representation of the environment and its regularities. The representation is both perceptual, as in the recognition of familiar persons, and conceptual, as in the belief in the continued existence of a person who is temporarily out of sight. The most significant achievement of this sensorimotor development, as Piaget has called it, is development of the realization that the world consists of enduring objects, located in a spatial framework, upon which the infant and other persons can act. It does not seem surprising that the child's earliest sentences are about agents, the actions they perform, the objects on which they act, and the locations of persons and objects. Cognitive development provides a foundation; put another way, the child can talk about only what he knows.[4]

Nevertheless, cognitive development is not all of language development. The child must find the linguistic means to express his ideas. Some concepts that seem fundamental to the cognition of the toddler are not expressed in language at all for some time. For example, the concepts of time and ordering—the knowledge that one event precedes or is simultaneous with another—are present in simple form in infancy, as when an infant sees his mother putting on a coat and cries in anticipation of being left. Nevertheless, whereas locations are talked about in stage I, time and ordering are not. In other examples, whether or not a concept is expressed linguistically is a function of the complexity of its means of expression in the particular language. For example, although most children ask yes/no questions in stage I, Finnish children do not (Bowerman 1973), because Finnish does not provide a simple means of formulating questions. A particularly clear example comes from the study of locative expressions produced by children bilingual in Hungarian and Serbo-Croatian, discussed in Chapter 3. Recall that locative expressions are marked in Hungarian considerably earlier than in Serbo-Croatian, presumably because the concept can be expressed more simply in the former language. In Reading 6.2, Slobin argues on the basis of this and other examples that, whereas cognitive development is the foundation for grammatical development, the two do not proceed in perfect synchrony. The means of expression may be relatively easy, as in yes/no questions in English, or difficult, as in yes/no questions in Finnish.

The Child as Linguist

The example of Hungarian and Serbo-Croatian suggests that suffixes and postpositions are simpler for the learner than prefixes and prepositions. Such bilingual examples provide a method for determining in general what makes a given linguistic means of expression simple or complex for the child. But bilingual children are not necessary for this comparison. We can compare various developments within a language (as Brown did

---

[4] See Edwards (1973) for a careful examination of the specific meanings expressed in early two-word utterances and a comparison with what is known of the cognitive development of the eighteen- to twenty-four-month-old child.

in his study of the development of the fourteen grammatical morphemes of English, discussed in Chapter 2), and we can compare the development of a concept in several languages, in which the meaning is relatively constant but the linguistic means is not.

Slobin (1973) has taken the latter approach. By reviewing a wide range of studies, he has been able to formulate a number of tentative generalizations, five of which will be considered here, with a sample of the evidence for each.

First is that the ends of words are particularly attended to. The comparison of Hungarian and Serbo-Croatian offers an example. In addition, accusative and dative inflections are acquired much earlier in Russian, Polish, Finnish, Hungarian, and Turkish, where they are expressed as noun suffixes, than in German, where they are expressed partly as articles that occur before nouns.

Second, rearranged and discontinuous structures are more difficult than continuous ones. English yes/no questions appear first in uninverted form: for example, *I can go?* At a later stage the same is true of *wh* questions. The present progressive, consisting of two parts, *is . . . ing*, separated by the verb, is first produced in the simpler form *-ing*. Similarly, in French, where the basic element is *ne . . . pas*, usually separated by the verb, the first negatives use simply *pas*. Note that in each example the element selected for use first is the element following the verb, in accordance with the first principle.

Third, overt and clear marking is easier than absence of marking or complex marking. The singular accusative case in Russian is sometimes signaled by the zero form of the morpheme (no suffix at all). However, Russian children select as their initial form (to overgeneralize) *-u*. The zero form is at least temporarily avoided. As the example suggests, a form that contains a vowel (and is hence syllabic) is preferred over a form that consists only of a consonant. The use of the masculine and neuter form *-om* for the instrumental case in Russian (discussed in Chapter 3), rather than the more frequent feminine *-oy*, shows a preference for forms that do not have a wide variety of meanings. The ending *-oy* has a number of other uses in Russian. A marking that is overt, rather than absent, syllabic, and relatively unambiguous, is simplest.

Fourth, regularities are simpler than exceptions, and consistent exceptions are simpler than inconsistent exceptions. In Chapters 2 and 3 many examples of the preference of the child for simple rules that apply to all instances were given. Even when exceptions are beginning to be mastered, the extent to which they follow a pattern will influence development. Recall the minimal-distance principle discussed in Chapter 5. Both *ask* and *promise* are exceptions to this principle. *Promise* consistently violates the principle, as in *John promised Bill to leave*, in which *John* and not *Bill* is the subject of leave. *Ask* is an inconsistent exception: In *John asked*

Bill to leave the principle correctly predicts that *Bill* will be the subject of *leave*, but, in *John asked Bill what to do*, *John* is the subject of *do*. Chomsky (1969) found that full comprehension of *promise* developed earlier than full comprehension of *ask*.

Fifth, semantic consistency aids in acquisition, and grammatical markers are used in semantically sensible ways. Even when an inflection is used incorrectly, it will be the semantically correct one applied to the appropriate type of word. Although Russian children make many confusions as to the proper suffix to employ within a given Russian case category, the child never uses one case instead of another: The child may use the wrong gender for the instrumental, but he does not use the accusative. English-speaking children may use the wrong preposition in a particular sentence, perhaps *on* instead of *over*, but they do not confuse prepositions with conjunctions or other parts of speech. Samoan children learn a particular inflection, the article, in stage I, earlier than inflections are generally acquired. In contrast to the situation in English, Samoan article selection is governed by a simple semantic principle: *le* is used before nonhuman common nouns, *'o* before proper nouns and pronouns. Thus the semantic feature "human" can be used to guide use of articles from a very early stage.

The fifth point concerns the relevance of semantic factors for syntactic development. Brown (1973) found that semantic complexity can predict some aspects of the developmental order of the fourteen grammatical morphemes of English. In particular, when predictions can be made on the basis of "cumulative complexity," they are invariably correct. That is, if one morpheme encodes all the concepts encoded by another morpheme and additional concepts as well, the second morpheme will be mastered after the first. Nevertheless, it seems in the majority of instances to be the syntactic complexity of the construction that governs acquisition. For example, as Ervin-Tripp has pointed out:

> . . . complex patterns such as the auxiliary system in English . . . are acquired in a relatively short period of time, obviously on the basis of transfer of patterns between items which do not share semantic features. I think it would be very hard to find any semantic commonality between *can*, *will* and *do*, which would be adequate to the rapid acquisition of the system by 2 year olds. . . . On the other hand, there are semantically related forms which do not have the same formal functions, such as *eat*, *eating* and *food*. It is hardly a surprise that we need some formal marker systems . . . to identify form classes, and that semantic unity is not enough. (Ervin-Tripp 1973:282)

The previous chapters have included many instances of phenomena that can best be viewed as evidence of an active, ongoing process of hypothesis testing by the child. The consistent use of such overregularizations as *comed*, early grammatical rules such as that underlying *Allgone sticky*, systematic misinterpretation of the structure of *The doll is easy to see*, and others show that the child for a time adopts incorrect hypotheses. But the same process must lead to the adoption of correct hypotheses as well. The Copernican model of the universe, with the planets traveling in circular orbits about the sun, was an incorrect hypothesis (the planets travel in eliptical orbits, which are quite different from circles), but it was a step in the right direction. And so is *Allgone sticky*.

One of the most significant steps in this process is the development of a transformational grammar, a grammar that distinguishes between deep and surface structure but that relates the two levels by means of transformations. Here it is particularly appropriate to think of the child as a linguist. He is formulating hypotheses about the corpus of speech he receives. The hypotheses are confirmed if they account for the corpus already available and successfully predict future sentences; they fail otherwise. Hypotheses that are confirmed become part of the grammar of the child; the others are rejected.

Suppose that children first formulate hypotheses about the corpus in the form of phrase-structure rules. They would work for a time, but inevitably they would become very complex. Generalizations that might unify a set of linguistic facts cannot be expressed in this way. Instead, the child must work with a large number of special cases. All of the arguments for formulating a transformational grammar discussed in Chapter 4 apply to the child as well as to the adult linguist. Transformations are simply more powerful.

Recall that one of the children studied by Bellugi (1965) first had a form of question that began *D'you want . . . ?* which always appeared in just that form and was pronounced as a single word. This form was viewed as the result of a phrase-structure rule. It does succeed in producing one type of adult question. But there are many other types of questions, and this approach would require an additional rule for every question type. Eventually the child switched to a transformation system, in which three transformations produced a wide variety of surface structures.

To claim that transformations are formulated by children because they are more powerful than phrase-structure rules leaves a great deal unexplained. For one thing, it does not explain how a child knows that transformations are more powerful or even that such rules can be formulated. However, as all languages appear to be transformational, this much knowledge may be part of children's innate capacity for language. Children may expect language to be transformational, but they have to learn when transformations are appropriate and what forms they take. A relevant linguistic fact is that there are restrictions on the kinds of operations that transformations perform. For example, no language has a transformation that permutes every pair of words in a sentence, that is, changes *My brother plays the flute superbly* to *°Brother my the plays superbly flute.* If a complex sentence is formed by conjoining two simple sentences, for example, conjoining *John came to visit* and *John stayed a month* to form *John came to visit, and John stayed a month,* and if the language allows pronominalization of one of two identical noun phrases, it is always the second *John* that is changed to *he,* not the first. So we have *John came to visit, and he stayed a month* but not *He came to visit, and John stayed a month* when *he* refers to *John.* The transformations that are actually found in languages are only a small subset of those logically possible. In other words, there are formal universals in the transformational component of language, and they may be part of children's capacity for language.

Comprehension and Syntactic Development

We have seen that there is fairly strong evidence against the adequacy of imitation and reinforcement as explanations of syntactic development and that the role of expansions is equivocal. What these three mechanisms have in common is the importance of the child's own productions. The child must either imitate the parent, say something to be reinforced, or say something to be expanded. Virtually any theory that places such importance on the child's productions will be subject to many of the same criticisms as can be applied to these three. In particular, the frequent superiority of comprehension over production, even with the aid of context, raises a very general problem for such a theory.

Psychologists interested in learning have to a great extent moved away from simple Pavlovian and Skinnerian responses in recent years. It is clear that in many domains overt responses need not occur for learning to take place, nor need reinforcement be present. A very simple demonstration is simply to carry a rat through a maze a few times, without giving him food or other reward. If at a later time the rat is hungry, he will learn the path through the maze more quickly than if he had not had the previous experience. Similarly, human subjects can observe a set of materials— numbers, geometric figures, and so on—and can learn something about the patterns in the stimulus set in order to recall them later or, more interesting, to recognize new instances of the same type. Learning of this kind is sometimes called "latent learning" (latent in the sense that no overt response occurs), sometimes "S-S learning" (learning that one stimulus is associated with another stimulus, as opposed to S-R learning, which is the association of a stimulus, such as a reinforcer, with a response). Language learning could be viewed as an instance of S-S learning. There is, however, a fundamental difference between viewing a particular instance of learning as a result of S-R learning and viewing it as an example of S-S learning. Reinforcement, a special case of S-R learning, does indeed offer an explanation if it is present and contingent; the behavior is fully accounted for by the structure of the environment. But to call an instance of learning "S-S learning" does not explain anything; it is simply to describe what has happened. How did the organism learn to associate the two stimuli and not others in the flood of stimulation encountered everyday? The problem is to develop models of how the child comes to make sense of the linguistic input.

One very basic point has been made by Macnamara (1972). Part of his argument is that at the beginning of language learning it is essential that the meanings of utterances addressed to the child be obvious. For the child to begin to "break the code" what is being talked about, the events and objects in the nonlinguistic environment, must be clear and match directly with what is said. Later, the child will be able to understand and learn by inference from what has been said before, just as adults can interpret novel utterances about remote events. But at first the adult must tell the child what he already knows or sees. Perhaps the most interesting aspect of maternal speech to young children is one that has been little examined, the semantics of such speech.

Once children have begun to master language, a very striking phenomenon occurs. On the whole, children are far more likely to make errors of comprehension than to be confused or to give up when confronted with new constructions. Passives may be interpreted as actives; *The doll is easy to see* will be given an erroneous interpretation, and many other examples could be given. The most basic concept of language, that the sound cues the meaning by means of some rule, is established very early. Just as simple rules are used in production, simple rules may also be used in comprehension. But the idea is there.

These considerations suggest that comprehension is a major focus of language learning. Kelley (1967) has formulated a general model of syntactic development along these lines. According to his model, hypotheses are continually being formulated and evaluated as the learner uses them to decode (or "parse") the sentences encountered. The learner uses his present grammar, together with any new grammatical hypotheses, to attempt to understand the sentence.

> To understand a sentence means to produce a correct analysis of that sentence. . . . To determine whether an analysis of an input sentence is correct [is determined by] whether a sentence analysis is consistent with what the child knows (on the basis of his general knowledge of the world and his particular knowledge of the situational context in which the sentence was spoken). If no analysis of a sentence is consistent in this sense with what the child knows, the sentence is simply discarded and not used at all. Only if the sentence is correctly understood is there any effect on the grammatical competence of the model.

When a sentence is correctly understood two things happen: first, all of the grammatical constructs used by the parsing algorithm to produce the correct sentence analysis are incrementally confirmed (including any grammatical hypotheses that were used); and secondly, the sentence itself may serve as the stimulus for the generation of some new hypotheses. (Kelley 1967:93–95)

As does Macnamara, Kelley places great importance on the match between the input sentence and what the child already knows or sees. An example might be a child who interprets a passive sentence like *The car is being pushed by the truck* as "car pushing truck." If the child actually sees a truck pushing a car, the proper conditions for learning have been established.

Communication and Language Development

One simple description of the early stages of language development is that there are many things missing. Children do not leave out just the elements that are often omitted by adults in casual speech. They leave out elements that are truly obligatory for adults. In stage I the child often omits major constituents of sentences: subjects, verbs, objects, locatives, and others. At the beginning of stage II, all of the fourteen grammatical morphemes studied by Brown (1973) are missing; later they are occasionally present, and only much later are they reliably present in the required contexts. As Brown points out, these omissions seldom impede communication:

This suggests to me that the child expects always to be understood if he produces any appropriate words at all . . . he would usually be right in this expectation as long as he speaks at home, in familiar surroundings, and to family members who know his history and inclinations. Stage I speech may then be said to be well *adapted* to its communicative purpose, well adapted but narrowly adapted. In new surroundings and with less familiar addressees it would often fail. This suggests that a major dimension of linguistic development is learning to express always and automatically certain things . . . even though these meanings may be in many particular contexts quite redundant. The child who is going to move out into the world, as children do, must learn to make his speech broadly and flexibly adaptive. (Brown 1973:245).

We simply do not have a theory which can account for this accomplishment. As Brown's own work on "sequiturs," discussed earlier in this chapter, shows, it is difficult to find instances in which communication is contingent on more advanced language. Studies of the way children vary their speech as a function of situation and addressee may prove enlightening in this respect.

Summary

The more we learn about language development, the less we understand how it works. The acquisition of language is one of the major feats of child development; language acquisition is a crucial test for any theory of learning. The concepts of imitation and reinforcement, though relevant, are inadequate as explanations. The creativity of the child and his relative independence from adult models and approval weigh against passive mechanisms of learning.

The verbal interchange between parent and child probably plays an important role in fostering language development. It is simpler than normal adult-adult speech, yet it remains above the level of the child's own productions, challenging his learning ability. The child's attention appears to serve a guiding role in determining the level of parental speech. Specific interchanges like expansions may also aid in development, but the evidence is ambiguous at present.

But most important is the role of the child himself. The emerging linguistic system expresses the concepts that have developed over the preceding year and a half. Mastering the linguistic means of expression of these concepts is not a simple task. In some way the child formulates hypotheses about the language about her and tests them, either by formulating utterances of her own or by attempting to comprehend new utterances. We can learn something of the process from comparisons that reveal which aspects of language are easier to master, for example, that suffixes are easier than prefixes. But even this information tells us more about the product of learning than about the process that makes it possible.

6.1   ON THE ROLE OF REINFORCEMENT
IN LANGUAGE ACQUISITION*

The proposition, "Syntactically correct utterances come to prevail over syntactically incorrect utterances through the selective administration of signs of approval and disapproval," is a testable one.

The proposition cannot be true for the natural case of parents and children at home unless parental approval and disapproval are in fact appropriately contingent on syntactical correctness. If the reactions are appro-

* From Roger Brown, Courtney Cazden and Ursula Bellugi, The child's grammar from I to III. In J. P. Hill (Ed.), *Minnesota symposium on child psychology*, Vol. II, pp. 70–71. Minneapolis: University of Minnesota Press, 1969.

priately contingent, then they may or may not have the effects proposed. For this analysis . . . [the] general plan was to contrast the syntactic correctness of the population utterances followed by a sign of approval—*that's right, very good,* or just *yes*—with the population of utterances followed by a sign of disapproval—*that's wrong* or *no.* The results are simply stated: there is not a shred of evidence that approval and disapproval are contingent on syntactic correctness.

What circumstances did govern approval and disapproval directed at child utterances by parents? Gross errors of word choice were sometimes corrected, as when Eve said *What the guy idea.* Once in a while an error of pronunciation was noticed and corrected. Most commonly, however, the grounds on which an utterance was approved or disapproved . . . were not strictly linguistic at all. When Eve expressed the opinion that her mother was a girl by saying *He a girl,* her mother answered *That's right.* The child's utterance was ungrammatical, but her mother did not respond to that fact; instead she responded to the truth of the proposition of the child intended to express. In general, parents fitted propositions to the child's utterances, however incomplete or distorted the utterances, and then approved or not according to the correspondence between proposition and reality. Thus, *Her curl my hair* was approved because the mother was, in fact, curling Eve's hair. However, Sarah's grammatically impeccable *There's the animal farmhouse* was disapproved because the building was a lighthouse, and *Adam's Walt Disney comes on on Tuesday* was disapproved because Walt Disney came on on some other day. It seems, then, to be truth value rather than [well-formed syntax] that chiefly governs explicit verbal reinforcement by parents—which renders mildly paradoxical the fact that the usual product of such a training schedule is an adult whose speech is highly grammatical but not notably truthful.

6.2 COGNITIVE PREREQUISITES FOR THE DEVELOPMENT OF GRAMMAR*

Why the precocious marking of locative expressions in Hungarian, then? . . . It seems unlikely that the structure of a particular language would draw attention more clearly to the possibilities of putting in, taking out, and so on, than would a child's everyday experience. It is difficult to imagine children *not* talking about such things. And, in fact, the cross-linguistic data suggest that children begin to express basic locative notions by noun-noun and noun-verb combinations at the two word stage in all languages. Two word utterances in Serbo-Croatian, Bulgarian, Russian, English, Finnish, Hebrew,

* From D. I. Slobin, Revised version of "Developmental psycholinguistics," in *A survey of linguistic science,* edited and copyrighted by William Orr Dingwall. College Park: University of Maryland Linguistics Program. Reprinted by permission of William Orr Dingwall. Revised edition in press with Greylock Publishers, 13 Spring St., Stamford, Conn., 06901.

and Samoan all seem to express the notions of 'in' and 'into,' 'on' and 'onto,' and 'from'—at first with no inflections or prepositions. This can be quite reliably assessed from context. . . . In addition, locative notions are expressed at early stages by prolocatives and demonstratives, such as the English "there," "innere," "on," and the like, and their equivalents in Bulgarian (Gheorgov, 1908), German (Leopold 1939; Park 1970), Finnish (Argoff, forthcoming), and other languages. . . . On the basis of current findings and theory (Furth 1969; Piaget, 1967, 1970), it seems to me that the pacesetter in linguistic growth is the child's cognitive growth, as opposed to an autonomous linguistic development which can then reflect back on cognition. As Piaget has put it: ". . . language is not enough to explain thought, because the structures that characterize thought have their roots in action and in sensori-motor mechanisms that are deeper than linguistics" (1967: 98).

The argument that language is used to express only what the child already knows can be supported by another line of evidence, coming from an examination of linguistic development from both a *formal* and a *functional* point of view. Studies which have considered the supposed intended meanings of children's utterances support a far-reaching principle which could be phrased as follows: *New forms first express old functions, and new functions are first expressed by old forms.* It turns out that this is a familiar principle in the psychology of cognitive development, and it is not surprising to find it in linguistic development as well. For example, Werner and Kaplan state (1963: 60):

> . . . wherever functional shifts occur during development, the novel function is first executed through old, available forms; sooner or later, of course, there is a pressure towards the development of new forms which are of a more function-specific character, i.e. that will serve the new function better than the older forms.

Numerous examples could be offered from grammatical development in support of this principle. . . .

We already have the locative example. The use of utterances in context indicates that locative relations are intended; when the appropriate new forms enter—be they prepositions, postpositions, inflections, or what have you—they will be new forms expressing old functions.

Roger Brown (1973) has performed a detailed analysis of the emergence of inflections in English. . . . At the beginning stage, when verbs occurred simply in their bare, uninflected form, Brown noted that they were used to express four kinds of meanings: (1) "naming an action or state . . . of temporary duration and true at the time of the utterance," or (2) referring to the immediate past, or (3) as a statement of the child's immediate wish or intention, or (4) as an imperative. The first verb markings to emerge were used to express just these functions: (1) the progressive -ing, (2) the past tense, and (3) catenative verbs ("gonna," "wanna," and "hafta"). The last function, the imperative, continues, of course to be expressed by an uninflected verb in English, but Brown notes that "please," as an imperative marker, entered at about the same time as these other verb markings. Brown also found that his three children understood the semantics of possession well before they attained the possessive inflection. In all of these cases, then, the appearance in child speech of a new formal device serves only to code a function which the child has already understood and expressed implicitly.

How does a child go about expressing a new meaning—that is how does he find the linguistic means for newly-developed cognitive notions? Here we have the other half of the principle proposed above: *New functions are first expressed by old forms.* Richard Cromer (1968) found many examples of this principle in studying the development of temporal expression in English. For example, shortly before emergence of the perfect tense, his subjects attached "now" and "yet" to statements about the past, producing utterances which performed the same function as the perfect tense (for example, "I didn't make the bed yet"; "Now I closed it"). Such forms were soon replaced by the perfect ("I haven't made the bed"; "I've closed it"). Here it is clear that cognitive development has given rise to semantic intentions for which new means of expression must be forged. In fact, children's temporary idiosyncratic linguistic forms often are cues to the fact that the development of a new notion has engendered a search for new means of expression. . . .

The picture we have so far, then, is the following: In order to acquire language, the child must attend both to speech and to the contexts in which speech occurs—that is, he must be trying to understand what he hears, and be trying to express the intentions of which he is capable. This means that he must have both cognitive and linguistic discovery procedures available—in order to formulate internal structures which are capable of assimilating and relating both linguistic and non-linguistic data, and which are capable of realizing intentions as utterances. The emergence of new communicative intentions must bring with it the means to decode those intentions in the speech the child hears, and this makes it possible for him to discover new means for expressing those intentions.

further reading

Braine, M. D. S. On two types of models of the internalization of grammars. In D. I. Slobin (Ed.), *The ontogenesis of grammar.* New York: Academic Press, 1971. Pp. 153–186.

Macnamara, J. Cognitive basis of language learning in infants. *Psychological Review*, 1972, **79**, 1–13.

Slobin, D. I. Cognitive prerequisites for the development of grammar. In C. A. Ferguson and D. I. Slobin (Eds.), *Studies of child language development.* New York: Holt, Rinehart and Winston, 1973. Pp. 175–208.

7

Semantic Development

Anyone who has spent much time talking with young children has learned that words often do not mean the same things to a child as to an adult. We have already seen examples of this in the first words of children (see Chapter 1). But even after the stage of the first words has passed, major differences in meaning remain. Chukovsky's observation, reported in Chapter 3, of a child who said *Can't you see, I'm barefoot all over!* is a good example. For this child, the meaning of barefoot was extended from bare feet to apply to a bare body. In another observation, a child commented that a mint candy made *a draft in the mouth.* For this child, the word *draft* primarily referred to a sense of coolness and not to the breeze that normally produces the coolness. Other differences are more subtle and require careful observation and questioning.

For a first example, the meaning of *more* and *less* can be assessed by asking children to make judgments of the form "what has more/less?" about glasses of water, apples on trees, and weights of blocks. At one stage in development (approximately three to four years) *more* is responded to correctly, whereas *less* is responded to in the same way as *more* (Palermo 1974).

Second, when asked to select the "big" one from two rectangles that differ in height and width, four-year-olds generally select the taller one, even when it is actually smaller in total area (Maratsos 1973a).

Third, the meaning of *before* and *after* can be assessed by asking children to act out sentences that describe two events, for example, *The elephant jumps before the dog sits down* and *After the dog sits down, the elephant jumps.* At one point, sentences with *before* are correctly interpreted but sentences with *after* are reversed. That is, *after* is interpreted to mean *before* (Clark 1971).

Fourth, certain verbs and adjectives are often used in inappropriate ways to describe actions. For example, Christy (Bowerman 1974) was watching her mother put her baby sister in a high chair; she said *No, mommy, don't eat her yet, she's smelly!* On another occasion she held a piece of paper over her sister's head and said *I gonna just fall this on her.* Peering with dissatisfaction into a partially filled bottle, she said *Full it up!* In each instance, her meaning could be expressed by an adult with a phrase of the form *make it full/fall/eat* or the specific words *fill, drop,* or *feed.*

Fifth, a child below the age of five years or so can correctly identify his left and right hands, but, when asked to identify the left and right hands of a person who is facing him, he will produce precisely the opposite of the correct response.

The semantic system of a language is the knowledge that a speaker must have to understand sentences and relate them to his knowledge of the world. It includes both knowledge of individual lexical items and knowledge of how the meaning of a sentence is determined by the meanings of individual lexical items and the structure of the sentence. Some aspects of this latter knowledge have already been discussed earlier in this book as part of the discussion of semantic relations in early child language. In the present chapter we shall consider the development of word meanings and some aspects of the development of sentence meanings past the earliest stages.

Semantic development is surely the least understood aspect of language development. This fact may seem surprising, for the study of vocabulary growth, one of the oldest lines of research on language development, would appear to contribute to an understanding of semantic development. In fact, interest in traditional studies of vocabulary growth has declined as the realization has grown that such studies miss many aspects of semantic development. First, the presence of a word in a child's vocabulary does not by itself tell an observer much about the meaning of that word to the child. We cannot assume identity of meaning for the child and for the adult. Second, vocabulary counts ignore important relations among word meanings, relations that make a vocabulary more than a list of words. And, third, vocabulary studies do not provide any information on the crucial process by which word meanings are combined into sentence meanings.

Semantic development is the aspect of language development most directly tied to the broader cognitive development of the child. The question How do children express their ideas? cannot be neatly separated from the question What kinds of ideas do children have to express? Therefore understanding of semantic development requires a deeper understanding of cognitive development.

Theories of Meaning

The most significant reason for our lack of understanding of semantic development is the fact that we do not really understand what it is that is being developed; that is, we do not understand adult semantic competence. In the instance of syntactic development, the existence of well-articulated theories of adult competence—for example, transformational grammar and case grammar—provides a framework for the collection and analysis of data from children. We lack this guiding framework in the study of the development of meaning.[1] In this section we shall consider some of the major issues in understanding meaning.

Reference and Meaning

There are many words for which, if asked the meaning, we might point to something in the world. For example, *Fido* refers to a particular dog, *red* to a range of colors, *cat* to a category of animals, and so on. That "something" to which a word or expression refers is its **referent**. A theory of meaning once widely held and still encountered is the referential theory: *The meaning of a word is its referent.* Words are symbols that stand for things other than themselves, things in the world, namely their referents.

Such a theory is attractive because it leads to a simple explanation of how words and their meanings are learned. *Fido* is learned by hearing *Fido* spoken while seeing a particular dog, *red* is learned by hearing *red* while being shown red objects, and so on. This process is entirely consistent with traditional views on learning. Nevertheless, the inadequacy of the referential theory is easy to demonstrate. Frege, in the nineteenth century, formulated a good example of the problem. The phrase *the morning star* and the phrase *the evening star* have different meanings yet the same referent: the planet Venus. That they have different meanings is shown by the fact that the sentence *The morning star and the evening star are the same planet* conveys information by linking together two expressions with different meanings.

Just as two expressions can have the same referent but different meanings, the converse can occur. Consider words such as *I, you, here,* and *there*. Suppose that I use the word *you* in a sentence spoken to a friend and that a few seconds later my friend uses *you* in a sentence to me. When I use the word *you*, it refers to my friends; when he uses the word *you* it refers to me. But that does not mean that the word *you* has different meanings (one for every person spoken to in the world). It *means* exactly the same thing, 'the person being spoken to.' And the word *I* means the speaker,

---

[1] Alston (1964) surveys several theories of meaning and some of the difficulties that they encounter.

whereas its referent changes constantly. Such words have constant meanings but many referents.

Even more damaging to the referential theory is the fact that many words either do not have referents or have referents that are difficult to identify. Such words and phrases as *unicorn* and the *present king of France* illustrate this category. The referential theory can be modified to permit reference to imaginary constructs such as unicorns, though this step raises problems of its own (Alston 1964). But this does not solve the problem of the meaning of the function words of language, such as *and, if, is,* and *but.* In fact, many philosophers who have worked with the referential theory have simply denied that these "little words" have any meaning in isolation. Yet we all have feelings about these words and their meanings. For example, we can talk about the difference between *and* and *but; but* seems to mean 'and, though you're not expecting this. . . .'

Of course, many words do have referents. And knowing how to use these words includes knowledge of their referents. However, Roger Brown (1958) has shown that even this simplest aspect of meaning is not so very simple. If every object had exactly one name and every name had exactly one referent, the situation would be quite straightforward. But neither condition is true. Almost all names actually refer to categories—the word *dog* refers to *all* four-legged animals of a certain type, the word *green* refers to the color of *all* green objects, and so on. Conversely, every object can be named with a variety of terms. A pencil I have used can be called a *pencil, a No. 2, a writing instrument, this worn, dull thing I used,* and many other terms. Some of them refer specifically to this pencil, some refer to larger categories—*a writing instrument,* for example. Brown (1958) uses the example of a dime, which can be called *dime, coin, money,* and *1952 dime,* among other names. Some of the terms refer specifically to the particular dime, some to categories. And those that refer to categories may refer to larger or smaller categories—compare *dime* with *coin.* Which one of these terms should be used? In fact, the name that is most commonly used by adults to children (and, in fact, by adults to adults) is the term that is more useful. *Dime* is the most useful name for this particular dime, because all dimes are equivalent for most purposes. But coins are not all equivalent for most purposes (they are equivalent for some, of course, such as making a decision by flipping a coin). On the other hand, the fact that the dime is a 1952 dime is unimportant (except for coin collectors). Learning about the referents of words is really a matter of learning about how the world is organized by human beings.

As a corollary to this conclusion, Brown clarifies an old question in the study of children's thinking: Is children's thinking more concrete than that of adults or more abstract? In Reading 7.1, he argues that studies of children's vocabularies are basically irrelevant to this question because "the sequence in which words are acquired is not determined by the cognitive

preferences of children so much as by the naming practices of adults"
(1958:20).

Bolinger (1968) has suggested a loose but useful view of meaning
as a system for segmenting reality. Word meanings serve to divide up the
world. *Reality* and *world* here mean not simply the concrete world of physical
objects external to the self but, rather, anything that may be talked about:
dreams, pain, ideas, memories, and so on. Certainly most of our speech is
not simply a running description of what is going on around us. We do not
say *Now I'm getting up; now I'm brushing my teeth; now I'm walking to
class; now I'm getting bored*. We talk about the past (*What a dull lecture
that was!*) or about the future (*If I get an A in this course I'll get into
medical school*) or about wishes (*If only this were the end of the term*) or
about many other situations far removed from the present one.

The ways in which meanings segment reality are not given in the
world; they too are arbitrary. The way in which English divides color into
blue and *green* does not correspond to any natural division in physics or
optics. Other languages divide it differently. There are many instances in
which the particular distinction is not yet settled. In English we have three
terms—*doctor, physician,* and *professor*—of which the last two have fairly
well-defind meanings but the first of which is still a matter of uncertainty
and, occasionally, controversy. Often when we think about meanings we
select particularly simple instances, like concrete nouns—*dog, sun, house,*
and the like. But the majority of words divide reality in complex and subtle
ways. That is why it is extremely rare for two words to be exact synonyms.
For example, we do not ordinarily say *I caught an illness* or *She caught an
ailment*. Instead we say *I caught a disease*. *Disease* has a more concrete
meaning, as a sort of separate entity. *To return* and *to take back* are not
perfect synonyms. *We took Junior back to the zoo* might refer to a second
trip to the zoo for an afternoon or it might refer to an inmate, whereas *We
returned Junior to the zoo* indicates that the zoo is indeed Junior's home.
This is the reason why dictionaries are always very long and always inadequate, as anyone who has tried to learn a second language using only a
dictionary has discovered.

Lenneberg (1967: ch. 8) has carried this argument further. He
argues that words are basically labels for categorization processes. They
do not refer to objects and events in the world directly; rather, they refer
to our cognitive organization of the world.

A question of growing interest in recent research in semantics and
child language is the extent to which categorization is arbitrary, differing
from language to language, or shared. Some distinctions seem to be so
natural as to be part of any natural language; for example, the distinction
between human and nonhuman. Later we will see another example of
commonality of semantic labelling across language in the area of color
naming. Macnamara has argued that "there are quite marked constraints on

what will be grouped together in a concept . . . (children) do not form bizarre concepts to include foot and floor and exclude all else." (1972, p. 3–4). Though research is just beginning in this area, it seems clear that there are perceptual and cognitive constraints on possible concepts.

One consequence of the view of meaning as a subtle division of reality is that determination of the meaning of a word for a particular speaker, such as a child, requires extended and careful observation of the speaker's use and comprehension of the word in a variety of linguistic and nonlinguistic contexts.

Relationships among Word Meanings

The vocabulary of a language is more than a list of words and their meanings. There are important relations among word meanings, some of which have been studied in detail by linguists, though they have largely been ignored until recently by psychologists.

The most obvious such relation is **synonymy**—having similar meanings. The two sentences *I saw an eye doctor yesterday* and *I saw an oculist yesterday* have the same meaning because they are identical except for *eye doctor* and *oculist* and these two words have the same meaning. Synonyms as good as these two are very rare (and are almost always technical terms). In virtually every instance two synonyms will differ in their meanings in some way. Consider the synonym *hitch* and *tether*; they both mean "to make fast." In some instances either may be used correctly. But, if the important aspect of the situation is making something fast to a vehicle in order to move it, we would use *hitch*, whereas, if the important aspect of the situation is connecting a vehicle to a post or other object in order to prevent its motion, we would use *tether*. And, if we think about it, this lack of perfect synonymy is not surprising. Why bother to have two words with exactly the same meaning? After all, the great merit of having so many words and so many syntactic processes is that we can express a tremendous variety of messages. Perfect synonyms are of little use in this respect.

The opposite of synonymy is **antonymy**—having opposite meanings. But the relation between synonymy and antonymy is really not this simple. Antonyms, like synonyms, share meaning. *Hot* and *cold* both refer to temperature and to extremes of temperature (compare *warm* and *cool*), *always* and *never* to extremes of frequency of occurrence, *full* and *empty* to extremes of fullness, and so on. Some words have two antonyms, for example, *noise-silence* and *noise-music*. The two antonyms share different parts of the meaning of *noise*.

One of the most important relations between meanings is that of **inclusion.** The meanings of *red*, *green*, and *blue* include that of *color*; the meanings of *apple*, *orange*, and *pear* include that of *fruit*; the meanings of *man*, *woman*, and *boy* include that of *human*; and so on. Another relation is **reciprocity.** *Buy* and *sell* are reciprocals, as are *give* and *receive.* What distinguishes these pairs from antonyms (which they are, in a sense) is that, whenever a sentence using one of them is appropriate, there is another appropriate sentence using the other member of the pair. For example, *John buys books from Bill* has the same meaning as *Bill sells books to John. He gave flowers to her* has the same meaning as *She received flowers from him.* There is a sort of "semantic passive"—as does the passive transformation in syntax, it presents the same meaning from a different point of view.

Relations like antonymy, inclusion, and reciprocity are crucial to understanding language, because they allow us to go beyond the particular words used in a sentence. As an answer to the question *Are there any apples there?* the reply *We don't have any fruit* makes sense only with the knowledge of the inclusion relationship between *apple* and *fruit.* The bizarreness of the sentence *°The bachelor saw herself in the mirror* results from the relation between *bachelor* and *male* and the contradiction between *male* and *herself.*

Word Meaning and Sentence Meaning

The given examples of relations among word meanings suggest that the meaning of a word should not be considered an indivisible unit. In many instances we should talk about part of a word meaning. Another reason for doing so comes from considering the process by which the meanings of individual words in a sentence are combined into the meaning of the sentence.

Most of the words of English have more than one meaning each. Many have literally dozens of meanings. In fact, the more common words of English tend to have the most meanings. If each word in a sentence has several meanings, it might seem that the sentence as a whole should have even more meanings. For example, a sentence consisting of five words with two meanings each should have thirty-two meanings. But, in fact, most of the sentences we hear have just one meaning each, and one we arrive at quickly without running through a long list of alternatives. One reason for the lack of ambiguity in sentences is the fact that only certain combinations are compatible.

The word *bat* is ambiguous; it may mean a kind of flying mammal, or it may mean an implement used in baseball. But the phrase *baseball bat* has no ambiguity at all; the use of *baseball* rules out one meaning of *bat.*

For this elimination, the relevant aspect of the meaning of *bat* is that part which refers to baseball. The phrase *baseball diamond* is also unambiguous due to this component of "baseball" in one meaning of the word *diamond.* Similarly, *the bat bit the girl* is unambiguous, because only one meaning of bat, containing a component which refers to animals, is compatible with the phrase *bit the girl.* The same component is responsible for the lack of ambiguity in *the snake bit the girl*, despite the fact that a tool used in plumbing work is also called a snake. In contrast, the sentence *I saw the bat* is ambiguous, because neither meaning of bat is ruled out by the remainder of the sentence. Of course, the particular meaning may be indicated by the preceding or following sentence or by the nonlinguistic context.

Thus, to account for certain semantic properties of sentences, such as ambiguity, anomaly, and the lack of either, we must talk about parts of meanings. These meanings are combined in ways that are determined by the syntactic structure of the sentence, and one result of the combination is the elimination of certain meanings.

Though there is no one generally accepted theory of meaning, several approaches to the problem of constructing such a theory seem particularly useful for understanding semantic development. The first approach, the most widely investigated, is based on the observations just discussed, which seem to require division of the meaning of a word into subunits. Borrowing the term from Bolinger, we can view this approach as an "atomic" theory of meaning. The meaning of each word is a collection of basic elements of meaning. The best-known such theory is that proposed by Katz and Fodor (1963; Katz 1966), in which the meaning of a word is said to consist of two parts.[2] The first is a set of **semantic features**, each of which expresses a part of the meaning of the word. For example, *bachelor* has, among other semantic features, the set (human) (male) (unmarried). *Wife* has, among other semantic features, the set (human) (female) (married). Semantic features appear in more than one dictionary entry. In many instances a feature may occur in a great many dictionary entries. The feature (living) occurs in the meanings of *dog, rose, plant,* and *man,* as well as in those of many other words. The appearance of a given feature in a set of words indicates that their meanings have something in common.

In addition to these semantic features, there are **selection restrictions** for every word, restrictions on possible combinations of words. *Bachelor's wife* obviously violates these restrictions, because *bachelor* includes the feature (unmarried) whereas *wife* includes the feature (married). One semantic feature for one of the senses of *bat* matches the selection restrictions of *baseball,* used as a modifier, so that the phrase *baseball bat* is not only meaningful but also unambiguous (because the other meaning of bat does not match the selection restrictions).

Two other major approaches to meaning take the basic insights of the feature approach as valid but argue that meaning is more complex than a set of semantic features and that additional structure is necessary to characterize meaning. A feature approach might define bird as (living)

---

[2] Bolinger (1965) and Weinreich (1971) discuss some of the problems of the particular theory proposed by Katz and Fodor.

(able to fly) (feathered). This representation correctly defines the set of birds, but it does not recognize any distinctions in importance among the features or in degree of typicalness among particular birds. Yet most people, if asked to visualize a bird, are likely to visualize a robin or similar bird; similarly, if we ask people to rate particular species of birds as to how well they represent the concept of birds, they are likely to rate robins as very "birdlike," turkeys less so, and penguins still less so. Similarly, although such color words as *red* can be used to describe wide ranges of colors, speakers of English agree in calling a very narrow range of colors the "best" red. Thus, the categories corresponding to words seem to have cores of instances that fit the labels most satisfactorily. Working from very different starting points, Rips, Shoben, and Smith (1973) and Rosch (1973) have concluded that the notion of centrality must be included in a description of particular concepts. Based on their work with adults, in which subjects must decide the truth or falsity of such sentences as *A robin is a bird*, Rips and his colleagues propose using *two* lists of features for each word, one specifying the features that define the category and a second list specifying the features that determine whether a particular instance is a good or bad example. For example, within a certain range, size is irrelevant for the definition of the word *dog*; dogs range from the very small to the very large. Yet our concept of a "good" dog is partially a function of size, cocker-spaniel size. Rosch, based on her work with children and adults investigating identification of and memory for color (to be discussed later in this chapter), has suggested that the core of the concept *red* is some sort of image of the best example of *red*. The difference between the approaches of Rips and his colleagues and Rosch is that the former emphasize that some *features* are more central than others, whereas the latter emphasizes that some *instances* are more central than others. They agree that a description of the meaning of a term should either include or actually be based on some sort of core concept.

A third approach to understanding meaning takes issue with the claim that the meaning of an item is simply the sum of the semantic features included. Relational information is also necessary (Norman *et al.*, 1975). Consider the word *pay*. Part of the meaning of this word is that money is transferred from one person (A) to another person (B). But there is an additional component: the fact that there is a previously established obligation on the part of A, because of some action or status of either A or B. If not, we would say not *A paid B* but *A gave money to B*. The meaning of *pay* thus involves a system of relations among A, B, money, giving, and obligation. It is not simply the set of elements that determines meaning, however, for the word *owe* also includes these elements, organized in a different way. The components making up the meaning of *pay* are joined in a structure that is important for the total meaning as the individual components, just as a sentence is not simply a collection of words but a structured assembly. Conventional dictionaries are based on a similar principle: Words are defined not by a list of synonyms, inclusion words, and the like but by sentences.

As a somewhat simplified illustration of the three approaches, consider the meaning of the word *cat*. A featural approach would specify such features as (mammal), (four-legged), and (purrs). A core-concept approach might specify a particular cat or type of cat. A relational approach would specify the relations between cats and such other concepts as that cats chase mice, are chased by dogs, eat meat, and so on.

Vocabulary Growth

Although vocabulary growth in itself tells us little about semantic development, the rapidity of the process is interesting in its own right. Many studies of vocabulary growth are reviewed by McCarthy (1954). The most comprehensive investigation is that of Smith (1926); the results of her study are shown in Table 7.1. The data on which this table is based were collected fifty years ago, however, and some caution is appropriate in generalizing the exact findings. The study of child development is continually changing;

TABLE 7.1   Vocabulary Growth as a Function of Age

Age (years, months)	*Number of Words*	*Increment*
0;8	0	
0;10	1	1
1;0	3	2
1;3	19	16
1;6	22	3
1;9	118	96
2;0	272	154
2;6	446	174
3;0	896	450
3;6	1222	326
4;0	1540	318
4;6	1870	330
5;0	2072	202
5;6	2289	217
6;0	2562	273

SOURCE: Adapted from M. E. Smith, An investigation of the development of the sentence and the extent of vocabulary in young children. *University of Iowa Studies in Child Welfare*, 1926, **3**, No. 5.

not only because of improvements in methodology and refinements in theory but also because of changes in the subject matter itself, children. Many aspects of development have increased in rate during the past half-century, ranging from the physiological onset of puberty (Tanner 1973) to intellectual performance on intelligence tests. The rapid rate of vocabulary development revealed in the table may be an underestimate of the growth of vocabulary today, although the findings do not differ greatly from those in Nelson's study (1973) of eighteen middle-class children, whose mean age at ten words was 1;3 and at fifty words 1;8.

Development of Word Meaning

The notion of semantic features has guided much research on the development of word meaning. Logically, there are two possibilities for the pattern of development. The first is that, initially, word meanings are too specific, are based on too many features. For example, a child who sees a particular dog and hears the word *dog* might define the word in terms of the particular features of that dog, perhaps color and size. In this instance development would require a process of abstraction. Irrelevant features would have to be eliminated. The contrasting possibility is that children begin with only partial meanings; that is, with only one or two features, perhaps overall shape. Development then consists of adding features. The first possibility predicts that early word meanings should be overspecific (*dog* would be applied only to certain dogs), whereas the second possibility predicts that early word meanings should be overextended (*dog* would be applied to dogs, cats, horses, and so on). The examples of meanings for the first words discussed in Chapter 1 suggest that overextension is more common and thus that development moves from few features to many features. However, this process is not universal. For example, proper names are hardly ever overgeneralized. Underextensions and overlaps (which combine over- and under-extensions) also occur, as was pointed out in the first chapter. Bloom (1973) reports that at 9 months her daughter Allison used *car* to refer only to cars moving on the street below as she watched from the window, not for cars standing still or for cars she was inside. All three types of nonadult usage occur for verbs and action words as well as for nouns. One of Bowerman's daughters used *off* only to refer to clothes and similar objects; the other daughter had used *off* at the corresponding age more broadly than would adults, applied to clothes and other appropriate contexts, and also to pulling stacked cups apart, unfolding newspapers, opening hinged boxes, and so on (Bowerman, in press). Another child used *cake* for any food which he could eat himself (Schlesinger 1974). With the very limited data we have available, it is not possible to judge whether overextensions or underextensions are more common.

The meaning of a word for a child tells us something about his language, but it is misleading to think of it as direct information about cognitive categories. That is, a child who applies the same term to dogs, cats, cows, and horses on the basis of shape may well be able to distinguish the four species. For example, he may know the appropriate noises made by each. Nevertheless, his semantic system encodes all these in a single category until additional specifications are added. Lack of a concept or distinction in language does not imply a corresponding omission in cognition; conversely, the presence of a concept in a child's thought does not necessarily imply its presence in his language.

Clark (1973) has elaborated a theory of semantic development, which she calls the **semantic feature hypothesis.** The hypothesis asserts that children acquire the meanings of words by sequentially adding specific semantic features. When the child first acquires a word, it has only some semantic features and thus it will be applied more widely than it would for an adult. From her survey of the early diary studies, she concludes that perceptual features are most common at this early stage (see Table 1.1), especially static perceptual features like size, shape, and texture, and also movement. Later features that are more abstract and not as directly perceptible are added. Certain general principles determine the order of acquisition of features. According to Clark's hypothesis, general features, which occur in many words, are acquired before specific features, which occur in few words. For example, the meaning of *brother* includes that of *boy*; all brothers are boys, but not all boys are brothers. The more general meaning of *boy* will be acquired first, and *brother* will be confused with it until the semantic features needed for *brother* are acquired. In fact, Piaget (1928; replicated by Elkind 1972) discovered precisely such a stage in the understanding of *brother*.

Pairs of antonyms, such as *high/low* and *long/short*, share most of their semantic features. For example, *long* and *short* both refer extension along the most extended dimension of an object. Only a feature of the form *plus/minus* distinguishes antonyms. According to the semantic-feature hypothesis the common features are acquired first, resulting in a stage during which antonyms are treated as synonyms.

Finally, Clark's theory predicts that the choice of which of the two meanings to attribute to both words (*long* or *short*) will not be random. The child selects the member of the pair that is linguistically simpler. Here Clark draws on the theoretical work of H. Clark (1970), who suggested that in many pairs of antonyms the positive member seems more basic. For example, such words as *long*, *big*, and *thick* can be used to name a dimension without implying quantity, whereas their antonyms *short*, *little*, and *thin* do imply a quantitative measure. The question *How long is it?* does not imply that the object is long, but the question *How short is it?* does presuppose that the object is short. The positive member of the pair can either refer to the dimension or can specify a greater extent along the dimension, whereas the negative member can be used to specify only lesser extent. H. Clark suggests that positive terms are acquired first because "the dimension itself has to be there before one can talk about greater or lesser extent along that dimension" (H. Clark 1973:90).

The universal phenomenon of overextension is very early speech is consistent with Clark's theory. However, as was pointed out in Chapter 1, semantic features are not limited to static perceptual features. Action— either the movement, the object, or the actions the child can perform on the object—is often central. Nelson (1974) in particular has argued for the primary role of function in the early use of words. And even at this early stage, such relational concepts as that represented by the *word* more, which are neither directly perceptual or functional, are present. But the value of the concept of semantic features for theory building and testing is independent of any particular definition of features. There are many different kinds of features, as the examples discussed in the remainder of this section illustrate.

A more serious difficulty with Clark's theory arises from cases of underextension and overlap. These phenomena, perhaps as common as overextension, cannot be accounted for by a model which postulates step-by-step addition of features. Children identify words not only with the appropriate features from the adult point of view but also with some that are irrelevant and which must be eliminated. One relatively common type of underextension results from the restriction of action words to the self at first (Bowerman, in press). The words *up* and *down* are likely to be used first for requests and comments on the child's activities, then for other people, and finally for inanimate objects.

Understanding these temporary semantic errors is not difficult. The child is surrounded by a world of complex objects and events. Sorting out which aspects of experience are relevant for a particular word is a difficult problem of hypothesis-testing and requires time. What is more difficult is to understand how the child ever arrives at the right solutions (Bowerman, in press).

The relationship of language to cognitive development is as difficult to understand here as it was in the case of syntactic development (Chapters 4 and 6). It is clear that semantic categories are not identical with cognitive categories, as was pointed out in the discussion of the first words of children. Cognitive categories and distinctions are more basic; they represent the total of the properties and features of the world which a person is capable of discriminating. Semantic distinctions are those cognitive distinctions which "make a difference, linguistically" (Schlesinger 1974: p. 144), in that they determine the speaker's choice of individual morphemes and rules of combination.

How does a cognitive concept become a semantic concept? One

possibility is that, at least initially, words are learned only as labels for concepts which have already been formed nonlinguistically. Nelson (1974) and Clark (1973) have proposed versions of this view, Nelson placing more emphasis on the functional properties of objects and Clark on their static perceptual attributes. A concept, or category, is essentially a perceived similarity among objects or actions which are not identical in every detail. According to the view presented above, judgments of similarity or lack of it are developed by the child nonlinguistically; the word is then attached to the category. Another position is that the child, as part of learning language, comes to see various experiences as similar if the language he is learning treats them as equivalent, as instances of the same concept. In effect, this position states that semantic and cognitive concepts are developed simultaneously in the development of word meaning. This position is closely related to the Whorf hypothesis, to be discussed in Chapter 9. In addition to these two positions—that the child attaches new words to already existing concepts, or that words are "invitations to form concepts"—there is the possibility of an ongoing and complex interaction between the development of semantic categories and the development of cognitive categories (Bowerman, in press). The three possibilities are not mutually exclusive. Perhaps some concepts develop relatively independently of language. Others may develop only because "language gives the child a little nudge" (Bowerman, in press). Still others may begin cognitively in a relatively primitive form, but the development is greatly influenced by linguistic input. Bowerman (in press) discusses possible examples of each type. The solution of this issue will require far more precise specification of the development of cognitive, that is, nonlinguistic, categories and discriminations than is presently available.

More and Less

Donaldson and Balfour (1968) first observed three-year-old children interpreting the terms *more* and *less* as synonyms—in particular, with the meaning of *more*. Their subjects responded as if they knew that *less* refers to quantity, just as *more* does, but without distinguishing the two terms. This work stimulated much of the current interest in semantic development. Although the experimental design used by Donaldson and Balfour has been criticized, an extensive experiment by Palermo (1974) has replicated the major findings. Palermo assessed preschoolers' understanding of *more* and *less* in five contexts: judging which apple tree had more/less apples, which glass had more/less water, which block weighed more/less, which rows of poker chips had more/less wheels, and finally which cup contained less candy (with the understanding that the child would receive the *other* cup). Performance on questions containing *more* was generally very good. In contrast, the children divided into two groups on the questions containing *less*.

About half of the children responded correctly on nearly all of the items. In contrast, about half of the three-year-olds and a quarter of the four-year-olds responded incorrectly consistently (at least six errors on the eight items with *less*), that is, selecting the object with *more* in response to a request to pick the object with *less*. Even when the children were motivated to obtain the larger amount, in response to the question about candy in the cups, those children who treated *less* as *more* generally (ten out of fourteen trials) gave the experimenter the cup with more candy and thus kept the cup with less candy. Very few children fell between these two extremes of performance.

Dimensional Terms

Dimensional terms—*big, little, long, short, thick,* and so on—have been extensively investigated (Donaldson and Wales 1970; H. Clark 1970; E. V. Clark 1972; Maratsos 1973a, 1974; Eilers, Oller and Ellington 1974). The full story of their development is far from clear. There is a general trend of development from the global terms *big* and *little* to terms that refer to single dimensions, like *tall* and *fat*. The pair *big/little* is extended to cover the domain of the more specialized terms. However, some of the more detailed predictions of E. V. Clark's hypothesis are not supported.

Eilers, Oller, and Ellington (1974) assessed the understanding of the terms *big, little, long, short, wide,* and *narrow* by children between 2;6 and 3;6; they simply asked them to "give me the _____ one" from a pair of appropriate objects. There were fewer errors on *big/little* than on *long/short* and fewer on *long/short* than on *wide/narrow*, confirming the trend from general terms to specific ones. But for all three pairs, correct responses were more likely to occur for the negative terms—*little, short, narrow*—than for the positive ones. That is, to the extent that both members of a pair shared the same meaning, it was more likely to be the negative meaning, contrary to some previous findings and to the semantic-feature hypothesis.

In such experiments, in which the child selects one of two objects, the selection may not be guided as much by the instructions of the experimenter as by the preferences of the child. Eilers and her colleagues explored this possibility in a second experiment, in which children were tested both for comprehension of the six dimension terms listed and for preferences independent of semantics. For the latter, children were simply given instructions of the form "Here are two cans. Give me one." The responses to these general instructions were very similar to the responses to dimensional terms. When these preferences were statistically removed from the comprehension data, no systematic trend to respond more correctly to either positive or negative terms was observed.

Eilers and her colleagues point out that the tendency to respond correctly to *little* rather than to *big* is not necessarily explained by the non-

semantic-preference tendency to select the smaller object. The reverse may
be true: The preference for small objects may result from the semantic focus
of the child on negative adjectives. "The importance of the preference
trend is in showing that it is difficult to rule out semantically irrelevant
factors from experiments investigating the learning of dimensional adjective meanings" (Eilers *et al.* 1974:201).

A finding by Maratsos (1973a) suggests that even the prediction that
performance steadily improves, first on general terms such as *big* and later
on specific terms like *long*, must be revised. The title of his paper provides
a succinct summary: "Decrease in the understanding of the word 'big' in
preschool children." Maratsos presented pairs of stimuli and asked the child
to select the big member of each. Some pairs consisted of squares of varying
height and width; others were pictures of animals varying in these dimensions. The overall proportion of correct responses dropped from 73 percent
at age three years to 37 percent at age four years and 23 percent at age
five years. Incorrect responses were virtually always in favor of the taller
rectangles. The taller rectangle was selected, even when it was clearly
smaller in area. One boy who consistently answered incorrectly in this way
took a short animal; stood it on its rear legs, making it taller than the other
figure; and exclaimed: "Look! Now *it's* the big one!" In another experiment,
Maratsos showed that preschool children generally respond to *big* and *long*
in the same way, which is more likely to be correct for *long* than for *big*,
and, furthermore, that even three-year-olds respond correctly to *long*.

Maratsos' findings suggest a three-stage development of the meanings of *big* and *long*:

1. At the first stage (age three years) *big* correctly refers to global size, and
    long correctly refers to one dimension.
2. At the second stage (age four to five years) *long* continues to be interpreted
    correctly, but *big* is treated as synonymous with *long* and in particular is
    related to the height of the stimuli.
3. In the third stage (after age five years) the two words are distinguished again
    and have their correct meanings.

Thus *long* is interpreted correctly as early as age three years, rather
than after the correct understanding of *big*. Research with two-year-olds
might uncover an earlier stage in which *big* is comprehended but not *long*,
but at the present time there is no evidence that this is so.

We have no idea why the characteristic error in interpretation of
big occurs in the second stage. It might be viewed as an overgeneralization
from the one-dimensional meaning of *long*. But in fact *long* has been correctly mastered for a year before this error occurs.

A valuable contribution of Maratsos' work is the examination of
cues that are irrelevant to adult meanings for the dimensional terms. Previous work has not pitted the individual dimensions of height, width, and

global size against one another in this way. For example, Eilers and her colleagues used, for comprehension of *big* and *little*, objects that differed in the same direction on two dimensions; for *long* and *short*, objects that differed only in the most extended dimension; and so on. Learning the meanings of words is not simply a matter of attending to the adult features; during the course of development quite different features may be used.

Before and After

E. V. Clark (1971) has studied the acquisition of the meanings of the relational conjunctions *before* and *after*. Her experiment included both a comprehension task and a production task. In the comprehension task, the children were asked to act out a sentence that described two events in a specific order, for example *The elephant jumps before the dog sits down* and *After the dog sits down, the elephant jumps*. Comprehension of these sentences developed through four stages. In the first stage, the response was independent of the particular conjunction used; instead the order of events acted out was identical with the order of mention in the sentences. Therefore, sentences of the form "E_1 before E_2" and "After E_1, E_2" were generally responded to correctly, whereas responses to sentences of the form "Before E_1, E_2" and "E_1 after E_2" were consistently wrong. In the second stage, sentences with *before* were correctly responded to, but sentences with *after* were still dealt with by means of the "order of mention" strategy. In the third stage, sentences with *before* were still generally correct, but sentences with *after* were consistently incorrect, showing that *after* was being treated as a synonym of *before*. In the fourth stage, the two words were recognized as being opposite in meaning.

The third stage is the most interesting. Additional evidence that *before* and *after* were synonyms comes from the production task, in which the experimenter acted out sequences of events and then asked such questions as *When did (event I) happen?* and *When did (event II) happen?* An appropriate answer to the second question would be *After (event I)*. The children had much more difficulty answering questions that called for *after* than answering questions that called for *before*; in a few instances they even used *before* in place of *after*.

Notice that, when *before* and *after* are treated as synonyms, most of the meaning is present. The semantic features "time" and "nonsimultaneous" are part of the children's meaning. Only a "plus/minus" feature remains to be acquired; Clark suggests the term "prior." As in the example of *more* and *less*, the particular meaning used for the two is the positive one.[3]

[3] For another interpretation of Clark's findings, see Amidon and Carey (1972). Other aspects of the semantics of time and ordering have been investigated by Hatch (1971), Sinclair and Fereiro (1971), Bronckart and Sinclair (1973), Cromer (1971), and Barrie-Blackley (1973).

Verbs and the Expression of Causation

The fourth example given at the beginning of this chapter concerns the use of verbs and adjectives in a special way. There are a number of verb pairs in English whose meanings differ primarily according to the semantic feature 'cause.' For example, *drop* means 'cause to fall,' *kill* means 'cause to die,' and so on. Verbs like *drop* and *kill* are called **causative verbs** for this reason. In the examples at the beginning of this chapter, non-causative verbs and adjectives were used as causative verbs. *Eat, fall,* and *full* were being used with an extra feature, that of cause. An examination of why these "errors" occur and of why they occur at this particular point in development is revealing.

English provides four ways to express causality of this type. For some combinations of verb or adjective meaning and causality, the lexicon of English provides a word that "bundles" the semantic feature of cause and the particular action into a single unit: for example, *drop* and *kill*. In other instances a more or less productive inflection is used to convert an adjective to a causative verb: for example, *sharp/sharpen, rich/enrich, legal/legalize*. A third method, the most general, is to use a syntactic construction of the form *make it fall/red/open* and so on. Finally, and most simply, some verbs can be used causatively as well as noncausatively, without modification, for example, *warm (The soup is warm/Warm the soup)* and *Open (The door is open/Open the door)*. Consideration of this fourth procedure suggests that the use of noncausative words like *eat* and *fall* as causatives by children is a kind of overgeneralization from words that do not undergo modification, analogous to the overgeneralization of the regular past tense to irregular verbs.

Bowerman (1974) has studied in detail errors of this type produced by her daughter. She concludes that the overgeneralization occurs when it does because specific syntactic and semantic developments are necessary prerequisites. She points out that true causative verbs are used from the earliest stages of language development: *break stick, mommy open,* whereas the novel causatives, noncausatives used as causatives, occur only later— at around twenty-four months for her daughter. Bowerman hypothesizes that, on the basis of experience with various causative and noncausative verbs, the child finally arrives at the generalization that certain verbs contain a "cause" feature. That is, the child analyzes the previously unitary meanings of such verbs as *break* and *open* into at least two parts, one of which is "cause." The creation of novel forms by analogy with existing ones provides the clearest evidence that such an analysis has been completed. Similarly, the creation of such forms as *doed* and *goed* constitutes the best evidence that the child has analyzed past-tense forms in the speech around him into two parts: the verb plus the past tense *-ed*. Just as *did* and *went* are replaced by *doed* and *goed,* the verbs *bring* and *keep* were replaced in Christy's speech by causative use of *come* (*Come her,* meaning 'Bring her here') and *stay* (*Mommy, can you stay this open,* meaning 'Can you keep this open').

In addition to this semantic step, certain syntactic prerequisites appear to be necessary for the creation of these novel causatives. Causative verbs are complex in a way similar to complex sentences. Just as complex sentences contain two or more main verbs (*I saw her walking away*), causative verbs have two verb-like semantic features: cause and the corresponding noncausative verb or adjective. This is shown most clearly in the third method of signifying causatives: constructions such as *Make it open* and *Get door open.* Strikingly, the use of noncausative verbs and adjectives as causatives emerged just after Christy began to produce causative constructions of this type. Both developments occurred considerably after she was producing three- and four-word sentences like agent-action-object-location. What is so difficult about *I can't get door open* and *I made it full?* It is probably the fact that these sentences, like causative verbs, relate two separate propositions: that somebody did something and that a certain event happened as a result. It is about this time that complex sentences in general emerge: *Watch me swinging* and *Christy fall down hurt self.* If this sequence of development is general (and Bowerman has some evidence that it is so), it suggests that the semantic ability to form novel causatives is related to the syntactic ability to join simple sentences into complex constructions.

The development of causative verbs is a good illustration of the diversity of sources of semantic features. Some seem to arise directly from the child's experience of the external world, but some, like cause, are the result of the child's analysis of previously acquired but as yet unanalyzed meanings, like the earliest meanings of *break* and *open.*

Verbs of Possession and Transfer

The set of verbs *give, take, pay, trade, spend, buy,* and *sell* provides a particularly good example of the importance of the nature of relations among the components of a word's meaning. Gentner (1975) divides this set into three levels of semantic complexity.

The verbs *give* and *take* are the simplest. Both contain the component 'transfer of possession from A to B.' In both another component is required, that of causal action. If the transfer were not caused by the action of either party, we would use a more neutral verb such as *lose* or *acquire.* The difference between the two verbs lies not in any difference of components but in the relationship of these two components. For *give,* it is party A who does something to cause the transfer of possession to occur; for *take*, it is party B. For *give*, the two components are related via party A, who is the agent of the causal action and the source of the object transferred. For *take*, two components are related via party B, who is the agent of the causal action and the goal of the transfer.

The verbs *pay* and *trade* are more complex. They include the two components transfer of possession and causal action; in addition, each requires additional information. *Pay* includes a component of social obligation and also a constraint that "object transferred is money." *Trade* includes two transfers of possession, one from A to B and one from B to A, and a component of mutual contract, which relates the two transfers. If the two transfers occurred as entirely independent transactions, we would not use the verb *trade*.

The verbs *buy*, *sell*, and *spend* are the most complex. They all include the components of cause, transfer of possession, social obligation, (the object being transferred in one direction creates an obligation to pay), mutual contract (the two parties agree to transfer an object in one direction and money in the other), and the constraint that "object transferred is money." The differences among the meanings of the three verbs, like the difference between *give* and *take*, hinge on how these components are related and especially on the party who is the agent of the causal action.

The components in the first group are most general, as they occur in the other verbs as well. The components in the second group are the next most general, as they occur also in the third group. The semantic feature hypothesis predicts that the order of acquisition should be *give* and *take*; then *pay* and *trade*; and, finally, *buy*, *sell*, and *spend*. In the stages before a child has completely acquired the meaning of a complex verb, his representation should contain some but not all of the necessary components. His interpretation of a more complex verb should resemble that for a simpler verb containing just those features.

Gentner (1975) provided children between 3;6 and 8;6 with two dolls (Bert and Ernie), each with its own set of toys and money. She asked the child to make the dolls act out sentences containing these verbs, for example, "Make Ernie buy a car from Bert." The results supported both major predictions. The verbs were mastered in the order given here. Furthermore, the pattern of errors indicates that the children assimilated the meanings of the complex verbs to those of simpler verbs. For example, children under five years typically acted out *buy* as if it meant *take* and *sell* as if it meant *give*. The object was transferred in the proper direction but with no awareness of the necessity for exchange of money. The fact that *buy* → *take* and *sell* → *give* demonstrates that the child has already incorporated the component of causal action into his representations and has related it properly to the component transfer of possession. Thus even the incomplete representation is a structured system of relations among components.

Egocentrism and Meaning

Preschoolers who can identify their own left and right hands are often unable to identify the left and right hands of a person facing them. They select the hands that are on their *own* left and right respectively. The feature that is missing from their meanings is not a perceptual one but rather an abstract relational one, relating meaning to perspectives that can change. Similarly, children somewhat older often go through a stage in which they cannot conceive of themselves as someone else's brother or sister. Such a child might correctly report that he has two brothers, but, when asked how many brothers a particular sibling has, he will answer just one. The *brother/sister* example and the *left/right* example reflect an inability to change perspective. They illustrate the important role of cognitive maturity in the development of word meanings. These examples are only a few instances of the young child's egocentrism, his inability to take another perspective in a wide variety of situations, linguistic and otherwise.

A more subtle instance of egocentrism in semantic development is shown in the development of the definite and indefinite articles *the* and *a*. Brown (1973, pp. 340–356) has studied their development in the spontaneous speech of three children, and Maratsos (1974c) has explored the development in detail with a larger number of three- and four-year-olds. At least two semantic dimensions are represented in the articles. The first is specificity/nonspecificity. If the speaker has a specific instance of a category in mind, he may use the definite article: *Can I borrow the car?* In contrast, the reference may be to any member of a class or to no member at all, as in *Why don't we buy a dog?* In the course of a conversation, an item may change from nonspecific to specific. For example, the sentence *Let's buy a dog* introduces a situation in which a particular dog may exist; later references to the dog will be specific, *Where would we keep the dog?* Nonspecific reference generally requires use of the indefinite article *a*. However, specific reference is not sufficient to justify use of the definite:

> Imagine someone who had just been bitten by a dog on the street and walked into a room full of people who knew nothing about it. Certainly the dog is a specific one for him. Nevertheless, the dog should initially be referred to with an indefinite, as in *a dog just bit me*. The corresponding definite reference, *the dog just bit me* would be unsatisfactory. It seems to imply that the listeners know what dog the speaker is talking about, when in fact they do not. Although the dog is a particular one for him, it is not yet a particular dog for his listeners until after he has introduced it verbally. Use of a definite reference implies that the speaker not only has a particular referent in mind, but that he also expects the definite reference to call up in his listener the same particular referent. (Maratsos 1974:447)

In other words, definite reference requires both specificity to the speaker and knowledge by the listener. If either condition is not present, the indefinite is used. Of course, the knowledge of the listener must be estimated by the speaker.

In Brown's examination of the naturalistic data from Adam, Eve, and Sarah, he found that the specific-nonspecific dimension was generally attended to in the early use of articles (about age three years). For example, Sarah referred to *the mailman* and Adam to *the trailer* when there was a single trailer in the context. Conversely, Eve requested *a bandaid* and Adam referred to a Q (*A wheel looks like a Q*). In both these cases, any instance of the class of bandaids or Qs is appropriate. However, a systematic error was observed in instances in which referents were specific to the speaker but not yet known to the listener. Sarah said *I want to open the door*; her mother replied *What door?* showing that it was unclear which door was intended. Adam, in retelling a story, said *The monkey hit the leopard* when *the leopard* had not yet been introduced to the listener. Here the points of view of the listener and the speaker diverged. What the three children did in many instances was to choose the article only on the basis of their own knowledge, as if the fact that the referent was specific to them implied that it was specific to the listener. The ability to view the situation from the perspective of another, as in *left/right* and *brother/sister*, had not yet been developed.

Maratsos (1974c) devised experimental tests of the command of these two semantic dimensions. In one procedure, the child was told a story about a lady who had a boy and a girl. The children were noisy, and the lady told them to be quiet. One of them started to laugh and make noise. The experimenter then asked *Who was making noise?* As a particular boy and girl had been established, the answer should have included a definite article, either *the boy* or *the girl*. Another version of the story included four boys and three girls, so that the information that one child was making noise did not specify a particular individual. The answer to the question *Who was making noise?* should have been answered with an indefinite article, *a boy* or *a girl*. Even if the child imagined for himself a particular boy or girl laughing, that referent would have been established for himself, not for the listener. Failure to take into account the lack of knowledge of the listener should lead to an egocentric error, the use of the definite article. On the basis of children's performance on these and other stories, Maratsos concluded that even three-year-olds had good control of the semantic dimension of specificity/nonspecificity for the speaker, despite the apparent abstractness of the dimension. But, like the children studied by Brown, those in Maratsos' experiment often erred on the dimension of knowledge of the listener, using *the* when *a* was appropriate, as in the second example. In Maratsos' sample, mastery of this second dimension began around the age of four and a half years, though there was great variation.

Most of the young child's communication is with very familiar people—parents, siblings, and friends—and the topic of conversation is a shared experience of some sort. Egocentric use of the article *the* reflects a kind of overgeneralization. A well-established mode of communication, based on an assumption of commonality of knowledge, is inappropriately applied to new communicative settings. We are reminded of Brown's (1973) view of the development of obligatory grammatical morphemes, discussed at the end of Chapter 6, as reflecting the gradual widening of the range of adaptation of child language.

Focal Colors and Color Naming

Speakers of English agree not only on the range of colors to which color words can be applied but also on the colors that are the best instances of these color terms (Berlin and Kay 1969). In fact, these best instances, or "focal colors," appear to be universal. Even though languages provide varying numbers of color words and the range of colors to which any term refers varies from language to language, the focal areas recur over and over again (Berlin and Kay 1969).

Heider (1971) has explored the development of color naming in the light of this discovery. Even three-year-olds, who do not yet use color words systematically, find the focal colors more attractive. When asked simply to "show me a color," they are far more likely to select a focal color than would be predicted by chance. When four-year-olds were asked to pick colors from an array that matched sample color chips, they were significantly more accurate with focal colors than with nonfocal colors. Furthermore, the colors selected to match nonfocal colors tended to err in the direction of focal colors.

Adults show great agreement on the location of focal colors. Is this knowledge something learned in addition to the category covered by the color term, or does the category grow out of the focal area? Heider (1971) tested three-and four-year-olds on their knowledge of color words by asking such questions as "show me the red one." Some of these young children responded completely inappropriately; the major question investigated was whether or not a focal color would be produced if *any* appropriate color was. That is, if the child produced a red color, would it be a focal red? And indeed the focal colors were produced far more often than would be predicted by chance. Thus, color terms may be learned first by being attached to the focal colors and later generalized to other colors (further evidence for this possibility has been found by Mervis, Catlin & Rosch 1975).

Given the cross-cultural similarities in focal-color naming and the special status of focal colors in the attending and matching behavior of preschoolers, it seems most reasonable to assume that the focal colors are defined by unknown perceptual and cognitive factors common to all human beings. The development of color naming then builds on these focal colors. Even though color words are later applied to broad categories of colors, the focal colors occupy a central place in color concepts. Rosch (1973) has argued that similar focal concepts occur in other aspects of semantic and conceptual development.

Expectations

Language communicates information about the speaker, as well as about the situation being described. This fact is obvious in the instances of tone, voice, and dialect, but certain words and constructions also convey information about expectations of the speaker. For example, the question *Did you see the broken headlight?* conveys a more positive expectation on the part of the questioner than *Did you see a headlight?* This expectation aspect of the meaning of the definite article can be demonstrated by showing adults a film of an accident in which no broken headlight is present. Viewers asked about the headlight with the definite article are more likely to respond affirmatively than viewers asked with the indefinite article (Loftus and Palmer 1974). The question *About how fast were the cars going when they smashed into each other?* elicits higher estimates of speed than does *About how fast were the cars going when they hit each other?* indicating that changes in a single word in a question can markedly affect answers to the question.

Although young children may be highly suggestible, it is not clear that their relatively short experience with the language is sufficient for them to learn the force of these subtle changes. Dale, Loftus, and Rathbun (1974) showed preschoolers filmed commercials and asked them questions about the films. The questions used were constructed to evaluate the effect of the definite/indefinite-article contrast, affirmation/negation in questions (*Didn't you see the bear?* seems to have a more positive expectation than *Did you see the bear?*), and the contrast between *some* and *any*. If the question was asked about an entity that was indeed present in the film, the form of the question did not matter. With high probability, the children responded *yes*. If, however, the question was asked about an entity that was not present in the film, the form of the question significantly affected the probability of a *yes* response. In particular, questions of the forms *Did you see the . . .* , *Did you see any . . .* , and *Didn't you see some . . .* were more likely to be answered *yes* than were other question types. Children are aware of the expectation conveyed by certain linguistic forms, like *the*. The expectation was not directly conveyed, as it would be in *I saw the car; did you?* It was implicit in the article. Though this expectation sense may appear to be secondary to the more literal meaning of the articles, it is acquired at least as early as the second semantic dimension explored by Maratsos (1974c), knowledge of the listener. As Dale and his colleagues point out, research of this kind has important implications for the obtaining and evaluation of eye-witness testimony from children and adults.

Word Meanings: A Summary

There is no single framework that covers all children, all word meanings, and all patterns of development. Some children treat *big* and *little* as synonyms meaning 'big'; others treat them as synonyms meaning 'little.' Some words are usefully described as bundles of semantic features (the dimensional terms, *before* and *after*), whereas others have to be discussed in terms of focal concepts (the color words) or relations among components (verbs of possession). And finally, in some instances development is the acquisition, gradual or sudden, of features and relations that permit performance more nearly approximating the adult norm, whereas in other instances (*big*) performance may actually deteriorate for a time. In some instances semantic development is tied rather closely to the child's level of cognitive maturity (*left/right*, the articles), whereas in others cognitive factors do not seem to play a role in determining the point of mastery. For example, a year-old infant has a fairly good idea of physical causality, yet cause does not emerge as a distinct semantic feature until at least age two years (Bowerman 1974) and seems to require a certain level of syntactic maturity. Semantic development is as varied as the concepts that language encodes.

Sentences and Beyond

Understanding a sentence requires integration of the meanings of the individual words into a sentence meaning. One aspect of this integration is the elimination of possible ambiguities, discussed earlier in this chapter. Although we generally think of the process as beginning with identification of the words and then proceeding to determine integrated meaning, this process is often partly reversed. Imagine listening to a conversation on a noisy telephone line. Parts of words are obliterated by the noise. Often a word cannot be completely identified on the basis of the acoustic signal alone, but identification is generally easy because we have heard other words in the sentence and can narrow down the range of possibilities. For example, after *the boy* a verb is extremely likely; after *the red* a noun is very probable. If the conversation is a sensible one and if we know something about the topic, stronger predictions can be made on semantic grounds. After *the boy* the verb *lectured* is unlikely, though grammatically correct.

Miller and Isard (1963) asked adult subjects to listen to three kinds of verbal strings through a masking noise:

Meaningful: The academic lecture attracted a limited audience.
Anomalous: The academic liquid became an odorless audience.
Scrambled: Liquid the an became audience odorless academic.

The anomalous strings have syntactic organization, though semantically they are nonsense. The meaningful strings are both syntactically and semantically structured. As the noise obliterated part of the signal, the subjects' ability to perceive the sentences depended in part on their ability to fill in the missing parts on the basis of what was heard.

Adult subjects do better on the anomalous strings than on the scrambled strings, reflecting their ability to use syntactic information. They do still better on the meaningful strings, reflecting their ability to use semantic information.

McNeill (1970) and Entwisle and Frasure (1974) have given children a similar task. Strings of the three types were constructed from a somewhat simpler vocabulary.

> *Meaningful*:   Bears steal honey from the hive.
> *Anomalous*:   Trains steal elephants around the house.
> *Scrambled*:   From shoot highways the passengers mothers.

The children, aged six to nine years, were asked to listen to tapes of these sentences with superimposed noise and to repeat the sentences as heard. Figure 7.1 illustrates the results of the Entwisle and Frasure experiment. At age six years there is little difference in performance on the three types of sentences. From age seven years on, performance is best on meaningful strings, next best on anomalous strings, and poorest on scrambled strings. Furthermore, the gaps among the various kinds of strings steadily increase. Given the relatively simple syntax of the sentences in this study, it is remarkable that performance on the anomalous strings, in which syntactic structure is the major aid, should continue to improve up to age nine years. This improvement may reflect a general ability to integrate in the way required for the task, as opposed to a specifically syntactic ability. The steady increase in superiority of meaningful strings is precisely what would be expected on the assumption that semantic development is the gradual addition of semantic features and selection restrictions to words already in the child's vocabulary. Certain words and meanings that would be ruled out by an adult are not eliminated by the child.

We do not listen to one sentence at a time. The process of semantic integration applies to sequences of sentences, as well as to each sentence individually. The particular form of a sentence or the way in which information is distributed among sentences is not as important as the total meaning expressed. These statements, reasonable sounding as they are, are something of a contrast to the heavily sentence-oriented theorizing of much linguistic research. But they are confirmed clearly by research on comprehension and memory. For example, adults generally cannot recognize or recall the particular syntactic form (active or passive, say) of a sentence

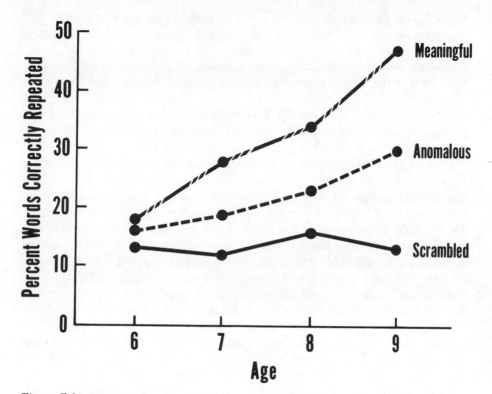

Figure 7.1   Percent of words repeated at four age levels as a function of syntactic and semantic structure.

SOURCE: A contradiction resolved: Children's processing of syntactic cues. In D. R. Entwisle and N. E. Frasure, *Developmental Psychology*, 1974, 10, 852–857, Figure 1. Copyright 1974 by the American Psychological Association. Reprinted by permission.

as well as they can recognize the meaning expressed (Sachs 1967). Experiments that provide subjects with a sequence of sentences have consistently shown that the subjects spontaneously integrate the sentences into a unified memory representation and do not remember the particular sentences used (Bransford, Barclay & Franks 1972). A common technique is to provide three sentences like:

> The bird is inside the cage.
> The cage is under the table.
> The bird is yellow.

If the listener is integrating these sentences, it will follow that the bird is under the table. The subject can be asked if the sentence *The bird is under the table* or *The cage is over the table* occurred. The latter is very similar to a sentence that did occur, though semantically it is quite the opposite. The former sentence did not occur but follows from an integrated representation. Studies with adults have consistently found that subjects will often accept the former type of sentence as having occurred before but not the latter.

Paris and Carter (1973) have investigated the development of this process of integration, sometimes called "constructive memory," in seven- and 10-year-olds. Each subject listened to number of three-sentence "stories" and was later asked whether or not certain sentences had occurred. Among these sentences were some that had actually occurred, some that had not but were similar in form to those that had occurred, some that were valid inferences from what had occurred, and some that were invalid inferences, for example, *The bird is on top of the table.* Both the seven-year-olds and the ten-year-olds often (better than 55 percent) "recognized" the inferential sentences as familiar. All other sentences were seldom so recognized (below 30 percent). Like adults, they spontaneously constructed a unified memory for the sets. Although the ten-year-olds were generally better at the task than the seven-year-olds, there was virtually no difference in this tendency to integrate and hence to "recognize" sentences that had not actually occurred. This is not to say that seven-year-olds have completed the process of development. The integration task in this experiment was a very simple one: Three sentences, immediately juxtaposed, on a common topic signaled by the identity of words, constitute the easiest possible integration task. The kind of integration required in reading fiction or technical prose requires far longer development.

Summary

It is easy to be impressed by the magnitude of the differences in semantic sophistication between child and adult. Words do not mean the same thing, and communication is often difficult. Yet the semantic abilities of young children are worthy of respect. By his third birthday, the average child has acquired nearly a thousand words. Though they do not have exactly the same meanings as they do for adults, they are typically used with consistent meanings that bear systematic relations to the adult meanings. Many components, or features, of meaning are involved, often in a complex relationship. Children somewhat older can use their semantic knowledge to fill in gaps of sentences as perceived and can integrate the information in several sentences to go "beyond the information given." The paths of semantic development are varied; they differ for individual words and for individual children. A full mastery of semantic competence requires many years; in a larger sense it continues throughout life.

7.1   IS THE CHILD'S THINKING CONCRETE
OR ABSTRACT?*

It is a commonplace saying that the mind of a child is relatively "concrete" and the mind of an adult "abstract." The words "concrete" and "abstract" are sometimes used in the sense of subordinate and superordinate. In this sense a relatively concrete mind would operate with subordinate categories and an abstract mind with superordinate categories. It is recorded in many studies of vocabulary acquisition that children ordinarily use the words milk and water before the word liquid; the words apple and orange before fruit; table and chair before furniture; mamma and daddy before parent or person, and so on. Very high-level superordinate terms like article, action, quality, and relation, though they are common in adult speech, are very seldom heard from preschool children. . . .

There are two extreme opinions about the direction of cognitive development. There are those who suppose that we begin by discriminating to the limits of our sensory acuity, seizing each thing in its uniqueness, noting every hair and flea of the particular dog. Cognitive development involves neglect of detail, abstracting from particulars so as to group similars into categories. By this view abstraction is a mature rather than a primitive process. The contrary opinion is that the primitive stage in cognition is one of a comparative lack of differentiation. Probably certain distinctions are inescapable; the difference between a loud noise and a near silence, between a bright contour and a dark ground, and so on. These inevitable discriminations divide the perceived world into a small number of very large (abstract) categories. Cognitive development is increasing differentiation. The more distinctions we make, the more categories we have and the smaller (more concrete) these are. I think the latter view is favored in psychology today. While there is good empirical and theoretical support for the view that development is differentiation, there is embarrassment for it in the fact that much vocabulary growth is from the concrete to the abstract. This embarrassment can be eliminated. . . .

It seems likely that things are first named so as to categorize them in a maximally useful way. For most purposes Referent A is a spoon rather than a piece of silverware and Referent B is a dime rather than a metal object. The same referent may have its most useful categorization on one level (Prince) for one group (the family) and on another level (dog) for another group (strangers). The categorization that is most useful for very young children (money) may change as they grow older (dime and nickel).

With some hierarchies of vocabulary the more concrete terms are learned first, but it often happens that a hierarchy develops in both directions from a middle level of abstraction. Psychologists who believe that mental

* From Roger Brown, How shall a thing be called? *Psychological Review*, 1958, **65**, 18–21. Copyright 1958 by the American Psychological Association. Reprinted by permission.

development is from the abstract to the concrete, from a lack of differentiation to increased differentiation, have been embarrassed by the fact that vocabulary often builds in the opposite direction. This fact need not trouble them, since the sequence in which words are acquired is not determined by the cognitive preferences of children so much as by the naming practices of adults. . . .

further reading

Bierwisch, M. Semantics. In J. Lyons (Ed.), *New horizons in linguistics.* Baltimore: Penguin, 1970.

Clark, E. V. What's in a word? On the child's acquisition of semantics in his first language. In T. E. Moore (Ed.), *Cognitive development and the acquisition of language.* New York: Academic Press, 1973.

Nelson, E. Concept, word and sentence: Interrelations in acquisition and development. *Psychological Review,* 1974, **81,** 267–285.

Phonology and Reading

One common method of teaching an adult a second language in the classroom is to begin with the sounds of the language being learned. When the student has demonstrated some mastery of these sounds, they are combined into words. When the words can be produced with fair accuracy, they are combined into sentences. Working "from the bottom up," the student must master each level before the next can be attempted.

The acquisition of language by children is very different. Children are working on the pronunciation of sounds, on acquiring words, and on sentence construction simultaneously throughout development. Complex sentences may be constructed of words with highly simplified pronunciations. Certain types of pronunciation are so typical of young children, for example, *wabbit* for *rabbit*, that they define "childish" language for most adults. Like the development of syntax and that of semantics, the development of the sound system of language, **phonology**, proceeds in a regular, step-by-step fashion, which is highly systematic at any particular point in development.

All the organs that are used in speech have other functions: The lips and tongue are used in eating and swallowing, the windpipe (or trachea) is the major pathway for air from the mouth and nose to the lungs, and so on. Because of this and because these organs are possessed by other animals, especially such higher primates as the orangutang and chimpanzee, it is often said that speech is simply an **overlaid** function, that is, a new use for an old structure. However, there are important differences in both the structure and function of these organs in man (Lenneberg 1967). For example, the muscles in the lips and tongue of human beings are more highly developed and more agile than the corresponding muscles in other animals. This added flexibility is of no use whatever in eating and swallowing but is extremely useful in producing rapid, articulate speech. The respiratory cycle is quite different during speech from what it is during normal breathing. The air intake is much larger but also much more rapid, whereas the outflow (primarily through the mouth, rather than the nose) is controlled by a different interplay of muscles.

In normal breathing, air flows through the windpipe, mouth, and nose in an unrestricted manner. Speech is produced by placing some kind of restriction in the way. All languages have two major types of sounds. In the first type, the air flows freely through the mouth cavity once it passes over the vocal cords (see Figure 8.1). These sounds are called **vowels.** In

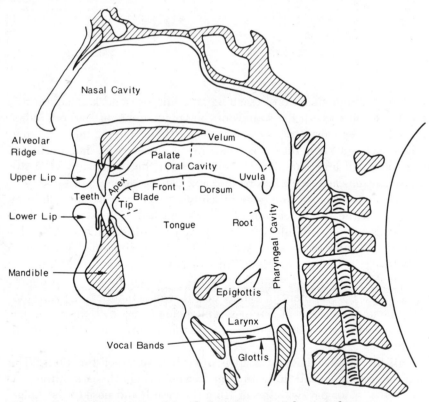

Figure 8.1 Cross-section of head showing principle speech organs.

SOURCE: W. Nelson Francis, *The Structure of American English.* Copyright © 1958, The Ronald Press Company, New York.

the second type of sounds, there is further obstruction in the way of the flow of air. These sounds are called **consonants.**

The basic vowel sounds are produced by vocal cords: two elastic membranes near the top of the windpipe. They function somewhat as the double reed functions in playing the oboe or the lips function in playing the trumpet. When they are held at just the right tension, not too loose and not too taut, air passing through them will set up a regular vibration, called **voicing.** Voicing is actually made up of many different sounds, each having a distinct frequency. The lowest of these is called the **fundamental frequency;** exact multiples of this frequency, or overtones, are also produced. Despite the fact that the air then passes unimpeded through the mouth, the sound may be modified greatly. This is parallel to the operation of various brass instruments—the lips are producing basically the same sound as the mouthpiece of the trumpet, French horn, or trombone, but the shape of the instrument determines the nature of the final note. Each particular way in which we can form our mouth cavity, which depends primarily on the positions of the tongue and lips, will emphasize some of the sounds emerging from the vocal cords. So, by moving the tongue and lips we can vary the frequencies that are emphasized and thus the quality of the produced vowel.

The chief characteristic distinguishing consonants from vowels is that the flow of air is closed off either completely or almost completely. When the flow is closed off, as in [t], it is called a **stop.** When the flow is partially blocked, it becomes very turbulent and produces a hissing sound, as in [s], which is called a **fricative.** The stops are produced by blocking the flow of air and letting pressure build up, then releasing it in a sudden burst. The fricatives are produced by moving the tongue or lips to a position very close to that of a stop but not quite the same. Notice that [t] and [s] are produced with the tongue in very similar positions.

The Sounds of English

English Vowels

The position of the tongue provides a useful categorization of vowels. The tongue may be moved in an up-and-down direction and also in a front-to-back direction. The difference between the sounds [i] and [u], as in *beat* and *cooed*, is that in [i] the tongue is raised to a position near the ridge just behind the upper teeth, that is, the **alveolar ridge.** This position is quite far forward for a vowel. For [u] the back of the tongue is raised to a position near the rear of the roof of the mouth, the **palate,** which is quite far back. The [i] sound is said to be a **front vowel,** [u] **a back vowel.** To produce [a], as in *cod,* the tongue is in its natural resting position, low and to the back of the mouth.

These three vowels are the extremes of the English vowels; all the other vowels fall between them along the front-back and low-high dimensions. There are twelve vowels in English (see Table 8.1). The mid vowel [ə], the most common, is often called the *schwa*.

TABLE 8.1   The Vowels of English[a]

	Front		
High	[i] b*eat*		[u] c*ooed*
	[ɪ] b*it*		[ʊ] c*ould*
	[e] b*ait*[b]	[ə] r*oses*	[o] c*ode*[b]
	[ɛ] b*et*		[ɔ] c*awed*
Low	[æ] b*at*	[ʌ] b*ut*	[a] c*od*

[a] Regional differences in American English are most commonly differences in vowel pronunciation. In some areas, for example, *cot* and *caught* are pronounced alike, combining the vowels symbolized by [a] and [ɔ] into a single sound type.
[b] The vowels of *bait* and *code* are diphthongs: combinations of simple vowels with glides (see discussion later in this chapter). The vowel of *bait* combines the simple vowel [e] with a [y]; the vowel of *code* combines the simple vowel [o] with a [w].

The position of the tongue determines the basic quality of a vowel. Four techniques are available for modification of the basic quality: nasalization, length, tone, and rounding. But only one plays a significant role in English. If you pronounce [i] and then [u], you will notice that for [i] the corners of the mouth are drawn back, whereas in [u] the lips are rounded and slightly protruded. The [u] sound is a **rounded vowel,** whereas [i] is unrounded. Four English vowels are rounded: [u], [U], [o], and [ɔ]; they are the back vowels, with the exception of [a]. It is neither logically nor physically necessary for only the back and not the front vowels to be rounded, although this is the case in English. For example, it is easy to produce a sound like [i] but rounded (try it); in fact this is a sound used in French. French has a series of rounded front vowels, as well as a series of unrounded ones, and this difference is enough to change meanings of words. *Fée*, 'fairy,' and *feu*, 'fire' differ only in that the second is pronounced with lips rounded.

English Consonants

The closure characteristic of consonants may occur at any position in the mouth. There are five important positions for English stops and fricatives.

1. *With the lips.* The [p] and [b] in *paste* and *baste* are stops produced with the two lips. They are called **bilabial stops.** English does not

have any bilabial fricatives. It does, however, have fricatives produced with the lower lip against the upper teeth: the [f] and [v] in *file* and *vile*. Because they are produced with the lips and the teeth, they are called **labiodentals.**

2. *With the tip of the tongue on the upper teeth.* English does not have any stops in this position, but it has two fricatives, the initial sounds in *thin* and *that*. These are quite distinct sounds, even though they are spelled in the same way. To distinguish them, the symbols [θ] (as in *thin*) and [ð] (as in *that*) are used. These sounds are called **linguadentals.**

3. *With the tip of the tongue on the ridge just behind the upper front teeth.* Because this ridge is known as the alveolar ridge, sounds produced in this way are called **alveolars.** The [t] and [d] of *tear* and *dare* are **alveolar stops,** whereas the [s] and [z] of *seal* and *zeal* are **alveolar fricatives.**

4. *With the entire front of the tongue on the forward part of the palate.* English does not have any stops of this type, but there are two fricatives, the final sounds of *hash* and *rouge*. These are written phonetically as [š] and [ž]. They are called **alveolopalatal fricatives,** as the tongue is near the juncture of the alveolar ridge and the palate.

5. *With the back of the tongue against the velum, that is, the soft palate.* English has two such velar stops, the [k] and [g] of *came* and *game*. Although English does not have any **velar fricatives,** many languages do, for example, the German *ch* as in *Bach*.

In addition to the stops and fricatives, there is a third, "combination" type of consonant. The first sounds of *cheap* and *jeep* are examples of these sounds. They are produced by first blocking the air flow as for a stop and then releasing it—not quickly as for a stop but slowly, so that the tongue is briefly in a position for a fricative. The initial sound of *cheap*, for example, is produced by starting with a [t] and then releasing it slowly so that an [š] is pronounced. These sounds are called **affricates** and are written [č] and [ǰ] respectively.

When some of the consonants we have discussed are voiced, the vocal cords are vibrating. This can be detected by holding a finger on the Adam's apple. Those consonants that are pronounced with vocal-cord vibration are called **voiced consonants,** those that are not **voiceless consonants.** In general, voiceless and voiced consonants occur in pairs, identical save that one is voiceless, one voiced: [p] and [b], [s] and [z], [č] and [ǰ], [θ] and [ð] and so on.[1] Vowels are almost always voiced. The only

---

[1] This is something of an oversimplification. The contrast between voiced and voiceless stops is realized as a contrast in voicing in certain contexts, for example, between two vowels, but in other contexts by means of other cues. For example, in initial position, the contrast between *pin* and *bin* is largely a matter of aspiration, both initial stops being, strictly speaking, voiceless. Nevertheless, the contrast is still generally considered one of voicing and not voicing, the use of other cues being generally governed by rules on the basis of context.

exception is the initial sound of *heat*. This sound is produced by starting the vowel without voicing, and then adding the voicing. Sometimes this is called a **voiceless vowel**, sometimes a **glottal** (using the vocal cords) **fricative**. We shall call it a glottal fricative because there is often some friction heard before the vowel starts.

There are three **nasalized consonants** in English: the [m] in *me*, the [n] in *no*, and the final sound of *walking* [ŋ]. Nasalized consonants are produced by letting air flow through the nasal cavity while pronouncing the sounds.

Table 8.2 summarizes the consonants on the basis of where constriction is produced, whether it is complete or partial, whether the sound is voiced or voiceless, and whether or not it is a nasal.

TABLE 8.2   Some Consonants of English

	Bilabial	Labiodental	Dental	Alveolar	Palatal	Velar	Glottal
Stops							
voiceless	p			t		k	
voiced	b			d		g	
Fricatives							
voiceless		f	θ	s	š		h
voiced		v	ð	z	ž		
Affricates							
voiceless				č			
voiced				ǰ			
Nasal							
All voiced	m		n			ŋ	

Liquids and Glides

Two additional groups of sounds, the **liquids** and the **glides**, fall between vowels and consonants and are sometimes classed with the former, sometimes with the latter. English has two liquids, [r] and [l]. Liquids are common in the languages of the world, but their pronunciation varies greatly from language to language and even within a particular language, depending on the context. The English [l], as in *lazy*, is most often pronounced with the tip of the tongue on the alveolar ridge but with air passing over the sides of the tongue. As there is neither complete closure nor any turbulence, [l] resembles a vowel. In [r] as in [l] it is the special shape of the tongue that gives it character. The tongue is raised toward the roof of the mouth, forming something like a cup shape. A related kind of [r] is heard in very rapid pronunciations of [t] and [d] in *butter* and *ladder*. Here the tongue flaps against the alveolar ridge. Some languages have trilled *r*s, in which the tongue flaps repeatedly against the roof of the mouth. The Spanish word *pero*, 'but,' has a single flap, whereas *perro*, 'dog,' has a trilled *r*. In some languages a trill is formed, not with the tongue, but with the uvula, which is the very back part of the velum.

The glides in English, [w] and [y], are characterized by movement of the articulatory organs. The glide [w], as in *wow*, is pronounced by starting in the position for [u], with the lips rounded and the tongue high and back. But, instead of producing [u], the vocal organs glide into the next sound of the word, the vowel [a]. After the [a] has been produced, the vocal organs glide back toward the position for [u]. The production of [y] is very similar, but it is the position for [i] from which, or to which, the vocal organs glide.

The Phoneme

Twenty consonants, two liquids, two glides, and twelve vowels in English have been listed. Let us look at one of them closely: [k]. This consonant occurs in the English words *key*, *ski*, and *caw*. How do we decide that [k] is a distinct consonant of English? There are two steps. First, we see that there are instances in which the presence of a [k], rather than of some other consonant, changes the meaning of a word (or, more accurately, morpheme). The words *key* and *tea* differ in just this way, and they demonstrate that [k] and [t] are different sounds. When we can find pairs of words that differ in just one sound and also in meaning, we can conclude that the sounds differ significantly. Such pairs of words are called **minimal pairs**. But there is another step necessary to identify the sounds of a language. The consonant [k] occurs in *ski* and *caw*, as well as in *key*; how do we know that these three *k*s are the same sound? The first answer that comes to mind is simply that they "sound alike." But this answer is not quite right; the different *k*s *are* different. A speaker of Arabic might object that the sounds in *key* and *caw* are quite distinct. In fact, [k] in *key* is pronounced with the tongue considerably further forward than it is in the pronunciation of the [k] in *caw*. In Arabic, there are minimal pairs that differ only in that one has the [k] of *key* and the other has the [k] of *caw*. Similarly, a speaker of Hindi might protest that *key* contains a different sound from the one in *ski*; and there *is* an important difference. If you hold your hand in front of your mouth when you pronounce the two words, you will feel a puff of air when you release the [k] of *key* but either no puff or a much weaker one when you pronounce the [k] of *ski*. The puff of air when a stop is released is called **aspiration**. It is often symbolized by a small raised h, as in [k^h]. In Hindi, there are minimal pairs in which the only difference is the presence or absence of aspiration.

"That's all very well," you might answer, "but Arabic and Hindi are not English. And in English the *ks* in *key*, *ski*, and *caw* are the same." And that is correct. Each language has its own way of deciding which sounds are the same and which are different. A class of sounds that are considered equivalent in one language is called a *phoneme* of that language. We have just seen that the three different sounds in *key*, *ski*, and *caw* are instances of the same phoneme in English. There are no pairs of words with different meanings that differ only in that one has the [k] of *key*, and one has the [k] of *ski*.

The relation between the pronunciation of a word and its meaning is arbitrary. It does not matter what the word that means 'a small device for opening locks' sounds like. But it does matter that the pronunciation of this word not be the same as the pronunciation of the word that means 'a beverage made from the leaves of a white-flowered plant grown in the Far East.' That is, *key* is different from *tea*, and that is all that matters. If the function of the sounds of a language is to distinguish different morphemes, the language needs only a small number of the unlimited number of possible sounds that a human being can make. English distinguishes only thirty-six different classes, or phonemes. Some languages have more; some have less. Each language selects certain aspects of sound as significant, treating others as irrelevant to meaning. To summarize, a phoneme is *a class of sounds treated as equivalent by a language.* Two sounds fall in different phonemes if there exists a minimal pair of morphemes that differ only in having the two sounds. They fall in the same phoneme if they do not contrast in this way. There are two basic ways in which sounds are combined into a phoneme. In the first, there are several sounds, but each is used in a specific context. We have seen that there are at least three [k]s: the unaspirated [k] in *ski*, the front aspirated [k] in *key*, and the back aspirated [k] in *caw*. These distinct "versions" of [k] are allophones of [k]. The first is always used after [s], the second before front vowels, and the third before back vowels. Because each allophone has its specific contexts, there can be no minimal pairs of words that differ only in having different versions of [k]. This type of combination of sounds into phonemes is called **complementary distribution.**

The other process of combination is **free variation.** As the term indicates, any of several possible versions of the phoneme can occur, with no change in meaning. This is actually just another way of saying that no two sounds are ever exactly identical. If you pronounce the word *key* ten times, there will be ten different positions of the tongue on the palate in pronouncing the [k] and ten different tongue positions for the vowel. These variations are simply ignored; the ten versions are in free variation. Both processes of combination can, and usually do, occur for a single phoneme.

Learning a language consists partly in changing your perception of speech sounds. Speakers of English can hear many very subtle differences between sounds (those that correspond to distinctions between phonemes) and at the same time cannot hear many other distinctions of the same physical magnitude (the distinctions between sounds within a single phonemic category). It is not clear yet whether this is due to sharpened perceptual ability at the boundaries of phonemes, diminished ability within categories, or some combination of the two.

Phonetic and Phonemic Transcriptions

It is important to distinguish between a **phonetic transcription** and a **phonemic transcription**. A phonetic transcription is simply as accurate a recording as possible of the exact pronunciation of an utterance. It is written with square brackets. For example, a phonetic transcription of *coat* might be [kʰ oʷ t], and a phonetic transcription of *skit* would be [skɪt]. The aspiration of [k] is indicated by the raised ʰ, and the rounding of [o] in *coat* is indicated by the raised ʷ. A phonemic transcription merely indicates the phoneme to which each sound belongs and is written with diagonal slashes. Phonemic transcriptions for coat and skit are /kot/ and /skɪt/. These phonemic transcriptions also indicate how the words are to be pronounced *if the general rules of English are known*: All initial voiceless stops are aspirated, and all back vowels except /a/ are sounded.

Phonetic and phonemic transcriptions serve very different purposes. A phonetic transcription can be read by a person totally ignorant of the language, assuming that he knows the principles of the transcription. Even if he does not know English, he will pronounce [tʰɛd] with approximately the same pronunciation with which a native speaker would pronounce *Ted*. The phonemic transcription /tɛd/, however, can be read only by someone familiar with the phonology of the language transcribed. Information about pronunciation that follows general rules, for example, the fact that initial stops are aspirated, is removed from a phonemic transcription. Only one symbol is needed for each phoneme. This distinction is important for the question of reading alphabets, which will be considered later in this chapter.

Producing, Perceiving, and Acoustics

The sounds of English have been described and classified in terms of their manner of production. A listener does not have any information about how the speaker has produced sounds. He receives only the acoustic signal through the air. The relation between the manner of sound production and the acoustic signal, as well as the relation between the acoustic signal and the sound perceived by the hearer, is complex and only partially understood. Sounds produced in similar ways often are quite distinct acoustically; conversely, sounds that are similar acoustically may be produced in distinct ways by the speaker. They comprise the subjects of the sciences of acoustic phonetics (Ladefoged 1962) and speech perception respectively. The acoustic signal is a continuous stream; it is not divided into distinct segments corresponding to phonemes or into words, even though we think we hear a sentence as a string of words. Listening to a speaker of a foreign language is often unsettling, just because his utterance appears to be a rapid, continuous stream. A division of the acoustic signal into segments corresponding to phonemes is impossible on purely acoustic grounds; within a syllable the acoustic signal is at every moment a function of *all* the phonemes of the syllable (Liberman 1970).

Prelinguistic Development

The development of language is customarily considered to begin with the appearance of the first words, near the end of the first year of life. Nevertheless, language does not emerge *in vacuo*. In a larger sense, the process of development begins at birth. When we think of the birth of an infant, our most characteristic image is of the birth cry. Within the first month or so other vocalizations than crying will begin to appear. Infants of a few weeks show a special sensitivity to the sound of the human voice; the voice is far more effective in arresting crying than are inanimate sounds, and it will be more effective in eliciting smiling and vocalizing in the following months (Wolff 1966). Recent research has demonstrated that even very young infants have remarkable perceptual and learning abilities; coupled with the ability to vocalize and with the special sensitivity to vocal sounds, they should lead to extensive learning about language in the first year. Nevertheless, the first year of life is the least understood period of language development, for both methodological and theoretical reasons.

Productive Abilities

Early vocalizations appear to develop through a sequence of four broad stages (Kaplan and Kaplan 1971). The transition between the stages may be abrupt or gradual, and the age at which each occurs varies greatly from child to child.

Stage 1: Crying   The first period begins with the birth cry and is characterized by cries and similar vocalizations. The cry usually has a rising and falling frequency contour and is part of a respiratory-inspiration-vocalization cycle that will be repeated about once a second. Many infants appear to have several variants of the basic cry, and parents may be able to infer a "meaning" for each cry, for example, hunger, pain, or boredom. However, at least one study (Muller, Hollien and Murry 1974) has revealed that, when tapes are played for parents removed from context (such as knowing how long it has been from the previous feeding), they are not able to identify the causes of the cries.

Stage 2: Other Vocalizations and Cooing At the end of the first month, vocalizations other than crying appear. They develop far greater variety than cries, partially through use of the articulatory organs (lips, tongue, and so on). By the end of the second month, a characteristic class of vocalizations often called "cooing" has emerged. Cooing sounds are generally similar acoustically to back vowels and are often rounded (that is, the lips are rounded). The term "cooing" undoubtedly arises from the frequent presence of the [u] sound. The relation between crying and cooing is not understood. The two are highly dissimilar acoustically, but some investigators have observed a transition from full crying through a kind of "fake crying," which temporarily precedes crying in the second month but then occurs independently to vocalizations that do not involve crying.

Stage 3: Babbling By the middle of the first year of life, though often earlier, vocalizations have become increasingly speechlike. Sounds like consonants become quite frequent, combinations of consonants and vowels appear, and later in this period intonation patterns similar to those of adults are heard.

Stage 4: Patterned Speech The last phase, beginning near the end of the first year of life, may more properly be regarded as the onset of "true" speech. The transition from stage 3 to stage 4 may be abrupt or gradual and may even include a period of complete silence from the child. The most striking characteristic of this transition is the *decrease* in variety of sounds produced by the child. The first words are constructed from a much smaller set of phonetic elements than were produced a few weeks earlier in babbling. Babbling may continue to occur after the onset of language, but the two activities are generally easy to distinguish.

A widely held position has been that, during the babbling stage, the infant produces an extremely wide range of sounds, including the sounds of the language he hears, sounds occurring only in other languages, and indeed sounds that do not occur in any known language. Therefore, arriving at the proper set of sounds for the language being learned is only a matter of narrowing down, of eliminating sounds. However, not all the sounds of English are babbled. Whereas non-English sounds may be produced, the range is not as wide as claimed. Thus, development of the full range of sounds requires the gradual addition, as well as elimination, of specific sounds (Irwin and Chen 1946; Oller, Wieman, Doyle and Ross, in press). It does appear, however, that the range of sounds produced at the beginning of stage 3 is similar for infants in different linguistic communities.

There is a great predominance of middle vowels, labial consonants (*b* and *m*), and back consonants (hard *g* and so on).[2]

Studies of individual children often reveal general patterns of development, for example, from back consonants to front ones, but few generalizations appear to hold across all children. One general observation concerns the structure of "syllables," that is, the units babbled. Generally vocalic (V) sounds are observed first, then consonant-vowel combinations (CV), then vowel-consonant-vowel (VCV) and vowel-consonant (VC) combinations, and, finally, reduplications (CVCV).

The babbling period is also characterized by suprasegmental variation, in pitch, stress, rhythm. From stage 2 on, utterances have characteristic intonation patterns, and from the beginning of stage 3 these intonation patterns come to resemble adult intonation patterns, both the standard rising-falling pattern of English declaratives and the level-rising pattern of English questions. Infants, during the babbling period, often mimic intonation patterns produced by adults. Just how distinct the development of segmental aspects (vowels and consonants) and suprasegmental aspects (stress, intonation, and rhythm) are is not known. It is possible that suprasegmentals are the first to convey meaning. A number of instances have been observed in which initial words are defined by their intonation patterns, rather than by segmental features. For example, one child used *ma'ma* (stress on first syllable) to call for his mother, *mama'* (stress on second syllable) for his father. Only later was the *m* corrected to *p* for the latter (Engel 1973).

Although intonation patterns may be used to define individual lexical items, they are apparently not used for sentence meaning at the one-word stage. That is, single words are not used consistently with two or more intonations to signal declaration, interrogation, or command until the period of two-word utterances (stage I) begins (Bloom 1973).

Receptive Abilities

Children often comprehend more than they produce. An extreme instance of this discrepancy is shown by children who, for various neuromuscular reasons, cannot produce speech at all yet who learn to understand language (and later to read and write) normally. Understanding the receptive abilities of infants is essential, for language learning must rest on the abilities of the infant to perceive and analyze the language about him.

Until recently it has been difficult to obtain reliable information on the receptive abilities of infants because of the general difficulty of experimentation with infants. Infants have very restricted response capabilities,

---

[2] These consonants may actually be unvoiced but unaspirated stops, as discussed in note 1 (Oller personal communication).

but this restriction often masks very considerable perceptual and cognitive abilities. As new and often ingenious techniques have been developed, they have greatly extended our impression of the infant's ability: for example, Bower's demonstration of depth perception and size constancy in the two-month-old (Bower 1966).

Very young infants have at least crude localization abilities for sound and will turn in the direction of a sound. Three-week-old infants become highly disturbed when they watch their mothers through a window if a speaker is used to displace the direction of the sound three feet to the left or right of the mother (Aronson & Rosenbloom 1971). Whether learned or innate, this localization ability is important for establishing eye contact between parent and child. By age three months, infants show a differential response to the mother's voice, compared to that of another adult female (Turnure 1971).

A number of observers have suggested that infants are first responsive to suprasegmental aspects of speech. During the babbling period, infants have been observed making the same responses to utterances that differ greatly in segmental content but have identical intonation patterns.

Recently, several experimental techniques have been devised to assess more precisely the perceptual abilities of infants. The most successful one uses the ability of infants to suck on a pacifier to control various aspects of their environment: to keep a light on, a movie in focus, or a mobile rotating (Bruner & Bruner 1968). The infant sucks to keep a tape recording playing. The tape consists of a repeated sequence of a syllable, for example, *pa, pa, pa* . . . Eventually the sucking rate will decrease as the infant becomes habituated to the sound. At this point the recording is switched to another syllable, like *ba, ba, ba* . . . (carefully recorded to be identical with the first syllable in loudness, duration, and fundamental frequency). Infants as young as six weeks old often respond to this shift with an increase in sucking; this increase may be interpreted as evidence that the infant has discriminated the two syllables, and hence can discriminate two consonants that differ only in voicing, and also that they are interested in the shift enough to resume sucking! (Eimas *et al.* 1971). Similarly, *ba* and *ga*, a contrast in place of articulation (Morse 1972); *va* and *sa*, a contrast in both voicing and placement of articulation (Eilers & Minifie 1975); and *a* and *i*, a vowel contrast in tongue height and placement, are discriminated by young infants (Trehub 1973). However, *sa* and *za*, in principle a contrast in voicing like *pa* and *ba*, are not discriminated, at least in this paradigm (Eilers & Minifie 1975).

Limited work has been done on the perception of suprasegmentals: stress, intonation, and rhythm. Infants discriminated *ba* with a rising intonation from *ba* with a falling intonation, all changes occurring only in the last .15 seconds of a .50-second syllable (Morse 1972). Infants also discriminate *ba'ba* (stress on first syllable) from *baba'* (Spring 1975).

Experiments with nonspeech sounds generally reveal that discrimination abilities are far superior with speech contrasts than with nonspeech contrasts of the same acoustic magnitude, suggesting that the human auditory system is especially sensitive to speech and speech-like sounds.

It is important to realize that discrimination, as assessed in these experiments, is not the same thing as recognition or comprehension. The ability to discriminate a contrast like *pa/ba* is necessary for attributing meaning to the contrast, but it is not sufficient. Much less is known about the ability of prelinguistic infants to attribute meaning to utterances. There is much anecdotal evidence for the recognition of meaning by infants during the second half of the first year of life, and this evidence often appears to rest on intonation. Controlled experimentation becomes possible only toward the end of the first year, leaving an unexplored period between ages four months (after which the sucking method is no longer useful) and one year. The basic technique used is to teach the child names for blocks of varying appearance. The names vary with respect to specific linguistic features. Then the subject is asked to give the experimenter a specific block, identified only by name. Obviously the task makes many demands in addition to the specifically linguistic ones, and it probably underestimates the infant's abilities. A study of Russian children revealed that the first contrasts that were reliably used to distinguish meaning were vowel contrasts (*a* versus *i*). This was followed by distinction on the basis of presence or absence of a consonant (*bok* versus *ok*), which was in turn followed by distinction between stop and continuant consonants (*mak* versus *bak*). A regular sequence of distinctions followed these early distinctions, but they belong more properly in the linguistic period, in the second year of life (Shvachkin: 1973). A replication with English-speaking children (Garnica 1973) revealed more variability than in the Russian study. Systematic investigation of the role of suprasegmentals in such learning has not been carried out.

Very little is known of the abilities of infants to understand specific words during the prelinguistic phase, though informal evidence suggests that such understanding does occur. Greenfield (n.d.) investigated a child's understanding of *dada* and *mama* by asking questions like *Where is dada?* with varying combinations of individuals present. By age nine months, the child generally responded by looking at the father if he was present. If the father was not present, either the mother or the child's sitter was the target. The defining feature of *dada* seems to be 'caretaker.' A few weeks later, the child began to respond to *mama* by looking at the mother. If the mother was not present, the child looked at the (female) sitter. The features 'male' and 'female' had been added. If techniques that do not require complex motor responses can be devised, it is likely that we shall find that the infant has a sophisticated semantic system long before the first words are produced.

Role of the Environment

Eventually the child speaks the language of the community about him. How the child manages this, that is, how the environment has this effect, is the great puzzle. We shall consider in turn the linguistic environment of the infant and the behavioral environment.

The babbling of infants from different linguistic communities cannot in general be distinguished (Atkinson, McWhinney, and Stoel 1970). This finding is not surprising, for the early meaningful utterances of children from distinct linguistic communities are almost indistinguishable in phonological makeup. The processes of babbling, like phonological development, are universal and somewhat independent of the immediate linguistic environment.

It is possible to increase the frequency with which three-month-olds vocalize by means of social reinforcement: smiling, rubbing the baby's stomach, and so on (Haugen and McIntire 1972). This fact has been emphasized by theorists who claim that the way others respond to the infant's vocalizations has a controlling effect on development. However, this research has established only that it is possible to increase or decrease the frequency with which a given type of already-present vocalization (all sounds, vowels, consonants) occurs, not that new sounds can be introduced.

People in the infant's environment provide models for imitation, but imitation does not seem to account for many prelinguistic developments. The sequence of sounds acquired during babbling bears little relation to the frequency of sounds in parental speech. In this development, as in syntactic and semantic development, the child *selects* the aspects of speech and language to be learned according to some, often not understood, strategy.

Prelinguistic Abilities and Language Development

Two contrasting views of the relation between prelinguistic abilities and language acquisition proper have been proposed. The first is the *selective-reinforcement*, or learning-theory, hypothesis. When the infant produces a sound that occurs in the language he is learning, he is reinforced, either by an external agent or by secondary reinforcement from the similarity of *his* productions to those that he has heard during feeding and other comforting situations. When he produces a sound that does not occur in the language, he is not reinforced; eventually such sounds simply disappear. Such a theory emphasizes the continuity of prelinguistic and linguistic development. The findings cited earlier are not consistent with this view. The range of sounds produced at the beginning of the babbling period is not nearly as wide as this theory assumes; not all the sounds of the language are produced and hence available for reinforcement. In addition, mothers in a natural setting do not reinforce sounds that approximate those of adult speech more than sounds that do not (Wahler 1969). The first words use only a small subset of the sounds that were babbled. When babbling continues after the onset of language, the contrast between the two is readily apparent: A wide range of sounds appear in babbling but only a restricted set in the first words. Jespersen characterized the contrast as the difference between "play" and "plan"; that is, the difference between playful non-goal-directed production and the intentional production of specific sounds:

> It is strange that among an infant's sounds one can often detect sounds— for instance k, g, h, and uvular r—which the child will find difficulty in producing afterwards when they occur in real words. . . . The explanation lies probably in the difference between doing a thing in play or without a plan—when it is immaterial which movement (sound) is made—and doing the same thing in fixed intention when this sound, and this sound only, is required. . . . (1925:106)

In contrast, linguists have tended to emphasize the discontinuity between early vocalizations and speech. Jakobson (1968) in particular has emphasized the restriction in range of sounds that accompanies the transition from babbling to speech. The evidence cited earlier is clearly more consistent with such discontinuity. However, Jakobson's theory is probably an oversimplification. Babbled syllables resemble the first meaningful words that the child will later produce in several respects: They generally begin with stops, rather than fricatives, and end either with vowels or unvoiced stops; glides are more common than liquids, front consonants more common than back consonants; consonant clusters are virtually absent (Oller *et al.*, in press). Thus babbling is subject to the same constraints as the child's first words; both are, to an extent, independent of the particular language heard. Oller and his colleagues conclude that "The child's phonetic production preferences antedate his meaningful speech, as evidenced by the babbling data. It would therefore seem reasonable to assume that phonological processes arc the *output* of an innate phonological acquisition device which reflects the child's production preferences."

Phonological Development

Not the least of the factors that often make child-adult communication difficult is the difference between the child's pronunciation of words and that of adults. The first words are constructed from a very restricted set of sounds. Particularly common are forms such as *mama, papa, dada,* and *didi.* Over the next two years, sounds are added in a gradual, step-by-step fashion.

Two approaches can be taken to understand the child's phonological development. One is to focus on the set of sounds used and on the gradual development of this set. The second approach is to consider the relations between the child's production and the word that he is trying to produce.

Determination of the phonemic inventory of the child is not easy. Ordinarily, the phonemes of a language are determined by establishing minimal pairs—pairs of words that differ in just one sound. For example, *pin* and *din* differ only in their initial consonant, establishing at least two consonants in English. The word *bin* establishes a third and so on. A procedure of this type is all but impossible with young children. Imagine asking an eighteen-month-old *Are these the same, pin and bin?* Instead, we can only record whatever the child says and try to guess which utterances have distinct meanings. Even the Shvachkin-Garnica technique, discussed earlier, is not appropriate because it assesses the limits of the child's speech discrimination, and not his phonemic groupings. Allophones of a single phoneme can often be discriminated even though they are treated as equivalent by the phonemic system of an adult or child speaker. The problems are multiplied by the fact that children are more variable in their pronunciation than adults. Because it is necessary to catch sounds "on the fly" and relate them to their presumed meanings, most of the relatively few studies of phonemic development that have been done have been studies by linguists of their own children (Burling 1959; Leopold 1953; Moskowitz 1970; Velten 1943). More recently, attempts have been made to gather information about larger numbers of children in order to establish general principles (Menyuk 1968; Warren 1975).

The most fundamental question about phonological development must be Is the sound system of a child's speech during development actually a structured, phonemic system? If so, then we can consider how the system develops.

The question can be answered affirmatively, with some caution because of the difficulties of studying phonemic development. Velten's daughter Joan, for example, near her second birthday had the following phonemes: /p/, /t/, /w/, /f/, /s/, /a/, /m/, /n/, and /u/ (1943). This does not mean that these sounds were the only sounds that she produced. She produced [b], as well as [p], for example. In fact, [b] occurred at the beginning and in the middle of words whereas [p] occurred in the final position. Because [p] and [b] were never contrasted, they were considered to belong to a single phoneme. The decision to call the phoneme /p/ or /b/ was arbitrary. And there was variation within the other phonemic categories as well. Words like *black*, *pat*, *spot*, *block*, *bite*, and *pocket* were pronounced /pat/ (with an initial b phonetically). There was also a great deal of free variation in the /a/ phoneme, so that words might sound like [bæt], [bayt], and [bat]. *New, knee, nail, no,* and *near* were all pronounced [nu].

An explicit theory of the order of phonemic acquisition was formulated by Jakobson in his historic 1941 book *Child Language, Aphasia and Phonological Universals* (first published in English as Jakobson 1968; summarized in Jakobson & Halle 1956: ch. 4). Jakobson proposed several principles governing the order of acquisitions, but the most striking concerns universals. The first three contrasts developed are generally oral-nasal (/b/ versus /m/), labial-dental (/p/ versus /t/), and stop-fricative (/p/ versus /f/). These contrasts are universal, that is, present in all (or nearly all) languages. Jakobson postulates that universal contrasts are acquired first. After this, development is described by the laws of "irreversible solidarity." There are consistent asymmetries in the phonemic systems of the languages of the world. For example, no language has back consonants without having front consonants; however, some languages have front consonants without having back consonants. Back consonants presuppose front consonants, in other words. Therefore, front consonants should precede back consonants in development. And, indeed, /p/ and /m/ appear before /k/ or /g/ in child speech. Furthermore, phonemes that are rare among the languages of the world, such as the /æ/ phoneme of English, are among the last to be acquired.

It is frequency in the languages of the world, more than how frequent the phoneme is in the particular language the child hears, that is important. The /æ/ phoneme is fairly common in English; it occurs in such common words as *bat, glad, sad,* and *at*. The fact that it is acquired by the child late demonstrates that mere frequency of exposure is not the variable that governs acquisition. Instead, there is an underlying connection between acquisition by children and cross-linguistic generalizations. Jakobson linked linguistic universals with language acquisition by means of the bold claim that the innate character of the latter explained the former, a claim that later was extended (by N. Chomsky, McNeill, and others) to syntax, as well as to phonology. On the basis of these considerations—universality of contrasts, the laws of irreversible solidarity, and frequency in the languages of the world—Jakobson established a universal ordering for the successive differentiation of distinctive features. This ordering is shown in Figure 8.2. No contrast can be acquired before every contrast on the branch leading to it has been acquired. Of course, the child learns only the contrasts present in the language about him.

Jakobson's theory is remarkable for its range and its daring. In fact, we do not have nearly enough evidence to draw any such firm conclusions. His order is clearly too rigid. Velten's study was the first to be conducted under the influence of the theory, and he found that the first three contrasts were not oral-nasal, labial-dental, and continuant-stop, as Jakobson had claimed, but, rather, labial-dental, continuant-stop, and oral-nasal. Nevertheless, it is remarkable that it is precisely these three features that emerged first. Ervin-Tripp has summarized the little evidence that is available:

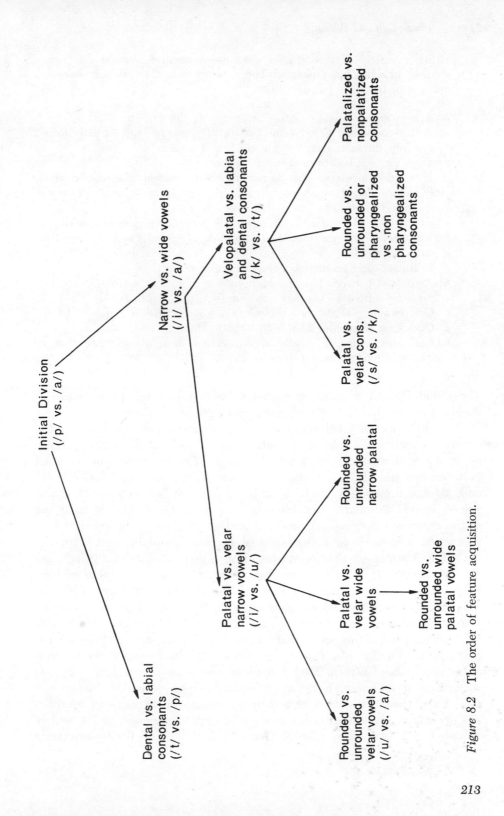

Figure 8.2 The order of feature acquisition.

Using a variety of case studies showing contrastive systems [phonemic studies] including some bilinguals before bifurcation of the systems—we can make some tentative generalizations:

a. The vowel-consonant contrasts are probably the earliest.
b. A stop-continuant (/p/ versus /m/ or /f/ contrast is quite early for all children, the continuant being a fricative or a nasal.
c. Stops precede fricatives in initial position.
d. If two consonants are alike in manner of articulation, one will be labial, the other dental or alveolar (e.g., /p/ versus /t/), resulting in the common lack of /k/.
e. Contrasts in place of articulation usually precede voicing contrasts.
f. Affricates (č, j) and liquids (l, English r) usually appear later than stops and nasals.
g. In Russian and French /l/ precedes a vibrant /r/.
h. A contrast between low and high vowels (e.g., /a/ versus /i/ or /y/) precedes a front versus back contrast (e.g., /i/ versus /u/).
i. Oral vowels precede nasal vowels, the contrast being acquired late.
j. Consonant clusters or blends are usually late.
k. Consonant contrasts usually appear earlier in initial position than in medial or final position. (1966:68–69)

These findings are, in general, consistent with Jakobson's predictions, although they can hardly serve to prove or disprove his theory.

An aspect of Jakobson's theory that is clearly not borne out by the evidence concerns the role of particular types of contrasts. Certain contrasts recur many times in a particular language. For example, the contrast between /p/ and /b/ is essentially the same as the contrasts between /t/ and /d/ and between /s/ and /z/. It is the contrast between voiceless and voiced sounds.[3] Similarly, the difference between /t/ and /s/ is the same as the difference between /d/ and /z/ and so on. This is the contrast that distinguishes stops from phonemes that do not completely interrupt the flow of air, the stop-continuant contrast. The nasal-oral contrast distinguishes /m/ from /b/, /t/ from /n/, and /ŋ/ from /g/. A small number of contrasts, or distinctive features, identifies all the phonemes of English. Figure 8.3 partially illustrates how the phonemes fit into a structure of distinctive features. Jakobson claimed that in every language the phonemes can be efficiently described in this way—that is, that these contrasts are universal and that the total number of distinctive features in the languages of the world is quite small, about fifteen. Each language draws some contrasts from this stock; English uses about a dozen. The description of particular phonemes as sets of such features—as prescribed by the theory of distinctive features—has important advantages in the study of (adult) languages and is widely accepted for this purpose. (See N. Chomsky & Halle 1968 for a particularly

---

[3] But see note 1.

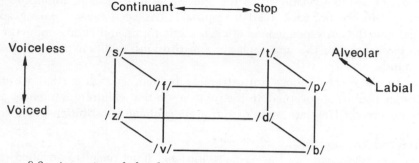

Figure 8.3 A portion of the distinctive feature structure of English consonant phonemes.

sophisticated account of the features.) Jakobson claimed in addition that children learn the phonemes of their language through a process of acquiring one contrast at a time, each contrast being added to the system in a unified, complete fashion. In some instances, this successive splitting actually does happen. For example, Burling (1959) found that his son acquired the voiced/voiceless contrast and almost immediately expanded his set of stops from three (/p/, /t/, /k/) to six (/p/, /b/, /t/, /d/, /k/, /g/). But this is more the exception than the rule. The presence of a contrast in a single pair of phonemes does not guarantee that the contrast will be used elsewhere. A single example from a child studied by Moskowitz (1970) illustrates this phenomenon. At the point in development observed, Mackie had mastered the voiced/voiceless contrast in the phoneme pairs /p/-/b/ and /t/-/d/. He had also mastered the stop-fricative contrast in the phoneme pairs /p/-/f/ and /t/-/s/. In addition, the labial-dental contrast had been mastered in the pairs /p/-/t/ and /b/-/d/. These three are sufficient to specify the six basic fricatives of English: /f/, /v/, /s/, /z/, /θ/, and /ð/. Yet Mackie had mastered only two fricatives: /f/ and /s/. Moskowitz summarizes the evidence:

> The situation suggests that *the learning of distinctive features per se is not a primary goal of Mackie's linguistic practice at this time*. Once learned, then, a feature does not necessarily spread rapidly throughout the system to all relevant segments. (1970:431)

Jakobson's theory is an impressive attempt to account for the emergence of the sounds and contrasts of language. There is still a great deal that it does not even attempt to explain. Suppose the child is trying to say *cake* and he does not yet produce the *k* sound in meaningful speech (though of course he may have produced it earlier during babbling). What sound does he use from his restricted inventory? In fact, *t* is overwhelmingly likely to be used: [teyt]. Jakobson's theory tends to treat the child's language in a vacuum, without relating it to the speech he hears and is attempting to produce. In recent years, another approach has been taken: looking specifically at the correspondence between adult forms and child productions. The basic data for this approach are **substitutions,** additions and deletions of sounds.

These substitutions are extremely regular, enough so that we can consider them rule-governed, in the same sense that children's sentences are rule-governed.[4] Here are some of the most common substitution processes:

1. Processes of substitution
   a. Final devoicing — Final consonants, if not completely omitted (see
      bag → [bæk] 3), are generally unvoiced.
   b. Initial stopping — Initial fricatives are changed to corresponding
      sandwich → [tæwɪš] stops.
   c. Gliding — Substitution of glides /w/ and /y/ for liquids
      rabbit → [wæbɪt] /l/ and /r/.
   d. Fronting key → [ti] — Substitution of front consonants for back ones.
      thick → [fɪk]
2. Processes of cluster reduction
   a. Deletion — Typically, when a stop is combined with a frica-
      stop → [tɔp] tive or a liquid, only the stop is produced.
      play → [pey]
   b. Epenthesis — Less frequent than a; both consonants may be
      blue → [bəlú] produced but with a vowel added between
      them.
3. Processes of final-consonant avoidance
   a. Deletion — Self-explanatory.
      cat → [kʰæ]
   b. Epenthesis — Less frequent than a; the consonant may be re-
      pig → [pʰigə] tained but a vowel added after it.
4. Processes of assimilation
   a. Assimilation — Some sounds are modified to make them more
      lamb → [næm] similar to other sounds. In the example, /l/ be-
      comes nasal, like /m/, but is still produced at
      the same point in the mouth as /l/; hence /n/.
      It is more common for early sounds to be
      assimilated to later ones, but the reverse fre-
      quently occurs.
   b. Reduplication — Assimilation is carried to the limit, an entire
      bottle → [baba] syllable being assimilated to another.

Processes 2a and 2b have the same effect: avoiding consonant clusters. Similarly, 3a and 3b have the same effect: ensuring that syllables are of the form consonant-vowel. Thus, these substitution processes might be stated as expressing a "preference" of the child: a preference for single con-

---

[4] The following discussion has been greatly aided by materials prepared by D. K. Oller.

sonants in CV syllables. The other processes may also be viewed as means for expressing preferences. For example, 1b and 2b reflect a preference for front stops in initial position. Translating these processes into preferences may provide more than just a more compact description. The phenomena listed here occur in children acquiring a variety of languages, not just English. Furthermore, they parallel the distribution of sounds produced in babbling, which also appears to be largely independent of the language heard by the child. All of the generalizations listed have been found by Oller and his colleagues to hold for babbling as well. Thus, it appears that babbling and the early forms of meaningful words reflect similar preferences, which are universal. For example, singleton consonants are more common than consonant clusters, and front consonants are more common than back consonants. These preferences may also underlie some aspects of the ordering proposed by Jakobson for phonemic acquisition, discussed earlier.

A particular child's substitutions are often so regular that we begin to think that she must "know" the correct pronunciation in order to guide her substitutions. Why the substitutions, then? Two obvious candidates are perceptual factors and articulatory difficulties. Undoubtedly both play a role, but they do not seem to account fully for the phenomena observed.

Consider perceptual problems first. Some discriminations are more difficult than others. Even adults have trouble discriminating *fish* from *thish* without visual cues from watching the speaker's mouth. Perhaps one sound is substituted for another because the two cannot be distinguished by the child. If sound A cannot be discriminated from sound B, the two should be used randomly; that is, substitutions will be two-directional. But, in general, substitutions are one-directional: /w/ is substituted for /r/ and never /r/ for /w/. The singleness of the direction of substitutions might be explained by a combination of failure to discriminate with some articulatory bias in favor of the substituted sound. The articulatory bias would, however, explain the substitution by itself; so the question remains whether a perceptual difficulty exists or not. Several kinds of evidence suggest that in a number of instances perception is not the problem. Children often respond negatively to adults' attempts to imitate their productions: ". . . a child asked if he could come along on a trip to the "mewwy-go-wound." An older child, teasing him, said "David wants to go to the mewwy-go-wound." "No, said David firmly, "you don't say it wight" (Maccoby and Bee 1965:67).

It is possible, of course, that the /w/ the child uses for /r/ is different from the /w/ he uses for /w/. Something like this is suggested by the following interchange:

THERAPIST: Johnny, I'm going to say a word two times and you tell me which time I say it right and which time I say it wrong:

/ræbɪt/, /wæbɪt/

CHILD: [wæbɪt] is [wayt] and [wæbɪt] is [waŋ]

Detailed phonetic studies, augmented by instrumental analysis, may confirm or disconfirm this hypothesis. If the differences indeed exist, it would be possible to determine whether or not the child can in fact discriminate, for example, the two /w/s. But, in any case, the problem does not seem to be a perceptual one. The child would have to be able to discriminate adult /r/ from /w/ in order to know which /w/ to use.

A few studies of the phonemic-discrimination abilities of children in the early phases of phonological development have been conducted. Edwards (1974) used the method developed by Shvachkin and modified by Garnica, discussed earlier in this chapter, for assessing the perception of fricatives and glides by children between 1;8 and 3;11. Like Garnica, Edwards found evidence for considerable variability in the sequence of perceptual development. Her results show that perception precedes production, often by a considerable interval, during which sounds are not produced, even though they are accurately discriminated. Furthermore, the order of development in perception is not identical with the order in production. For example, /l/-/r/ is discriminated before /w/-/y/, but the order is reversed in production.

To the extent that perceptual factors do not fully account for patterns of substitution, we may infer that in some sense the child does "know" the correct pronunciation of many words, even though he cannot produce them. This claim is supported by the fact that the child must be understanding the words he hears in their adult forms; else he would not be trying to produce them. There is another kind of evidence that suggests that, in many instances, children know the correct adult forms. When a new phoneme is acquired, it is often (though not always) generalized to other words when appropriate but not to words in which it is not appropriate. For example, when /k/ is mastered, it may be applied to many words formerly pronounced with /t/; [teyt] changes to [keyk] and so on. The child does not have to hear all the words with /k/ again, yet words that were correctly pronounced with /t/ retain the /t/.

An alternative explanation for the child's form of words is articulation, the production of the sound. Sounds like the /č/ of *church* and the /ǰ/ of *judge* must be more difficult to produce than simple stops or fricatives. Though articulatory difficulty must account for some substitutions, there are clearly many instances in which this is not the problem. Despite the broad similarities of babbling and early speech, many sounds that were produced in the former stage are not produced in the latter. Even if it is granted that babbling and speech are different processes, there is evidence within speech that the problem is not purely a motor problem. A child may pronounce *shop* as [sɔp], suggesting that he cannot produce the /š/ phoneme, but the same child may pronounce *chair* as [šɛr], clearly producing the /š/. There is a kind of simplification going on in both examples, but it is not a matter of either being able or not being able to articulate a sound.

The difficulty of producing a sound is not an absolute quantity. The production of speech requires a constant and rapid movement of the articulatory organs from one position to another. The difficulty of producing a sound depends on its immediate phonetic context. We need to know more about the emergence of sounds in relation to specific contexts; whether or not and how sounds appear first in one context and then in others. It seems likely that sounds are not produced for certain words in certain contexts yet are produced in similar contexts for other words. The problem remains.

Perhaps the clearest evidence that not all substitution processes are the results of perceptual and articulatory factors (though surely many are) comes from instances in which a child who regularly substitutes one sound for another in her spontaneous speech is able, when asked, to imitate successfully words containing both sounds. Both the perceptual ability and the articulatory ability are present (Eilers and Oller 1975).

It seems to me that in these instances the substitutions should be thought of as *linguistic* simplifications, not as perceptual or motor simplifications. The child is working with a linguistic system that reduces the number of contrasts to be attended to and simplifies programming for the articulatory organs (Oller 1974). This simplification reduces the load on the child's long-term memory for linguistic structure. To put it another way, we can think of children as having certain preferences with respect to the ways in which syllables and words are constructed. They are aware of elements and words that are different from these preferences, but in the production of their own words the adult forms are "bent" in the direction of their own systems, in a fashion similar to the way in which children's imitations of sentences are syntactically modified to fit their own grammars.

Underlying Representations

In the preceding discussion of phonology, we have assumed that a morpheme can be adequately represented as a sequence of phonemes. For example, *cat* consists of the three phonemes /kæt/, *glasses* of the six phonemes /glæsəz/, and *critic* of the six phonemes /krɪtɪk/. Recent work in phonology (Schane 1973) has demonstrated the limitations of this approach.

In the description of syntactic structure we saw that a description of the surface structure of a sentence does not capture all the important aspects of it and that a distinction has to be drawn between deep and surface structure. Similarly, the actual pronunciation of a morpheme is only a partial description, and a distinction must be drawn between the **underlying representation** and the **phonetic representation** of the morpheme. Deep structure and surface structure are related by transformations; underlying representations and phonetic representation are related by **phonological rules:**

Underlying	Phonological rules	Phonetic
representations	$\longrightarrow$	representations

The reasons for the adoption of such a theory in linguistics are similar to those that led to the postulation of deep and surface structure: primarily, that broader and deeper generalizations can be made. Only one kind of evidence will be considered here (Langacker 1973: ch. 6). Morphemes vary in pronunciation, depending on the linguistic context. Consider the plurals of three common nouns: *cats* [kæts], *dogs* [dogz], *glasses* [glæsəz]. The plural morpheme has three different pronunciations; that is, three different phonetic representations. It is not difficult to state the conditions in which each form is used. After any of the consonants [s z š ž č ĵ] the proper form is [əz], after any consonants [p t k] it is [s], and in all remaining contexts is [z].

This description is correct as far as it goes. But it misses the point that this variation is not an isolated variation. Support we assume that the underlying representation of the plural morpheme is always /z/. If we add it to /dog/ we get [dogz], to /bra/ [braz], producing the correct phonetic representations. Now for *glasses*. If we add /z/ to /glæs/ we get [glæsz]. This is not the phonetic representation. A schwa must be inserted between the [s] and [z]: [glæsəz]. This is done according to a phonological rule that inserts a schwa whenever the final consonant of the root is similar to the ending in location of articulation and type of consonant. The sounds [s z š ž č ĵ] are all produced at approximately the same location as the [z] of the plural morpheme, and, like the [z], they are fricatives or affricates containing fricatives.

This rule is not entirely *ad hoc*. The past tense in English, too, has three regular forms: *helped* [hɛlpt], *hugged* [hʌgd], *rotted* [ratəd]. We can assume that the underlying representation of the past-tense morpheme is always /d/, which accounts for *hugged*. In *rotted*, a schwa is added. As in the plural, a schwa is added whenever the ending consists of a single consonant (in particular, /d/) that is produced at the same location and in the same manner as the final consonant of the root. The location is different from that of the plural, and the rule is being applied to stops, rather than to fricatives and affricates, but the principle is the same. The rule stated covers the past tense, as well as the plural.

The remaining form of the plural is /s/, as in *cats*. The underlying /z/ is changed into [s]. This is the result of a phonological rule that states that, if there are two obstruants (stops or fricatives̄) in a cluster, *all* components of the cluster must be either voiced or voiceless. The first consonant in the cluster determines which it will be. Because the final /t/ in *cat* is voiceless, the voiced /z/ must be changed to voiceless [s]. This rule also explains the [t] in the past-tense form *helped*. The /p/ is voiceless, and the rule changes /d/ to [t].

The three plural endings, then, all derive from a simple underlying representation; the variation among them is completely regular and may be explained with just two rules. Both of the rules play an important role in many other parts of the description of the phonology of English. As we have seen, they account for the variation in phonetic representation of the past-tense morpheme. As another instance, consider the variation in the third-person singular morpheme: *pats* [pæts], *stabs* [stæbz], *teaches* [tiyčəz]. Assuming an underlying /z/ for this morpheme, we find that the two rules account for the variation.

Variation in phonetic form occurs in roots of words, as well as in suffixes. The root *critic* occurs in the words *critical* and *criticize*. The final /c/ of the root is pronounced [k] in *critical*, [s] in *criticize*. This alternation is not unique to this pair; it occurs in *medical-medicine, romantic-romanticize*, and in other pairs. In each instance, the variation is irrelevant to the meaning of the root morpheme, and it is simplest to assume that the underlying representation has a /k/ and that a phonological rule changes the /k/ to [s] in certain specified contexts.

Vowels in morphemes also vary in their phonetic representation. It is extremely common in English for unstressed vowels to be **reduced,** that is, changed to a schwa when they are unstressed. Consider the vowels in the morpheme *telegraph* and some of its related forms: *telegraph* [téləgræf], *telegraphic* [téləgræflk], *telegraphy* [təlégrəfiy]. In the first two forms, the second vowel is reduced; in the third, the first and third are reduced. This variation is completely predictable on the basis of the stress pattern of these words. They are introduced by the phonological rules; the underlying representation of the morpheme is simply /tɛlɛgræf/. Notice that this representation is *never* the phonetic representation. Some phonological rule or rules always applies to reduce one or more vowels.

Hardly anything is known about the development of such dual-level phonological competence. Phonological rules are generalizations across morphological systems. According to the analysis presented earlier, the plural [s] and the past tense [t] are common instances of a devoicing rule, and the plural [əz] and the past tense [əd] are common instances of a rule that inserts a schwa. Baird (personal communication) has found that forms that are related in this way, such as [s] and [t], are not acquired simultaneously in development. It seems likely that individual inflectional processes are learned first and more general phonological rules later. Anisfeld (1969) found that adults could generalize abstract phonological rules to nonsense words.

A particularly interesting source of evidence on the development of phonological knowledge comes from studies of invented spellings by preschoolers (Read 1971). Some preschool children invent their own systems, relatively uninfluenced by the standard system. Their spellings are highly consistent and sensitive to quite subtle aspects of English phonology. An especially intriguing finding concerns the expression of the past tense. At age three or four years phonetic spellings are most common: MARED for *married*, LAFFT for *left*, HALPT for *helped*. Around the age of five or six years a change occurs: WALKD for *walked*, HAPPIND for *happened*, STARTID for *started*. Spelling becomes relatively consistent for this morpheme, as if the children had formulated a generalization—a common underlying representation—for the various forms of the past tense. The new spelling is also closer to the conventional spelling, but Read feels that explicit teaching is not a major factor here:

> It would be incorrect, I think, to attribute all of this development to adult teaching. The girl who wrote the last class of examples attended a Montessori school . . . where the practice was to accept all of the children's writing with a minimum of correction. Her mother . . . followed much the same practice at home . . . In fact, almost all of these children got correction from their parents only when they asked; that seems to have been a necessary condition for the spontaneous spelling to occur at all. Of course the child has used information from adults—but this information apparently has been "filtered" through the child's own notions, which exert a powerful influence on what he writes. (Read 1970:27)

It is very likely that preschoolers (and perhaps the older children as well) have not yet mastered the dual-level system fully and that representations of lexical items are close to phonetic representations for a considerable period. In a few special cases, such as the children studied by Read, we can observe something of the transition occurring, but for the most part it takes place internally and unnoticed. In terms of both increasing vocabulary and increasing sensitivity to words and their relationships, the learning of reading must have wide-ranging effects on phonological development.

Underlying Representations and Spelling

The writing system, or **orthography,** of English is generally classified as phonemic (or alphabetic). In a fully phonemic orthography, each phoneme of the spoken language is represented by a characteristic letter. (In other systems, a single character may represent a syllable of the spoken language, as in the Japanese Kana system, or a word, as in the ideographic system of Chinese). A purely phonetic orthography would be highly undesirable, because it would indicate many nonmeaningful details, such as the puff of air after the initial /t/ of *tap*, and the lack of this puff after the /t/ of *stop*. Of course, English orthography is far from being a purely phonemic system, and its deviations from pure "alphabetism" have been much maligned. The discrepancies, however, have many advantages.

If you will look over the examples in the last section, you will see that in most instances the phonetic variations introduced by the phonological rules are ignored in the conventional orthography. Each morpheme is spelled in a uniform fashion, even though it may be pronounced in several ways, that is, have several phonetic representations. The root *critic* is always spelled with a final *c*, *telegraph* is always spelled with two *e*'s and an *a*, and the plural morpheme (aside from irregular forms like *oxen*) is spelled *s* or *es* (an improvement over three forms).

Chomsky and Halle (1968) argue for the postulation of underlying representations that are often quite different from phonetic representations and that, in fact, generally resemble the conventional spellings of the morphemes. Other linguists have argued that a sweeping generalization of this type goes too far, that many features of English orthography are the residue of historical change in English (as writing systems typically reflect the pronunciation of earlier stages in the development of a language), rather than aspects of phonology that are valid for the present-day speaker of English. Nevertheless, there is agreement that many aspects of English orthography, like those discussed here, reflect the tendency of the writing system to express morphemes, and hence meaning, directly. To the extent that this is so, how can a reader correctly pronounce what is printed? The orthography does not directly indicate the pronunciation, as would a purely phonemic system. But in those instances in which the orthography does indicate the underlying representations, it does determine pronunciation, because the reader can bring to bear what he knows of the phonology of English, in particular the phonological rules. This procedure is efficient because the variation in pronunciation is generally predictable according to the phonological rules.

One very important advantage of a writing system of this type concerns dialect differences. It appears that many dialect differences arise from changes in phonological rules, rather than from differences in underlying representations. Because the conventional orthography reflects underlying representations and ignores phonetic variation, it can serve for both British and American English and for the range of English dialects throughout either country.

Reading and Learning to Read

Reading and learning to read are complex activities, drawing on perceptual, cognitive, linguistic, educational, and social processes. In this section we shall consider only the contribution of linguistics and the study of child language to an understanding of reading, particularly the question of spelling. We shall not consider directly what Jeanne Chall (1967) called "the great debate," the controversy over the relative merits of phonic, look-and-say, and other pedagogical methods for teaching reading. Smith (1973) has provided a review of current psycholinguistic approaches to reading.

The first important contribution of linguistics to reading was the concept of phonemes as the smallest distinctive units of sound. Just as the speaker of a language learns to make the relevant distinctions among phonemes, he learns to distinguish among the printed symbols of the alphabet; the core of the learning process is the establishment of associations between symbols and phonemes. Leonard Bloomfield (1933), one of the originators of the concept of the phoneme, was among the first to suggest this view of reading, and it was developed more fully by Charles Fries (1963).

Often the learning of reading is described as the establishment of **grapheme-to-phoneme correspondences.** Just as different sounds may be functionally equivalent (allophones), many different visual configurations may be functionally equivalent in representing a given letter. For example, the three /k/s discussed earlier can be represented by K, k, *k*; and many other versions of the printed symbol are possible. Learning the letters of the alphabet, then, is a matter of learning the relevant discriminations among categories of printed symbols, or **graphemes.**

In practice, this view emphasizes discrimination training on sounds and letters by means of materials that focus the learner's attention on key elements of words, teaching a child that the visual difference between *can* and *cat* corresponds to the auditory difference between /kæn/ and /kæt/, for example. To the extent that a language has a purely alphabetic (that is, phonemic) writing system, such an approach is entirely feasible. The writing system of English is only partially alphabetic, however, and this fact has produced varying responses by reading theorists.

The first response has been to use only a small subset of the vocabulary of English, one that does follow a regular grapheme-phoneme correspondence.

> To assist beginning readers in the understanding the relation between the sounds (phoneme) and the letters (graphemes) that stand for the sounds in words, linguists have classified words according to their basic phoneme-grapheme patterns, such as *man, fan, can* and *cat, fat, sat.* Through the inductive study of these regular phoneme-grapheme patterns, beginning readers quickly and easily gain insights into these sound-spelling relationships. Through this linguistic approach to beginning tasks, pupils become independent readers from the outset. (Rasmussen & Goldberg 1964:8–9)

Such an approach, if followed rigorously, produces sentences like *Dan can fan the fat cat.* So exclusively is attention paid to the phoneme-grapheme correspondence that other aspects of language are seldom considered. Often the attempt to work into a sentence many words of similar form and spelling results in sentences that are either artificial—*Sam, Ann, Mat, and Tab ate fish and mints* (Sullivan 1966:48)—or include constructions that are probably not in the children's competence, like *Al and the big man began to dig in the big man's pit* (Rasmussen and Goldberg 1964:62). Reading is more than the identification of words; their meanings must be combined in ways determined by the syntactic structure of the sentence. If the syntactic pattern is unfamiliar to the reader, the sentence will not be understood, no matter how well the sentence may be read aloud.

Although there is little research comparing the oral language patterns of children with their ability to read various written language patterns, the research of Strickland (1962), Ruddell (1965), and Tatham (1970) strongly suggests that reading, as one type of linguistic performance, draws on the same linguistic competence that underlies speaking and listening. Ruddell constructed passages incorporating either high- or low-frequency constructions in the children's oral language (*A spaceman could fix the small hole* versus *The leader gave the men short breaks because they needed rest*) and found that the former were better understood, as measured by the **cloze technique.** In the cloze technique, a single word is removed from each sentence, and the subject is asked to fill in the missing word. Effectively, it is a test of the subject's ability to use the syntactic and semantic structures of the remainder of the sentence to identify the missing word. Tatham compared the comprehension of single sentences written at two levels of syntactic complexity, measured by correct selection from three alternative illustrations of the meaning of the sentence, and concluded:

> A significant number of second and fourth graders comprehend material written with frequent oral language patterns better than material written with infrequent oral language patterns . . . it is logical and in keeping with linguistic knowledge to use children's patterns of language structure in written materials to facilitate learning the concept that spoken and written language are related. (1970:424)

Nevertheless, it is probably possible to oversimplify syntax. The natural input to the child learning his first language is somewhat beyond his own level of achievement. This fact, together with the general superiority of comprehension over production, suggests that reading materials should not be totally bound by children's productions. To be sure, constructions that are clearly not understood by children should be generally avoided. Carol Chomsky's work (discussed in Chapter 5) has identified a number of these constructions. For an example involving both vocabulary and syntax, compare *Mother scolded Sam for taking a cookie, and I would have done the same* with *Mother scolded Sam for taking a cookie, although I would have done the same*. The relation between *and/although* and the phrase *done the same* is not realized until fairly late in childhood. But any syntactic simplification of reading materials must be achieved in a way that preserves interest. The discussion of the role of attention in Chapter 6 also suggests that perhaps a major means of evaluating materials should be the children themselves; if a book really holds the interest of the reader, it must be doing something right.

A second response by reading theorists to the nonexistence of regular phoneme-grapheme correspondence in English has been to look for higher-order regularities. It is often possible to identify regular correspondences between pairs of printed symbols and single phonemes, pairs of phonemes, or even longer sequences of graphemes and phonemes. For example, although the letter *e* has several possible pronunciations, the sequence *el* is almost always pronounced [ɛl] as in *help, bell,* and *belt.* Similarly, although the letter *c* has several pronunciations, the sequence *cl* at the beginning of a word is invariably pronounced [kl]. Gibson and her colleagues (1962) have suggested that these higher-order invariants may be the basic units of reading. By using such higher-order regularities, it is possible to enrich greatly the vocabulary to be used in reading materials, and this helps to avoid some of the problems discussed. Nevertheless, the stubborn facts of English orthography imply an ultimate limitation to this approach.

The third, and most sweeping, response to the lack of a perfectly regular phoneme-grapheme correspondence (even of sequences of phonemes and graphemes) in the conventional writing system of English is simply to abandon this system. The best-known example of this response is the Initial Teaching Alphabet (i.t.a.) developed by Sir James Pitman (Pitman and St. John 1969). The i.t.a. is not perfectly phonemic, but it is much closer to a perfectly phonemic system than is our present writing system. The phoneme /u/, which is spelled in no less than seventeen distinct ways (in *ruby, rule, do, move, fruit, bruise, group, through, moon, wooed, loose, rheumatism, flue, maneuver, grew, canoe,* and *two*), is represented by the single symbol ω in i.t.a. Recognition of printed symbols is facilitated by elimination of capital letters. A larger lower-case shape is used, rather than a distinct shape, as is common in the conventional orthography. Figure 8.4 illustrates the complete i.t.a.

The three approaches just discussed—restriction to a subset of English vocabulary, use of higher-order invariants, and the construction of a more nearly alphabetic writing system—share a common emphasis on phoneme-grapheme correspondences. The phonological theory discussed in the previous two sections leads to a fundamentally different view of the reading process. English spelling indicates underlying representations fairly directly and phonetic representations—actual pronunciations—indirectly, via the phonological knowledge that is part of the competence in spoken language possessed by any fluent speaker. The goal of reading is understanding, which includes determining the morphemes of the sentence. If morphemes have constant underlying representations, despite varying pho-

b	bee		bat	bat
c	kee		cut	cut
d̦	dee		d̦et	debt
f	ef		fit	fit
g	gay		got	got
h	hay		hunt	hunt
j	jay		jest	jest
k	kay		aks	axe
l	ell		lip	lip
m	em		mous	mouse
n	en		nævy	navy
p	pee		pens	pence
r	ray		rist	wrist
ɼ	er		fiɼst	first
s	ess		sord̦	sword
t	tee		tiet	tight
v	vee		velvet	velvet
w	way		wun	one
z	zed (or zee)		zeɛbra	zebra
ʂ	zess		horseʂ	horses
ch̦	chay		ch̦urch̦	church
ŋ	ing		siŋ	sing
ʃh	ish		ʃhaft	shaft
th̦	ith		th̦aut	thought
ɹh	thee		ɹhis	this
wh	whay		whær	where
ʒ	zhee		meʒuer	measure
y	yay		yot, sity	yacht, city
æ	aid		cæs	case
a	at		caʃh	cash
ɑ	ahd		cɑm	calm
ɑ̦	ask		cɑ̦sl	castle
e	et		net	net
ɛɛ	eed		nɛɛt	neat
i	it		nit	knit
ie	ide		niet	night
o	ot		not	knot
œ	ode		nœt	note
u	ut		tuf	tough
ue	ued		tuen	tune
ω	oot		tωk	took
ǀω	ood		tωth̦	tooth
au	aud		taut	taught
ɔi	oid		tɔi	toy
ɑu	owd		tɑun	town

Figure 8.4 A comparison of the initial teaching alphabet with traditional orthography.

netic representations, then a writing system that indicates the underlying representation of the morpheme most directly is most appropriate. A spelling that indicates pronunciation directly requires two steps: one to determine the pronunciation and then one to determine the morpheme.

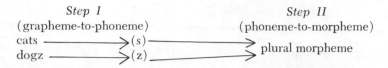

Step I
(grapheme-to-phoneme)
Step II
(phoneme-to-morpheme)

But a spelling that indicates the underlying representation requires only one step:

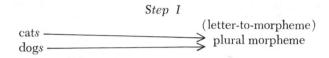

Step I
(letter-to-morpheme)

In many instances, this is the kind of spelling system we have in English.

To illustrate this point, MacDonald (1970) has pointed to some irregularities in the use of the i.t.a. There are sufficient symbols in the i.t.a. to permit a one-phoneme, one-symbol correspondence. However, Pitman does not always depart from the conventional orthography. The phoneme /č/, for example, is usually written ɟh in words such as *which* and *church*. However, in the words *question* and *nature*, the phoneme is written *t* just as in the conventional orthography. MacDonald comments:

> One would normally assume that with just such cases as "question" or "nature" there is need to reflect the phonetic sounds of the words if one is seriously interested in facilitating youngsters' reading practice. . . . In actual practice Pitman appears to apply his alphabet with attention to fine-grained phonetic differentiation in the vowels while leaving the consonant sequences less altered from the conventional orthodox form. (1970:320)

Question is related to *quest* and *nature* to *natal* and *nativity*; in each instance there is a *t* in the underlying representation. The i.t.a. implicitly preserves the underlying representation because it facilitates the identification of the morphemes. There are many other examples of departures from the consistent application of i.t.a. that preserve parts of the underlying representations.

Beginning readers and later readers may differ on just this point: whether or not sound is a necessary intermediary between print and meaning—what Smith (1971) has called "mediated word identification," as opposed to immediate identification. The i.t.a. is intended only as a temporary alphabet to facilitate initial reading. After a period of a few months to two years, the reader is switched to conventional orthography. Gillooly (1975) has carefully reviewed the evidence on the effects of different writing systems on learning to read. In the early stages, phonetic writing systems like i.t.a. and the traditional writing system for German have an advantage of a limited sort. Word-recognition skills are better, as is spelling. But paragraph-meaning scores are not superior. And, by the fourth grade, children read traditional orthography better than simplified ones. There are several factors at work here. One is that traditional orthography encourages grouping letters in meaning-relevant, rather than sound-relevant, ways, and this grouping leads to larger clusterings. A second factor extends beyond the single-word level. Part of learning to read well is learning *not* to look at everything on the page. Presumably in an orthography that is based on meaning, one can form expectations as to where to look for maximum information.

The evidence for the claim that an orthography like the traditional one for English is read better in the fourth grade than a phonemically based one comes primarily from cross-national comparisons. Since German spelling is relatively more phonemic than that of English, the superior performance of American fourth-graders may be due to the traditional, that is, partially meaning-based, writing system. A direct comparison of readers using the two writing systems cannot be made, because that i.t.a. is not used in the fourth grade; a transition is made sometime during the first two years. The really crucial question is Does early use of i.t.a. help or hinder in the long run? To my knowledge, there is really no good evidence on the question, evidence that would compare children's reading comprehension at intermediate levels on the basis of their initial spelling systems. In mature readers, that is, adults, the nature of the writing system does not seem to affect reading speed. A given amount of content is read in about the same amount of time, even with orthographies as dissimilar as English and Chinese. A particularly interesting ability to examine would be the acquisition of new words. By this I mean the ability to read, not words that are already in the reader's vocabulary, though never before encountered in print, but words that are genuinely new to the reader. As Brown (1958) and others have pointed out, the ability to decode letters to a sound sequence that has never before been heard is not very useful. A system based on meaning is more likely to be of help if the new word is at least partially composed of familiar morphemes. In the long run, after all, reading is supposed to be a way to learn new things.

One solution to this spelling problem that has not been tested extensively but would appear to have much to recommend it is simply to let children make up their own spelling systems. The idea of giving children a more active role in learning to read is not new—in *Teacher*, Sylvia Ashton Warner (1962) describes letting children make up their own vocabularies, then showing them how to spell the words. In other approaches children have experience in dictation, thus determining the syntax of the reading materials. Read (1971) has studied the writing systems spontaneously invented by bright preschoolers, and Carol Chomsky has suggested that children be encouraged to invent such systems. "The natural order is writing first then reading what you have written" (1972a:120). In fact, the spellings invented by children are quite sensitive to many aspects of the sound system of English, even though they are quite different from those of an adult. Consider the child who is trying to spell *wet*. He begins with an r, which is reasonable, because he generally pronounces r identically with w. For the vowels, children seem to rely heavily on letter names. So, in trying to write the sound e, he must choose from letters whose names are pronounced [ey], [iy], [ay], [ow], and [yuw]. The natural selection is [ey] or a. T is the final letter selected, and the child finishes with rat, which he reads as *wet*. Other regularities crop up; there is more consistency than one would expect. The learner is getting practice in thinking about how words sound, systematically representing sounds, and learning that writing is fun. Later will come the discovery of the myriad printed words about him—on street signs, food labels, books, billboards, and more. Now he tries to read these words and runs into certain problems, but he is ready to ask for help. He has the basic idea of reading. Although such a program has been tried only informally, it deserves further exploration.

Silent and oral reading are probably more distinct activities than is usually thought. Skillful readers undoubtedly omit a great deal of phonological processing when they read silently. One of the fundamental goals of "speed reading" instruction is to eliminate "silent vocalizing," which suggests that most of us still retain some vestiges of phonological processing in silent reading.

Practice in reading aloud may be useless, or worse, in developing silent reading. For beginning readers there may be no difference, and oral reading may be useful to the teacher. But once past this stage oral reading may be a hindrance. Reading aloud adds two tasks to the process of reading: not only the motor task of speech production, but also an additional mental task. In those instances in which the printed symbols determine the morphemes directly, without passing through an auditory stage, the application of phonological rules to determine phonetic representations is unnecessary. Oral and silent reading each serve important functions, but it must be realized that practice in oral reading may not facilitate silent reading.

The child of six or seven years who is beginning to read has probably not yet mastered the dual-level phonological system of English fully. There are two alternative implications for the teaching of reading that can be drawn from this fact. The first is that beginning reading should be taught in the traditional manner, emphasizing phoneme-symbol (grapheme) correspondences and reading aloud. As this process is mastered and the child's vocabulary increases, he will develop a dual phonological system of underlying and phonetic representations "automatically" (as all normal adult speakers of English do), and he will also change "automatically" to a reading process that identifies morphemes directly on the basis of spelling. This approach is essentially how reading is taught currently.

A second possibility is deliberately to enrich the child's vocabulary to include the word groups that will enable him to construct the underlying representations of words, as in *industry-industrial, medicine-medical, sign-signature,* and so forth. The child's attention should be drawn to the fact that words of similar meaning are spelled alike, even though the pronunciation differs. Carol Chomsky has suggested several exercises that might be useful for this purpose. Some of them are discussed in Reading 8.1.

A combination of approaches seems most promising. At the very earliest stages, an attempt to enrich vocabulary might be confusing. However, once the fundamentals of the reading process have been mastered, the teacher need not wait for the child to increase his own vocabulary. Methods like those discussed can be used.

Perhaps the most important implication of these theoretical considerations is the primacy of meaning in learning to read. The goal of reading is to understand meaning. Understanding may occur directly or indirectly, but it is always the goal. Undoubtedly one of the reasons for the success of the television show *The Electric Company* in teaching reading is the fact that every printed message is accompanied by contextual information that clearly signals the meaning, as well as by the actual pronunciation.

Reading and Language Development

Learning to read draws on the knowledge of spoken language already acquired by the child. But the relationship between language and reading runs both ways. Carol Chomsky (1972b) has collected evidence that suggests that the amount of exposure to reading, both the child's own reading and reading to the child by adults, is highly correlated with linguistic development in the years five to ten and that this correlation is not simply owing to such variables as IQ, father's education, and so on. Although her evidence is not yet conclusive, it does suggest that the child's language-learning ability comes to school with him, so to speak, and that the materials encountered in school are an important input for further learning. The learning is accidental, in the sense that no direct attempt is made to teach the grammatical structures tested. The point is that the children are able to take advantage of the richness and variety of language encountered. Note that, if this conclusion is valid, it runs counter to the approach discussed earlier, of simplifying structures to the level of the child. Learning can only take place if the child is exposed to *new* aspects of language. Simplification and enrichment are not mutually exclusive strategies, of course; the real problem of instruction is to find the most effective balance between the two.

A second way in which reading may affect language development is more direct. Much of the evidence for the claim that traditional English orthography reflects meaning directly, and hence is superior to a sound-based system, comes from complex derivational forms, like *critical-criticize*. The richness of the vocabulary encountered in intermediate reading, if not in beginning reading, may provide the essential input for the child to develop the dual-level phonological representations of words claimed by N. Chomsky and Halle and other linguists—a meaning-related level and a sound-related level. Furthermore, learning to read promotes an awareness of language, an analytical ability, that would be difficult to instill in any other way.

A third way in which language may be affected by learning to read is through communication. In many situations young children are not very effective communicators. Underlying their difficulties is the pervasive problem of egocentrism, as Piaget has described it. Young children have great difficulty in seeing situations from any perspective other than their own. We have already seen examples of this problem in describing semantic development in Chapter 7. In a larger sense, this problem of egocentrism, of not being able to get outside one's own perspective and into the shoes of the listener or reader, remains with us throughout life. One of the most interesting sections in Vygotsky's book *Thought and Language* (1962) concerns the special nature of written language in this respect. Vygotsky compares "inner speech," talking for one's self, with talking to others. Inner speech can be highly abbreviated and rapid. It is something like talking to someone you know very well about a familiar topic; much can be left out. But talking to another person requires filling in much additional information. When we consider writing, we realize that it is just that much farther removed from inner speech. The reader is not present, so we have no immediate feedback, either verbal or nonverbal. In fact, the writer may not even know who the reader will be. No assumptions can be made about the specific knowledge of the reader. In Vygotsky's words, "the change from maximally compact inner speech to maximally detailed written speech requires what might be called deliberate semantics—deliberate structuring of the web of meaning" (Vygotsky 1962:100). The alternation between reading and writing is probably of great value here. Both Piaget and Vygotsky would agree that a great aid to overcoming egocentrism is switching roles, actual experience at seeing things from different perspectives. Shantz and Wilson (1972), in fact, used this as a tool for fostering oral-communication skills. Second graders participated in a communication task requiring one child to describe a picture to another so that the second one could pick it out or draw it himself. The children took turns being sender, receiver, and observer. The program produced significant gains in communication ability. This finding suggests that writing should not just be something the child does for his or her teacher but rather that children should sometimes read what they and other children have written. Only in this way will the child eventually be able to conceive of the reader and his informational needs, as he writes.

Summary

From the beginning of life, human infants show a special sensitivity to, and keen discrimination abilities for, the sound of speech. The vocalizations of infants follow a similar developmental path, relatively independent of the linguistic community. When children begin to form meaningful utterances, the phonological aspect, like the syntactic and semantic aspects, is systematic. The differences between the child's forms and those of the adult are not solely a matter of perceptual and articulation difficulties; rather, they reflect the workings of a rule-governed system that is essentially simpler than that of the adult. This system—both the elements available to the child and the ways in which they are used—appears to be quite similar in the early stages for children acquiring different languages. Little is known of the development of the dual-level phonological system of English, but an understanding of this process would be valuable for understanding the process of learning to read.

8.1 PHONOLOGY AND TEACHING SPELLING*

The examples which follow suggest several types of "spelling lessons" that can be constructed to bring out a number of [the meaning-preserving] features of [English spelling]. These samples are intended primarily to indicate a general approach. In practice, of course, vocabulary would have to be adapted to the abilities of individual classes.

Children could be asked, for example, to fill in the missing reduced vowel in a list such as column (1), and then to justify their choices by thinking of related words which retain vowel quality. They would then produce something like column (2).

(1)	(2)
dem_cratic	democracy
pres_dent	preside
prec_dent	precede
comp_rable	compare, comparison
comp_sition	composer, compose
hist_ry	historical, historian
janit_r	janitorial
manag_r	managerial

* From C. S. Chomsky, Reading, writing, and phonology. *Harvard Educational Review*, 1970, **40**, 305, 307–308. Copyright 1970 by President and Fellows of Harvard College. Reprinted by permission.

(1)	(2)
maj_r	majority
ill_strate	illustrative
ind_stry	industrial
imm_grate	migrate
cons_lation	console
ab_lition	abolish
comp_tent	compete

Or, simply given column (2), they would be asked to think up other forms of the words, and to characterize the specific ways in which the vowel sounds shift around. Anything that focuses their attention on related words and con-comitant pronunciation shifts ought to be good practice for finding specific related words when they need them.

Another helpful exercise involves consonants which are silent in some words but pronounced in others. For example:

(1)	(2)
muscle	muscular
sign, (design)	signature, signal (designate)
bomb	bombard
condemn	condemnation
malign	malignant
soften	soft

Children could be given column (2) and asked to think of related words in which the underlined consonant becomes silent. Or, conversely, they could be given column (1) and asked to think of related words in which the silent consonant is recovered phonetically. Or they could be given the words in column (1) orally and asked to name the silent consonant. For those who can't do it, the column (2) word can be elicited or, if necessary, pointed out as helpful evidence.

Exercises such as these are to be construed as samples of a par-ticular approach which can be extended as the need arises. However, it is perhaps much more to the point for the teacher to develop a way of dealing with spelling errors that the children produce day by day than to equip herself with preselected word lists. Most important is that she transmit to the child the notion that spelling very often is not arbitrary, but rather corresponds to something real that he already knows and can exploit. A good way to handle misspellings that come up in class is to search with the child for a systematic reason why the word should be spelled the way it is, if indeed one can be found. In many cases, such a reason can be found. Often this will mean simply bringing a relation between two familiar words to the child's attention. To use some examples drawn from the spontaneous writing of a group of third and fourth graders, the child who misspells *president* as *presedent* needs to have pointed out that it is related to *preside*. The child who misspells *really* as *relly* needs to think of *reality* to get it right. *Apon* is more likely to be written *upon* if the child realizes that it is a combination of *up* and *on*.

Immagrate will become *immigrate* if it is connected with *migrate*. *Medisin* will lose the *s* and acquire a *c* if it is connected to *medical*.

Sometimes a related word that could help settle the difficulty for the child is a word he doesn't know. *Illustrative*, for example, may be no part of the vocabulary of the child who writes *illastrate* for *illustrate*. In such cases, it may make better sense to introduce the new word than to have him memorize a seemingly arbitrary spelling for his familiar word.

further reading

Ferguson, C. A. and Slobin, D. I. *Studies of child language development*. New York: Holt, Rinehart and Winston, 1973.

Ingram, D. Phonological rules in young children. *Journal of Child Language*, 1974, **1**, 49–64.

Schane, S. A. *Generative phonology*. Englewood Cliffs, N.J.: Prentice-Hall, 1973.

Steinberg, D. D. Phonology, reading, and Chomsky and Halle's optimal orthography. *Journal of Psycholinguistic Research*, 1973, 2, 239–258.

9

The Functions
of Language

Language is *the* uniquely human characteristic.[1] How is it related to man's very considerable cognitive abilities? The belief that language is somehow essential for thinking is widely held and apparently sets in at an early age, as the following dialogue with a preschooler (my son Jonathan, age 2;11) about his younger sister illustrates:

> J. D.: She's not crying.
> P. D.: She knows she's going to get dinner.
> J. D.: No, she doesn't; she can't talk.

Psychologists have had what can only be called a love-hate relationship with language. On the one hand, language is often seen as a controlling, distorting influence on thought. Although this view was foreshadowed by German philosophers like von Humboldt in the eighteenth century, it was first formulated in modern times by the American linguist Edward Sapir, who wrote:

> Human beings do not live in the objective world alone, nor alone in the world of social activity as ordinarily understood, but are very much at the mercy of the particular language which has become the medium of expression of their society. It is quite an illusion to imagine that one adjusts to

[1] A different opinion from Mark Twain: "Man is the only Animal that blushes. Or needs to" (from *Following the Equator*).

reality essentially without the use of language and that language is merely an incidental means of solving specific problems of communication or reflection. . . . We see and hear and otherwise experience very largely as we do because the language habits of our community predispose certain choices of interpretation. (1958:162)

Sapir's student Benjamin Lee Whorf argued this position most widely and vividly, and it is often called the "Whorf hypothesis" (Whorf 1956).

On the other hand, language is often viewed as a great liberating force for human reasoning, for it frees the mind from total dependence on the immediate appearance of reality in all its detail, allowing generalization and abstraction, as well as consideration of new possibilities. Jerome Bruner, a psychologist, wrote:

> In effect, language provides a means, not only for representing experience, but also for transforming it. . . . Once the child has succeeded in internalizing language as a cognitive instrument, it becomes possible for him to represent and systematically transform the regularities of experience with far greater flexibility and power than before. (1964:4)

Sapir and Bruner, along with most psychologists, are in agreement that language plays a predominant role in thinking. Only one major psychological theorist, Jean Piaget, has opposed this view. He believes that

> a symbolic function exists which is broader than language and encompasses both the system of verbal signs and that of symbols in the strict sense . . . it is permissible to conclude that thought precedes language . . . language is not enough to explain thought, because the structures that characterize thought have their roots in action and in sensori-motor mechanisms that are deeper than linguistics. (1967:91, 98)

There is an alternative formulation of the question of language and thought that may be more fruitful. Human beings use the flexible structure of language for a wide variety of functions: communicating, reasoning, and memorizing, among others. What are the relations among these functions of language, and how do they change with development?

The Whorf Hypothesis

Whorf, like many linguists of the early twentieth century, was struck by the differences among languages. He argued that linguists had for too long restricted their attention to the European languages, which are all quite similar. He thought that they could be lumped together under the heading Standard Average European (SAE), in contrast to the American

Indian languages, which are radically different both from SAE and often from one another. These differences led him to propose two hypotheses:

1. All higher levels of thinking are dependent on language. This is **linguistic determinism:** That is, language determines thought.
2. Languages differ drastically; therefore the world is experienced differently by speakers of different languages. This is **linguistic relativism:** The picture of the universe is different for individuals in different linguistic communities.

In Whorf's writings, these two hypotheses are generally found together; in fact, it is not clear that Whorf really distinguished them. Although most research on this issue has concerned itself with the two together, they are actually independent claims. It is possible that one of them may be true and the other false. Suppose language determines thought but that the languages of the world are all the same, or at least similar insofar as the aspects of language that affect thought are concerned. In this instance the linguistic-determinism hypothesis would be true and the linguistic-relativism hypothesis would be false. On the other hand, it may be true that speakers of different languages picture the world differently but that this is the result not of language but of general culture or environmental differences. In that case, the linguistic-determinism hypothesis would be false and the linguistic-relativism hypothesis true.

Returning to the Whorf hypothesis as usually stated—linguistic determinism plus linguistic relativism—we may ask what kinds of differences between languages led to this extreme position? One important way in which language deals with experience is by categorizing it. There are two very important ways in which this is done. Words in general stand for categories, or classes, of objects, actions, or properties—not for particular ones. A large category of objects is grouped together under the label *house.* A category of colors is grouped together under the heading *green.* A category of actions is grouped together under the label *to touch.* These are all instances of **lexical categories** (*lex-,* 'word').

The second way language represents categories is by means of various grammatical devices. The suffix *-ed* indicates that some aspect of experience is in the category of the past tense; that is, of all possible situations, some fall into a category that requires *-ed* for its description. English categorizes *houses, cats, democracy,* and *lightning* together; all are named by nouns that are used in certain specific ways in sentences. These are both instances of **grammatical categories.**

Languages differ in how they categorize the world by means of these devices. One language may simply not have a term equivalent to a term in another language. Many languages do not have a word equivalent to the English word *atom.* English does not have a word equivalent to the German word *Weltanschauung* ('all-encompassing world view'). A more important difference is that languages often differ in providing superordinate terms for classes. For example, English has the word *bird*, which covers all birds, whereas several South American Indian languages do not, although they have words for specific kinds of birds. On the other hand, English does not have a single word that encompasses both fruits and nuts, whereas Chinese does. There are many such differences among languages.

A third difference, and one that is very useful for experimental investigation, is that languages make different splits in various experiential realms. The color continuum provides the best example of this. Colors vary in hue. All languages draw distinctions among colors, and they do it in various ways. Gleason (1961) compares the division of hues by speakers of English, Shona, and Bassa (see Figure).

English

purple	blue	green	yellow	orange	red

Shona

cips^wuka	citema	cicena	cips^wuka

Bassa

hui	ziza

Consider a color that we would call "yellowish green"; it falls near the boundary between two English color categories, green and yellow. If such a color were presented to an English speaker to be named, his response would take longer than if a pure yellow or a pure green were presented (Brown and Lenneberg 1954). But such yellowish green would probably be a good example of *cicena* to a Shona speaker, and he could give a name for it quickly and easily. Languages not only divide up the color continuum differently; they also distinguish colors that are good examples of categories from colors that are more difficult to name in different ways. (Whorf's theorizing and the research by Brown and Lenneberg and others that grew out of it were accomplished before the research of Berlin and Kay 1969 on similarities of color naming, discussed in Chapter 7. We shall return to the implications of these new findings later.)

The second way in which a language categorizes the world is at the grammatical level. This is more interesting than lexical categorization, because speakers of a language are even less aware of it. Every language embodies a variety of mandatory observations and classifications. These classifications are shown most clearly when we compare different languages. A most vivid example of this comparison was provided by Whorf's teacher, Sapir (1958). As Sapir commented, the natural view is to assume that, when we want to communicate an idea, we take an inventory of the elements of the situation and their relations and that our linguistic task is merely to find the particular words and fit them together according to the rules of the language. Suppose an individual sees a stone falling. Assuming that, like ourselves, he is a speaker of English, he will analyze this situation into two parts: the stone and the act of falling. They are combined by means of English grammar to produce the sentence *The stone falls*. What could be more natural?

A Russian might wonder why it is necessary to specify whether the stone must be conceived of in a definite or an indefinite manner—that is, why we must say either *the stone* or *a stone*. *Stone falls* is acceptable Russian and Latin. A Kwakiutl Indian would agree that definiteness is important, but he might wonder why we do not indicate in some way whether the stone is visible or invisible to the speaker at the time of speaking, as he would do in his description. He would also wonder why we do not indicate something about the position of the stone—is it nearer to the speaker, the listener, or some third party? And he would wonder why we insist on expressing the fact that only one stone falls. A Chinese could describe the situation most economically, with *stone fall*, in which there is no indication of number, visibility, definiteness, and the like. Of course, extra pieces of information can be provided in each language, but we are concerned with what is *required*.

So far the fundamental analysis of the situation into *stone* and *fall* has been unchallenged. But in the Nootka language (spoken on Vancouver Island), the situation would be analyzed differently. The two elements in Nootka are, first, an element indicating general movement of a stone and, second, an element indicating a downward direction. Imagine that we had in English an intransitive verb *to stone* referring to the movement of a stone-like object. Then the English sentence *The stone falls* would be reassembled by a Nootka speaker into something like *It stones down*. Instead of analyzing the situation into an object and its activity, the Nootka speaker selects a generalized notion of the movement of a particular class of objects and a direction.

The Whorf hypothesis is a grand and sweeping statement. In an age worried about the use of language to deceive and distort, in propaganda and advertising, it has a certain appeal.[2] We have all had complex ideas or emotions that were impossible to put into words; our language has seemed too rigid and unbending.

---

[2] The General Semantics Movement, although of independent origin, is very similar in orientation; see Hayakawa (1964).

But Whorf's arguments have been criticized extensively by linguists and psychologists, especially Eric Lenneberg (Lenneberg and Roberts 1956). Whorf's reasoning is basically circular. He notices that a language is different from our own, and from this difference he infers that the speakers of that language think differently. Finally, he concludes that the differences in thinking arise from the differences in language. Actually, differences in language prove only that languages differ. Without an independent measure of the thought patterns themselves, no conclusion can be drawn.

Outside observers, like Whorf, are usually too sensitive to metaphors that may be completely dead for the speakers of the language. Imagine a Japanese coming to the United States to study the natives and how they think. How quaint of the Americans to think of sleeping as a period of fasting, which we terminate in the morning with *breakfast*. How very food-oriented! The word *everybody* must indicate that we always think of people in material terms. Too often, Whorfian analysis takes such metaphors, of which speakers of the language are no longer aware, as meaningful and important indicators of the thought of the speakers.

The German word *Weltanschauung* can be "borrowed" in English; we can talk about fruits and nuts; we can even learn to distinguish among the many kinds of snow for which Eskimos have distinct names. The absence of a single word does not preclude either consideration of the category or the naming of it. Language and language users are creative. We can construct English phrases with approximately the same meanings as single words in other languages. Perhaps the differences among languages are based simply on which categories are easily available to speakers of each language: "Languages differ not so much as to what *can* be said in them, but rather as to what it is *relatively easy* to say in them" (Hockett 1954: p. 122). This more modest version of the hypothesis has come to be known as the *weak* Whorfian position, although Whorf himself never espoused it.

Cognitive Consequences of Grammatical Differences

So, despite the eloquence of Whorf's writing, his own arguments are not very convincing. Much effort has gone into designing experiments that might give us some information about the hypothesis. The experiments have tried to relate specific aspects of a given language to specific sorts of behavior. They appear rather disappointing in contrast to the grand sweep of the Whorf hypothesis.

Only one study (Carroll and Casagrande 1958) has been conducted on the cognitive consequences of grammatical structure. This is undoubtedly owing to the difficulty of devising suitable behavioral measures. In a pair of experiments in the southwestern United States, the cognitive correlates of both lexical and grammatical categories were examined. English has two verbs, *to spill* and *to pour*, that differ according to whether the action is accidental or intentional. However, either can be used with both liquids and solids. That is, we can say *I spilled the milk*, and *I spilled the sugar*. Hopi also has two verbs: *wehekna* ('to pour liquid') and *wa:hokna* 'to pour sand or other nonliquid loose things.' But either verb may be used for both accidental and intentional spilling and pouring.

In the experiment, three pictures were presented to the subjects: peaches being poured from a box, coins being spilled from a pocket, and water being spilled from a pitcher. The subjects were asked to decide which two of the three pictures went together. Speakers of English should have grouped the second and third pictures together (*spilling*), whereas speakers of Hopi should have grouped the first two pictures (*wa:hokna*). Carroll and Casagrande devised a number of such items. The subjects included fourteen Hopi adults, all fluent in Hopi, though most also spoke English; twelve rural New England adults of comparable education to that of the Hopi; and fifteen Harvard University graduate students. Table 9.1 presents the results for the twelve sets of stimulus pictures for which there were clear predictions. These data provide some support for the hypothesis, as the Hopi speakers chose the "Hopi choice" more often than English speakers. However, they selected the English choice even more often than the Hopi choice.

TABLE 9.1   Picture Grouping by Speakers of Hopi and English (percentages)

	Hopi Choice	*Anglo Choice*	*Other Choice*
Hopi speakers	34	47.6	18.4
Rural Anglos	21.5	59.0	19.5
Harvard graduate students	18.8	63.9	17.3

SOURCE: Adapted from Table 2 of John B. Carroll and Joseph B. Casagrande, The function of language classifications in behavior. In Eleanor E. Maccoby, Theodore M. Newcomb and Eugene L. Hartley (Eds.), *Readings in social psychology* (3rd Ed.), p. 26. Copyright 1947, 1952, © 1958 by Holt, Rinehart and Winston, Inc. Reprinted by permission of Holt, Rinehart and Winston, Inc.

The second experiment investigated grammatical categories. In Navaho, there is a class of verbs that all have something to do with handling —the verb for *carry*, for example—and, whenever one of these verbs is used, an ending that depends on the shape or rigidity of the object being handled must be added to the verb. To ask a person to hand oneself an object, one must use the word *sanleh* for a long, flexible object like a piece of string; the word *santiih* for a long, rigid object like a stick; the word *sanilcoos* for a flat, flexible object like a piece of paper; and so on. In this way objects are grouped in categories according to their shapes and rigidity. Navaho children are able to use those verbs and endings appropriately by the age of three or four years. However, there are no words for these categories in Navaho, nor are the Navaho able to tell why they use a particular form with a given object. Carroll and Casagrande reasoned that, because Navaho speakers are required to pay attention to form, they are more likely to group objects according to form than are English speakers.

The procedure was quite simple. A pair of objects that differed in both color and form, like a yellow rope and a blue stick, were presented to the child. Then a third object, which had one characteristic in common with each of the two objects, in this instance a blue rope, was presented, and the subject was asked to tell the experimenter which object of the pair went best with this third object.

The subjects were Navaho children between the ages of three and ten years. As most of them were at least slightly bilingual in English and Navaho, the children were divided on the basis of tests into a Navaho-dominant and an English-dominant group. The results are shown in Table 9.2. The data from the Navaho-dominant and English-dominant children support the hypothesis that speaking Navaho leads to an increased tendency to group on the basis of form. However, there are more data to be reported. In order to have an extra control group, Carroll and Casagrande administered their experiment to a group of white middle-class American children of similar ages in the Boston area. Their results are shown in the last column of Table 9.2. The Boston children acted more as Navaho speakers were expected to than the Navaho speakers did. The effect of these data is to render the results of the experiment with Navaho children completely unclear.

There is one possible explanation that does permit us to salvage a bit of the experiment and the hypothesis. We know from studies of white children that young children—aged three to six years—normally group more on the basis of color than on the basis of form; with increasing age, there is an increasing amount of grouping on the basis of form. It has also been found that children of higher socioeconomic status make this transition to form grouping earlier. The transition to form grouping thus seems to be a good indicator of cognitive maturity. In this experiment, both the Navaho-dominant and the English-dominant children showed an increased tendency to group on the basis of form—to respond with the a choice—as age increased. But the increase began earlier for the Navaho-dominant children. Furthermore, neither of the Navaho groups could really be considered "middle class," as were the Boston children. One explanation for these results is that the transition from color grouping to form grouping is natural for all children, and it may be facilitated in several ways. In particular, learning to speak a language like Navaho, which requires the speaker to

TABLE 9.2   Object Grouping by Speakers of Navaho and English
(percentages)

Original Pair[a]	Third Object	Navaho Dominant	English Dominant	White
a. Yellow rope	blue rope	70.7	39.5	83.0
b. Blue stick		29.3	60.5	17.0
a. Blue rope	yellow rope	70.7	39.5	80.7
b. Yellow stick		29.3	60.5	19.3
a. Yellow stick	blue stick	71.2	44.2	76.6
b. Blue cylinder		28.8	55.8	23.4
a. Yellow stick	blue stick	72.4	44.2	77.1
b. Blue oblong block		27.6	55.8	32.9

[a] The "Navaho" choice is indicated by a.
SOURCE: Adapted from Table 3 of John B. Carroll and Joseph B. Casagrande, The function of language classifications in behavior. In Eleanor E. Maccoby, Theodore M. Newcomb and Eugene L. Hartley (Eds.), *Readings in social psychology* (3rd Ed.), p. 29. Copyright 1947, 1952, © 1958 by Holt, Rinehart and Winston, Inc. Reprinted by permission of Holt, Rinehart and Winston, Inc.

pay attention to form, facilitates this development. But so does practice with toys of the form-board variety, which middle-class American children are likely to have experience with. Even if this explanation is correct, the role it assigns to language is much less sweeping than that of the Whorf hypothesis.

This experiment illustrates a fundamental problem of cross-cultural experimentation. Language users in two different linguistic communities are separated by more than their languages; many of their attitudes, experiences, and interests are different. But it is just the relations between language and these other factors that we are interested in. As both groups of variables vary, it is generally impossible to draw any inferences.

Cognitive Consequences of Lexical Differences for Perceptual Continua

One solution to this problem is to restrict experimentation to a single linguistic community and to explore cognitive consequences of lexical categories, in particular the division of perceptual continua, such as color. The color space can be specified with three dimensions—hue, brightness, and saturation—and this space divided into a small number of classes by the set of color names in a given language.

Brown and Lenneberg (1954) were the first to use color chips to test the Whorf hypothesis. In their study, they investigated how easily colors can be named using several measures, including length of name given to the color, the time necessary to give the name, agreement among subjects on the names, and others. All their measures were correlated highly, and they concluded that colors differ in their **codability** in English. Next they asked a second group of subjects to remember colors for varying lengths of time and then to recognize them in a large array. The more codable colors, that is, those more easily named, were indeed more accurately remembered. This result demonstrates a relation between the set of verbal labels supplied by English and a nonverbal behavior, memory. However, the positive correlation between codability and accuracy of recognition was very low (0.25) when the interval was short (seven seconds) and rose as the task became more difficult (0.49 when four colors had to be recognized after three minutes).

This experiment was repeated with Zuñi Indians, with similar results. Although the codability of individual colors in Zuñi is quite different from that in English, those colors that were easily named in Zuñi were most accurately remembered by the Zuñis.

An even better predictor of memorability for colors is the measure **communication accuracy,** devised by Lantz and Steffire (1964). They suggested that memory be viewed as a process in which an individual communicates to himself through time, using the brain as a channel. Remembering is similar to communication between separate individuals. If an item can be communicated successfully to another individual, it can be remembered well. Their measure, communication accuracy, was obtained by asking subjects to make up a description of a color that would enable another person to pick it out of an array of colors. Then the descriptions were given to another set of subjects to use in selecting colors. By observing how well the second group of subjects was able to select the original color on the basis of the descriptions, a measure of how accurately each color can be communicated can be obtained. Then Lantz and Steffire performed the recognition experiment with the set of colors used by Brown and Lenneberg and with another very different array. On both arrays communication accuracy was correlated positively (0.32–0.86) with recognition accuracy; that is, those colors that could be accurately communicated from one individual to another could be remembered and recognized accurately.

Lantz and Steffire concluded that their formulation of the relation between language and behavior emphasizes the *productivity* of language— that new descriptions can be formed spontaneously and effectively. *Blue* may be short and conventional, but under many circumstances *light sky blue with a tinge of pink* will communicate more effectively. They argue that the role of dictionary words and grammatical categories is greatly overrated.

Their experiment has been repeated with deaf and hearing adults and with hearing six-year-olds, with similar results (Lantz and Lenneberg 1966). Although just which colors have the highest and lowest communication accuracy varies from group to group, those colors with high communication accuracy are always recognized most accurately. Communication accuracy appears to be an excellent predictor of recognition accuracy.

As in Brown and Lenneberg's experiment, the correlation between communication accuracy and recognition accuracy was weakest (0.51 and 0.32 for the two arrays) for the easiest task (one color for five seconds) and stronger (0.65–0.86) for the more difficult tasks (four colors for five and thirty seconds). Like the earlier study, this experiment is evidence only for the influence of language on memory.

In recent years, interest in the Whorf hypothesis has generally declined. The disappointing results of the studies just described are one reason; another is the growing interest in language universals. The similarities among languages are now of more interest than the differences. The striking findings of Berlin and Kay reveal that even in the domain of color names, languages do not label colors in a completely arbitrary fashion. Though the boundaries between color areas vary widely, the focal areas— up to eleven in all—recur in historically unrelated languages. The universality of these focal areas, together with Heider's (1971; Rosch [Heider] 1973) research with preschoolers, discussed in Chapter 7, suggest that in the domain of color names, at least, the Whorf hypothesis is nearly exactly the opposite of the truth: Rather than linguistic differences in color naming causing perceptual and cognitive differences in the treatment of colors, it appears that universal aspects of the human perceptual and cognitive apparatus lead to universal aspects of color naming.

This change in emphasis also fits well with the growing tendency to formulate the problem of language learning as one of mapping concepts already developed nonlinguistically into language, or to explore possible interactions between language and cognition in development. Some of the issues in this difficult area have been discussed in Chapters 4, 6 and 7. Although the questions are far from being settled, or even formulated satisfactorily, it seems clear that the direction of influence is not simply from language to cognition.

Language and Memory

That language plays an important role in memory is not surprising to anyone who has tried to remember a license-plate number, paint color, or collection of waxed fruit. The most useful strategy in each instance is to convert the items to be remembered into linguistic form. In the previous section we saw that the evidence is ambiguous with respect to the effect of different ways of encoding experience in language; but it is clear that the variable of language versus no language has a powerful effect on memory. Encoding of experience in language is not sufficient, however. The use of language for memory requires an active process of rehearsal as well. Have a friend show you a telephone number, randomly chosen from a directory.

Under normal conditions, it is a trivial task to remember the number for thirty seconds. But if you are also given another three-digit number, say 886, and instructed to count backward by threes for thirty seconds, the task of remembering becomes extraordinarily difficult. Counting backward interferes with the process of rehearsal of the telephone number.

Young children are not able to use the efficient mnemonic strategy of naming plus rehearsal, even when they know the appropriate names. Kindergarteners shown a series of three pictures of familiar objects neither name the objects nor remember them very well, in contrast to older children, who name the objects and remember them. Children a year or two older can be instructed to name pictures and rehearse the names, which leads to superior recognition. However, when the instructions to rehearse are dropped, they return to their nonrehearsing behavior, and recognition performance drops (Keeney, Canizzo and Flavell 1967). In other words, children of this age have all the component abilities for the use of rehearsal —naming, rehearsal, the use of the rehearsed name for recognition—yet they fail to select and integrate these functions spontaneously. Mastery of the linguistic system is only a first step; an additional measure of cognitive maturity is necessary to use language in memory and other domains (Flavell 1970).

The use of language for memory is not an unmixed blessing. The word is not reality. Language has evolved to be as flexible and multipurpose as possible; in practice this means that there is seldom an exact fit between reality and language. In consequence, the encoding of reality in verbal form often results in distortion. A classic demonstration of this distortion is an experiment by Carmichael, Hogan, and Walter (1931), later replicated by Herman, Lawless, and Marshall (1957). Ambiguous figures, such as (1) shown below,

1.

were presented to adult subjects, who were told that they would later have to reproduce them as accurately as possible. Each figure was named as it was presented. One group was given the label "curtains in a window" another group the label "diamond in a rectangle." The subjects tended to distort the figures in their reproductions to conform better to the verbal labels. The example figure was often reproduced as shown in (2) below

2.

by the first group and as shown in (3)

3. $\diamond$

by the second group. Though it is easier to remember verbal labels than these drawings, the result is not always increased accuracy.

If the use of language for memory were a skill that emerged gradually, it would be expected that this kind of distortion in memory would be of less magnitude in children. It is interesting that many psychologists have commented on the keen perceptual skills of children and their ability to remember pictures and perceptual attributes of objects and events better than verbal descriptions (Entwisle and Huggins 1973; Jones 1973).

Even if the influence of language were limited to memory (a considerable oversimplification, as will be seen in the remainder of this chapter), language would play an important role in cognition. Our thinking is seldom based on the here and now; we think about the past and future, our dreams and wishes, what we have been told, and what we have told others. Even if cognition were independent of language, the raw material upon which it operated would be heavily verbal.

Language and Egocentrism

The appearance of Piaget's *The Language and Thought of the Child* (1955; first edition in French, 1923) marked the beginning of one of the most productive careers in psychology, just now drawing to a close.[3] In this work Piaget sought to determine the functions of language in the life of a child. He began by examining the free speech of kindergarten children. His first conclusion was that there are two major categories of speech. The first he called **egocentric speech:** speech that, whether uttered in solitude or in the presence of others, can be judged to lack a primary communicative intent. There is no real attempt to take the role of the listener (hence the term "egocentric") or to adapt the message to his informational needs. The second category is **socialized speech,** which includes those utterances that do appear to possess genuine communicative aims.

Piaget distinguished three subclasses of egocentric speech. One he called **repetition,** or **echolalia.** The child repeats, for his own pleasure, his own utterances and those of others. This even occurs in the context of conversation. (All of the following examples are from Piaget 1955: ch. 1.)

---

[3] Ginsburg and Opper (1969) offer a particularly clear and readable exposition of Piaget's theory of cognitive development.

Jac says to Ez: "Look; Ez, your pants are showing." Pie who is in another part of the room, immediately repeats: "Look, my pants are showing and my shirt, too."

That this is repetition, and not communication, is shown by the fact that Pie's comment is simply not true.

The second subclass is **monologue.**

The child talks to himself: Lev sits down at this table alone: "I want to do that drawing there. . . . I want to draw something, I do. I shall need a big piece of paper to do that."

It is interesting that in Piaget's definition of this type of egocentric speech, he uses the phrase "as though he were thinking aloud." However, he does not follow up this concept, which was to be the central concept of Vygotsky's analysis (1962).

The third subclass, one that is investigated in some detail in Piaget's book, is the **collective monologue.** In such exchanges, children "take turns" talking but without any apparent intention that other children should hear and respond. Anyone will serve as an audience.

(The children are busy with their drawings and each one tells the story which his drawing illustrates.)

LEV: "It begins with Goldilocks. I'm writing the story of the three bears. The daddy bear is dead. Only the daddy was too ill."
GEN: "I used to live in Salève. I lived in a little house, and you had to take the funicular railway to go and buy things."
GEO: "I can't do the bear."
LI: "That's not Goldilocks."
LEV: "I haven't got curls."

This is a conversation in that the children are all speaking about the same things, their pictures, but each is talking for himself.

Piaget distinguished five subclasses of socialized speech. The first he called **adapted information.** It is the basis of true dialogues. The primary distinction between this and the collective monologue is that the child actually talks about the topic of the other person's original comment.

EZ TO PIE: "You're going to marry me."
PIE: "No, I won't marry you."
"Oh, yes, you'll marry me."
"No."
"Yes . . ."

There is a clash of wills here, but it is not egocentric speech, as the children realize that there is a difference of opinion about this important question.

Another category is **criticism**. Although "critical" remarks usually assert the superiority of the speaker or deprecate others, as in "I've got a much bigger pencil than you," they are not egocentric in Piaget's non-evaluative sense. There is communication, as arguments and quarrels usually result. Piaget's three remaining categories are self-explanatory: **commands, questions,** and **answers.**

The coefficient of egocentric speech is that proportion of spontaneous utterances that are egocentric. However, the category of answers must be eliminated for the total number of utterances, for they are almost always answers to adult questions and hence vary in number for extraneous reasons. Piaget found the coefficient to be about 45 percent. Later investigations have seldom obtained coefficients of egocentrism as high as these. One reason may be the fact that the kindergarten where this study was performed (the Maison des Petites, at the J. J. Rousseau Institute, Geneva, where many of Piaget's studies have been done) was one that placed great emphasis on individual activity and vary little on organized group activity.

In another study with children in the early school years (Piaget 1955: ch. 3), one child was given a body of information by the experimenter and told to relate this information to a second child of the same age. Based on the results, Piaget came to two conclusions. First, children in these age groups do not communicate material very clearly, primarily because, in their egocentrism, they fail to adapt to the role of the listener and his needs. And second, as listeners, they do not understand very well information that is adequately expressed, again because of egocentric factors. Interestingly enough, they almost always have the illusion that they have been understood or have understood.

The experiment was performed with the transmission of an explanation of a kind of faucet and also with a story. The following is one of several stories used.

Once upon a time, there was a lady called Niobe, and she had twelve sons and twelve daughters. She met a fairy who had only one son and no daughter. Then the lady laughed at the fairy because the fairy had only one boy. Then the fairy was very angry and fastened the lady to a rock. The lady cried for 10 years. In the end she turned into a rock, and her tears made a stream which still runs today.

Here is one child's rendition of this story, with Piaget's comments:

Geo (8 years old) tells the story of Niobe in the role of the explainer: "Once upon a time there was a lady who had twelve sons and twelve girls, and then a fairy, a boy and a girl. And then Niobe wanted to have some more sons" than the fairy. Geo means by this that Niobe competed with the fairy, as was told in the text. But it will be seen how elliptical is his way of expressing it. "Then she (who?) was angry. She (who?) turned into a rock, and then her tears (whose?) made a stream which is still running today."

Young children typically use gestures and pronouns that convey little information: *this, something, there, she* as in the example, and so on.

The central concept of Piaget's analysis, which was to become even more important in his later theorizing, is the concept of egocentrism. The young child is the unwitting center of his universe. Only his own point of view can really matter, for he is unaware that there are other points of view. Piaget's later investigations convinced him that egocentrism is a pervasive characteristic of cognition in the preschool years. We have already seen some examples in the area of semantic development (Chapter 7). In one investigation, the child faced a scale model of a landscape and was asked to represent the appearance of the landscape from positions other than his own by, for example, selecting from a series of photographs the one that depicts what the landscape looks like to a doll sitting on the opposite side. Four- and five-year-old children persistently chose a picture depicting their own point of view; children a few years older were able to represent other perspectives.

In a revised edition of his book (Piaget 1959), Piaget included some additional studies on the effects of other people on the nature of the child's speech. He found much greater egocentrism in speech to adults than in speech to other children. Piaget's interpretation has broad implications for understanding development:

> The adult is at one and the same time far superior to the child and very near to him. He dominates everything, but at the same time penetrates into the intimacy of every wish and every thought . . . there is no frontier separating his ego from her (his mother's) superior ego . . . the child's egocentric speech is greater with the adult than with other children. . . . The playfellow, on the other hand, both resembles and is very different from the child's ego. He is like him because he is his equal in what he can do and what he knows. But he is very different just because, being on the same level with him, he cannot enter into his most intimate desires or personal point of view as a friendly adult would. . . . Where the superiority of the adult prevents discussion and cooperation, the playfellow provides the opportunity for such social conduct as will determine the true socialization of the intelligence. (1959:257–258)

This finding and Piaget's interpretation are extremely interesting and deserve further exploration. They are particularly suggestive concerning the role of peer interaction in learning, both in and out of the classroom.

Two factors might underlie egocentrism in communication: lack of **social will** and lack of **cognitive skill** (Kohlberg, Yaeger & Hjertholm 1968).

Many examples of egocentric speech in spontaneous settings seem to reflect a lack of communicative intent. The observations from the story-and-explanation study seem to show a lack of the cognitive skill necessary to communicate complex information. Collective monologues seem to involve both factors. Piaget believes that both factors arise from the young child's inability to differentiate his own perspective from those of others, but he does not consider the distinction closely. At times Piaget claims that egocentric speech does have a communicative function, one that the child is unable to realize effectively for cognitive reasons. With development comes the necessary skill for communication, and egocentric speech thus drops out in favor of adequate social speech. But at other times Piaget offers a negative characterization of egocentric speech: speech without communicative function or intent. This latter formulation in particular has led to extensive criticism of Piaget's views on the role of such speech, the best-known of which is that by Vygotsky (1962).

Russian Views of Language and Cognition

Since Pavlov, Russian psychologists have generally distinguished the "second-signal system" of language from the "first-signal system" of other physical stimuli (this distinction was introduced in Chapter 3). A recurrent theme in much Russian research with children is the emergence of this second-signal system. This research is often said to focus on the development of "verbal control," but it is quite the opposite of the verbal control assumed by the Whorf hypothesis. Language is believed to free the organism from dependence on immediate events in the environment and allows mental planning and voluntary behavior.

Such a view of the role of language in the development was first elaborated by Lev Vygotsky (1962; original Russian edition, 1934), who summarized his overall analysis of development as follows:

1. In their ontogenetic development, thought and speech have different roots.
2. In the speech development of the child, we can with certainty establish a preintellectual stage, and in his thought development, a prelinguistic stage.
3. Up to a certain point in time, the two follow different lines, independently of each other.
4. At a certain point these lines meet, whereupon thought becomes verbal and speech rational. (1962:44)

Vygotsky's innovation was the concept of **inner speech:** speech for oneself, speech gone underground, unarticulated. Inner speech is not talking to oneself in words and sentences, although this does occur, as when we carefully rehearse a speech silently. Inner speech is the process of thinking in **word meanings:**

Inner speech is not the interior aspect of external speech—it is a function in itself. It still remains speech, i.e., thought connected with words. But while in external speech thought is embodied in words, in inner speech words die as they bring forth thought. Inner speech is to a large extent thinking in pure word meanings. It is a dynamic, shifting, unstable thing, fluttering between word and thought, the two more or less stable, more or less firmly delineated components of verbal thought. (Vygotsky 1962:149)

Inner speech has a very different structure from external, or social, speech: It is highly abbreviated and consists primarily of predicates. These characteristics follow from the fact that inner speech serves a totally different function from that of social speech. In social speech, it is necessary to make one's *topic*, the psychological subject, clear in order to be understood. But, in inner speech, the topic is already known. We know what we are thinking *about*; what is of interest is *what* we think about it. Thus it is the *comment*, the psychological predicate, that is novel. In this respect, inner speech resembles social communication between two people on a topic of mutual concern. When two people have been waiting for a long-overdue bus and one of them spies the bus coming, he is unlikely to say *The bus is coming at last*; more likely he will say simply *It's coming* or *At last!*

Vygotsky's attempts to understand the development of inner speech led him to differ with Piaget on the nature of egocentric speech. Piaget had observed that egocentric speech gradually declines in frequency with age and finally disappears around the age of six or seven years. According to Piaget, egocentric speech simply withers away: one manifestation of the general phenomenon of declining egocentrism in the early school years. The child learns how to communicate, how to take into account points of view other than his own. The order of development, according to Piaget, is

presocial speech → egocentric speech → social speech

Vygotsky claimed that egocentric speech does not indicate lack of intent to communicate or an egocentric lack of awareness of the listener's perspective. Instead, failure to communicate arises from the fact that egocentric speech has a different function from that of social speech, namely *self-guidance*. It is vocalized because the young child cannot direct his actions verbally in covert fashion, as adults do. With development, the vocalization disappears, and egocentric speech goes underground to become inner speech. The order of development, according to Vygotsky, is

socialized speech → egocentric speech → inner speech
                              ↘ communicative speech

The language of the child is oversocialized at first, not undersocialized, as Piaget maintained. Language is primarily social in origin. At first the child does not distinguish between communication with others and communication with the self. Then egocentric speech develops. It is a hybrid form: It has the structure and function of inner speech but is vocalized as social speech. Gradually the child's ability to use egocentric speech for self-guidance increases. The speech becomes increasingly streamlined and effective for this purpose. The end point of such an abbreviation process is the complete internalization of egocentric speech as inner speech.

Vygotsky reports several experiments in support of his views on this question. He argues that Piaget assumed that egocentric speech is a result of insufficient socialization. So, by weakening the social constraints, we can cause the incidence of egocentric speech to *increase*. In such situations the possibility for truly socialized speech would be diminished, and the proportion of egocentric speech, which is not really intended for communication, should increase. For Vygotsky, the prediction is the reverse. The young child's awareness of the distinction between himself and another as a listener is sufficiently confused that he can produce only self-guiding speech in a social context. When the social constraints are weakened, for example, when the listener is less like the self or less able to understand the self, the frequency of egocentric speech should *decrease*.

Vygotsky manipulated a number of factors that might effect the nature of the social setting. He placed children with deaf-mutes, with children speaking a foreign language, with strangers, at separate tables, and even alone in a room. In every instance the coefficient of egocentric speech dropped considerably. Thus the feeling of being heard and understood—which is an essential condition for social speech—is crucial for egocentric speech also. This finding contradicts those of Piaget, who claimed that egocentric speech occurs because the child always assumes that he is being understood.

Interpreting Vygotsky's results is difficult because he does not report either the details of his experiments or the means used to compute the coefficients of egocentric speech. Does egocentric speech alone decrease in his situations, or do all kinds of speech diminish? Which specific types of egocentric and nonegocentric speech are observed? Because of Vygotsky's untimely death at the age of thirty-eight years, we have little more than the hastily collected essays and lecture notes that constitute his posthumously published book.

Vygotsky suggests another source of evidence for his interpretation of egocentric speech. According to Piaget, egocentrism is something that must be eliminated from the language of the well-adjusted adult. Egocentric speech should decrease in quality, as well as in quantity, during this period. That is, the egocentric speech observed should be decreasingly egocentric, just as the overall frequency of egocentric speech is decreasing. Vygotsky observed the opposite trend. Egocentric speech becomes increasingly egocentric, as it becomes better and better adapted to its function.

It is least egocentric at age three years and most egocentric at age seven years, despite the steady decline in frequency. Especially when the child encounters difficulties, highly egocentric speech can be observed. A five-and-a-half-year-old boy was drawing a streetcar when his pencil broke. He tried to continue working but failed because of the broken point. He muttered to himself *It's broken*, then put aside the pencil, took up watercolors, and began to draw a broken streetcar, continuing to talk to himself from time to time about his picture.

More recently, Kohlberg, Yaeger, and Hjerholm (1968) obtained more evidence in support of many of Vygotsky's conclusions. They have demonstrated clearly a curvilinear relation of egocentric speech (which they prefer to call "private speech") to age, not the monotonically decreasing relation that follows from Piaget's interpretation. The increase in private speech in early childhood reflects the emergence of a new ability in the child; the decrease a few years later reflects the internalization of this function. They also observed an increase in private speech with increasing task difficulty.[4]

Communication

We learn language in a social setting. Children talk to adults and hear adults talking with one another. Communication would seem to be the most obvious function of language. Piaget's investigations, however, suggest that language is not a very effective communication system for young children. This is a consequence of the second aspect of egocentrism mentioned earlier: lack of the cognitive skill necessary to adopt the perspective of another.

Communication of a specific object, event, or relationship to another is the simplest kind of communication, but it poses serious problems for the speaker. As Brown (1958) has pointed out, referents, whether objects, events, or relationships, do not have single names (recall the discussion in Chapter 7). A speaker has considerable latitude in the name he selects. His choice must be partially determined by the set of alternatives from which he must distinguish the intended referent. A pencil in a box of pebbles may be identified with the label *writing implement*; in a collection of pens, crayons, and so on, the word *pencil* is adequate; but in a box of pencils that have been used to varying degrees, the phrase *the four-inch*

---

[4] Vygotsky's work has been carried on by his student, the distinguished neuropsychologist A. R. Luria. Although Luria's theoretical innovations are extremely suggestive (Luria 1959), the inability of other investigators (Miller, Shelton & Flavell 1970; Bronckhart 1973) to replicate his major empirical findings makes it difficult to evaluate his work.

pencil may be required. The difficult cognitive task for the speaker is to consider the set of alternatives from which the listener must select the intended referent and to provide the listener with the appropriate information.

A very simple game situation (Glucksberg, Krauss and Weisberg 1966; Glucksberg and Krauss 1967) can be used to assess the ability of children and adults to communicate a single referent. Two children (or adults) are seated at a table, separated by an opaque screen. Each has a collection of six blocks on the table before him. Each block has a distinctive novel line drawing. The drawings are designed to be difficult to name but relatively easy to distinguish. Two examples are

One subject, the decoder, must select one block at a time from the set of six on the basis of a verbal message provided by the other subject, the encoder.

With the six forms used in this experiment, adult performance is nearly perfect. Children's messages are much less successful. Although preschool children understand the game and can play successfully, provided the referents are easy to encode (for example, colors or familiar animals), their selection of blocks with the novel drawings is virtually random. A 50 percent success level is not attained until approximately the seventh grade. Young children's messages are shorter than those of adults and often are highly idiosyncratic: for example, *mother's dress*. The idiosyncratic descriptions are not meaningless; when the children are later given their own descriptions and asked to serve as decoders, their performance is considerably higher. This is a good example of egocentrism; the child's solution to the problem is quite adequate *if* the other child knows everything the encoder knows.

When children are given adult messages, their selections are more accurate than the selections of adults who are given children's messages; in other words, children are better decoders then encoders. Encoding may simply be the more difficult task, as it requires the selection of appropriate distinctive features. Another explanation, consistent with Piaget's findings on egocentrism in speech to children and adults, is that having an understanding mother, as most children do, does not provide any motivation for less egocentric productions on the part of the child, whereas the child is constantly attempting to understand the messages of others.

A particularly striking difference between children and adults on this task is shown by their respective reactions to feedback from the decoder about his own understanding. When the decoder requests further information, for example, *I don't understand which one you mean,* adult encoders are likely to provide completely new descriptions or to elaborate previous messages, whereas children are more likely simply to repeat the descriptions or remain silent. Peterson, Danner, and Flavell (1972) have compared the effectiveness of various types of feedback, including facial expressions. Young children are unlikely to respond appropriately to facial expressions of puzzlement, though they will at least try to improve their communications in response to specific directions of the form *Tell me some more about it.*

The most extreme variety of egocentrism is shown by the youngest children, kindergarteners and first-graders, who occasionally use pointing, saying "This one" and pointing to one block, despite the presence of the opaque screen, which renders this strategy useless. One equally egocentric decoder replied to such a message by asking "Do you mean that one?" and pointing; he was given the reply "Yes." As Piaget had observed, whether the children are communicating or not, they assume they are understanding and being understood.

Despite these findings, the egocentrism of young children's communications should not be overestimated. Young children are, in many instances, able to make significant adjustments in their speech according to the characteristics of the listener. Like adults, four-year-olds produce fewer, shorter, and simpler sentences when speaking to two-year-olds than when speaking to other four-year-olds or adults (Shatz and Gelman 1973). When three-to-five-year-old children are shown a set of toys and allowed to ask for one from an adult who either sees the toys or places his hand over his eyes and the children's descriptions are then scored as adequate or not for a blindfolded observer, they do much better (75 percent) in the blocked-vision condition than in the normal-vision condition (27 percent). The toys are easily and uniquely named: a red and a green duck, boy and girl dolls, and so on. Therefore the cognitive task of selecting identifying features is extremely easy. The task requires only that the child be aware of the increased information that is required by a listener who cannot see the display (Maratsos 1973b).

Mueller (1972) introduced pairs of three-to-five-year-olds to each other and allowed them to play together. In general, the children played and communicated successfully without difficulty. Almost all the utterances provided adequate information to the listeners, and 85 percent of them received replies or at least attracted the listeners' attention. The difference between successful communication in this natural and unstructured setting, as assessed by the maintenance of the verbal exchange, and the failure of children of this age in laboratory communication tasks as described must lie primarily in the fact that, in playing together, the two children in each pair shared a common context of toys and books and of interests. Speech was about the "here and now," which was shared by the listener. Once again, language development can be seen to consist in part of a widening of the range of settings in which communication is possible (Brown 1973).

Pragmatics

Description of a referent situation, as in the Glucksberg and Krauss experiment, is one of the simplest functions of language. In recent years, linguists, anthropologists, and sociologists have sought to understand the full range of functions language serves in a social context. The term pragmatics is often used to refer to "the study of the use of language in context, by real speakers and hearers in real situations" (Bates 1974:277). Language may be used to command, placate, query, impress, threaten, or establish rapport with the listener; and this is only a partial list. Knowing how to use language often requires more than knowing how to assemble a syntactically well-formed sequence with a given literal meaning. We have already seen an example of this in the discussion of the functions of questions and other sentence types in Chapter 5. A particular sentence type may serve a variety of functions, depending on the topic, the relationship of the speaker and the hearer, and other aspects of the situation.

Lakoff (1972) has provided a good example of the subtlety of pragmatic knowledge in her discussion of modal verbs (*can, may, shall,* and *must*). Normally *you must* imposes an obligation, *you should* offers advice which may be ignored by the listener, and *you may* gives permission for something the listener already wants to do. *You may* is customarily the most polite; *you must* the most rude. But in certain situations the rules are quite different. In particular, a host at a dinner party who offers a guest a special dish saying *you must try this is* actually being far more polite than if he said *you should try this* or *you may try this.*

Gumperz and Hymes (1972) include a number of studies of the way in which language, situation, speaker, topic, listener, and other variables affect the use of language. Surprisingly little is known about the development of pragmatic knowledge by children, though much research is currently underway (Bates 1974). Bates (in press) presents a general view of pragmatics in child language.

Language and Representation in Cognitive Development

A major change occurs in the thinking of the child at the age of six or seven years. It is no coincidence that schools around the world begin at this age, for the child is now ready. The change is apparent in many cognitive domains, but one of the most striking is the acquisition of con-

servation. Piaget (Piaget and Szeminska 1952) first discovered that, when children below the age of six are presented with two equal rows of clay pellets

A   .   .   .   .   .
B   .   .   .   .   .

which they judge to be equal, and if the experimenter then rearranges the pellets (without concealing anything) to

A   .   .   .   .   .
B   .   .   .   .   .

the children will select row A as having more pellets. Similarly, if two beakers of water, equally full, are presented, children judge them to be equal, but, if the contents of one beaker are then poured into another, taller and thinner beaker, resulting in a higher water level, the taller beaker will be judged to contain more water.

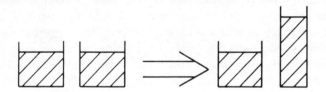

What children of this age (up to about six or seven years) lack is the realization that quantity is invariant, even though the shape or appearance of the substance can vary. Quantity is conserved, but children do not attain this concept, **conservation,** until the age of six or seven years.

The acquisition of conservation is only one particularly striking aspect of the cognitive advance occurring at six or seven, which is a major focus of research on children's thinking. Piaget's own explanation is based on the concept of **reversibility:** Events in the environment can be physically or mentally undone. One type of reversibility is **negation:** The child comes to know that the quantities of liquid in the two beakers are equal because, as many children express it, "If you were to pour the water back, it would be the same." Another type of reversibility is **compensation,** which is based in turn on **decentration.** The young children can attend to only one dimension at a time, length in the pellet experiment or height in the liquid experiment. With development, he can attend to both dimensions in each situation (decentration) and can then realize that a change in one dimension, length, is exactly compensated by a reverse change in the other dimension, density, so that there is no change in quantity.

Bruner (1964) has theorized that the course of cognitive development is basically the history of the evolving use of modes of representation. Representation should be understood literally: How does the mind represent reality to itself in thinking? Children between the ages of two and six years are primarily dependent on images for representation. They are more likely to use imagery and the perceptual properties that images are based upon in solving a problem, and their images seem to have greater vividness and detail. Children's performances on classification tasks illustrate well the quality of their thinking. When young children are given a group of pictures to be sorted into categories, they are likely to group on the basis of color, shape, or size. Around the age of six or seven years, there is a shift from reliance on perceptual or iconic properties to reliance on symbolic representations. Older children are more likely to group using a superordinate word, for example, "They are all tools."

The greatest limitation of iconic representation is its static quality. It is not possible to rearrange or combine the elements of an image. Before the transition from iconic to symbolic representation occurs, the amount of water in a conservation experiment will be judged on the basis of a single, directly observable property—usually the height of the water level. The use of language for representation (and Bruner seldom considers symbols other than linguistic ones) revolutionizes cognition because it is so flexible. "In effect, language provides a means, not only for representing experience, but also for transforming it" (1964:4). Bruner is not entirely clear on the extent to which his use of the term "transforming" is literal or metaphorical, but it is at least some of each. The basic idea is that the linguistic representation of an event, in the form of a phrase or sentence, can be manipulated and that various inferences can be drawn. This gives the child's cognition far greater flexibility and power than it had at the previous, iconic stage.

Several kinds of evidence can be offered for this view, including one concerning conservation specifically. Frank (reported in Bruner 1964) hypothesized that, if transitional-age children, children developing symbolic techniques of representation, could be shielded from the misleading iconic rendering of the situation so that they could represent the situation verbally *before* they see it, their language could serve as a guide.

The children, four-, five-, six-, and seven-year-olds, were all given the standard conservation-of-liquid-quantity test first. Then Frank gave a screened version of the test, in which the actual pouring was concealed by an opaque screen. First, the child inspected two partially filled standard beakers and agreed that they contained equal amounts of water. Another beaker, wider but of the same height, was then shown to the child. The experimenter poured from one of the standard beakers into the wider beaker behind the screen. The child, who could not see the water level in either the remaining standard or the new beaker, is asked which had more to drink, the standard or the wider beaker, or did they both have the same amount? Figure 9.1 illustrates the results.

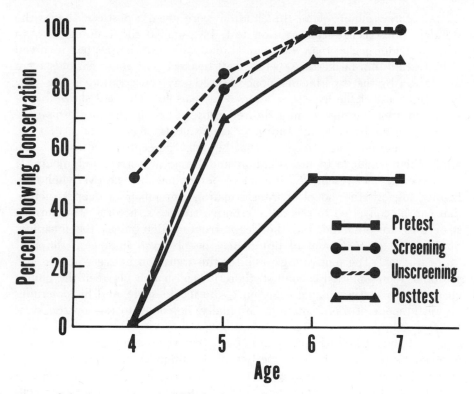

Figure 9.1 Percentage of children showing conservation of liquid volume on a pretest, during screening, upon unscreening, and on a posttest run after completion of the experiment.

SOURCE: The course of cognitive growth. In J. S. Bruner, *American Psychologist*, 1964, **19**, 1–15, adapted from Figures 6 and 7. Reprinted by permission of the American Psychological Association.

With the screened beakers, there was a striking increase in correct equality judgments. Correct responses jumped from 0 to 50 percent among the four-year-olds and from 50 to 100 percent among the six-year-olds. When asked to justify their responses, most children replied with something like "It's the same water" or "You only poured it."

Then the screen was removed, and the children were asked again which beaker had more water, or were they the same. All the four-year-olds changed their minds. The perceptual display overwhelmed them, and they decided that the wide beaker held less water. But almost all the five-year-olds stuck to their original judgments. In fact, they often explicitly mentioned the difference between appearance and reality: "It looks like more to drink, but it is only the same because it is the same water and it was only poured from there to there," to quote one. And all the six- and seven-year-olds stuck with conservation.

A few minutes later the children were given a posttest. It was the standard, unscreened conservation test, but, unlike the training test, in which a wider beaker than the original one was used, the posttest involved either a tall, thin beaker or several small beakers. The four-year-olds were unaffected by the experiment—none showed any conservation in the new task. But most of the five-, six-, and seven-year-olds who had showed conservation after the unscreening showed conservation in the posttest.

On the basis of this and other experiments, Bruner argues that the younger children, when freed of what he calls "perceptual seduction," can apply their language to the situation and arrive at correct judgments. If the screen is not present, the impact of perception may be overwhelming. Bruner suggests the model of transformational grammar: a deep structure that can be converted to several alternative surface structures. The surface structures are observed, but the deep structure determines the meaning. Similarly, a given amount of liquid may be observed in several different "appearances." The motivating force for the transition between iconic and symbolic representation is conflict; there is a mismatch between the child's current means of organizing experience, the iconic mode, and his emerging linguistic mode of representation. Gradually, he comes to rely on the symbolic encoding, not the direct perception.

Language clearly plays an important developmental role, according to Bruner's theory. Certain properties of cognition are made possible because of language: for example, overcoming dependence on perceptual attributes in the conservation task (for others, see Bruner, Olver & Greenfield 1966). However, mere possession of language is not enough; the child must learn to rely on language. Bruner offers the screening-unscreening conservation experiment as evidence that the use of language can bring some children to conservation if they have a chance to deal with the situation first in purely linguistic terms.

In Frank's experiment, the role of language was basically implicit; little can be said about precisely what kinds of language were used or how. A more direct approach to these questions has been taken by Sinclair de-Zwart (1969). Bruner pointed out that preconservational and conservational children differ in the language they use to describe various stimulus materials. The younger children do not attend to both dimensions at once; they say *That one is tall, and that one is little*. But the older children use more sophisticated language. They speak of one glass's being *taller but thinner* than another. Bruner suggested that training children to use language appropriate to the demands of the task would improve their performance on it.

On this point Piaget and his coworkers, including Sinclair de-Zwart disagree strongly. According to Piaget, language reflects, rather than determines, cognitive development; therefore special linguistic training will not help children whose level of cognitive development has not yet reached the point at which they can comprehend the relevant concepts represented by the words.

Sinclair de-Zwart tested Bruner's suggestion that nonconserving children can be taught language expressions characteristic of conserving children and that this training will lead to conservation. This test required, as a first step, identifying changes in the children's descriptive language that occur with the acquisition of conservation. A number of sets of materials were used for this purpose. In one, two dolls were given equal or unequal amounts of clay, equal or unequal numbers of marbles, or pencils that varied in length and thickness. Each child was asked to describe these arrangements spontaneously; then the examiner asked the child to arrange the objects according to some verbal instructions, in order to test comprehension. Then all the children were tested to determine whether or not they conserved. Essentially no differences in comprehension between the conservers and nonconservers were found. But there were three principal differences in the spontaneous descriptions produced by the two groups.

Children who conserved used *more relational terms*; they said things like *One has more than (a plus que) the other* or *One has more, and the other has less.* The other children almost always failed to use these terms; the predominant response was of the type, *one has got a big bit (a beaucoup), the other a little bit (un peu).*

Children who conserved used more *highly differentiated* terms. They often used appropriate pairs of terms for specific dimensions, like *long* and *short* (*long* and *court*) and *fat* and *thin* (*gros* and *mince*). Nonconservers used undifferentiated terms for the two dimensions; *fat* (*gros*) might be used for a long and thin pencil and *small* (*petit*) for a short and thick one.

Children who conserved produced *coordinated descriptions*. If objects differed on two dimensions, children who did not conserve tended to mention only one of the differences. For example, when one doll had four small marbles and one had two big ones, such a child stated *One has got a lot of marbles and the other only two.* When such a child *did* mention both dimensions, it was usually in a four-part uncoordinated description: *This crayon is long; the other is short; this crayon is thin; the other is fat (Ce crayon est long; l'autre est court; ce crayon est mince; l'autre est gros).* In contrast, the conservers coordinated the dimensions, saying *This pencil is longer but thinner; the other is short but thick (Ce crayon est plus long mais plus mince; l'autre est court mais gros).*

The descriptive patterns used by a child were a better clue to his conservation ability than was his age. An eight-year-old who did not conserve used descriptive patterns characteristic of the five-year-olds, who typically did not conserve.

Next an attempt was made to teach nonconservers to use the expressions used by the conservers. The training process has not been described in great detail, but it appears to involve the examiner's first giving instructions to the child and then the child's instructing the examiner. Easiest to teach was the use of differentiated terms, then the use of relational terms, and finally the use of coordinated descriptions. This is interesting because, of the three aspects, the last and most difficult—coordinated descriptions— was most highly correlated with conservation.

Of the children who did learn to use these expressions, very few made the transition to conservation. Children who had given partial-con- servation answers in the pretest were able to express their arguments more clearly and also more consistently in the posttests. And those who did not show conservation on the pretest, those who indicated that water level determines quantity, began spontaneously to mention both dimensions— height and width—and even occasionally to mention the convariance of the two dimensions. But conservation itself was *not* achieved by these children. One said: *There the water goes up because the glass is thin; the other glass is shorter and wider, and there is less to drink there.*

These results demonstrate that language training can at best con- tribute *indirectly* to the acquisition of conservation. Language can lead the child to focus on the relevant dimensions of the task situation. The observed changes in the justifications for the answers given indicate that language can aid in the storage and retrieval of relevant information. But, in addition to the selection, storage, and retrieval of relevant cues, cognitive integration and coordination are necessary for conservation, and language training does not appear to contribute to them directly.

In a similar, but must more extensive, study of the relationship between conservation and dimensional language, Peisach (1973) found that comprehension of dimensional language is necessary, but not sufficient, for conservation, a finding consistent with that of Sinclair-de-Zwart. The use of language for cognitive purposes requires a mature level of cognitive functioning.

Holland and Palermo (1975) taught kindergarteners who made the "less is more" error (Chapter 7) the correct meaning of the terms *less* and *more*. Previous research suggested a relationship between mastery of these concepts and successful performance on the conservation task, in which the term *more* is used extensively. Although most of the children were success- ful in the language training phase, and generalized their knowledge to materials and situations not directly trained, no change occurred in con- servation scores.

Deafness and Cognitive Development

A very different approach to the question of the role of language in cognitive representations and functioning has been taken by Hans Furth (1966; 1971), who has compared the performances on various cognitive tasks—concept attainment, memory, conservation, rule learning, and others—

by deaf children, who in the vast majority of instances have not mastered English in either its oral or printed forms, with those of hearing children. He has found that, in a surprising variety of situations, the performances of the deaf are fully comparable to those of hearing children. Conservation, for example, is only moderately retarded (1 to 2 years) if at all in deaf children; the available evidence is mixed. Furth interprets this evidence as support for the contention, based on the theoretical work of Piaget, that language is not necessary for thought.

The issue may not be settled, however. Many deaf children acquire some form of manual communication, either the fully developed American Sign Language or some simplified signing system (Moores 1974). Manual communication appears to be a truly linguistic system (Stokoe 1960) and may well serve deaf children in ways similar to the ways in which oral language serves hearing children (Kohl 1966; Spence 1971). Best (1973) found that deaf children with more exposure to sign language performed more similarly to hearing children on various classification tasks than those with less exposure to signing. Many of the experiments comparing deaf and hearing subjects have to be repeated, with careful attention to the signing abilities of the subjects.

The Importance of Modality

Blank (1974) suggests that the influence of language on the young child's thinking has been greatly underestimated because of focusing only on problems of visual-spatial processing. She argues that the sensorimotor skills available to the preschooler are generally sufficient for his purposes. But in other areas these skills are not as useful, and therefore the child has more opportunity and motivation to use language. One such area is that of temporal concepts. Preschoolers can learn to look for candy under a board with two circles and not under a board with one circle; this learning requires no use of language. But learning to look under a board that flashes once and not under the board that flashes twice is much harder and can only be accomplished by children who can apply appropriate verbal labels, for examples, "one" and "two." Similarly, in typical studies of communication, the problem is virtually always in the visual modality. Removing the visual information can drastically affect the speech produced. For example, three-year-olds were taught a simple form-discrimination task, to learn to look under the circle and not the triangle. Afterward each child was asked, "Which one had the candy?" When the objects remained in place, most of the subjects simply pointed, but, when the objects were first removed, most of the subjects offered the relevant attributes: *the round one, the circle.* Blank also points out that verbal instructions are much more helpful in problems requiring tactual discrimination than in visual problems. She suggests that the child may first become aware of the usefulness of language when facing tasks involving the nonvisual spheres and only later may begin to transfer this awareness to the visual modality. . . . With a reduction in the visual component (through the use of other sensory modalities or through removing the visual stimuli), the word not only assumes greater prominence, but often it becomes essential to the task of communication. (1974:239)

Blank's work has shown that the limitation of work on language and thinking in young children to a narrow range of primarily visual-spatial thinking has been unfortunate.

Summary

The investigations reported in this chapter illustrate clearly the distinction between the structure of language and its functions. Mastering the linguistic system is not the same thing as putting it to work. Language is not successfully used for many functions for a considerable period after the essential mastery of structure. One function that is present from the beginning of language—communication—is extremely inefficient in early childhood. The use of language in each area—memory, communication, representation, and others, such as categorization (Oliver and Hornsby 1966)—is tied to the level of cognitive functioning. Like any tool, language requires an intelligent hand to guide it.

Two models have been suggested for the emergence of language as a tool of thinking. The first, more widely investigated, is that the ability to use language for many functions emerges approximately simultaneously with the many cognitive advances that occur in middle childhood, around the age of seven years. Whether it is cognitive advance that explains the improvement in using language or the reverse remains a fundamental problem for developmental psychology. But the internalization of language in inner speech seems to tie all these advances together. Though this process of internalization is difficult to study, it is surely one of the major milestones of human development.

A second model, suggested by Blank, does not postulate a broad breakthrough in the use of language on many fronts. Instead, this model views the advance as a more gradual process, one that begins in narrowly circumscribed domains, in particular those with little visual-spatial content, and only gradually is transferred to other domains.

Only further research on a wider range of problems can settle this issue. But perhaps the models are simply different perspectives on the same process: Blank's model emphasizes the beginning of the process and the internalization model its culmination.

further reading

Flavell, J. H. Developmental studies of mediated memory. *Advances in Child Development and Behavior*, 1970, **5**, 182–211.

Moore, T. E. (Ed.) *Cognitive development and the acquisition of language.* New York: Academic Press, 1973.

Piaget, J. Language and thought from a genetic point of view. In *Six psychological studies*, trans. by A. Tenzer. New York: Random House, 1967.

Vygotsky, L. S. *Thought and language.* Trans. by E. Hanfmann & G. Vakar. Cambridge, Mass.: M.I.T. Press, 1962.

Dialect Differences and Language Development

The Gileadites seized the fords of the Jordan and held them against Ephraim. When any Ephraimite who had escaped begged leave to cross, the men of Gilead asked him, "Are you an Ephraimite?," and if he said "No," they would retort, "Say Shibboleth." He would say "Sibboleth," and because he could not pronounce the word properly, they seized him and killed him at the fords of the Jordan. At that time forty-two thousand men of Ephraim lost their lives. (*Judges* 12:5–6: New English Bible)

All too often language serves as a barrier, rather than as a flexible and efficient means of communication. We do not all speak the same language. Even within a particular language community individuals do not speak in exactly the same way. Such variations within a single language are called **dialects.** Dialect differences are often interpreted as indicators of real or imagined differences in education, religion, morality, social class, race, attitudes, and other aspects of life. Shaw's *Pygmalion* is about a benevolent use of this interpretive tendency; the story from *Judges* represents the other side of the coin.

Dialect differences arise whenever a group of individuals communicate more among themselves than with individuals outside the group, at least on certain topics. Thus dialects of a limited sort often develop on the basis of profession. Different occupations have different things to talk about. But the same concepts will be labeled with different words. The words *forecast, prognosis,* and *prediction* have very similar meanings, but one is associated with meteorology, another with medicine, and the third with the sciences. McNeill has studied the dialect used by astronautical engineers in "Speaking of Space" (1966).

Age differences lead to dialect differences. One age group may deliberately coin new words and phrases and new meanings for existing words and phrases. These age differences are preserved by the tendency of speakers to continue using the language they learned when young, although the general language may have changed since then. Old people tend to continue to use words that have been generally replaced in the language.

Although profession, age, and many other factors affect language, two factors determine the most significant dialect differences. One is geography. Even in the United States, which has a remarkable uniformity of language for a country its size, there are considerable differences, which are primarily geographic in nature. The word *greasy* rhymes with *fleecy* in the northern part of the country, whereas in the South it rhymes with *easy*. In some parts of the East and South, *r* is not pronounced at the ends of words or before consonants. In such regions, *par* rhymes with *pa*, and *startle* with *throttle*. In the northeastern part of the country, *stoop* is often used for *porch* and *comforter* for *blanket*. The words *hotcakes, pancakes,* and *griddle cakes* are associated with particular regions. Generally speaking, the greatest differences occur on the East Coast of this country and gradually become weaker as one proceeds inland.

The second major factor determining dialect differences is social class. Bolinger (1968) has contrasted geography with social class as, respectively, the horizontal and vertical coordinates of language. These differences are most pronounced when a society is stratified, and, in a very real sense, American society is divided into classes. There is a strong tendency for people to classify other individuals on the basis of their language, and this classification can be strongly evaluative in nature. Differences in speech are often cultivated for just this reason, to influence the opinion of others. Ethnic-group differences are usually classified as social-class differences.

Profession, age, geography, and social class are all factors that lead to the use of different dialects by different persons. There is also a factor that leads to the use of different dialects by a single speaker: the particular situation in which a speaker finds himself. Every speaker will modify his speech in a way that he feels appropriate for the setting. In most societies, for example, there is a standard formal dialect. In India, formal Hindi has some Sanskrit added to it. In standard formal English, there is much less use of contractions than in informal English—"Let us begin" versus "Let's start." Near synonyms are selected for the appropriate situation:—*begin* and *rise* are the formal equivalents of *start* and *get up*. In standard formal English, adverbs ending with *-ly* are common and may be placed either before or after the verb they modify—*They left quickly* or *They quickly left*.

Informal English tends to place the adverb after the verb or change to a different form of modifier, also placed after the verb—*They left quickly* or *They left right away.*

Sociolinguistics

The study of dialect is a job both for the linguist and for the sociologist. In the past, there has been a division of labor. Linguists have focused primarily on geography and sociologists on the role of social class. Each may miss important facts and generalizations that the other would notice, so it is important that both be involved in such studies. Increasingly in recent years, there has developed the new field of **sociolinguistics,** drawing on the techniques and concepts of both parent disciplines. Foremost among the sociolinguists is William Labov (1970a; 1970b), who has added much to our knowledge of sociolinguistic theory and method and also to our knowledge of a specific dialect of English, Black English, to be examined later in this chapter.

In addition to the variability among individuals characteristic of social-class and ethnic-group dialects and, to the variability within individuals because of situational factors, there is a third kind of variability inherent in the use of language by a single speaker in a single situation. Many aspects of language are fundamentally probabilistic, not absolute. Although we often tend to perceive probabilistic phenomena as "all or nothing," the variability is there. A good example is the pronunciation of the -*ing* morpheme in words like *working* and *living*, which has been studied in detail by Labov. Most people will perceive the speech of another person as *always* including [ɪn] of [ɪŋ]. In fact, everyone, including English teachers, uses both forms with some probability. The probabilities are a function of both the social class of the speaker and the situation in which the speech is produced. That is, the same aspects of language that vary in shifting from relatively more formal to relatively more informal speech—what Labov calls "style shifting" (see Reading 10.1)—also distinguish social levels of English.

In a study of dialect differences in New York City, Labov obtained samples of speech under conditions of casual speech, careful speech, and reading style. He calculated the proportion of times -*ing* was pronounced [ɪn] in these three situations for four groups of white speakers: lower-class, working-class, lower middle-class, and upper middle-class. Figure 10.1 illustrates the results.

The four lines of the figure clearly reflect differences among the four groups. But equally important are two findings that hold for all the groups. The first is that there are no points corresponding to either 100 percent or 0 percent use of [ɪn]. That is, speakers in all groups produced some instances of both pronunciations in each situation. And, second, each group showed regular style shifting in the same direction. They all used

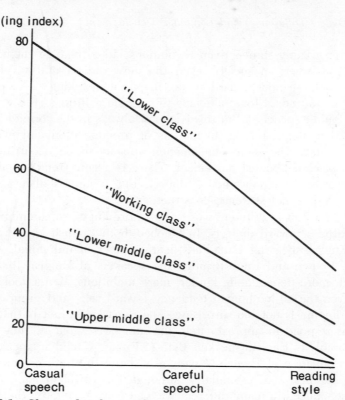

Figure 10.1 Class and style stratification of (ing) in *working, lining,* and so on, for white New York City adults. From Labov, W. *The study of nonstandard English.* Copyright © 1970 by the National Council of Teachers of English. Reprinted by permission of the publisher and W. Labov. p. 19, fig. 2.

[ɪŋ] most in the casual condition, less in the careful condition, and least in reading.

Labov has found the same patterns of variability for the pronunciation of [d] for *th*, for the absence of *r* in such words as *park* and *car*, and for some grammatical features such as the use of *ain't* and double negatives.

Attitudes toward Dialect Differences

A language is a coherent system of rules. Two dialects of a given language are somewhat different systems of rules. By definition, dialects have a great deal in common with one another. Dialects are not foreign languages but alternative versions of the same language.

Social-class and ethnic dialects are simply dialects, like any other kind of dialect. Unfortunately, they have not always been viewed in this way. There is a strong tendency to see nonstandard dialects as the result of isolated deviations from the standard language, resulting from failure to master the standard dialect. This failure in turn may be blamed on inadequate environment, genetic differences, or other factors.

Social values and attitudes related to language are not only strong but also remarkably stable. Even revolutions fail to change them in most instances. In American society, even the most radical and revolutionary figures do not use nonstandard syntax in public speaking or in print. Of course, it is traditional for politicians to sprinkle a little of the vernacular into their public speeches. But this is almost always in the form of vernacular vocabulary items, seldom in matters of pronunciation and even more rarely in syntax. The same phenomenon appears to be occurring in the American black-nationalist movement. There is a new trend toward using some aspects of the nonstandard dialect, but it almost always involves vocabulary items, not sentence construction.

To put this in different words, the entire linguistic community often shares attitudes toward dialects. In Quebec, both English and French are spoken. English-speaking Canadians hearing tapes of individuals speaking Canadian French and English judge the speakers of English to be more intelligent, more dependable, kinder, more ambitious, better looking, and taller. Given the all-too-human tendency toward self- and group-glorification, this finding is not too surprising. The remarkable fact is that French Canadians respond in approximately the same way; that is, they respond more favorably to English speakers than to French Canadian speakers. The negative evaluation of French Canadian is shared by both communities in Quebec (Lambert 1967). Similarly, although the vowel in *mad, bad,* and *glad* is pronounced in many different ways in New York City, there is general agreement that, the higher the tongue (pronouncing the vowel closer to that of *beard*), the lower the status of the speaker. These two examples are both instances of a phenomenon that has long been familiar to sociologists: the adoption of majority norms by members of the minority, even when they are highly unfavorable to the minority.

These attitudes can and do change. French-speaking Canadians have become increasingly concerned with preserving their linguistic heritage and so have many black Americans. But the changes are slow. Often an educated, culturally conscious elite can change its view, but it will have difficulty in affecting the majority of the group.

It is often true that the people who most strongly condemn a form in the speech of others are among the people who are most likely to use it in their own casual speech. This is undoubtedly owing to the fact that they are the ones who are struggling most actively to overcome this trait and therefore most conscious of it. This situation often leads to what has been called **hypercorrect speech**—adopting the standard form even more strongly than the high-prestige group. In studies of the pronunciation of *r* in such words as *heard, guard,* and *car,* lower middle-class speakers sharply increased their pronunciation of *r.* In reading sentences their score was almost identical to that of upper middle-class speakers, and in reading word lists it actually exceeded that of upper middle-class speakers. This tendency for such speakers strongly to condemn the nonstandard form is particularly important for the educational process, because American school teachers have traditionally been drawn from the lower middle class (although this is increasingly less true).

Of course, there is no logical reason or necessity for such unfavorable attitudes. There are many situations in the world that demonstrate that a pluralistic situation can exist successfully. There are more children in the world who experience part of their schooling in languages that are not their mother tongues than children who do not. And in most instances this does not mean that the mother tongue is stigmatized. Swahili is the school language in Tanzania, although a substantial proportion of the children in this region are native speakers of languages other than Swahili. The Kerman area of Iran is an example of a pluralistic dialect situation. Kermani Persian is the native dialect of the children, whereas Standard Persian is the dialect of the schools. There is no stigma attached to speaking Kermani with family and friends, but Standard Persian is used in school and with people from other areas of Iran.

Black English

Despite our long-standing belief in the pluralism of American society, we have always been less than tolerant of differences. Nowhere is this clearer than in the area of language differences. The dialect of English spoken by many black Americans is probably the best known example, but it is hardly the only one. Yiddish, which was once the native language of literally millions of Americans is now nearly extinct in this country. In the southwestern part of the country and in parts of New York City, a nonstandard dialect of English arises as the result of contact between Spanish and English speakers. In fact, Chicano Spanish is viewed as a nonstandard and, indeed, "inferior" dialect of Spanish by speakers of European Spanish.

The dialect spoken by many black Americans is both the most widespread nonstandard dialect and the one we know most about. Labov (1966), in his path-breaking studies of language use in New York City, and Stewart (1964), working in Washington, D.C., have provided reliable and useful sociolinguistic knowledge about this dialect. The dialect is now, by general agreement, called Black English. The term is in some ways unfortunate: Not all blacks speak a version of the dialect (in fact, we do not even know how many do); furthermore, many of its features are present in other southern regional dialects. The term is a convenient abbreviation and, like all abbreviations, somewhat false. However, it is shorter than Nonstandard Negro English or Black Nonstandard English. Labov (1972) argues that since black Americans speak a wide range of dialects, a more specific label is needed; he proposes the term Black English Vernacular for the dialect we are concerned with here. For brevity's sake, we will continue to use the term Black English.

From a linguistic point of view, the differences between Black English (BE) and Standard English (STE) are not great. In general, the deep structures of sentences and the underlying representations of lexical items are the same in the two dialects. And so are most of the rules that operate on them: transformations on deep structures and phonological rules on underlying representations. Some rules are different, however; a rule may be present in one dialect but not in the other, or the conditions for a rule's application may differ. We shall consider a few of the most obvious differences (following Labov 1970a); Reading 10.2 contains a carefully annotated sample of BE, with emphasis on syntactic differences.

In STE the present progressive is marked in two ways; *He is going* contains the auxiliary *be* and the affix *-ing*. In BE only the second element is necessary: *He going home*. In the so-called present perfect, *I have lived here* is the STE form, whereas either *I have live here* or *I lived here* is permissible in BE. Some possessives do not contain the *'s* marker; *This is John mother* in BE, in contrast to *This is John's mother* in STE. Notice that, because of the order of the nouns, the BE form is unambiguous in referring to the mother of John. When the second noun (the object possessed) is deleted, the BE form does mark the possessive with *'s*: *This is John's* is the possessive, whereas *This is John* has a quite different meaning.

In the three constructions just discussed, STE marks a feature twice (*be* + *ing* for the present progressive, *have* + *en* for the present perfect, and *'s* + order for the possessive), whereas BE marks the feature just once. The converse also occurs. Double and triple negatives, as in *Didn't nobody see it*, are common in BE. *Or either* is sometimes used as just *either* in STE. Neither dialect should be viewed as a "simplified" version of the other.

Agreement between subject and verb in person and number is not obligatory in BE; *She have a bike* and *They was going*. Many common irregular verbs are not marked for the simple past tense. For example, the past tense forms of *come* and *see* are *come* and *see* respectively. This is not to be interpreted as the lack of a past tense or as an indication that the speakers of BE do not have a concept of the past. The two tenses are negated differently: *I don't see it* is the present tense, whereas *I ain't see it* is the past tense form of the negation.

There are some instances in which BE makes a grammatical distinction that STE does not make or that can be indicated in STE only by use of a complex construction. The most important is the use of the uninflected form of *be* to indicate habitual or general state. *He be workin'* means that he generally works, perhaps that he has a regular job. *He be with us* means that he is generally with us, perhaps that he lives here. In contrast *He workin'* can mean simply that he is working at this moment and *He with us* that he is here now.

The verb *be* (in its inflected forms) is often not present in constructions that call for *be* in STE. These constructions include sentences with predicate nouns (*He a friend*), predicate adjectives (*He tired*), and the present-progressive tense described (*He workin' with us*).

Although some linguists have interpreted the absence of *be* to reflect a difference in deep structure between the two dialects, Labov and other linguists have argued that the assumption that *be* is not present in the deep structure is unjustified. The verb *be* does appear in many contexts as the last word in sentences like *There he is* (not *There he*); in tag questions and in negatives, like *He ain't here, is he?*; in the past tense, as in *She was here*; and in other contexts. These facts indicate that *be* is present in the deep structure but that it is deleted by a transformation or transformations in certain specified contexts, in the process of conversion to the surface structure. The verb *be* is deleted in just those instances in which contraction is possible in STE—*He's a friend, He's tired, He's with us* but not *There he's*. The absence of *be* may be viewed as a result of contraction to *he's* by the same rule that exists in STE, followed by deletion of a final *s*, which is a very common phenomenon in BE.

David, he say "Here I come" illustrates the common use of a pronoun following the noun subject of a sentence in BE. This structure does occur infrequently in STE. It serves to focus attention on the "topic" of the sentence.

Labov has asked speakers of BE to repeat the sentence *Ask Albert if he knows how to play basketball.* The most common response is the production of *Ask Albert do he know how to play basketball.* In Chapter 5 the structure of English direct questions was outlined. The declarative *He knows how to play basketball* has a corresponding direct question of the form *Does he know how to play basketball?* But, when this question is indirect, that is, embedded in a sentence, it takes the form *if he knows how to play basketball.* The question transformation and the transformation that supplies *do* if necessary are not applied in STE. But in BE these transformations are applied consistently to both direct and indirect questions. Here we have a common kind of difference between dialects: not the presence or absence of a transformation in a dialect but simply a change in the conditions under which it is applied. A similar difference exists for imperatives. The direct imperative *Don't do that* becomes *I told you not to do that* in STE but retains its form in BE: *I told you don't do that.*

The phonological differences probably contribute more than syntactic differences to difficulties in understanding between speakers of the two dialects. Many of these differences involve consonants at the ends of words. In BE the liquid [r] is dropped before consonants and at the ends of words. As a result, *sore* and *saw* are **homophones** (words pronounced alike), as are *court* and *caught*. Similarly, [l] may be omitted in the same contexts. Thus, *toll* and *toe* are homophones, as are *help* and *hep*.

Consonant clusters at the ends of words are often simplified, especially if the cluster ends with [t], [d], [s], or [z]. *Past* and *passed* are homophones with *pass, called* with *call, hits* with *hit,* and so on. In many of these examples it is not easy to determine whether the difference is a phonological or a syntactic one. Is the final *d* of *called* deleted because of a phonological rule or because the simple past tense is not inflected in BE? Is the *s* of the third-person singular form *hits* deleted because of a consonant-cluster simplification rule or because number agreement is not obligatory between subject and verb? Both views account for some of the evidence and leave other forms unexplained.

In most instances there is no distinction between [ɪ] and [ɛ] before nasals and liquids: *Pin* and *pen* are homophones, as are *cheer* and *chair.* Often the sounds [ay] and [aw] are changed to the simple vowel [a]. In this instance, *find, found,* and *fond* are homophones.

The fricative [θ] in final position is changed to [f]; thus *with* and *bath* are pronounced [wif] and [baef], respectively.

It is still a matter of disagreement whether differences in pronunciation, that is, phonetic representations, arise from differences in underlying representations or from differences in the phonological rules that convert underlying representations into phonetic representations. This is a question that has important implications for the teaching of reading, which will be discussed in the final section of this chapter. However, it does seem clear that the majority, even if not all, of the differences are in the rules and that in those instances the underlying representations are the same in both dialects. An example of such a difference follows.

Many speakers of BE pronounce *risk* as [rɪs] and *test* as [tɛs]. From consideration of these forms alone there is no evidence that the final consonant is present in the underlying representations of these words. The most common plural forms for these words are [rɪsəz] and [tɛsəz]. Again, it does not appear that the final consonants are present. But suppose a suffix, *-y* or *-ing,* is added. Now the forms are pronounced [rɪskiy] and [tɛstɪn], in which the final consonants are present. The final consonants sometimes appear even in the root word, when it is followed by a word that begins with a vowel. The observed forms can best be accounted for with the assumption that the underlying forms are identical to those in STE, together with two phonological rules, one unique to BE, and one shared with STE:

Underlying representations:	/tɛst/	/tɛst + z/	/tɛst + In/
	↓	↓	↓
1. *Consonant-clusters:* simplification [st] → [s] if followed by anything except a vowel	[tɛs]	[tɛsz]	[tɛs tIn]

2. [ə] *insertion:*   [tɛs]   [tɛsəz]   [tɛs tIn]
    the rule (also in STE)
    that inserts the vowel
    between two consonants
    with the same point of
    articulation

In addition to syntactic and phonological differences, BE and STE have somewhat distinct vocabularies. Many slang expressions in STE originated in BE: *cool* and *dig* in the 1940s and *rap* and *right on* in the 1960s (Burling 1973). But many others remain distinctively black: *crib* for 'house,' *hammer* for 'beautiful girl,' and a good many colorful terms for whites. Beyond lexical and structural differences, there are different patterns of the use of language: Labov (1970a) has studied patterns of requesting and politeness, and there are such characteristically black verbal activities as "toasting," "sounding," and "signifying" (Burling 1973). Stewart (1970) and Burling (1973) have traced the history of Black English, a fascinating story of the interaction of various West African languages and English, reflecting the basic processes of language change around the world and throughout history.

The significance of research on Black English must be carefully understood, for misunderstandings are common. A few years ago this newspaper headline appeared: "English a Foreign Language to Negroes" (Allen 1970). At least four errors are captured in these six words. Black English is a variety of English, just as Standard English is. Second, two dialects of a single language have far more aspects in common than they have in contrast. Third, not all blacks speak a version of Black English. And, fourth, speakers of one dialect are likely to be familiar with other dialects.

Many features of BE are common to other dialects. Williamson (1972) has collected examples from nonblack speakers of many constructions similar to Black English: omission of the copula in *You mad*, from an English teacher at a southern university; omission of the auxiliary in *You running parties in there is what you doing*, from an Alabama police officer; omission of *have* as an auxiliary in *How long you been out?* from President Eisenhower; and more. Nevertheless, the existence of a distinct dialect is clear enough. Some features, such as the use of *be* with the sense of 'habitual,' are probably limited to black speakers, as are certain characteristic intonation patterns. Many other features may be used occasionally by other speakers but are used more consistently by black speakers. Indeed, white dialects must be affected by Black English in many cases.

In its omission of certain morphemes required in STE, BE bears a superficial resemblance to the language of children acquiring STE. Brown has considered the hypothesis that BE and child STE represent fundamentally similar "simplifications" of STE. On the basis of a careful analysis, he concludes that such a similarity does not exist. Omission in child language is produced by relatively simple rules; the patterns of BE are generated by rules which are different and are fully as complex as those of STE.

Black Children and Language Development

At this point it would be appropriate to look at detailed longitudinal linguistic studies of the development of language by black children, studies of the type done by Brown, Braine, Bloom, and so on for white children. There are none. Labov has worked primarily with black adolescent boys and, to a lesser extent, with black eight- and nine-year-olds. By this age he finds a well-developed linguistic system.

Unfortunately, this lack of knowledge of language development in young black children has not prevented many psychologists, educators, and others from formulating hypotheses or even dogmatic conclusions. There is a widespread belief that the well-documented academic failure of many black children is owing to an impoverished or retarded language. This view, often called the **verbal-deficit hypothesis,** can be summarized as follows: Because black children from the ghetto hear very little language, much of it ill formed, they are impoverished in their means of verbal expression. They cannot formulate complete sentences; they speak in "giant words." They do not know the names of common objects, they lack crucial concepts, and they cannot produce or comprehend logical statements. Sometimes they are even reported to have no language at all.

It is entirely possible that some black children do have difficulties in language development. We know that many aspects of cognitive development are slowed by extreme poverty and other social factors. Nevertheless, the verbal-deficit hypothesis as just stated is based on shaky assumptions and evidence. First is the implicit assumption that language plays a predominant role in thinking. As we have seen in Chapter 9, this claim continues to be controversial. Second, the hypothesis does not distinguish between structure and function. Are these children deficient in their mastery of the linguistic system or in their ability to use language in classification, problem-solving, communication, memory, and other cognitive tasks? Third, observed differences between the speech of middle-class white children and that of poor black children confuse race and social-class factors. Although the methodological problems are great because of the overrepresentation of black Americans in the lower social classes, they must be overcome because race and social class are quite different variables. (Studies of social-class variations in language belong more properly in Chapter 11 than in this one.) And, finally, Labov (1970b) has provided a well-reasoned critical analysis of some "observed differences."

Labov questions the sample of speech from black children available to most investigators. Simply placing a black child in a room with a large, albeit friendly, white adult may produce a defensive withdrawal from the situation, not a fluent sample of speech. Even placing the child in a room with a black adult who is familiar to the child may not draw out the most representative speech from the child. But the situation changes drastically when the procedure is modified:

> . . . in the next interview with Leon, Clarence
> 1. brought along a supply of potato chips, changing the "interview" into something more in the nature of a party;
> 2. brought along Leon's best friend, 8-year-old Gregory;
> 3. reduced the height imbalance (when Clarence got down on the floor of Leon's room, he dropped from 6 ft. 2 in. to 3 ft. 6 in.);
> 4. introduced taboo words and taboo topics, and proved to Leon's surprise that one can say anything into our microphone without any fear of retaliation. (Labov 1970b:8)

This procedure led to large quantities of active, argumentative, fluent speech from eight-year-old Leon.

Many instances of "illogical" speech from black children are actually misinterpreted dialect differences. Multiple negations, such as *He doesn't know nothing*, are often pointed to as examples of the lack of logic in the mind of the child. Many languages of the world use multiple negation— for example, Russian and Old English, a forerunner of modern English— whereas others use only single negation (modern English). BE falls in the former category, STE in the latter. Both types of languages are "logical"; that is, they can be used to convey meaning quite precisely, as long as the listener *knows the rules of the language.*

The verbal-deficit hypothesis is contradicted by the observation by many social scientists and others familiar with black culture that there is great emphasis on verbal fluency. There are several stylized types of aggressive verbal behavior, such as "basing" and "sounding" (see the annotations for Reading 10.2), and, in general, superior verbal fluency is a mark of distinction.

This observation is supported by the results of one of the few trustworthy cross-ethnic-group comparisons of mental abilities, conducted by Stodolsky and Lesser (1967). They were not so much interested in overall level of cognitive abilities—which they knew to be partially a function of socioeconomic status (SES)—as in the pattern of these abilities. Are there characteristic patterns of abilities for ethnic groups? To determine the answer, they administered four tests—verbal, reasoning, number, and spatial-conceptualization tests—to four ethnic groups in New York City, Chinese, Jewish, Black, and Puerto Rican first graders at two SES levels. The tests were constructed to be as culture-fair as possible, references to giraffes or xylophones were eliminated in favor of references to fire hydrants, buses, and so on. They were administered in the primary languages of the children by examiners who were of their ethnic groups. Stodolsky and Lesser found that there was indeed a characteristic pattern of abilities within each ethnic group. The absolute level, but not the pattern, was a function of SES. The verbal abilities of the black children, far from being a handicap, were clearly their greatest strength; in fact, only one other group exceeded their average score on verbal ability. A replication study with Chinese and black first graders in Boston produced the same results. It is difficult to reconcile this high assessment of black children's verbal abilities at age six or seven years with the low assessment implicit in the verbal-deficit hypothesis at age three or four years.

A number of experimental studies have been conducted to determine the language abilities of black children, especially with respect to knowledge of STE in comparison with BE. The results are not entirely consistent, reflecting a number of procedural difficulties. Most of the investigators have not checked whether or not their black subjects are actually Black English speakers; often they have not been as careful in constructing stimulus materials, especially recordings of BE, as they might have been; and, finally, race and social class have often been confounded, as in comparisons of white middle-class and black lower-class children. Nevertheless, there is good evidence that black children have a considerable knowledge of STE. In fact, Copple and Suci (1974) found that black five- and seven-year-olds were better at completing sentences in STE than in BE. Frentz (1971) found that black children's comprehension (assessed by a picture-pointing task) was as good in STE as in BE. Anastasiow and Hanes (1974) asked elementary-school children to repeat (STE) sentences and found that, when reconstructions from STE in BE were considered correct, there were no differences between black lower-class and white middle-class children. In a particularly interesting study, Johnson (1974) compared the performance of black and white children on standard language tests and in their use of language in natural settings. He administered the Wechsler Preschool and Primary Scale of Intelligence and the Illinois Test of Psycholinguistic Abilities (to be discussed in Chapter 11) and also gathered one-and-a-half-hour samples of spontaneous speech from his sample of four-year-olds. Several measures were applied to the spontaneous speech, including measures of complexity, vocabulary, and concepts. Johnson also controlled for general intelligence by matching his groups on a relatively nonverbal intelligence test. There were only very modest differences between the black and white children on the standardized tests, and there were no differences at all in spontaneous speech.

The Role of Peers

Stewart (1964) has observed that there is not just one black dialect of English in the Washington, D.C., area but a whole series of them. At one extreme there is a dialect that is fairly close to the STE in Washington.

Stewart calls this dialect **acrolect** (from Greek *acro*, meaning 'apex'). At the other extreme is the dialect that is most different from STE, which is called the **basilect** (from Greek *basi*, meaning 'bottom'). The features of BE discussed earlier are found most regularly and completely in the basilect. In between basilect and acrolect there is a range of dialect levels, and most Washington black speech falls into this middle range. Of course, any individual speaker will shift between levels depending on the situation. However, in addition to the influence of the situation, there is a strong and interesting age pattern.

According to Stewart, the consistent use of the basilect is largely restricted to young children. At about the age of seven or eight years the dialect begins to shift. Many of the features of higher levels of the dialect series begin to appear in speech. Some verbs begin to be marked in the past tense, for example. As a result, the speaker now functions at a dialect level that is higher in the series than the basilect, although he may still be quite far from the acrolect.

This dialect shift appears to take place quite automatically, independently of formal education. Schooling does not seem to be the cause or to affect it greatly. It is more than coincidental that this shift coincides with a change in the informal social structure of the peer group. At about this age boys make the transition from "small boy" to "big boy." Both adults and big boys regard the basilect as the natural way for younger children to talk, so that a boy who wants to join the older age group is motivated to change his speech. This rapid dialect shift is much less common among girls, which may be related to the fact that age grading as "small" or "big" is much less rigid for them than for boys.

Such an influence of the peer group raises a puzzling and difficult question: From whom do children learn language? Stewart has written:

> It is easy to find cases involving second- or third-generation Washington Negro families in which the parents are speakers of a quite standard variety of English [the acrolect], but where the children's speech is much closer to that of the newer immigrants (from the South) [the basilect or something close to it]. The explanation seems to be that heavy postwar immigration has dialectally swamped much of the younger generation of native Washingtonians. This phenomenon, incidentally, seems to support the theory that children learn more language behavior from members of their own peer group than from their parents, and suggests that educatory concern for the quality of "language in the home" may be misplaced. (1964:16–17)

Labov has found similar phenomena in children of both races in the New York area. In many middle-class areas of northeastern New Jersey many parents are from New York City and speak a dialect that drops *r*s before consonants and at the ends of words. But almost all their children pronounce the *rs*. It is the local group of the children's peers that determines the new generation's speech patterns.

There is a long-standing split on this question between linguists and psychologists. Linguists, in general, have argued that children speak more as their peers do than as their parents do. Children of immigrants, who have been raised in a home where one language is spoken but who play and go to school with children speaking another language, speak the latter language. Psychologists, on the other hand, have offered evidence that the speech of first children is generally superior to that of later children, and they have argued that this is because of their greater opportunities for conversation with parents.

This apparent disagreement is probably the result of failure to distinguish between competence and performance. Immigrant children have no difficulty in understanding their parents; in other words, they have linguistic competence in both languages. The fact that they speak only one of them is a social fact, not a psycholinguistic one. Furthermore, age may be important in the way that Stewart has suggested: There are specific periods in which peer-group influence is especially strong.

It is easy to speculate on the roles of parents and peers in the language development of lower-class children of either race, given the larger size of families in this setting. In addition, a large proportion of mothers work, leaving the children with even less adult contact. At the present time, however, we can only speculate. Another unknown is the role of television. In our society a higher proportion of time is spent watching television in the lower SES levels. Television provides a supply of verbal stimulation to the child, but this verbal stimulation is not contingent on the child's actions or speech. Does this help or hinder language development?

Language and Indian Children

Concern for disadvantaged groups in the United States has been overwhelmingly focused on black Americans. We have emphasized just one aspect of a problem, ignoring the fact that blacks do not constitute the majority of the poor in this country or even the majority of people with an essentially different culture. Chicanos, Puerto Ricans, poor whites and others are all just beginning to take their place in American life. Other groups, such as Franco-Americans in northern New England, are less recognized at the present time. In many of these groups, as among blacks, the larger problem of being a minority culture in the United States is manifested in a language problem. Typically this problem is not a black problem, an Indian problem, or a chicano problem but is in large part a problem of prejudice arising from the inability of the larger society to accept linguistic diversity.

Except for blacks, we have very little reliable linguistic and sociolinguistic research to inform us. In particular, we know very little of language development in these settings. The present section, concerned with American Indians, is focused on the functions of language, not just on the structure. Differences in linguistic structure are often more immediately striking, and we can forget that how human beings *use* language is also, in part, an aspect of their culture.

The phrase "the vanishing American," once applied to the native American population, is far from the truth. The Indian population is increasing at a rate considerably faster than the population of the country as a whole. It has been estimated that the low point was reached in the 1890s, at around 240,000. The 1960 census reported more than a half-million Indians, and the estimate for 1970 is nearly 600,000 (Osborn 1970). Many live on or near reservations, but in recent years there has been a major move to large cities; nearly half of all Indians are now estimated to be living in urban settings. By virtually any objective measure, the plight of the American Indian is appalling. Unemployment on the reservation is in excess of 40 percent (Osborn 1970), at least six times the national average. Family income is less than one third the national figure. The average schooling of young adults on the reservations is eight years; the national average is approximately twelve years. Infant mortality is higher, and the average life span is far lower: forty-two years, in contrast to seventy years for the country as a whole. And so on down the list.

Occasionally *Indian* is referred to as a specific language, but, in fact, there is no single Indian language. There has always been tremendous linguistic diversity on the North American continent, at least as great as the diversity throughout the Eurasian area. The passage of time has extinguished many of the languages, but a survey in 1941 found 149 native languages, not counting local and regional dialects, spoken by Indians north of Mexico. It is all too easy for an outsider to assume that all the members of any group are identical. Many Indians speak only English. Others, like the isolated Miccousukee of the Florida Everglades, did not have a school in which English was taught until 1962. We do not know how many speakers there are for each Indian language, how many speakers are monolingual or bilingual in English as well, and how many no longer speak the Indian languages at all. We do know that until recently the trend was definitely away from the Indian languages. One survey estimated that about 55 percent of the Indian languages and dialects still spoken were spoken only by the older members of the communities. At the present time, there are several Indian languages that are on the increase.

On the whole, people who have been interested in language and the American Indian child have focused on English as a second language. As ethnocentric as the belief that a good command of the English language is necessary for survival in our society is, there is a considerable element of truth to it. The Indian who has difficulty with English will have difficulty dealing with sales clerks, understanding the procedures associated with voting, registering an automobile, or making a purchase on the installment plan.

When schools were first organized for Indian children during the last part of the nineteenth century, there was a deliberate attempt to obliterate any and all traces of the native languages (Osborn 1970). Many boarding schools were established with the specific goal of removing children from the influence of their parents. In many instances Indian children were punished for slipping back into their native languages, sometimes by having their mouths scrubbed with strong laundry soap. English was taught by rigorous use of imitation and repetition. In the late 1920s and the 1930s, a move away from the boarding schools began. But it is only in recent years that the idea has taken hold that Indians have a right to both cultures: not just modern American middle-class society and English but also native arts, philosophies, and languages. One of the first schools to attempt to put this belief into practice is the Rough Rock school on the Navaho reservation. The goal of this school is "to instill a sense of pride in being Indian. We want to show them that they can be Indian and American at the same time, that they can take the best from each way of life and combine it into something viable" (Conklin: 1967). At Rough Rock the children are encouraged to use their own language. For several hours each week Navaho is taught in classes. Some portions of regular classes, such as those in arithmetic and social studies, are held in Navaho. English is taught formally twice a day. There are situations in which English is required, like asking for food in the cafeteria.

Rough Rock was a pioneering institution. Many other bilingual and bicultural programs for Indian children have been established since then, partly thanks to the impetus of the Bilingual Education Act of 1968.

Many Indian children have difficulties in school. In the early elementary-school years, Indian children do fairly well. But from about the fourth grade on they begin to fall behind. And, not surprisingly, the dropout rate increases in the upper elementary and secondary years. The problem is not one of intelligence or educational ability. When measures are used that are not dependent on the English language or on specific experiences in middle-class American society, for example, Piaget-type tasks or tests of prereading perceptual skills, Indian children do very well (John 1972).

A very common observation is that Indian children are very reluctant to talk in class and that they participate less and less in school as they grow older. The classroom situation depends on dialogue between teacher and pupil, both for instruction and for the pupil's demonstration of mastery. But, rather than viewing these facts as evidence of a deficiency in the children, we ought to consider the possibility of a cultural difference in the norms of language use; just as the dialect spoken by many black children is not deficient English but a different English.

Susan Phillips (1972) has investigated the patterns of speech usage in one particular setting: the Warm Springs reservation in central Oregon. Though the details of her observations may not be applicable to all Indian groups, her major point, that how language is used is determined by culture, is a general one.

From the very beginning, there are differences between Indian and other children in the classroom. Indian first graders are slower to begin to follow the basic rules of the classroom: They do not remember to raise their hands before speaking, they wander around the room without the teacher's permission, and they talk to other students even when the teacher is talking. They are consistently more interested in what their fellow students are doing. Indian pupils seldom bid for the teacher's attention as other pupils are likely to do. Instead, they are more concerned with attracting their fellow students' attention. They are also more likely simply to disobey a specific direction, for example, the direction not to put feet on chairs. In general, Indian children are less likely to accept what is the fundamental rule of the classroom: that the teacher is in charge.

Throughout the school years Indian pupils are reluctant to participate in any activity that involves verbally responding to the teacher in front of other children. They hardly ever volunteer to speak, and when they are called on they reply in low, almost inaudible voices. On the other hand, when the teacher is available for student-initiated communication while the pupils are working on their own assignments and projects, Indian children will initiate verbal contact with teacher as often as other children do.

When the class is divided into small groups that run themselves in order to complete various projects, Indian children become fully involved and talk a great deal with one another. They are often more successful than other children in organizing and dividing up the work. Observations of play reveal the same preferences. Indian children are not willing to be leaders or to interact with a leader in a one-to-one fashion. But if they can organize into teams, they participate wholeheartedly in competition.

So it is not surprising that teachers think that Indian children will not talk, especially if a class is organized so as to rely on one-to-one dialogue with the pupil under the direction of the teacher. This organization may work well with many American children, reflecting the culture of the majority children, but it is inappropriate for Indian children and frustrating for both pupils and teachers.

Many teachers working with Indian children modify their teaching styles in response to their pupils' characteristics. There are fewer word games requiring one child to give another child commands. There is no "show and tell," which requires a child to talk before the entire class. In the upper grades teachers are more likely to organize group projects than to lecture to the pupils or to ask individuals questions before the rest of the class. To be sure, this accommodation only postpones the problem until high school, when Indian students are typically outnumbered by others and teachers are likely to use methods appropriate for the others. And it may be that certain subjects are learned only in one kind of classroom situation, though we do not know this empirically.

School is only a part of any child's life and not the most important part at that. Phillips proposes that we examine the broader culture in which these children are growing up to understand their behavior in the classroom. Using language is essentially a matter of making choices; we have considered choices of lexical items and grammatical structure, but the most fundamental choice of all must be whether or not to talk. What are the general conditions for the use of language in learning and other social settings? And do these conditions illuminate the performance of the Indian children in the classroom? Phillips studied just one Indian group, but her general findings are probably typical of many, though not all, Indian groups.

Indian children are not brought up exclusively by parents, as are middle-class American children. Grandparents, uncles, and other relatives are involved. Indian children also spend a great deal of time with other children: brothers, sisters, cousins, and so on. These peer relationships typically continue to be the strongest friendship bonds throughout life.

Indian girls are taught skills around the home, and Indian boys are taught outdoor skills earlier than most middle-class children. Girls are doing some cooking and housecleaning before the age of eight years. Responsibilities are accompanied by early independence. By age ten or eleven years the children often spend afternoons and evenings with other children, without having to ask permission of or later to account for their time to parents. They may decide to live with other relatives for weeks or months. In general, there is considerable self-determination and little disciplinary control.

Indian culture is characterized by certain processes of learning. One important process is simply watching. Young children are often present at adult activities and conversations as silent but attentive observers. Indian society is not as age-segregated as our own. This process of silent observation appears to be one of the traditional means of learning. For example, the older women reminisce about being required to watch older relatives tan hides when they were young.

In a second process of learning, an older relative may divide up a task into small segments and have the child carry out some portion. Young girls are often given the task of moving furniture for housecleaning. Such activities require very little verbal instruction, but the children are completely free to ask questions, which they do. This process of learning is hardly unique to Indians, but it seems to be used more by them.

One major difference between the learning of skills by Indian and other children is that, for the former, there is very little testing of the children before they have mastered the skills. In many instances the child takes it upon herself to test the skill when she is alone. Failure will thus not be seen by others. When the child succeeds, the fruits of learning—a tanned hide, a piece of beadwork—can be shown to others.

Thus, many of the skills that Indian adults wish to pass on to their children are learned through a three-stage process: observation; supervised participation; and, finally, private, self-initiated testing. The use of language is very limited and occurs primarily in the form of the child's questions to adults. The final demonstration of learning is likely to be a matter of material evidence or a physical expression.

The contrast between the classroom and broader culture could hardly be clearer. In the classroom the assumption is that one learns through making mistakes in front of others. The Indian children have no chance to observe others performing successfully before they must respond. There is no opportunity to practice and to decide for themselves when they know enough. The emphasis on verbal communication and demonstration of mastery is a complete change.

The role of the teacher is also novel. Indian social activities are generally open to all and are not directed by a single person by means of verbal instructions. Either a set of ritual procedures is followed, or there may be a group of people who collectively direct the activities. There are no soloists in the dancing or drumming. If speeches are being made, anyone who wants to may say a few words. A person is not leader by virtue of heredity or other external status; he leads because he has demonstrated ability in some activity and because other individuals have chosen to follow his suggestions. Leadership is not permanent; if the people choose not to follow a leader's plans, he is no longer a leader.

The classroom teacher differs from the typical Indian leader on all points. The teacher is not chosen freely by individuals but rather is imposed from outside. The fact that the teacher is usually not Indian adds to the problem, though it is not the crucial element. The frequent indifference to the directions and orders of the teacher on the part of Indian children is not surprising. It is less a matter of hostility or disrespect than a failure to see why the teacher *should* be obeyed. This is particularly true in relation to the teacher's most important power: deciding who shall participate in which activities and when. To summarize, the Indian children studied by Phillips do not participate verbally in the classroom because the social conditions for participation that they have learned in their larger culture are lacking in the classroom. Though the details of the mismatch between culture and classroom studied by Phillips may be unique to certain Indian groups, mismatches can and probably do occur for children in many settings.

Dialect and Reading

The discussion of reading in Chapter 8 involved children learning to read their native language. Speakers of a nonstandard dialect or language face a more difficult task. In recent years, much attention has been given to alternative strategies for teaching reading to these groups. Three particularly good reviews of some of these approaches are by Baratz and Shuy (1969), DeStefano (1973), and Burling (1973). Not surprisingly, most attention has been paid to speakers of Black English, given the all too well-documented failure of the schools to teach many black inner-city children how to read successfully.

Broadly speaking, at least four alternative policies may be conceived: teaching reading of the standard dialect exclusively, teaching STE by means of foreign-language techniques, teaching reading in the non-standard dialect, and teaching pupils to read in their own dialect materials written in STE.

Exclusive Use of Standard Dialect

The first approach is essentially the current policy in most schools. It amounts to a complete rejection of the languages the children bring to school with them. It is only one of the many ways the schools, and society in general, reject the family and heritage of the black child. Furthermore, it confuses two quite distinct tasks: learning to read and learning a second dialect.

What actually happens is instructive. A black child may read the printed words *We were going . . .* as *We was going . . .* or *I didn't have any* as *I don't have none.* These readings will be taken to be erroneous. They are difficult or impossible to eradicate and together with many similar errors lead to anxiety, frustration, and ultimately even poorer reading performance. In fact, the child has accurately and correctly "translated" the printed words into his own dialect. If anything, these errors are the best possible evidence that the reader has successfully decoded the *meanings* of the sentences. The achievement is in some ways more impressive than that of the STE-speaking child who pronounces *were* and *didn't have any,* for the latter child has more guidance from the spelling.

Relatively phonic approaches to teaching reading particularly penalize the nonstandard speaker. Only confusion can result from an explanation that *u* denotes the sound in *sure,* whereas *o* denotes the sound in *shore*—for children who pronounce the words identically. Use of an initial alphabet such as the i.t.a. exaggerates the problem. One defense of the traditional orthography of English is that it is equally illogical for all dialects!

Teaching a Second Dialect

An alternative approach would be to teach STE as an oral language to speakers of BE, perhaps by means of foreign-language techniques, and then to teach reading using materials in the standard dialect. Such an approach at least separates the two issues confounded in the first. It assumes that the ability to speak STE is a useful one and that reading is learned most efficiently in a dialect the child knows. This policy has been propounded in recent years under the label of **bidialectalism**. Nevertheless, it is a questionable one. The problem is the first step, teaching STE as a second dialect. Elementary-school programs for teaching foreign languages have become quite popular in recent years, but they have not been notably successful. There are several factors responsible for this lack of success. One is that there is very little psychological or pedagogical research on teaching foreign languages to young children. Another is that opportunities to practice with the new language or dialect are usually lacking. Many elementary-school programs have failed because they have provided only three to five hours a week of instruction, without other opportunities for the children to use the language. The same situation is likely to arise in the teaching of STE as a second dialect. Many of the students will simply leave this dialect behind at school every afternoon.

Motivation is perhaps the most important factor in learning a new language. Foreign languages are learned best by learners who think highly of speakers of that language. For example, those students who admire French and French culture learn French most successfully. Now young children are likely to have quite neutral feelings about a second language like French or Spanish. But young black children are likely to have strong negative feelings about white speakers of STE. And, if anything, such feelings are likely to be increased by the rejection of their own language in the schools. However bidialectalism is labeled, it is most likely to come across to the children as "It is alright to speak in that crude way at home and to your friends if you really want to, but while you are in this classroom, you had better speak correctly" (Burling 1973:135).

There are valuable elements in the policy of bidialectalism though. It is at least a beginning toward a policy of linguistic pluralism. It seeks to offer the pupil a choice of dialects for different settings. Perhaps the central flaw is an assumption about language that is easy to make and is captured in the phrase "learning to talk": that language is a matter of production. The importance of the comprehension side of language use is often overlooked. In particular, the belief that all members of our society need to be able to communicate with one another hardly requires that we all *speak* the same way. Reading, writing, speaking, and listening are the most important ways of using language, but we do not have to use the same dialect for all purposes. Black children come to school with a considerable ability to comprehend STE (but how many teachers have the ability to comprehend BE?); does teaching them how to read and write in STE require changing their oral language? Surely not.

Use of the Native Dialect Exclusively

Many people have argued that a genuine acceptance of linguistic pluralism means that the native dialect of the pupil ought to be used for all instruction, including reading, even if it means preparation of special materials. The Center for Applied Linguistics (Baratz & Shuy 1969), in particular, has developed programs and materials for speakers of Black English. Such a policy eliminates an irrelevant task—learning a second dialect—from the context of learning to read.

For most Americans, questions of linguistic diversity are a new concern. We forget that diversity is the normal state in the world. For example, there are more children who receive at least some of their schooling in a language or dialect other than their native tongue than children who do not. There is a considerable body of evidence on the question of sequencing language and reading instruction (Tucker 1974). Use of the native language for initial instruction has been found to be successful in many settings. For example, a program in Chiapas, Mexico, introduced reading to children in their native Indian languages. When they had successfully mastered the initial materials, they were placed in the first grade, where all subsequent instruction was carried out in Spanish. Later reading tests showed that the children who had first been taught to read in their native tongues read Spanish better than their peers who had been instructed solely in Spanish. Other programs, in Sweden, the Philippines, and elsewhere, have also been successful.[1]

Despite such successes, some difficulties can be foreseen in extending such an approach to our own society. First, we have assumed that there is only *one* Black English. Little is known about variations in this dialect, but we would expect to find at least some regional variation. Individuals within a single black community vary in dialect (recall Stewart's findings in Washington, D.C., discussed earlier). If the variation is of sufficient magnitude, different sets of beginning reading materials will be necessary. A second possible difficulty is parental and community attitudes. Parents who have succeeded in mastering, or are attempting to master, STE and wish their children to do the same are not likely to look with favor on an educational program that appears to reinforce the use of BE. The assumption is often made that, if children are at one point encouraged to use one dialect (BE), their chances of eventually mastering a second (STE) are

---

[1] Nevertheless, it *is* possible to learn to read in a second language without difficulty. In the Montreal program (Lambert and Tucker 1972); English-speaking Canadian children enter kindergarten in a "total immersion" French program and learn to read in French in the first grade. The reading skills are generalized to English with remarkably little difficulty. As Lambert and Tucker point out, the success of this remarkable program depends on a number of factors that would not hold for STE and BE in our country.

diminished. There is really no evidence for this assumption. The converse is certainly possible: The teacher's acceptance of the child's dialect may serve as a model for the child's later acceptance of that of the teacher.

A similar argument has been raised against the use of sign language by young deaf children (discussed in Chapter 3). A growing body of evidence demonstrates that early use of sign language facilitates later acquisition of English in its spoken and written forms. Though the cases of deaf children and black children are different in many ways, this evidence lends at least some plausibility to the hypothesis that early use of BE will serve as a basis for later acquisition of STE.

There is a larger issue embedded in the question of attitudes. Whatever our goals for our society, it remains a fact that access to education, knowledge, and jobs often requires some command of STE. Black parents can hardly be faulted for feeling that the use of BE in schools for their children is an attempt to keep their children "in their place." Put somewhat differently, using the native dialect exclusively may be asking these children to pay the price of our liberal beliefs. In fact, hardly any programs of this type have actually been attempted; in virtually every instance, community reaction, black, white, or both, has prevented or terminated the program.

If, as seems essential, the goal is to educate all children to read materials printed in STE, an additional, transitional program is necessary. Stewart (1969) has suggested a three-stage process. In the first stage, reading materials would be in BE syntactic form: *Charles and Michael, they out playing.* At the second stage, the most important syntactic features of STE would be introduced, such as the inflected forms of the verb *be*: *Charles and Michael, they are out playing.* And, in the third stage, sentences would be brought into full conformity with STE: *Charles and Michael are out playing.* A transitional program of this type would reintroduce teaching a second dialect into teaching reading, but in a much more controlled way than is common at present. As such a program has not been attempted on any major scale, we cannot yet tell if the transition would cause any difficulties.

The problem of orthography is also a difficult one. It would be possible to use a writing system reflecting the children's own pronunciations at first. Gradually, the system would be changed to the standard orthography. Stewart has suggested a compromise solution, in which BE pronunciations would be indicated by minor changes in the conventional English spellings, with frequent use of the apostrophe as a cue for differences between dialects. Some examples are *ben'* for *bend, bendin'* for *bending, 'bout* for *about,* and *'posed to* for *supposed to.* The apostrophes serve as indicators of where later instruction will occur.

STE Material Read in the Native Dialect

The fourth approach is to teach children to read STE materials in their own dialects. In fact, this is what many black children spontaneously attempt, reading *we were going* . . . as *We was going* . . . This proposal seems at first unreasonable. On the one hand, it asks for readers to make "errors," to say things that are not on the printed page. And, on the other hand, it requires the speaker of a nonstandard dialect to "translate" between dialects.

First, the matter of errors: Any fluent reader of English, asked to read a passage aloud quickly, will make errors, will produce words that are not identical to the printed words. But these errors often leave the meaning unchanged. Contractions may be formed, synonyms may be substituted, and compound sentences may be broken up. Good readers are constantly guessing ahead as to what comes next. Only if the guess is clearly wrong will the reader correct himself; otherwise, he is not aware of any error. Goodman (1967) has dubbed reading a "psycholinguistic guessing game." Good readers "play" better than poor readers. Thus, the long-term goal of reading instruction is to free the reader from total dependence on the printed page. Understanding must be based both on the printed page and on the reader's knowledge of the language and the subject matter. There is no inherent reason for tying sound inflexibly to symbol.

English and American children read the same printed materials, yet their pronunciations differ. Because the underlying representations of morphemes are identical in the two dialects, speakers can convert the printed forms to the correct phonetic representations in their respective dialects, using their knowledge of phonological rules. Thus, the question of "translation" is really just a particular instance of the general principle that sound and symbol are related by relatively complex principles. To be sure, BE and STE differ more substantially than do British and American English. Yet the example of Chinese can set the issue in perspective. Written Chinese is uniform throughout the country, though the spoken language varies considerably. In fact, it can be argued that the term Chinese really covers several distinct *languages*, not just dialects.

This fourth alternative eliminates the need for special materials (in the orthographic sense; culturally relevant content is still necessary) and guarantees that all children will have access to books, magazines, and newspapers that are overwhelmingly in STE. Perhaps the most serious difficulty for advocates of this policy is the need for flexibility. A teacher's criterion for correct reading must vary with the individual child. A child who normally pronounces the plural form of *was* as *were* and then reads *were* as *was* must be recognized as having made an error, though a speaker of a dialect that pronounces the plural of *was* as *was* must be recognized as having read correctly. In addition to varying criteria for individual children, the teacher must distinguish between key indicators of reading ability and the much larger and more noticeable range of dialect differences. Labov offers an example:

> For the teacher to make this distinction, it is necessary that he know what correct reading sounds like. If a Negro child reads *He always looked for trouble when he read the news* as *He a'way look' fo' trouble when he read* (rhyming with *bed*) *de news*, the teacher should be able to judge that he is reading correctly. But if he clearly articulates *He always looked for trouble when he read the news*, yet rhymes *read* with *seed*, he is not reading correctly and has to be stopped. (Labov 1970a:44)

Some General Considerations

The goal of reading is understanding, the extraction of meaning from the printed page. The choice of materials and methods for reading instruction must always be made on the basis of how well the goal is served.

One way to devise better reading materials for speakers of nonstandard dialects would be to have the children prepare them themselves. The "language experience" approach (Lee and Allen 1963) seems at least as appropriate for nonstandard speakers as for the standard speakers for whom it was devised. The teacher writes down the words, sentences, and stories of the children and uses these materials as a basis for explaining how language is written. Too often in beginning reading instruction, the essential two-way nature of the process is slighted. We write things down so that others will read them; what we read has been written down by other people. In addition to keeping the reading materials close to the dialect of the learner, this approach gives her the opportunity to express, as well as to receive.

One cannot help thinking that questions of orthography, teaching method, and the life are only a small part of the larger problem. Labov and Robins (1969) have found in New York that there is a striking relationship between reading ability and membership in street groups. Boys in early adolescence who participated in street groups were significantly less successful in reading than those who were not, though the former were no less verbally skillful or intelligent than the latter. Labov and Robins argue that the major factor in reading failure among Black English-speaking boys is the conflict between black adolescents' street culture and the school culture. Schooling is seen as hostile and irrelevant to their lives.

Burling has eloquently summarized the fundamental dilemmas for anyone concerned with linguistic diversity in our society:

> If all Americans spoke alike, I would find America a less interesting place in which to live. Thus, I will always be uncomfortable when offering advice on how to teach standard English to nonstandard speakers, and I will always

feel that the only humane solution to the problem will be a change in our attitudes and our society. . . .

Until this change comes about we will have to respond as best we can to the student who asks our help in learning a new kind of English, but when we teach him standard grammar or a prestigious pronunciation, we are merely teaching him to conform to the demands of those with power. . . . When we help a man learn to read, however, we do far more. . . .

Nothing can ever fully take the place of the language that we learn from our parents and from our earliest friends. For each of us, this language has special emotional connotations, and I would like to work toward the time when we can all respect one another's varied linguistic heritage. Of course, a man's language will grow and change as he encounters new people and as he studies new subjects. No one continues to speak like a five-year-old all his life. But we learn most successfully and we move most easily into new experiences when we can build upon what we already know. If teachers could appreciate the child's own language and recognize its irreplaceable value, they would be able to work together with the child, helping him and helping his language to grow and develop. . . . (Burling 1973:160–161)

Summary

With the decline of the "melting pot" theory of American society, social scientists have begun to explore and appreciate the diversity of culture and language in the country. Recognition of Black English as an autonomous dialect of English has been delayed by strongly negative attitudes toward it and its speakers. The language abilities of many black children have been seriously underestimated. The shift away from a "deficiency model" to a "differences model" in the long run benefits all children, as we realize that linguistic communities can differ not only in phonology and syntax but also in vocabulary, semantics, and ways of using language in learning.

An educational system should capitalize on the capacities children bring to school, rather than penalize them. How best to do so, for example, how best to teach reading, is a question requiring a combination of imagination and careful research on psychological and pedagogical issues. The question how best to use both the children's native dialects and the dialect of the larger society is basically one for empirical investigation in this way. However, it is probable that, even more important for the success of the educational enterprise than matters of reading materials and methods, are the larger social factors of our society: the extent to which members of all parts of the society share a sense of opportunity and the feeling that the educational system exists to help provide opportunity. Only major changes in our society can fully resolve the problem of dialect and education.

10.1 STYLE SHIFTING*

One of the fundamental principles of sociolinguistic investigation might simply be stated as *There are no single-style speakers.* By this we mean that every speaker will show some variation in phonological and syntactic rules according to the immediate context in which he is speaking. We can demonstrate that such stylistic shifts are determined by (a) the relations of the speaker, addressee, audience, and particularly the relations of power of solidarity among them; (b) the wider social context or "domain": school, job, home, neighborhood, church; (c) the topic. One must add of course that the stylistic range and competence of the speaker may vary greatly. Children may have a very narrow range in both the choices open to them and the social contexts they respond to. Old men often show a narrow range in that their motivation for style shifting disappears along with their concern for power relationships [for example, old men no longer trying to make it].

We apply the principle stated above in a very concrete way when carrying out research with face-to-face interviews. We do not judge the absolute stylistic level of the speaker by some absolute standard of "casualness." We know that, as long as we are asking questions and receiving answers, the speaker is using a relatively "careful" or "consultative" style, and that he possesses a more "casual" or intimate style with which he argues with his friends or quarrels with his family. There are techniques for obtaining casual speech in an interview situation, but the soundest approach is to observe the speaker interacting with the peers who control his speech in everyday life when the observer is not there.

Well-developed social variables show a systematic range of style shifting which is correlated to the amount of attention paid to speech. We can easily observe such style shifting in certain longstanding variables which are common to almost all dialects of English. The *th* of *thing* and *that* can appear as a smooth fricative "*th*" sound, the standard variant; as a "*t*"-like sound lightly or strongly articulated; as a combination of these two; or as a zero as in *Gimme 'at.* For most Americans, the proportions of these forms are nicely blended and graded for each stylistic level—at different absolute levels for different social groups and different religions. Similarly, the alternation of *-ing and -in'* in unstressed syllables is a systematic stylistic variable for most Americans—again at different levels for different classes and regions.

At one time, the dialect areas of the eastern United States were sharply divided into r-less and r-pronouncing areas, according to whether consonantal r is pronounced in words like *car* and *card.* But in the last two decades the r-pronunciation of "general American" has become accepted as the standard of broadcast networks and of careful middle class pronunciation almost everywhere. As a result, we find that the new "prestige" pronunciation of r in final and preconsonantal position has become a sociolinguistic variable in the older r-less areas. Almost all younger and middleaged speakers will show some styles shifting with r, so that in the more formal styles they will use more r and in casual speech practically none at all.

The grammatical variables that show style shifting are quite well-known in general, though we usually lack the exact knowledge of where and when these features are used to signal change of style. Some are well-established stereotypes, like *ain't*. Although dictionaries may vary in the way they label *ain't*, most native speakers are quite clear in their sociolinguistic approach to this word—in their social evaluation of the form. To make the point clear, imagine a community in which *ain't* is the formal style and in which people correct *isn't* to *ain't* when they are careful. Such a community would be very odd indeed—obviously not a part of the same American speech community in which we all live.

The "double negative" or negative concord is an important stylistic marker; it allows nonstandard speakers to express negatives in a particularly emphatic fashion by reduplicating the negative forms (*Nobody don't know about that*) and at the same time register their adherence to the nonstandard form which is stylistically opposed to the standard (*Nobody knows anything about that*).

The passive has two forms in English, which are closely allied but perhaps not equivalent in meaning. If we ask "What happened to him?" the answer can be "He got run over" or "He was run over." The colloquial form is clearly the former; nonstandard dialects depend almost entirely upon this got-passive, to the exclusion of the be-passive. As a result, the be-passive has acquired a standard, rather careful flavor which it would not have if there were no opposing forms.

In all these examples, we can easily demonstrate the meaning of the stylistic alternation by observing the direction of correction in false starts. In almost every interview, one will find speakers making corrections like "Nobody told him noth—anything about it." No matter how rare or how common such corrections may be, we find that they uniformly run in the same direction, since the more formal style is associated with a mental set in which greater attention is paid to speech and the less formal style with a casual and spontaneous use of language in which the minimum attention is given to the speech process.

10.2 AN ANNOTATED TRANSCRIPTION OF A SAMPLE OF BLACK ENGLISH*

. . . (an) original Black English passage, which is a dramatized enactment of a situation occurring in the ghetto. In this passage we have simply transcribed and edited a section from a phonograph record (Street and Gangland Rhythms, Folkways 5589) and arranged it as a quasi-drama. The record contains the reasonably spontaneous speech of six pre-adolescent Harlem boys. We have made no grammatical changes in the text so that at places it may appear that certain forms are importations from Standard English. . . . Our annotations indicate those places where there exist clear-cut contrasts between the grammatical systems of Standard English and Black English. Phonological differences are not annotated except where they affect grammatical form. Differences in the semantic context of lexical items have not generally been noted.

Dumb Boy

(Scene I)

CALVIN: One day I was walking. Then I met Lennie. Lennie say,[1, 2] "Calvin, what happened to your lip?" I said, "Nothing." And then Lenn came over to me and he say,[1, 2] "What you mean by nothing?" Like he always say[2] because he's always interested in me and me and him[5] is[6] good friends. So I told him what happened.[3] "This guy named[3] Pierre, he[7] about fifteen . . ."

LENNIE: Yeah?

CALVIN: He came over to me . . .

LENNIE: Uh huh.

CALVIN: And he hit me in my[8] lip because . . .

LENNIE: Yeah?

CALVIN: I . . .

LENNIE: Done[9] what?

CALVIN: Had done copied[9] off his paper in school.

(Scene II)

LENNIE: What's that guy[12] name?

CALVIN: Pierre.

LENNIE: Where[4] he live at?

CALVIN: Around our block.

---

* Reprinted with permission from Walt Wolfram and Ralph Fasold, Toward reading materials for speakers of Black English: Three linguistically appropriate passages. In J. C. Baratz & R. W. Shuy (Eds.), *Teaching black children to read*, pp. 144–147, 152–154. Washington, D.C.: Center for Applied Linguistics, 1969.

LENNIE: How old is he?

CALVIN: About the size of the other guy named Pierre around our block.

LENNIE: Well, tonight it's[13] gonna be a party at 118th Street where I live at. You bring him around there, hear?

CALVIN: I surely will.

LENNIE: Okay. . . .

(Later)

CALVIN: So when I walked in there, everything was silent.

LENNIE: Is that the guy over there?

CALVIN: Yeah.

LENNIE: Hey you, what[4] you hit my little brother for?

PIERRE: Did he tell you what happened,[3] man?

LENNIE: Yeah, he told me what happened.[3]

PIERRE: But you . . . but you should tell your people to teach him to go to school, man. I know I didn't have a right to hit him. But he was copying off me and the teacher said. . . . I forgot to tell the teacher.

LENNIE: What[4] you mean you forgot to tell the teacher? What[4] you mean to tell my parents to make him go to school to learn? What[4] you mean by that? What[4] you mean?

PIERRE: Just like I said, man, he can't be dumb, man. I don't be[14] with him all his life.

LENNIE: You basing or you sounding?[15]

PIERRE: I ain't doing neither[10] one.

LENNIE: That's more like it. But we[7] gonna deal tonight.

PIERRE: If you can't face it, don't waste[16] it. If you can't face it, don't waste[16] it.

Annotations

1. Some verbs, like "come" and "say," are not marked for past tense in Black English narratives, even when the context is past time.

2. Black English lacks the *-s* suffix which marks the present tense with third person singular subjects in Standard English.

3. When the suffix *-ed* is realized by a stop following a base form which ends in a consonant, the stop is not pronounced (thus, the pronunciation /neym/, for Standard English /neymd/). This reflects a Black English phonological pattern in which syllable final consonant clusters in Standard English correspond to simple consonants in Black English (see note 16). The pattern illustrates how phonological constraints in Black English affect the presence of certain grammatical categories.

4. Sentences which would have a pre-posed verbal auxiliary in Standard English due to the formation of a content question generally have no auxiliary at all in the corresponding Black English sentence. For example, the "do" which would appear in the Standard English equivalent of questions like *What do you mean by nothing?* is absent for this reason.

5. In coordinate noun phrases, the distinction between objective and subjective forms of the pronoun is often neutralized, so that the "objective" form may function as a grammatical subject.

6. Occasionally (and particularly with coordinate constructions), the singular conjugated forms of "be" ("is," "was") occur with the plural subject in Black English.

7. The present tense form of the copula frequently is not realized in a number of different syntactic environments in Black English. Generally, where the contracted form of the copula may occur in Standard English the stative condition is indicated simply by word order in Black English.

8. In Standard English, sentences like "kiss her on the cheek" and "punch Jack in the stomach" involving a verb of physical contact, a personal nominal reference and body part, the definite article "the" is used with the body part although it belongs to the same person referred to by the personal noun or pronoun. In Black English, the possessive pronoun is used in these constructions instead of the article.

9. The use of "done" plus the past tense of a verb is a construction indicating completed action. Some speakers occasionally include a form of "have" as in "had done copied . . ."

10. In Black English, negation is typically marked not only in the main verb phrase but also in each indefinite determiner or indefinite pronoun in the sentence, as well as in certain adverbs like "hardly" and "never."

11. An embedded imperative may be retained in its original quoted form instead of being realized in an infinitive construction (e.g., "I told you don't do that no more" instead of "I told you not to do that no more").

12. Black English lacks possessive -s so that possession is indicated only by the order of the items.

13. "It," in Black English, can be used as an "expletive" or "resentative" in addition to its function as a pronoun referring to a specific object or participant. In this usage it is equivalent to Standard English "there."

14. The form "be" can be used in Black English as a verb [to] denote(s) interaction or habituation.

15. The expressions "basing" and "sounding" refer to types of aggressive verbal behavior. "Basing" is a kind of back-talk and "sounding" refers to a special type of ritual insult.

16. The items "face" and "waste" have rhyming endings in Black English because the final stop member of a syllable final consonant cluster is frequently absent.

further reading

Burling, R. *English in black and white.* New York: Holt, Rinehart and Winston, 1974.

Labov, W. *Language in the inner city: Studies in the black english vernacular.* Philadelphia: University of Pennsylvania Press, 1972.

Lambert, W. E. & Tucker, G. R. *Bilingual education of children: The St. Lambert experiment.* Rowley, Mass.: Newbury House, 1972.

Measuring Language Development

Therapeutic disciplines—medicine, psychotherapy, education, and others—are highly dependent on their assessment measures and diagnostic techniques. Tests define the problem for us ("Poor children score low on the Stanford-Binet Intelligence Scale") and also measure how effective our educational programs are ("Professor X's preschool raises IQ scores by twelve points"). In the area of language, measures of development serve at least three functions: diagnosis of children with suspected difficulties in one or more aspects of language development; evaluation of their progress during therapy, and research on normal children, exploring the effects of various environmental factors (birth order, amount of television watched, and so on) on language development. In this chapter we shall review some of the currently available measures of language development and shall discuss some areas of application under the third topic listed.

An assessment measure is fundamentally a small sample of behavior that is interpreted in standardized ways. The goal of the sampling procedure and the interpretation is to be as informative as possible; that is, they should be maximally predictive of language in other settings. If we know that two aspects of language are acquired approximately simultaneously, then only one need be tested. Thus, information about the normal course of development must be the foundation for test development. However, this consideration suggests that it may be a mistake to attempt to develop tests to serve all three functions listed in the preceding paragraph. Until we know whether or not children with language disabilities follow the same sequence of development as normal children, there is no basis for predictions based on normal language development. Similarly for evaluation of therapy: The normal sequence of development may be A, B, C; but a child who has mastered only A may be taught C without having mastered B. Different tests may be required for different purposes.

In fact, most presently available tests have been developed in clinical settings because most recent research on normal language development has ignored the possibility of individual differences. Only recently have there been attempts to construct tests based on knowledge of normal language development. As we have little experience with any of them, it is too soon to decide whether or not a single test can be useful with both normal and language-disabled children.

A related issue is the interrelatedness of various aspects of language development. Is there a single dimension of language development, or are the separate components independent in a statistical sense? Informally it seems that articulation and syntactic development are largely independent of each other. Some children articulate clearly relatively primitive language, whereas others produce highly developed, complex sentences in an almost unintelligible manner. It is suggestive that among children with language disabilities, disturbed syntax is almost always accompanied by disturbed articulation, but that articulation difficulties are often not accompanied by disturbed syntax. It is probably unrealistic to seek a single measure, a "linguistic age," that can represent language development. But just how many distinct components exist is far from clear. Vocabulary is probably distinct from syntactic development, and the ability to use language effectively for communication (see Chapter 9) is probably distinct from both.

There are two approaches to language assessment. The first is analysis of spontaneous speech; the second is the use of structured situations, that is, tests. Each has its limitations, and the two should be thought of more as complementary than as mutually exclusive.

Analysis of Spontaneous Speech

Analysis of spontaneous speech has two primary advantages. The first is that research on normal language development has focused most intensively on spontaneous speech and that therefore there is a larger body of normative data. The second is that any testing situation must be to some extent artificial and constraining, whereas conversation with a child seems less so than the interrogation typical of structured texts. A finding by Prutting, Gallagher, and Mulac (1975) illustrates this point. They compared the results produced on the expressive portion of the Northwestern Syntax Screening Test (to be discussed) with an analysis of spontaneous speech a group of four- and five-year-old language-delayed children. In the test children were shown pictures and asked to name them. Prutting and his colleagues found that 30 percent of the structures that were failed on the test were produced in spontaneous speech. They argue that the test requires many other psychological operations besides mastery of specific grammatical constructions.

Analysis of spontaneous speech also has its limitations. Some of these have been discussed in the Introduction and in Chapter 5. The most serious are, for productive abilities, the sampling problem and, for comprehension, the availability of contextual cues for successful understanding.

Both the size of the sample and the method by which it is to be obtained are still open to question. The standard sample used in much clinical work is 50 to 100 utterances. Yet the most informative basic research on language development has been based on far larger samples—300 to 800 utterances, and in some cases even larger. Such large samples are clearly out of the question for clinical use, especially with children who are delayed, shy, or both, yet the limitations of the small sample are serious. Especially with small samples, the nature of the speech obtained is likely to vary greatly with the situation. Cazden (1970) has reviewed a number of studies that show that both the quantity and quality of the speech produced by children vary with the topic of conversation, the task the children are engaged in, and the age of the listener and his familiarity. To consider a single point, questions of the form "What do you see?" and "What is he doing?" tend to elicit one-word answers. If there are very many such interchanges in the sampling situation, the sample will have a shorter Mean Length of Utterances (MLU) and display a smaller variety of constructions than would be observed otherwise. The sampling situation is best viewed as a conversation, rather than as an interrogation.

Writing a full grammar for each child is not practical, because of the difficulty of doing so and the time required. Instead, only selected aspects of language can be assessed. MLU is a traditional measure of language development. Different investigators have used somewhat different procedures for computing MLU, but the rules of Brown (1973), summarized in Table 2.1 of this book, are likely to become the standard. Tyack and Gottsleben (1974) have provided a very clear guide for teachers and clinicians collecting language samples and analyzing them. Though crude, MLU appears to be the best single indicator of language development for children with MLU under about five. Its validity can be demonstrated in two ways. First, Shriner (1969) found that MLU is highly correlated with psychological scaling judgments of development. He asked adults to rate a large number of samples of children's speech (fifty utterance samples) on a seven-point scale of development and compared their ratings with several quantitative measures: MLU was the most highly correlated. Second, the work of Brown (1973) and others has shown that many specific aspects of syntactic development are correlated with MLU. Brown and Fraser (1964), for example, found that the auxiliary is added to the progressive (advancing from *I going* to *I am going*) at about an MLU of 3.2.

The most serious objection to the use of MLU is that it is highly dependent on situation; that is, it has limited reliability unless the situation is carefully controlled. All the measures discussed in this section suffer from this problem, MLU perhaps less than most because it is based on all the utterances of the sample, whereas some of the other measures look only at instances of particular constructions.

Several other measures have been proposed for the examination of particular aspects of grammatical development, in attempts to devise measures of the complexity of sentences, not just their length. Some of them (Frank & Osser 1970) include a measure of the number of transformational operations in the generation of the sentence. However, research with adults has cast doubt on the equation of complexity with number of transformations (Fodor and Garrett 1966).

Lee and Canter (1971) have developed a comprehensive scheme for measuring the complexity of sentences. Attention is focused on eight aspects of sentences: indefinite pronouns and noun modifiers, personal pronouns, main verbs, secondary verbs, negatives, conjunctions, interrogative reversals, and *wh* questions. Within each area knowledge of the normal course of development is used to establish a developmental weighting of various forms. For example, the earliest personal pronouns are the first and second person: *I, you,* and so on. A sentence containing such a pronoun is scored 1 point. The third-person pronouns are more advanced and receive a score of 2 points. The plurals (*those, these*) receive 4 points, reflexives (*myself, himself*) 5 points, *wh* pronouns (*who*) 6 points, and the pronoun *whatever* 7 points. Each sentence is scored for the eight aspects, and a total complexity measure is computed for that sentence. The mean score for a fifty-utterance sample constitutes the "developmental sentence score" (DSS). Though more time-consuming than MLU, this measure is at least practical for individual children and provides far more information. It is possible to compute means for the eight aspects separately to determine particular areas of difficulty. Lee and Canter have obtained standardization data from a sample of 160 white middle-class children between 3;0 and 6;11.

In common with virtually all other measures of spontaneous speech, the DSS evaluates all instances of particular constructions as equally valid; that is, no attempt is made to determine whether or not a construction is a productive part of the child's language. The work of Brown and others suggests that the occurrence of particular forms should be evaluated with respect to the number of contexts in which the form is required. The analysis scheme of Tyack and Gottsleben (1974), which is somewhat similar to the system of Lee and Canter, is one of the few that does this to some extent. It is also more suitable than the DSS system for work with very young children. The DSS analysis is based on fifty "complete" sentences, in which the term "complete" means that the sentence "must have at least a noun and verb in subject-predicate relationship" (Lee and Canter 1971: 317). Young children produce a large proportion of utterances that do not fit this criterion. Thus, the language of children with MLU below 3.0 or so is probably better analyzed with Tyack and Gottsleben's system.

The existence of dialect differences raises problems for all measures so far proposed. It is hardly fair to penalize a child for not producing a structure that is not present in his dialect. One solution to this problem would be to restrict the measures to features of language that are shared by all dialect groups. More practical is to develop alternate forms, as Osser, Wang, and Zaid (1969) did, viewing *if he knows* and *do he know* as equivalent indirect-question forms. Still better would be to base tests for children on norms established in their own linguistic communities.

Testing

The limitations on analysis of spontaneous speech are essentially twofold: First, it is an inefficient use of time, and, second, only certain aspects of language development—primarily productive vocabulary and syntax—are observed. The desire to probe more deeply and more widely in a limited period of time has led to the development of many tests of language development.

The Testing Situation

Psychological tests are not measuring devices like yardsticks, which can be applied objectively and reliably to produce unambiguous numbers. The performance of a child on a test is the product of an interaction between two human beings in a particular setting. Most tests are administered by an adult—usually a strange adult—alone in a room with a child. There are many factors that can lead to children not performing as well as they might.

Familiarity with the testing situation is an important determinant of success. Testing is, after all, a bizarre sort of activity. At first, it may be intimidating and anxiety-producing for the child. The importance of the familiarity of the testing situation is highlighted by the findings of Johnson (1974), discussed in Chapter 10. Johnson found that social-class differences and race differences appeared much smaller when based on analyses of spontaneous speech than when based on a standardized test of language development. Children simply retested on an intelligence test generally do better, often by about five points (Zigler and Butterfield 1968). Familiarity with the examiner may also affect performance. Several studies have revealed that, if the examiner begins by spending several sessions with the child, playing and talking with him, the child will eventually score higher on the test (Cazden 1970). Zigler, Abelson, and Seitz (1973) found that the opportunity to play with the examiner and to establish rapport significantly improved scores on the Peabody Picture Vocabulary Test (to be discussed) and that this improvement was particularly marked among poor children. The way in which the test is administered may greatly affect the child's motivational level. Zigler and Butterfield (1968) found that relatively modest changes in the procedures for administering the Stanford-Binet Intelligence Scale—beginning with an easy item, returning to an easy item whenever the child missed two consecutive items, and "gentle encouragement" to respond—raised scores 5 to 8 points.

Similarities between the child and the examiner may affect performance. A number of studies (Moore and Retish 1974) have found that black children score higher on various tests when they are administered by black examiners, though other studies have not revealed this difference (see Sattler 1970 for a review). The language or dialect of the test may also be significant. A test that counts the use of multiple negatives as an error or requires the use of *if* in such contexts as *I ask Alvin if he knows how to play basketball* is inappropriate for use in determining how well many black children have acquired the language of their community. Children who are bilingual in Spanish and English, like Puerto Rican children in New York City, score higher when tests are administered in Spanish. Dialect is not always a determining factor, however. Quay (1972; 1974) has administered the Stanford-Binet Intelligence Scale in two dialects to black preschoolers and school-age children; she has found no significant difference in performance between children administered the test in black English and those administered the test in Standard English. Probably more important than the particular dialect used are the manner of administration of the test and the possible bias in its content. For example, a vocabulary test may ask about objects that are unknown. Pictures are often used in language-comprehension tests. Yet Sigel, Anderson, and Shapiro (cited in Cazden 1972) found that poor black preschool children had more difficulty categorizing pictures of objects than the objects themselves. Culturally specific values may be embedded in tests, as when the child is asked "Why do you need to wash your face and hands?"

The three most widely used measures of language development are the Stanford-Binet Intelligence Scale, the Peabody Picture Vocabulary Test and the Illinois Test of Psycholinguistic Abilities. Although the Stanford-Binet is seldom specifically labeled as a language test, it is often used as an evaluation measure in preschool programs that claim to emphasize language development. And, indeed, the test is often attacked as an intelligence test on the grounds that it is excessively verbal. Most of the terms require comprehension of complex verbal instructions, and many require verbal responses. However, the test also taps memory, reasoning, and other cognitive factors that should be distinguished from language development.

The Peabody Picture Vocabulary Test

The Peabody Picture Vocabulary Test (PPVT; Dunn 1965) is well described by its name. The child is presented with four simple line drawings at a time and asked, "Put your finger on the picture of the word I have just said." The words proceed from common to rare. The test is quickly administered, is easy to score, and does not require verbal responses, as it is a receptive-vocabulary test. Table 11.1 contains a sample of the vocabulary lists and the norms for various ages. As a vocabulary test, the PPVT is carefully designed and well standardized (although the list appears to be overloaded with nouns, relative to children's vocabulary as a whole). However, it is widely used as a general language-assessment tool. The implicit assumption in this use is that vocabulary growth alone reflects language development; there is little or no supporting evidence for such an assumption, no correlation between vocabulary growth and other aspects of language development. The reader should judge for himself the extent to which the PPVT is culture-loaded, that is, assumes a specific cultural background on the part of the child.

Like other vocabulary tests, the Peabody views the acquisition of a word as an all-or-nothing affair. No attempt is made to assess the changes in meaning that often occur after the word has entered a child's vocabulary. In addition, line drawings or photographs are used, though all children are not equally familiar with the conventions of two-dimensional representation (Yoder 1974).

The PPVT is often used, not only as a measure of general language development, but also as a general intelligence test, probably because of the speed and ease of its administration. And, indeed, PPVT scores correlate quite highly (typically in the 70s) with Stanford-Binet IQ scores, which is the customary validation technique for intelligence measures.

Illinois Test of Psycholinguistic Abilities

By far the most commonly used assessment device is the Illinois Test of Psycholinguistic Abilities, or ITPA (Paraskevopoulos & Kirk 1969). The ITPA is composed of twelve subtests, which are defined and illustrated in Reading 11.1. The present version of the ITPA is a revision of the widely used experimental edition (McCarthy & Kirk 1961). The revision included changes in the names of the subtests, modification of items for easier administration, extension of the age range, and the addition of three subtests: Auditory Closure, Sound Blending, and Visual Closure.

TABLE 11.1   The Peabody Picture Vocabulary Test, Form A

1. car	16. drum	31. nest	46. dial
2. cow	17. leaf	32. caboose	47. yawning
3. baby	18. trying	33. envelope	48. tumble
4. girl	19. force	34. picking	49. signal
5. ball	20. bat	35. badge	50. capsule
6. clock	21. bee	36. goggles	60. bronco
7. clown	22. bush	37. peacock	70. stunt
8. key	23. pouring	38. queen	80. coil
9. can	24. sewing	39. coach	90. submerge
10. chicken	25. wiener	40. whip	100. amphibian
11. blowing	26. teacher	41. net	110. encumbered
12. fan	27. building	42. freckle	120. tartan
13. digging	28. arrow	43. eagle	130. gauntlet
14. skirt	29. kangeroo	44. twist	140. raze
15. catching	30. accident	45. shining	150. pensile

Norms (no. correct)	Age
20	2;6
25	2;9
30	3;1
35	3;5
40	3;10
45	4;5
50	5;1
60	6;10
70	8;9
80	10;8
90	12;11
100	15;7

SOURCE: Adapted from L. Dunn, *Peabody picture vocabulary test*. Minneapolis: American Guidance Service, 1965.

The subtests of the ITPA are constructed in accordance with a theory originated by Osgood (1957a; 1957b), which specifies the basic processes of language behavior in terms of three dimensions: modality (auditory, visual, motor), type of process (receptive, organizing, expressive), and level of organization (representational, automatic). There is, however, little evidence in support of this model, of either an experimental nature or derived from factor-analytic studies of the test (Burns & Watson 1973). Several of the subtests appear to have little to do with language at all. It is common for only a subset of the tests to be used—most often,

Auditory-Vocal Association, Verbal Expression, and Grammatic Closure. Many aspects of language are not assessed at all, for example, comprehension of various syntactic constructions.

Tests of Articulation and Discrimination

Tests of articulation are the best developed of the types of assessment being considered. Typically the child is asked to name pictures of familiar objects, which have been carefully selected to include the sounds of interest. Particular sounds are generally tested in initial, medial, and final positions (Templin & Darley 1964; Fisher & Logemann 1971). Articulation tests generally score the child's production as correct or incorrect. A careful comparison of the target words with the child's productions will generally reveal regular patterns of substitution (see Chapter 8). Even children with apparently severe articulation disorders are often found to be following regular rules of substitution (Compton 1970).

Corresponding to tests of productive articulation are tests of auditory discrimination (Templin 1957). Pairs of familiar objects whose names are words with similar pronunciations, except for single sounds, like *string* and *spring*, are shown simultaneously to the child, and he is asked to point to the picture in each pair named by the word the examiner then produces. This procedure is limited by the supply of available English words; some contrasts are not easily illustrated in this way. Eilers and Oller (1975) have developed a more general procedure, in which familiar words are paired with nonsense words, *rabbit* and *wabbit*, for example.

Tests of Grammatical Development

The research of the past few years has inspired clinicians and other investigators to attempt to devise more adequate measures of grammatical development. A wide range of tests (reviewed in Yoder 1974) have been proposed, though none of them has been sufficiently tested or "normed" to be considered definitive yet. Most of the tests are based on the procedure devised by Fraser, Bellugi, and Brown (1963) for assessing comprehension and production of grammatical contrasts, although we have seen in Chapter 5 that both the comprehension and production tasks raise serious difficulties. For example, in the Northwest Syntax Screening Test (Lee 1969) children are given twenty pairs of sentences such as *The girl will drink/ The girl is drinking* which test comprehension (in the example, of the future versus the present progressive) by requiring the children to point to an appropriate picture (either a girl with a full glass or a girl actually drinking). They are also given twenty additional sentence pairs, which the children first listen to and then use to name pictures. The Miller-Yoder test (Miller and Yoder 1973), widely used with retarded and other language-disabled children, assesses comprehension of a wider range of grammatical contrasts. The Assessment of Child's Language Comprehension Test (Foster, Giddan and Stark 1973) tests comprehension in a similar fashion but adds the desirable feature of actually checking to be sure the children are familiar with all vocabulary items used in the syntax test. The Auditory Test for Language Comprehension (Carrow 1968) is a particularly comprehensive survey of vocabulary, morphological, and syntactic items and provides an equivalent set of items in Spanish.

Other Aspects of Language

Surely one of the most important implications of research in linguistics and psycholinguistics is the richness of language and language use. Knowing a language includes knowing vocabulary, syntactic patterns, the phonological system, semantic relationships, the ways in which language can be used as a tool for memory and problem solving, and more. Yet vocabulary, articulation, and syntax have been far more extensively explored in tests than, for example, meaning or the use of language for memory.

Meaning is particularly difficult to assess. The cloze technique, requiring the child to fill in a missing word in a sentence, might be useful here. A version of the cloze technique is used in the Auditory-Vocal Association subtest of the ITPA, in which a child must complete such test statements as *I sit on a chair; I sleep on a* _____ and *An elephant is big; a mouse is* _____. In such a problem the child must use his knowledge of meaning and of the relations among the meanings of the words in a sentence to identify correctly the missing word.

Tests of memory span for sentences may also be useful in the investigation of semantic development. There is much evidence that meaningful material is easier to remember than material that is not meaningful, because it forms a coherent whole. The difference between memory for strings of unrelated words and memory for sentences is a measure of the child's ability to integrate a sentence semantically. Syntactic structure must, of course, be carefully controlled, as in the studies of Miller and Isard (1963) and Entwisle and Frasure (1974), discussed in Chapter 7.

Virtually no attention has been given to assessment of the abilities of children to use language for cognitive purposes, as discussed in Chapter 10, though it would be relatively simple to test the use of language for memory by means of procedures of the type developed by Flavell and his associates. Such abilities may be good predictors of the abilities of children to profit from the educational experience.

Sex Differences

In addition to the uses of tests for diagnosis of difficulties in language development, valid and reliable means of assessing language development would illuminate a number of questions about normal language development. In the next three sections we shall consider three questions of both theoretical and practical interest: Are there differences between boys and girls in language development? How similar is the process of language development in twins? Are there differences between poor and middle-class children in language development? Each question, in one way or another, involves the ways in which genetic endowment and environment jointly determine the course of language development. The available evidence is based on a narrow range of measures, but it is suggestive for further research.

That females are superior in verbal processes is a widely held generalization among both laymen and psychologists. A number of studies done in the 1920s and 1930s (reviewed in McCarthy 1954) suggested that sex differences begin very early. However, these early findings are weakened by the use of crude measures and small samples. In most instances the observed differences were small. Although our understanding of language development has increased greatly in the past twenty years, very few studies of sex differences in language development have been conducted. Maccoby and Jacklin (1974) have provided an exceptionally comprehensive and careful review of sex differences in all aspects of psychological development. The limited amount of data available on language suggests that the advantage of females may be smaller than believed or even non-existent.

Below the age of one year, most studies have found no differences between boys and girls on measures of the amount of vocalizing or vocal responding to mothers' behavior, though Lewis and Freedle (1972) found that three-month-old girls responded more than boys. Between one and two years, there are no reported differences in amount of vocalization, but girls develop vocabulary more rapidly than boys. Nelson (1973) found that the mean age at fifty words in her sample was eighteen months for girls and twenty-two months for boys.

The period between two and four years is especially interesting, because it is in this period that the major features of syntax are mastered. Girls talk more frequently, both to mothers and to other children. Girls are rated higher in language development than boys by their teachers. However, experimental tests of language development, as opposed to these measures of quantity of language development, do not show such a strong trend. Clarke-Stewart (1973) found girls' comprehension, as well as vocabulary, to be higher at seventeen months. But the overwhelming majority of the dozen or so studies of vocabulary and sentence comprehension have found no differences between boys and girls (see Maccoby and Jacklin 1974, Table 3.3). The largest sample was tested by McCarthy and Kirk (1963) as part of the standardization process for the ITPA. Seven hundred children between two and a half and nine years were tested. No differences were found on either the Vocal Encoding (now called Verbal Expression) subtest or the Auditory-Vocal Automatic (now called Grammatic Closure) subtest. Differences in favor of girls were found on the Auditory-Vocal Association subtest at five and six years only.

In the early school years few differences have been reported. Even the vocabulary differences diminish or disappear. One exception to this generalization is provided by research at the Stanford Research Institute, where it was found that in a sample of poor children in compensatory programs from kindergarten through second grade (the Follow-Through program), girls tested higher on a variety of tasks. But, on the whole, it is the absence of differences on such measures as length of response to pictures, verbal free association, vocabulary, articulation, and linguistic complexity that is striking in this age range. Several studies that have examined the ability to use language in the senses discussed in Chapter 9, as opposed to mastery of linguistic structure *per se*, have been reported. There are no differences in the amounts of egocentric speech produced while constructing designs for adults, retelling a story, communicating the rules of a game, and other communication measures (see Maccoby and Jacklin 1974, Table 3.3). Girls have better memory for verbal content, either words or sentences, after age seven years (see Maccoby and Jacklin 1974, Table 2.21), though there are no differences in memory for objects and digits. The evidence on reading ability is highly ambiguous. Some studies have found girls superior, some have found no differences, and a few have found boys superior.

Around the age of ten or eleven years, girls establish a definite pattern of superior verbal performance, which continues through the high-school and college years. Actually, tests that are basically tests of knowledge, such as the SAT Verbal (the College Boards) do not show differences, but tests of more specifically verbal skills, such as spelling, punctuation, comprehension of complex written texts, comprehension of logical relations expressed in verbal terms, and some measures of verbal creativity do show a consistent, though modest, difference of about one quarter of a standard deviation in favor of girls (Maccoby and Jacklin 1974).

Maccoby and Jacklin propose three distinct phases in the development of sex differences. Before the age of three years girls may be in advance of boys, though this is largely based on very old studies. This early advantage may be short-lived, for studies of preschoolers do not typically show differences. By age three years boys have caught up, and few differences are observed until adolescence—though, if there are differences, they usually favor the girls. Finally, in adolescence, girls are generally ahead. Maccoby and Jacklin also discuss the possible sources of sex differences in psychological functioning; their book is fundamental for anyone interested in sex differences.

An additional implication of the research on sex differences is that talkativeness and qualitative development of language are not the same thing. Unfortunately, this point has not been tested directly, but it seems to follow from findings about the greater talkativeness of preschool-age girls, together with the absence of differences in development of linguistic abilities.

Language Development in Twins

Twinning, the process by which two human beings are born with the greatest of all biological bonds, has always fascinated people. Psychologists are no exception. Since the beginning of developmental psychology, twins have been regarded as a very special case of great interest. In general, psychologists have asked two broad questions about twins: First, what is the effect of being a twin on psychological development? And, second, are identical twins more similar to each other than are fraternal twins? The second question is one means by which we can obtain information about the importance of genetic factors in development. Two kinds of twins occur: identical (monozygotic, or MZ) twins, resulting from a single fertilization, so that the twins have identical genetic endowments, and fraternal (dizygotic, or DZ) twins, resulting from two distinct fertilizations, so that the twins share, on the average, 50 percent of their genetic endowments. To the extent that genetic endowment determines an individual's development, identical twins should show greater similarity, or concordance, in development than fraternal twins. For this comparison, it is necessary to consider only same-sex fraternal pairs, for identical twins are always of the same sex.

No longitudinal studies of the language development of twins have been published. The onset of language appears often to be delayed in twins. Lenneberg (1967: ch. 6) compared a number of studies using somewhat different criteria and estimated the frequency of delay to be 47 percent in fraternal twins and 65 percent in identical twins. Although we do not know how many singletons would be classified as delayed by the criteria used, there would surely be fewer than these figures represent. Day (1932) reported that "the mean length of response for five-year-old twins is slightly below that of three-year-old singletons." Her measure, computed in words, was based on a sample of fifty consecutive utterances. One limitation in interpreting this result is the fact that twinning is correlated with social class, size of family, spacing between children, and other variables that may influence language development. Comparisons of twins with singletons should match singletons to twins on these and other variables that may affect language development.

Such a careful comparison was made by Koch (1966); however, her study included only six-year-old children. Her tests included a verbal-ability test (the verbal subtest of the Primary Mental Abilities test) and an "error analysis" of a sample of speech (defined as 400 consecutive words). The following errors were counted: lack of subject-verb agreement in number; faulty case; incorrect plurals (probably overregularizations); improper forms of tense, adjectives, adverbs, and prepositions; "faulty word order and sentence structure; incomplete sentences or omissions of essential words; confused references; and garbled or misused words" (Koch 1966:55). Clearly, the measure was a rather global one. Koch distinguished six types of twins: identical males (MZm), identical females (MZf), fraternal same-sex males (DZSSm), fraternal same-sex females (DZSSf), fraternal opposite-sex males (DZOSm), and fraternal opposite-sex females (DZOSf). As have a number of other investigators, Koch found that differences remained between twins and singletons in the school years but that they were much reduced over the differences reported at the beginning of the language-development period. On these language measures and others the singletons generally scored higher than fraternal twins, who in turn scored higher than identical twins. The differences were not great but were significant in about half the cases. An analysis by sex was revealing. On the syntax-error count, girls performed consistently better than the corresponding boys; for example, DZSSfs were superior to DZSSms, MZfs to MZms, and DZOSfs to DZOSms. This finding is in contrast to those from the comparison of singletons, in which the boys were consistently superior. Boys were also superior on the verbal subtest of the Primary Abilities test, whether they were singletons, DZSSs, or DZOSs. Only the identical twins reversed this pattern; MZfs were superior to MZms. Koch considers a number of explanations for the differences among groups, including both the social relationships of twins and singletons and physical development. A plausible hypothesis is that the differences remaining in the early school years are the long-term effects of the greater probability of birth difficulties and problems in the early physical development of twins.

The absence of evidence on the actual process of language development in toddler and preschool-age twins greatly hampers attempts to explain the differences observed. Informally, many observers have noted the unique communication systems worked out by twins, which often serve to exclude other children and adults from communication with them. But, whether they are genuinely different systems or simply abbreviated versions of a standard system, which could be developed by any two individuals in close contact with each other, is unknown at present.

Research on the second question posed at the beginning of this section compares identical and fraternal twins not with respect to overall level of achievement but rather with respect to the correlation between the two members of a pair. It has long been observed that the developmental history of identical twins is more synchronous than that of fraternal twins. This similarity holds for such physiological milestones as height, change in voice for boys, and first menstruation for girls—and for some psychological milestones as well. Lenneberg (1967) presents evidence that the onset of language is such a milestone. In identical twins, development began normally in 35 percent of the sample and was delayed in both twins in 65 percent of the sample; in other words, the agreement, or concordance, was perfect. In fraternal twins, development began normally in 53 percent of the sample, was delayed identically in 35 percent of the sample, and was delayed in just one twin (or significantly more delayed in one twin) in 25 percent of the sample.

Koch (1966) does not report the correlations between twin pairs for her measures of language development. However, the correlations for the full Primary Mental Abilities test (including five subtests) were .79 for identical twins, .45 for fraternal same-sex pairs, and .52 for fraternal opposite-sex pairs. These figures are consistent with other studies of verbally loaded intelligence tests, such as the Stanford-Binet, and strongly suggest a genetic influence on mental development, including language.

Chubrich and Mann (1971) have examined language development in twins at a more detailed level. Their measures, all based on the children's productions, included articulation, such inflections as those for the third-person singular and the past tense, and such aspects of syntactic development as pronouns and negation. Eight pairs of twins, four identical and four fraternal, were followed for nine months, beginning at approximately 3;7. Considerably greater agreement in age of attainment was found for the identical twins than for the fraternal twins on both the inflections and the syntactic items. Little difference was found for the articulation tests.

One possible explanation for such results is that parents expect and actually foster differences in fraternal twins, whereas they do not for identical twins. This hypothesis may be evaluated by examining miscategorized twins. The diagnosis of category is usually based on the attending obstetrician's judgment, which is in turn largely based on his examination of the placenta (or afterbirth). This judgment is not always accurate but is generally accepted by parents. A more accurate determination requires elaborate blood testing and other procedures, which are seldom carried out except in research projects. Do twins who are miscategorized resemble the type of twins they are believed to be by their parents, or do they resemble twins of their correct type? One pair of twins in Chubrich and Mann's sample had been miscategorized as fraternal but was in fact identical. Measures of language development were extremely close for this pair; in other words, the pair resembled other identical pairs, rather than the fraternal pair they were believed to be.

Waterhouse (1973) has taken another approach to understanding the role of the environment in determining twin concordance in development. She has examined maternal speech to twins, scoring nine factors, including rate of questions, answers to children's questions, expansions, repetitions of child utterances, and so on. For half of the measures, mothers of fraternal twins showed greater variance in style of speaking to the two twins than did mothers of identical twins, but, for the other half of the measures, it was the mothers of identical twins who showed greater variance. So there is no clear trend revealing a substantial difference between mothers of identical and fraternal twins in this regard. Waterhouse also compared identical twins who had been categorized correctly and incorrectly (as fraternal twins). If the greater concordance between identical twins reflects parental expectation and treatment, the identical twins who had been categorized as fraternal twins should have shown greater variance within pairs than did identical twins who had been categorized correctly. In fact, the reverse was true.

Thus, the evidence currently available, though based on an extremely small sample, suggests that identical twins show greater concordance in language development than do fraternal twins and that this concordance is not the result of parental expectations and treatment. It should be noted that these observations, based on measurements taken part of the way through the process of language development, are ambiguous. The demonstration of a genetic influence on development at this point does not necessarily imply a genetic influence on the end point of language development. It is entirely possible that we are observing a genetic influence only on the *rate* of development, not on its end point. The example of height is instructive. A random sample of fifteen-year-old Americans today would yield a higher mean height than a random sample of fifteen-year-old Americans 200 years ago. Although a sample of thirty-year-olds today would be taller than a sample of thirty-year-olds 200 years ago, the change in height over two centuries has been greater for fifteen-year-olds than for thirty-year-olds. The reason for this change is improved nutrition, so that Americans mature physically faster today than two centuries ago. The idea that an individual's genetic endowment exerts a control over rate of maturation is well established; rate of development shows some consistency in families. The findings from twins may be interpreted as evidence that language development is in part a maturational process, representing the unfolding capacity of the human brain (Lenneberg 1967).

Social-Class Differences

A third possible source of differences in language development, social class, as manifested in the contrast between poor and middle-class children, has the most important practical implications. The failure of many poor children to succeed in school is all too obvious; one pervasive explanation is that the language development of these children is impaired by poverty and that this impairment in turn hampers learning. Ginsburg calls this view "the conventional wisdom": "[A] deprived environment retards children's speech, this inferior speech leads to deficient thought, and deficient speech and thought result in school failure" (Ginsburg 1972: 58).

One line of reasoning for this view runs as follows. On the whole, social-class differences on standard tests, like the Stanford-Binet or the Bayley Infant Scales, do not appear before two and a half or three years of age (Golden *et al.* 1971). It is only about the time that language emerges as a complex system for the expression and understanding of messages that social-class differences are reliably observed. Thus, the problem must be one of either learning language or learning how to use language.

Social class itself can hardly be a direct cause of language development or retardation; presumably some of the many variables that are correlated with social class, such as the speech heard by the child or child rearing practices, may affect language development. But the data available on social class differences in language development are surprisingly ambiguous. In this section, we shall distinguish three broad dimensions of language development: vocabulary, syntactic development, and development of the functions of language. Many of the data are limited in usefulness, either because of the crude measures used or because of the frequent confounding of social class and race or dialect in particular studies.

The cross-ethnic-group study of patterns of ability (Stodolsky and Lesser 1967) discussed in Chapter 10 offers a particularly clear demonstration of social-class differences. The lower-class sample in each of the four ethnic groups scored significantly lower on all tests, including the verbal test, than did the middle-class sample from the corresponding group. The tests were essentially vocabulary tests; they included both a productive test of naming, using pictures, and a definition test, using questions of the form *What is a* _____? and *What do we mean when we say* _____? All children were tested in their native languages or dialects, and words that seemed to show social-class bias (*sonata* for the middle-class children, *welfare* or *stickball* for the lower-class children) were carefully excluded. Thus, the revealed differences appear to be genuine and not artifacts of the testing procedure. In fact, there is a considerable body of evidence supporting this finding for vocabulary development. Stodolsky (1965) found significant differences among groups of black children from welfare, lower-class, and middle-class families on the Peabody Picture Vocabulary Test. Templin (1957) found similar variations in vocabulary growth in preschool and school-age children.

There is much less evidence for social-class differences in the acquisition of syntactic competence. The lack of good indexes of syntactic development has hampered many studies. Templin (1957) assessed the language of 480 white children between three and eight years of age. She recorded fifty utterances in a play situation and classified them in six categories. A simple sentence without phrase is illustrated by *He goes*, a functionally complete but structurally incomplete sentence by *Down there* (in response to a question about where a toy goes), as imple sentence with phrase by *He runs with great speed*, a complex sentence by *She watches the movie while he gets the popcorn* (one subordinate clause), and a compound sentence by *He plays the clerk, and she gives him the popcorn.* Elaborated sentences have several subordinate clauses; incomplete sentences omit subjects or verbs. (Examples are from Ginsburg 1972.) On the whole, Templin found few and minor social-class differences. The lower-class children produced proportionately more simple sentences without phrase. But all types of sentences were produced by both groups of children. This finding raises a general issue. What does it mean if lower-class children produce fewer subordinate clauses than middle-class children, a finding reported by both Templin and Loban (1963)? As the lower-class children produce *some* subordinate clauses, they have the necessary competence. Unfortunately, the tendency to report only group means obscures the more interesting questions, which are whether or not some children do not produce certain constructions at all and whether or not these children tend to fall more in one social-class group than another. Of course, even if some children do not produce relative clauses, the question of their ability to comprehend relative clauses, which would also reflect linguistic competence, remains open.

Loban (1963) reported a number of social-class differences in syntactic development, based on a study of 338 children. However, his procedures are open to serious question (Ginsburg: 1972). First, his sample included both black and white children, confounding race with social class. Furthermore, many of his findings are reported as the contrast between the thirty most proficient children and the twenty-four least proficient, exaggerating the differences. Although most of the former were middle-class and most of the latter lower-class children, the significance of Loban's findings is far from clear, because we do not have the figures for these two social-class groups as a whole.

Osser (1966; cited in John and Moskowitz 1970) observed that lower-class black children had a more limited range of syntactic constructions than middle-class white children. Osser analyzed the children's syntax by means of a transformational grammar, and he eliminated dialect differences by establishing equivalences between various Standard English and Black English constructions, for example, *if he knows* and *do he know.*

Paraskevopoulos and Kirk (1969) report a study of the relations between ITPA scores and social class. Unfortunately, their results are reported as correlations between the two, rather than as mean differences. But the correlation between social class and the Grammatic Closure subtest is a modest .23.

Dewart (1972) tested comprehension of active and passive sentences, as well as sentences of the form *The wolf is happy/easy to bite,* by five- and six-year-old middle-class and working-class children in Belfast. The middle-class children performed significantly better on passives and complex sentences; both groups had little difficulty with simple actives.

Parisi (1971) tested three- to six-year-old Italian children's abilities to comprehend various constructions, using the procedure devised by Fraser, Bellugi, and Brown (1963). No differences were observed between the social-class groups up to age 3;6; thereafter a difference emerged, and it became sizable by age five years. One wonders about the possible existence of dialect differences in Rome that might be responsible for some of the differences observed, however.

Of the studies mentioned, only those by Osser (1969), Paraske-vopoulos and Kirk (1969), and Dewart (1972) clearly support the generalization of social-class differences in syntactic development. At least as many studies have failed to find differences. LaCivita, Kean, and Yamamoto (1966) asked lower-middle- and upper-middle-class elementary-school children to guess the meanings of nonsense words in such sentences as "Ungubily the mittler gimmled" and required each child to analyze each nonsense sentence syntactically and to produce a word of the same part of speech as the underlined nonsense word (a verb in the example); the lower-middle-class children were expected to do less well. In fact, the two groups of children performed equally well.

Shriner and Miner (1968) investigated the mastery of morphological rules by middle-class and lower-class white preschool children. Both expressive and receptive tests were included. The expressive test was based on Berko's technique (1958) and included plural and possessive inflections for nouns and the third-person singular, the present progressive, and past-tense inflections for verbs. The receptive test included noun pluralization only and required a pointing response from the child. No differences were found between the groups on either expressive or receptive items.

Cazden (1970) compared the MLU of black children in a Boston day-care center with the same measure as reported by Brown, Cazden, and Bellugi (1969) in their studies of generally middle-class white children; she concluded that "the lower class Negro children seem to be undergoing grammatical development at a similar rate" (1970:82).

Findings of no difference are probably more significant than findings of differences. Many of the problems associated with assessing children's language discussed in Chapter 10 and earlier in this chapter, such as unfamiliarity with the tester and the testing situation, expectancy effects, and so on, probably bias the results against poor children, so that observed differences are ambiguous. They may reflect genuine social-class differences or extraneous factors in the assessment situation. But findings of no difference, if valid measures are used and a reasonable sample tested, are unambiguous.

These findings on social-class differences provide further support for a fundamental difference between vocabulary and syntax learning. Recall that Ammon and Ammon (1971) found that vocabulary, but not syntax, could be developed through imitation training. Cazden has proposed that "the acquisition of grammar and the acquisition of vocabulary require different kinds of environmental assistance" (Cazden 1968:12).

To the extent that any aspect of language determines whether or not a child can profit from school, it should be the ability to use language for specific functions. Cazden has put it very well: "Discussions of the goals of education, like analyses of child language, too often focus on language form when they should be concerned with language use" (Cazden 1970:97). Heider (1969) tested the communication abilities of middle-class and lower-class ten-year-olds in a task similar to that of Glucksberg and Krauss (1967), discussed in Chapter 9. Consistent differences in encoding style were found: Middle-class children tended to describe one part of the stimulus at a time and in purely descriptive terms, for example, *It has an opening at the top.* Lower-class children described the entire stimulus at once, in ways that went beyond the actual stimulus: *It looks like a hat, He looks like someone hit him.* The middl-class children were superior encoders, as measured by giving encoded messages from both groups to other decoders, and superior decorders, as measured by giving the same messages to both groups.

Similarly, Krauss and Rotter (1968) found that middle-class seven- and eight-year-olds were more accurate decoders than lower-class children, whether the messages were encoded by middle-class or by lower-class children. And, conversely, middle-class encoders were responded to more accurately than were lower-class encoders, whether the listeners were middle-class or lower-class. Baldwin, McFarlane, and Garvey (1971) extended the study of Krauss and Rotter by using meaningful pictures, rather than nonsense forms, and by testing fifth graders. Again, middle-class children were more successful than lower-class children.

The consistency of these results is strong evidence for a social-class difference in communication ability. A somewhat different interpretation is suggested by the findings of Heider, Cazden, and Brown (1968): The difference may be more one of motivation than of ability. In the experiment of Heider and her colleagues the decoder could ask the encoder for more information. Decoders made nearly twice as many requests to the lower-class encoders as to the middle-class encoders. Eventually the former were virtually as successful in identifying the stimulus picture with the lower-class encoders as with the middle-class ones. Thus the performance of the lower-class children was far superior to their performance in a standardized situation, in which the amount of "probing" was controlled or eliminated. However, this finding was not confirmed by Baldwin, McFarlane, and Garvey (1971), who also permitted decoders to ask for more information. Social-class differences were not eliminated by this procedure.

Such studies of communication effectiveness are global; information about specific aspects of language in communication is needed. The use of nouns and pronouns appears to be important for communication. In a study of the free speech of five-year-olds, Hawkins (1969) found that middle-class children tended to use nouns, whereas lower-class children made much more use of pronouns. Nouns are easily and flexibly modified—*these two very long railroad trains.* Modification of pronouns is extremely limited. The ability to add further information by means of modification is very useful for communication. Hawkins also found differences in the use of pronouns. Lower-class children, in describing a picture, tended to use pronouns that referred directly to the situation: *They're playing, and he kicks it.* The speaker seems to assume that the listener can see the picture (another example of egocentrism). In contrast, middle-class children used pronouns that referred to previously mentioned nouns: *The boy kicked the ball, and it broke the window.*

Pozner and Saltz (1974) have suggested that many of the observed differences in communication effectiveness may result from limitations on vocabulary, rather than from a general inability to handle the communication situation. They have attempted to devise a situation in which vocabulary problems are minimized. Furthermore, they have attempted to explore two specific dimensions of language: conditional communication and egocentrism. In their experiment, conducted with white fifth graders, subjects learned to play a simple game, of a conditional nature, with the experimenter. In one game, the rule was as follows: If the experimenter placed a white circle on his game sheet, the child had to place his penny on the red circle on his own game sheet, and, if the experimenter placed a black circle on his sheet, the child had to place his penny on the green circle. All subjects were able to name the relevant aspects of the game: colors, shapes, and so on. Furthermore, they were all able to explain the game back to the experimenter. Thus, all subjects began the communication phase with a demonstrated mastery of the rules of the game and the relevant vocabulary.

In the communication task, the communicator—the child who had learned the game from the experimenter—explained the game to a second child, called the "listener," so that the latter could then play the game with the experimenter. Pozner and Saltz found that there were no differences in the abilities of middle-class and lower-class children as listeners. The two groups were equally able to learn the rules from the communicators, as measured by the total number of errors. But the middle-class children were much more effective as communicators. Analysis of the descriptions produced by the communicators showed that lower-class children were much more likely (54 percent versus 3 percent) to omit part of the critical conditional statement, for example, by giving only half of the condition: "If the experimenter does A, you do B." This difference occurred despite the fact that the lower-class children had demonstrated their understanding of the rules and their ability to reformulate them for the experimenter before beginning the communication phrase. Thus the problem was not one of understanding the conditional or even of having the ability to express it; it was apparently a problem of realizing the need for expression. Such a difficulty might be viewed as an example of egocentrism. Further evidence that the performance of lower-class children is more hampered by egocentrism is the fact that about one quarter of these subjects produced information that was simply inaccurate for the listener, though accurate for the communicator. For example, one communicator told a listener to put his coin on the figure that was closest to the blackboard, though the different orientation of the listener rendered this information invalid. None of the middle-class children produced such comments. Note that in this procedure there was no possibility for feedback from the listener to the communicator, which might lead to more adequate messages from the communicator.

One of the most distinctive aspects of the educational process is that discourse is primarily about events and objects that are not immediately present. They are remote in time and space. Thus, the use of language for memory may be central for schooling. McCarver and Ellis (1972) compared white middle-class and black lower-class five-year-olds on their ability to use labeling as a mnemonic aid for pictures. Despite an enormous difference between the two groups in vocabulary (44 PPVT "IQ" points), no significant differences were found in short-term memory performances. Furthermore, the effects of instructions to label aloud the six pictures presented on each trial were similar for the two groups. As other investigators have found, the rehearsal strategy increases memory for the last few items in the list to be remembered and decreases memory for the first few items, presumably because rehearsal of the final items either interferes with or replaces rehearsal of the older items. McCarver and Ellis found this pattern to hold for both groups.

Possible explanations for social-class differences in language development are more common than actual evidence for the differences and are beyond the scope of this discussion. Hess and Shipman (1965), Tulkin (1972), and Bee (1974: Part III) are good sources on this subject.

Summary

Translating findings from basic research on the general patterns of language development into procedures for assessing the development of individual children will not be an easy task. It may be more effective to develop tests for particular purposes—diagnosing specific language disabilities or assessing the progress of normal development—than to try to develop a single battery of tests for all purposes. Tests of articulation and vocabulary are well established, and a number of attempts to devise tests of grammatical development have been published. Other aspects of language, such as semantic development and the use of language for memory, have not been extensively tested.

Two widely held generalizations about individual differences in language are not as well supported as supposed: the superiority of females over males, which is difficult to demonstrate in the preschool and elementary-school years, and the poor performance of children from poverty environments, which appears to be limited to vocabulary, as opposed to syntactic, development. There is a small amount of evidence for the claim that identical twins are more similar in language development than same-sex fraternal twins, supporting the view of language development as, in part, a genetically controlled maturational process.

11.1   SUBTESTS OF THE ILLINOIS TEST OF PSYCHOLINGUISTIC ABILITIES*

Functions Tested at the Automatic Level

A. The Receptive Process (Decoding)

There are two tests at this level which assess the child's ability to comprehend visual and auditory symbols.

Auditory Reception (Auditory Decoding)   This is a test to assess the ability of a child to derive meaning from verbally presented material. Since the receptive rather than the expressive process is being sampled, the response throughout is kept at the simple level of a "yes" or "no" or even a nod or shake of the head. . . . The test contains fifty short, direct questions printed in the *Manual*. Typical items are: "Do dogs eat?" "Do dials yawn?" "Do carpenters kneel?" "Do wingless birds soar?"

Visual Reception (Visual Decoding)   It is a measure of the child's ability to gain meaning from visual symbols. In this test there are forty picture items, each consisting of a stimulus picture on one page and four response pictures on a second page. The child is shown the stimulus picture for three seconds with the directions, "See this?" Then the page of response pictures is presented with the directions, "Find one here." The credited choice is the object or situation which is conceptually similar to the stimulus. The other choices include pictures with varying degrees of structural (rather than functional) similarity or pictures which are associated with the stimulus or with the acceptable choice.

* From S. A. Kirk, J. J. McCarthy and W. D. Kirk, *Examiner's manual: Illinois test of psycholinguistic abilities* (Rev. ed.), pp. 9–13. Urbana, Ill.: University of Illinois Press, 1968.

B. The Organizing Process (Association)

At the representational level this process is represented by the ability to relate, organize, and manipulate visual or auditory symbols in a meaningful way.

Auditory-Vocal Association   This test taps the child's ability to relate concepts presented orally. . . . A sentence completion technique is used, presenting one statement followed by an incomplete analogous statement, and allowing the child to complete the second statement appropriately. There are forty-two orally presented analogies, such as, "I cut with a saw; I pound with a _____." "A dog has hair; a fish has _____."

Visual-Motor Association   The organizing process in this channel is tapped by a picture association test with which to assess the child's ability to relate concepts presented visually. The child is presented with a single stimulus picture surrounded by four optional pictures, one of which is associated with the stimulus picture. The child is asked, "What goes with this?" (pointing to the stimulus picture). "Which one of these?" (pointing to the four optional pictures). The child is to choose the one picture which is most closely related to the stimulus picture, such as a sock belonging with a shoe, or a hammer with a nail.

C. The Expressive Process (Encoding)

This process at the representational level involves the child's ability to use verbal or manual symbols to transmit an idea. There are two subtests, one requiring vocal and the other manual responses.

Verbal Expression (Vocal Encoding)   This test taps the child's ability to express ideas manually. . . . In this test fifteen pictures of common objects are shown to the child one at a time and he is asked to, "Show me what we do with a _____." The child is required to pantomime the appropriate action, such as dialing a telephone or playing a guitar.

Functions Tested at the Automatic Level

. . . [N]o effort has been made to measure purely receptive or purely expressive processes at this level. The following subtests are basically "whole level" tests which measure the child's ability to perform automatic, non-symbolic tasks.

A. Closure

The following tests assess the child's ability to fill in the missing parts in an incomplete picture or verbal expression (or the ability to integrate discrete units into a whole).

Grammatic Closure   This test assesses the child's ability to make use of the redundancies of oral language in acquiring automatic habits for handling syntax and grammatic inflections. In this test the conceptual difficulty is low, but the task elicits the child's ability to respond automatically to often repeated verbal expressions of standard American speech. . . . The test measures the form rather than the content of the missing word, since the content is provided by the examiner.

There are thirty-three orally presented items accompanied by pictures which portray the content of the verbal expressions. . . . Each verbal item consists of a complete statement followed by an incomplete statement to be finished by the child. The examiner points to the appropriate picture as he reads the given statements, for example: "Here is a dog; here are two _____." "This dog likes to bark; here he is _____."

Supplementary Test 1: Auditory Closure   This is basically a test of the organizing process at the automatic level. It assesses the child's ability to fill in missing parts which were deleted in auditory presentation and to produce a complete word. . . . In this test the child is asked, "What am I talking about: bo--le? tele--one"? There are thirty items ranging in difficulty from easy words such as "airpla--" to more difficult ones such as "ta-le--oon" and "-ype--iter."

Supplementary Test 2: Sounding Blending   This test provides another means of assessing the organizing process at the automatic level in the auditory-vocal channel. The sounds of a word are spoken singly at half-second intervals, and the child is asked to tell what the word is. Thus he has to synthesize the separate parts of the word and produce an integrated whole. . . .

Visual Closure   This test assesses the child's ability to identify a common object from an incomplete visual presentation. There are four scenes, presented separately, each containing fourteen or fifteen examples of a specified object. The objects are seen in varying degrees of concealment. The child is asked to see how quickly he can point to all examples of a particular object within the time limit of thirty seconds for each scene.

B. Sequential Memory

The two following tests assess the child's ability to reproduce a sequence of auditory or visual stimuli. They are tests of short-term sequential memory.

Auditory Sequential Memory   This test assesses the child's ability to reproduce from memory sequences of digits increasing in length from two to eight digits. . . .

Visual Sequential Memory   This test assesses the child's ability to reproduce sequences of nonmeaningful figures from memory. The child is shown each sequence of figures for five seconds and then is asked to put corresponding chips of figures in the same order.

further reading

Maccoby, E. E. & Jacklin, C. N. *The psychology of sex differences*. Stanford: Stanford University Press, 1974.

McCarthy, D. Language development in children. In L. Carmichael (Ed.), *Manual of child psychology*. New York: Wiley, 1954, Pp. 452–630.

Yoder, D. E. Evaluation and assessment of children's language and speech behavior. In M. V. Wisland (Ed.), *Psychoeducational diagnosis of exceptional children*. Springfield: Charles C Thomas, 1974. Pp. 329–379.

APPENDIX: Exploring the Language of Children

Young children are not the docile experimental subjects that rats and college students are. This is part of their charm. Long, tedious, rigid experimental procedures are simply not feasible. As a result, many of the studies discussed in this book are easy to repeat. Such replication is valuable for two reasons. First, many findings are surprising in themselves, either because the child is more capable than may have been thought, as in Wieman's finding (see Chapter 2) that stress is consistently used to distinguish new and old information even in stage I, or because the child is less capable, as in Carol Chomsky's finding (see Chapter 5) that sentences of the form *The doll is easy to see* are systematically misinterpreted. Second, there are remarkable similarities that hold among children in many instances, especially similarities of sequence. These sequences may be verified by administering two or more procedures to the same children and asking, in effect, whether or not some children have achieved A but not B whereas no children have achieved B but not A.

Projects that I have asked students to undertake fall into two categories: experimental investigations and naturalistic observation and analysis of a child's speech. Often the class divides itself into small groups (three or four) for these projects, in order to help one another find subjects, administer the procedures in standard fashion, and discuss and interpret the results. In addition, if time permits, after the replications are completed, each group is asked to formulate an unanswered question about language development and to propose an empirical investigation that might provide some information on the question. The class as a whole then considers the proposed experiments and selects the one that appears most interesting (and feasible) and conducts the study.

Results of studies as reported in journal articles and books are abstractions from the actual behavior of children in particular settings. Replication of published studies provides a "feel" for the actual nature of responses—which are confident and which tentative, which items are easy and which are hard—and the variability among children. Going beyond replications of published studies to the proposal of new studies has as its goal the conversion of the student from a passive observer to an active investigator.

The following general instructions are given.

General Testing Instructions

Once you have obtained permission, you should arrange a time (or two times if necessary) when it is possible for you and your subject to be more or less alone in some room. It is much better if the parents or siblings are not present. Tell the child you want him to play some games with you and that you want him to try as hard as he can. Often, if you introduce yourself as a student and tell the child you are doing this for school work, you can get excellent cooperation. Follow the instructions given as closely as possible. If you feel you must deviate in some way, do so, but indicate this in your report and indicate how and why you changed the procedure. If the child's attention seems to be wandering, you may, of course, stop the testing and chat or play with him for a period of time. If necessary (and this is particularly likely with younger children), break the testing into two sessions, to be given on different days. Do not force the child to do anything he does not want to do. You may urge and encourage if he is resistant, but do not force him. The subject should always have the right to terminate the testing if he does not want to continue.

Afterward, show the parents the child's answers and tell them that, as far as you know, the responses are typical of children his age. You might suggest that they try asking the child some of the same questions in a year or two and note the differences. If the parents seem surprised at the fact, for example, that their four-year-old child cannot identify someone else's left and right hands, you might mention that adults often overestimate how much children of this age know. Do not attempt to diagnose the child as an individual, and do not say anything that an anxious parent might construe as a judgment of the relative intelligence of the child.

Parental Permission

You must get the signature of one of the child's parents before you question the child. The reason for this is an ethical one: You are invading the family's privacy. Even though what you are doing cannot harm the child or the parents, they might think that it can, and the harm will have been done.

Children are not laboratory animals; they are people, and you have a responsibility to act maturely, as a professional. Each child has the right to refuse to participate, and his parents have the right to refuse to let you question him at any point in the interview. If you do not complete the procedure with a particular child, indicate why in your report, make a copy of the blank data sheet, and find another subject.

You should explain to the parent that you are a student taking a course about children. Assure her that the project is for your own training, that the results will not be used for any other purpose, and that you are not studying individual children or comparing one child with another but, rather, are trying to learn about the things that are true of all children. Then let her (or him) read the signature form and sign it.

Parental Permission Form

_____ has my permission to ask questions

of my child, _____, as part of a class project at (name of school). I understand that the result of this observation will be used only for the purpose of training students to become good observers and interviewers of children, and that my child is not being compared with other children on an individual basis. The student has adequately explained the nature of the questions to be asked. The class is under the direction of (name of instructor), who may be contacted at (telephone number).

(signed) _____

(date) _____

Miniexperiments

Only a handful of experiments for replication are suggested here. New experiments are constantly appearing in the literature, and the instructor should keep an eye out for techniques suitable for class projects. As a general rule, sheets should be prepared and duplicated for each student, indicating explicitly what is to be said and shown to the child and providing space in which the child's responses may be recorded. The first experiment is specified in this way; others are described more briefly.

Comprehension of Verbs of Possession

Words do not always mean the same thing for children as for adults. The differences are often most easily observed in comprehension errors; the systematic nature of these errors reveals something of the process of semantic development. In this project we shall look at the comprehension of a set of verbs that have to do with possession and change of possession. This experiment is suitable for children between 3;6 and 8;6.

Procedure. Introduce two dolls, Bert and Ernie. Place each doll down next to his pile of toys and money: pennies, cars, airplanes, boats, and so on. Be sure that each doll has an identical set of objects. Then ask the subject to perform the following actions. The objects named are not important. Nor is it necessary that the dolls actually move the objects. Just keep track of which objects and coins move from one location to another.

1.	Make Bert give Ernie a car.	correct	incorrect	(explain)
2.	Make Ernie take an airplane from Bert.	correct	incorrect	(explain)
3.	Make Ernie pay Bert for a boat.	correct	boat from Bert to Ernie	other error (explain)
4.	Make Bert buy a boat from Ernie.	correct	boat from Ernie to Bert	other error (explain)
5.	Make Ernie sell a car to Bert.	correct	car from Ernie to Bert	other error (explain)
6.	Make Bert trade an airplane to Ernie for a cat.	correct	a. airplane from Bert to Ernie *or* car from Ernie to Bert, but not both b. car from Bert to Ernie *and* airplane from Ernie to Bert	other error (explain)

The incorrect responses indicated for items 3–6 specify the most common mistakes, which can usually be interpreted as the results of assimilation to simpler verbs. For example, the error indicated in item 4 reflects misinterpretation of *buy* or *take*.

Comprehension of Syntactic Forms

One of the best ways to explore the child's comprehension is to ask her to demonstrate with dolls or other toys the action described in a sentence. In Chapter 5 of this book we reported a number of studies of this type; Bellugi-Klima (1971) has suggested a wide range of such comprehension tests, and undoubtedly more can be constructed. Many of these tests may be attempted with children as young as two and a half years or even younger. The general procedure is to place the objects on the table before the child, identify them, and demonstrate the action. This is done so that the only contribution the child must make is the transition from syntactic form into action. The simplest test is of active sentences. Place a toy cat and a toy dog on the table and ask the child to show "The dog chases the cat" and conversely (though not necessarily in this order).

Before the possessive inflection appears in children's speech, they appear to produce possessive constructions—for example, *mommy dress.* Comprehension of the possessive may be tested by showing the child a small boy doll and a larger man doll (identifying the former as the son and the latter as the father) and asking her to point to "the boy's daddy" and then "the daddy's boy."

Understanding of singular and plural endings on nouns and verbs may be tested by showing the child two girl dolls lying down and asking the child to show "the girl walks" and "the girls walk."

Reflexive pronouns, as in *He hurt himself,* do not appear in children's speech until a late period. Comprehension of reflexives may be tested by showing the child two dolls and a washcloth, demonstrating the action of washing, and asking the child to show "John washed him" and "John washed himself."

Passive sentences are not only late in appearing in children's speech; they also seem not to be comprehended before age four years or so. They may be tested by the same method used for active sentences: asking the child to show "The cat is chased by the dog" and "The dog is chased by the cat." Comparison of the performances of particular children on various comprehension tests often reveals a regular sequence of development, comparable to the regularity of sequence observed in children's productions.

The Meaning of Left and Right

This experiment is suitable for children between four and seven years old. Ask the child to show you his left hand and then his right hand. Next, while facing the child, ask him to point to *your* left hand and then to *your* right hand.

The "Easy To See" Construction

This experiment is suitable for children between four and eight years old. Place a blindfolded doll on the table in front of the child. Ask "Is this doll easy to see or hard to see?" If the child responds, "Easy to see," ask "Would you make her hard to see?" If the child responds "Hard to see," ask "Would you make her easy to see?" Then ask, "Why was she hard to see in the beginning? What did you do to make her easier to see?" Chomsky's *ask/tell* experiment, described in Chapter 5, is longer and more elaborate to stage but even more interesting.

Analysis of Spontaneous Speech

Despite the problems in drawing conclusions about children's linguistic competence from studies of their productions (see Chapters 1, 4, 5, and 6), one of the most enlightening exercises that can be undertaken is the observation and analysis of a child's free speech. It is difficult to specify a suitable age. The child should be producing at least a moderate quantity of multiword utterances sufficiently clearly so that the observer (perhaps with the help of the child's parent) can identify the words. However, the child should not be too advanced, or the analysis will be impossible with a small corpus and limited time. The most efficient procedure is probably to collect a limited sample of fifty utterances and to compute MLU (following the rules given in Table 2.1) as a screening measure. If the MLU is not over about 2.0, it is feasible to attempt to describe the linguistic system as a whole. If the MLU is longer, say between 2.0 and 3.5, the system will be too complex for this task; instead, such specific subsystems as negations, questions, and noun phrases may be analyzed. The particular grammatical terminology and notation used for this purpose is not important; the goal is to describe the kinds of combinations of words that can occur and the constraints on the order of words in such combinations.

At least 200 utterances should be collected and preferably more. Learning to elicit speech from a young child is a highly personal process and depends on the personalities of both the child and the interviewer. There are no hard-and-fast rules. But it is best to keep in mind that the goal is a conversation, not an interrogation. Questions are likely to elicit one-word replies, if any. More productive is to begin playing with toys or reading a book. Most young children do not like being left out of any interesting activity and will soon join in. Since more than one session may be necessary to gather a sufficient corpus, it is a good idea to bring along a few new toys and books each time a visit is made. If possible the speech of the child should be both taped and recorded by an observer; neither alone is likely to give a complete record. In addition, relevant contextual information for disambiguating sentences should be recorded.

An interesting extension of this investigation is to compare the child's productive speech with either his imitations or his comprehension ability. For selected aspects of syntax, sentences may be prepared for imitation or comprehension, and the child's ability to imitate or comprehend may be compared with his use of the feature in spontaneous speech.

References

Allen, V. F. A second dialect is not a foreign language. In J. E. Alatis (Ed.), *20th Georgetown University Round Table*. Washington, D.C.: Georgetown University Press, 1970. Pp. 189–202.

Alston, W. P. *Philosophy of language*. Englewood Cliffs, N.J.: Prentice-Hall, 1964.

Amidon, A., and Carey, P. Why five-year-olds cannot understand before and after. *Journal of Verbal Learning and Verbal Behavior*, 1972, **11**, 417–423.

Ammon, P. R., and Ammon, M. S. Effects of training black preschool children in vocabulary vs. sentence construction. *Journal of Educational Psychology*, 1971, 421–426.

Anastasiow, N. J., and Hanes, M. L. Cognitive development and acquisition of language in three subcultural groups. *Developmental Psychology*, 1974, **10**, 703–709.

Anisfeld, M. Psychological evidence for an intermediate stage in a morphological derivation. *Journal of Verbal Leaning and Verbal Behavior*, 1969, **8**, 191–195.

Antinucci, F., and Parisi, D. Early language acquisition: A model and some data. In C. A. Ferguson and D. I. Slobin (Eds.), *Studies of child language development*. New York: Holt, Rinehart and Winston, 1973. Pp. 607–619.

Ashton-Warner, S. *Teacher*. New York: Bantam, 1962.

Atkinson, K., McWhinney, B., and Stoel, C. An experiment on the recognition of babbling. *Papers and reports on child language development*, Committee on Linguistics, Stanford University, 1970, No. 1.

Bach, E. *Syntactic Theory*. New York: Holt, Rinehart and Winston, 1974.

Bach, E., and Harms, R. T. (Eds.). *Universals in Linguistic Theory.* New York: Holt, Rinehart and Winston, 1968.

Baird, R. On the role of chance in Imitation-Comprehension-Production test results. *Journal of Verbal Learning and Verbal Behavior,* 1972, 11, 474–477.

Baldwin, T. L., McFarlane, P. T., and Garvey, C. J. Children's communication accuracy related to race and socioeconomic status. *Child Development,* 1971, 42, 345–357.

Bar-Adon, A., and Leopold, W. F. (Eds.) *Child language: A book of readings.* Englewood Cliffs, N.J.: Prentice-Hall, 1971.

Baratz, J. C., and Shuy, R. W. (Eds.) *Teaching black children to read.* Washington, D.C.: Center for Applied Linguistics, 1969.

Barrie-Blackley, S. Six-year-old children's understanding of sentences adjoined with time adverbs. *Journal of Psycholinguistic Research,* 1973, 2, 153–165.

Bates, E. Acquisition of pragmatic competence. *Journal of Child Language,* 1974, 1, 277–281.

————. Pragmatics and sociolinguistics in child language. In D. Morehead and A. Morehead (Eds.). *Language deficiency in children: Selected readings.* Baltimore: University Park Press, in press.

Bee, H. *Social issues in developmental psychology.* New York: Harper & Row, 1974.

Bellugi, U. The development of interrogative structures in children's speech. In K. Riegel (Ed.), *The development of language functions.* University of Michigan Language Development Program, Report No. 8, 1965. Pp. 103–138.

————. The acquisition of negation. Unpublished doctoral dissertation, Graduate School of Education, Harvard University, 1967.

————, and Brown, R. (Eds.). *The acquisition of language.* Monographs of the Society for Research in Child Development, 1964, 29, No. 92.

————, and Fischer, S. A comparison of sign language and spoken language. *Cognition,* 1972, 1, 173–200.

————, and Klima, E. S. The roots of language in the sign talk of the deaf. *Psychology Today,* 1972, 6, 61–76.

Bellugi-Klima, U. Some language comprehension tests. In C. S. Stendler (Ed.), *Language training in early childhood education.* Urbana, Ill.: University of Illinois Press, 1971. Pp. 157–169.

Berko, J. The child's learning of English morphology. *Word,* 1958, 14, 150–177.

Berlin, B., and Kay P. *Basic color terms: Their universality and evolution.* Berkeley: University of California Press, 1969.

Best, B. J. Classificatory development in deaf children: Research on language and cognitive development. Occasional Paper No. 15, Research, Development and Demonstration Center in Education of Handicapped Children, University of Minnesota, 1973.

Bever, T. G. The cognitive basis for linguistic structures. In J. R. Hayes (Ed.), *Cognition and the Development of Language.* New York: Wiley, 1970. Pp. 279–362.

Bierwisch, M. Semantics. In J. Lyons (Ed.), *New Horizons in Linguistics.* Baltimore: Penguin Books, 1970.

Blank, M. Cognitive functions of language in the preschool years. *Developmental Psychology*, 1974, **10**, 229–245.

Bloom, L. *Language development: Form and function in emerging grammars.* Cambridge, Mass.: M.I.T. Press, 1970. (a)

———. Semantic features in language acquisition. Paper presented at the Conference on Research in the Language of the Mentally Retarded, University of Kansas, February, 1970. (b)

———. Why not pivot grammar? *Journal of Speech and Hearing Disorders*, 1971, **36**, 40–50.

———. *One word at a time.* The Hague: Mouton, 1973.

———. Talking, understanding, and thinking. In R. L. Schiefelbusch, and L. L. Lloyd (Eds.), *Language perspectives—acquisition, retardation, and intervention.* Baltimore: University Park Press, 1974.

———. Language development. Chapter prepared for *Review of Child Development Research*, Vol. 4. University of Chicago Press, in press.

———, Hood, L., and Lightbown, P. Imitation in language development: If, when and why. *Cognitive Psychology*, 1974, **6**, 380–420.

Bloomfield, L. *Language.* New York: Holt, Rinehart and Winston, 1933.

Bogoyavlenskiy, D. N. The acquisition of Russian inflections. In C. A. Ferguson and D. I. Slobin (Eds.), *Studies of child language development.* New York: Holt, Rinehart and Winston, 1973. Pp. 284–292.

Bolinger, D. The atomization of meaning. *Language*, 1965, **41**, 555–573.

———. *Aspects of language.* New York: Harcourt, 1968.

Bornstein, H. A description of some current sign systems designed to represent English. *American Annals of the Deaf*, 1973, **118**, 454–463.

Bower, T. G. R. The visual world of infants. *Scientific American*, 1966, **215**, 80–92.

Bowerman, M. *Early syntactic development: A cross-linguistic study with special reference to Finnish.* Cambridge, Mass.: Cambridge University Press, 1973.

———. Learning the structure of causative verbs: A study in the relationship of cognitive, semantic and syntactic development. *Papers and Reports on Child Language Development*, Committee on Linguistics, Stanford University, 1974, No. 8, 142–178.

———. Semantic factors in the acquisition of rules for word use and sentence construction. In D. Morehead and A. Morehead (Eds.), *Language deficiency in children: Selected readings.* Baltimore: University Park Press, in press.

Braine, M. D. S. The ontogeny of English phrase structure: The first phrase. *Language*, 1963, **39**, 1–13.

———. On two types of models of the internalization of grammars. In D. I. Slobin (Ed.), *The ontogenesis of grammar.* New York: Academic Press, 1971.

———. Children's first word combinations. *Monographs of the Society for Research in Child Development*, in press.

Bransford, J. D., and Franks, J. J. Sentence memory: A constructive vs. interpretive approach. *Cognitive Psychology*, 1972, **3**, 193–209.

Bronckart, J. P. The regulating role of speech: A cognitive approach. *Human Development*, 1973, **16**, 417–439.

————, and Sinclair, H. Time, tense and aspect. *Cognition,* 1973, **2,** 107–130.

Bronowski, J., and Bellugi, U. Language, name and concept. *Science,* 1970, **168,** 669–673.

Brown, R. How shall a thing be called? *Psychological Review,* 1958, **65,** 14–21.

————. The development of wh questions in child speech. *Journal of Verbal Learning and Verbal Behavior,* 1968, **7,** 277–290.

————. Derivational complexity and order of acquisition in child speech. In R. Brown, *Psycholinguistics.* New York: Free Press, 1970.

————. The first sentences of child and chimpanzee. In *Psycholinguistics: Selected papers of Roger Brown.* New York: Free Press, 1970. Pp. 208–231.

————. *A first language: The early stages.* Cambridge, Mass.: Harvard University Press, 1973.

————. The development of the human child's native language. In A. Silverstein (Ed.), *Human communication: Theoretical explorations.* Hillsdale, N.J.: Lawrence Erlbaum Associates, 1974.

————, and Bellugi, U. Three processes in the child's acquisition of syntax. *Harvard Educational Review,* 1964, **34,** 133–151.

————, Cazden, C., and Bellugi, U. The child's grammar from I to III. In J. P. Hill (Ed.), *Minnesota Symposium on Child Psychology.* Vol. 2. Minneapolis: University of Minnesota Press, 1969. Pp. 28–73.

————, and Fraser, C. The acquisition of syntax. In U. Bellugi and R. Brown (Eds.), *The acquisition of language.* Monographs of the Society for Research in Child Development, 1964, **29** (Serial No. 92), 43–79.

————, and Hanlon, C. Derivational complexity and order of acquisition. In J. R. Hayes (Ed.), *Cognition and the development of language.* New York: Wiley, 1970. Pp. 11–53.

————, and Lenneberg, E. H. A study in language and cognition. *Journal of Abnormal and Social Psychology,* 1954, **49,** 454–462.

Bruner, J., May, A., and Greenfield, P. Early words: Action and the structure of language [film]. New York: Wiley, 1973.

Bruner, J. S. The course of cognitive growth. *American Psychologist,* 1964, **19,** 1–15.

————, and Bruner, B. M. On voluntary action and its hierarchical structure. *International Journal of Psychology,* 1968, **3,** 239–255.

————, Olver, R., and Greenfield, P. *Studies in Cognitive Growth.* New York: Wiley, 1966.

Burling, R. Language development of a Garo and English speaking child. *Word,* 1959, **15,** 45–68.

————. *English in black and white.* New York: Holt, Rinehart and Winston, 1973.

Burns, G. W., and Watson, B. L. Factor analysis of the revised ITPA with underachieving children. *Journal of Learning Disabilities,* 1973, **6,** 371–376.

Cambon, J., and Sinclair, H. Relations between syntax and semantics: Are they "easy to see"? *British Journal of Psychology,* 1974, **65,** 133–140.

Carmichael, L. (Ed.). *Manual of child psychology.* New York: Wiley, 1954.

————, Hogan, H. P., and Walter, A. A. An experimental study of the effect of language on the representation of visually perceived form. *Journal of Experimental Psychology,* 1932, **15,** 73–86.

Carroll, J. B., and Casagrande, J. B. The function of language classifications in behavior. In E. E. Maccoby, T. M. Newcomb, and E. L. Hartley (Eds.), *Readings in Social Psychology*. (3d ed.) New York: Holt, Rinehart and Winston, 1958, pp. 18–31.

Carrow, M. W. The development of auditory comprehension of language structure in children. *Journal of Speech and Hearing Disorders*, 1968, **33**, 99–111.

Cazden, C. Environmental assistance to the child's acquisition of grammar. Unpublished doctoral dissertation, Graduate School of Education, Harvard University, 1965.

————. The acquisition of noun and verb inflections. *Child Development*, 1968, **39**, 433–438. (a)

————. Some implications of research on language development for preschool education. In R. D. Hess and R. M. Bear (Eds.), *Early Education*, Chicago: Aldine, 1968. (b)

————. The neglected situation in child language research and education. In F. Williams (Ed.), *Language and poverty*. Chicago: *Markham*, 1970. Pp. 81–101.

————. *Child language and education*. New York: Holt, Rinehart and Winston, 1972.

Chall, J. *Learning to read: The great debate*. New York: McGraw-Hill, 1967.

Chapman, R. S., and Miller, J. F. Word order in early two and three work utterances: Does production precede comprehension? *Journal of Speech and Hearing Research*, 1975, **18**, 355–371.

Chomsky, C. S. *The acquisition of syntax in children from 5 to 10*. Cambridge, Mass.: M.I.T. Press, 1969.

————. Reading, writing, and phonology. *Harvard Educational Review*, 1970, **40**, 307–308.

————. Write now, read later. In C. B. Cazden (Ed.), *Language in early childhood education*. Washington, D.C.: National Association for the Education of Young Children, 1972. Pp. 119–126. (a)

————. Stages in language development and reading exposure. *Harvard Educational Review*, 1972, **42**, 1–33. (b)

Chomsky, N. *Syntactic structures*. The Hague: Mouton, 1957.

————. *Aspects of the theory of syntax*. Cambridge, Mass.: M.I.T. Press, 1965.

————. Deep structure, surface structure, and semantic representation. In D. Steinberg and L. A. Jokobovits (Eds.), *Semantics: An interdisciplinary reader in philosophy, linguistics and psychology*. Cambridge: Cambridge University Press, 1971. Pp. 183–216.

————. *Language and mind* (2d Ed.). New York: Harcourt, 1972.

————, and Halle, M. *The sound pattern of English*. New York: Harper & Row, 1968.

Chubrich, R. E., and Mann, M. B. Selected phonological, morphological, and syntactic measures for identical and nonidentical same-sex twins. Paper delivered to the American Speech and Hearing Association, November, 1971.

Chukovsky, K. *From two to five*. Translated by M. Morton. Berkeley: University of California Press, 1968.

Clark, E. V. On the acquisition of the meaning of "before" and "after." *Journal of Verbal Learning and Verbal Behavior*, 1971, **10**, 266–275.

———. On the child's acquisition of antonyms in two semantic fields. *Journal of Verbal Learning and Verbal Behavior*, 1972, **11**, 750–758.

———. What's in a word? On the child's acquisition of semantics in his first language. In T. E. Moore (Ed.), *Cognitive development and the acquisition of language*. New York: Academic Press, 1973.

Clark, H. H. The primitive nature of children's relational concepts. In J. R. Hayes (Ed.), *Cognition and the Development of Language*. New York: Wiley, 1970.

———. Space, time, semantics, and the child. In T. E. Moore (Ed.), *Cognition and the acquisition of language*. New York: Academic Press, 1973. Pp. 27–63.

Clark, R., Hutcheson, S., and van Buren, P. Comprehension and production in language acquisition. *Journal of Linguistics*, 1974, **10**, 39–54.

———. Performing without competence. *Journal of Child Language*, 1974, **1**, 1–10.

Clarke-Stewart, K. A. Interactions between mothers and their young children: Characteristics and consequences. *Monographs of the Society for Research in Child Development*, 1973, **38**, No. 153.

Compton, A. J. Generative studies of children's phonological disorders. *Journal of Speech and Hearing Disorderism*, 1970, **35**, 315–339.

Conklin, P. Good day at Rough Rock. *American Education*, 1967, **3**, 4–9.

Copple, C. E., and Suci, G. J. The comparative ease of processing standard English and Black nonstandard English by lower-class Black children. *Child Development*, 1974, **45**, 1048–1053.

Cromer, R. F. The development of temporal reference during the acquisition of language. Unpublished doctoral dissertation Harvard University, 1968.

———. Children are nice to understand: Surface structure clues for the recovery of a deep structure. *British Journal of Psychology*, 1970, **61**, 397–408.

———. The development of the ability to decenter in time. *The British Journal of Psychology*, 1971, **62**, No. 3, 353–365.

Curtiss, S., Fromkin, V., Krashen, S., Rigler, D., and Rigler, M. The linguistic development of Genie. *Language*, 1974, **50**, 528–554.

Dale, P. S. Language development: Structure and function. New York: Dryden Press, 1972.

———, Loftus, E. F., and Rathbun, L. The influence of the form of the question on the eyewitness testimony of preschool children. Unpublished paper, University of Washington, 1974.

Day, E. J. The development of language in twins: I. A comparison of twins and single children. *Child Development*, 1932, **3**, 179–199.

Descartes, R. Discourse on method, part V. In E. S. Haldane and G. R. T. Ross (Eds.), *The philosophical works of Descartes*. New York: Dover, 1955

DeStefano, J. S. *Language, society, and education: A profile of Black English*. Worthington, Ohio: Charles A. Jones Publishing Company, 1973.

de Villiers, J. G., and de Villiers, P. A. A cross-sectional study of the acquisition of grammatical morphemes in child speech. *Journal of Psycholinguistic Research*, 1973, **2**, 267–278. (a)

————, and de Villiers, P. A. Development of the use of word order in comprehension. *Journal of Psycholinguistic Research*, 1973, **2**, 331–341. (b)

———— and ————. Competence and performance in child language: Are children really competent to judge? *Journal of Child Language*, 1974, **1**, 11–22.

Dewart, M .H. Social class and children's understanding of deep structure sentences. *British Journal of Educational Psychology*, 1972, **42**, 198–203.

Donaldson, M., and Balfour, G. Less is more: A study of language comprehension in children. *British Journal of Psychology*, 1968, **59**, 461–472.

————. and Wales, R. J. On the acquisition of some relational terms. In J. R. Hayes (Ed.), *Cognition and the development of language*. New York: Wiley, 1970.

Dunn, L. *Peabody picture vocabulary test*. Minneapolis: American Guidance Service, 1965.

Edwards, E. Sensory-motor intelligence and semantic relations in early child grammar. *Cognition*, 1973, **2**, 395–434.

Edwards, M. L. Perception and production in child phonology: The testing of four hypotheses, *Journal of Child Laguange*, 1974, **1**, 205–219.

Eilers, R. E., and Minifie, F. D. Fricative discrimination in early infancy. *Journal of Speech and Hearing Research*, 1975, **18**, 158–167.

————, Oller, D. K., and Ellington, J. The acquisition of word-meaning for dimensional adjectives: The long and short of it. *Journal of Child Language*, 1974, **1**, 195–204.

————, and Oller, D. K. The role of speech discrimination in developmental sound substitutions. Paper presented to the Society for Research in Child Development, Denver, April, 1975.

Eimas, P., Siqueland, E. R., Jusczyk, P., and Vigorito, J. Speech perception in infants. *Science*, 1971, **171**, 303–306.

Elkind, D. Children's conceptions of brother and sister. *Journal of Genetic Psychology*, 1962, **100**, 129–136.

Engel, W. v. R. An example of linguistic consciousness in the child. In C. A. Ferguson and D. I. Slobin (Eds.), *Studies of Child Language Development*. New York: Holt, Rinehart and Winston, 1973. Pp. 155–158.

Entwisle, D. R., and Frasure, N. E. A contradiction resolved: Children's processing of syntactic cues. *Developmental Psychology*, 1974, **10**, 852–857.

————, and Huggins, W. H. Iconic memory in children. *Child Development*, 1974, **44**, 392–394.

Ervin, S. Imitation and structural change in children's language. In E. H. Lenneberg (Ed.), *New directions in the study of language*. Cambridge, Mass.: M.I.T. Press, 1964. Pp. 163–189.

Ervin-Tripp, S. Language development. In L. W. Hoffman and M. L. Hoffman (Eds.), *Review of child development research*. Vol. 2. New York: Russell Sage Foundation, 1966. Pp. 55–105.

————. Some strategies for the first two years. In T. E. Moore (Ed.), *Cognition and the acquisition of language*. New York: Academic Press, 1973. Pp. 261–286.

———. The comprehension and production of requests by children. *Papers and Reports on Child Language Development*, Committee on Linguistics, Stanford University, 1974, No. 8, 188–196.

Feldman, C. The effects of various types of adult responses in the syntactic acquisition of two- to three-year-olds. Unpublished paper, Department of Psychology, University of Chicago, 1971.

Ferguson, C. A., and Slobin, D. I. *Studies of child language development*. New York: Holt, Rinehart and Winston, 1973.

Fernald, C. D. Control of grammar in imitation, comprehension, and production: Problems of replication. *Journal of Verbal Learning and Verbal Behavior*, 1972, 11, 606–613.

Fillmore, C. J. The case for case. In E. Bach and R. T. Harms (Eds.), *Universals in linguistic theory*. New York: Holt, Rinehart and Winston, 1968.

Fisher, H., and Logemann, J. *The Fisher-Logemann Test of Articulation Competence*. Boston: Houghton-Mifflin, 1971.

Flavell, J. H. Developmental studies of mediated memory. *Advances in Child Development and Behavior*, 1970, 5, 182–211.

Fleming, J. D. The state of the apes. *Psychology Today*, 1974, 8.

Flores d'Arcais, G. B., and Levelt, W. J. M. (Eds.), *Advances in Psycholinguistics*. New York: American Elsevier, 1970.

Fodor, J., and Garret, M. Some reflections on competence and performance. In J. Lyons and R. J. Wales (Eds.), *Psycholinguistics papers*. Edinburgh: Edinburgh University Press, 1966. Pp. 135–154.

Foster, R., Giddan, J. J., and Stark, J. *Assessment of children's language comprehension*. Palo Alto: Consulting Psychologists Press, 1973.

Frank, S., and Osser, H. A psycholinguistic model of syntactic complexity. *Language and Speech*, 1970, 13, 38–53.

Fraser, C. Bellugi, U., and Brown, R. Control of grammar in imitation, comprehension, and production. *Journal of Verbal Learning and Verbal Behavior*, 1963, 2, 121–135.

Frentz, T. S. Children's comprehension of standard and Negro nonstandard English sentences. *Speech Monographs*, 1971, 38, 10–16.

Fries, C. C. *Linguistics and reading*. New York: Holt, Rinehart and Winston, 1963.

Furth, H. *Thinking without language*. New York: Free Press, 1966.

———. *Piaget and knowledge: Theoretical foundations*. Englewood Cliffs, N.J.: Prentice-Hall, 1969.

———. Linguistic deficiency and thinking: Research with deaf subjects 1964–69. *Psychological Bulletin*, 1971, 75, 58–72.

Gardner, R. A., and Gardner, B. T. Teaching sign language to a chimpanzee. *Science*, 1969, 165, 664–672.

——— and ———. Early signs of language in child and chimpanzee. *Science*, 1974, 187.

Garnica, O. K. The development of phonemic speech perception. In T. E. Moore (Ed.), *Cognition and the acquisition of language*. New York: Academic Press, 1973. Pp. 215–222.

Gentner, D. Evidence for the psychological reality of semantic components: The verbs of possession. D. A. Norman, D. E. Rumelhart, and the LNR Research Group, *Explorations in Cognition*. San Francisco: Freeman, 1975. Pp. 211–246.

Gherogov, I. A. *Ein Beitrag zur Grammatischen Entwicklung der Kindersprache*. Leipzig: Engelmann, 1908.

Gibson, E. J., Pick, A., Ossar, H., and Hammond, M. The role of grapheme-phoneme correspondence in the perception of words. *American Journal of Psychology*, 1962, **75**, 554–570.

Gillooly, W. B. The influence of writing-system characteristics on learning to read. *Reading Research Quarterly*, 1975, **8**, 167–199.

Ginsburg, H., and Opper, S. *Piaget's theory of intellectual development: An introduction*. Englewood Cliffs, N.J.: Prentice-Hall, 1969.

———. *The myth of the deprived child*. Englewood Cliffs, N.J.: Prentice-Hall, 1972.

Gleason, H. A. *An introduction to descriptive linguistics*. New York: Holt, Rinehart and Winston, 1961.

Gleitman, L. R., Gleitman, H., and Shipley, E. The emergence of the child as grammarian. *Cognition*, 1972, **1**, 137–163.

Glucksberg, S., and Krauss, R. M. What do people say after they have learned to talk? Studies of the development of referential communication. *Merrill-Palmer Quarterly*, 1967, **13**, 309–316.

———, ———, and Weisberg, R. Referential communication in nursery school children: Method and some preliminary findings. *Journal of Experimental Child Psychology*, 1966, **3**, 333–342.

Golden, M., Birns, B., Bridger, W., and Moss, A. Social-class differentiation in cognitive development among black school children. *Child Development*, 1971, **42**, 37–45.

Goldin-Meadow, S., and Feldman, H. The creation of a communication system: A study of deaf children of hearing parents. Paper presented to the Society for Research in Child Development, Denver, April, 1975.

Goodman, K. S.   Reading: A psycholinguistic guessing game. In H. Singer and R. B. Ruddell (Eds.), *Theoretical models and processes of reading*. Newark, Del.: International Reading Association, 1970. Pp. 259–272.

Gumperz, J. J., and Hymes, D. *Directions in sociolinguistics*. New York: Holt, Rinehart and Winston, 1972.

Haldane, E. S., and Ross, G. R. T. (Eds.), *The Philosophical Works of Descartes*. New York: Dover, 1955.

Hatch, E. The young child's comprehension of time connectives. *Child Development*, 1971, **42**, 2111–2113.

Haugan, G. M., and McIntire, R. W. Comparisons of vocal imitation, tactile stimulation, and food as reinforcers for infant vocalizations. *Developmental Psychology*, 1972, **6**, 201–209.

Hawkins, P. R. Social class, the nominal group and reference. *Language and Speech*, 1969, **12**, 125–135.

Hayakawa, S. I. *Language in thought and action*. (2d ed.). New York: Harcourt, 1964.

Heider, E. R. Style and effectiveness of children's verbal communications within and between social classes. Unpublished doctoral dissertation, Department of Social Psychology, Harvard University, 1969.

―――. "Focal" color areas and the development of color names. *Developmental Psychology*, 1971, **4**, 447–455.

―――, Cazden, C. B., and Brown, R. Social class differences in the effectiveness and style of children's coding ability. Project Literacy Reports, No. 9. Ithaca, N.Y.: Cornell University Press, 1968.

Herman, D. T., Lawless, R. H., and Marshall, R. W. Variables in the effect of language on the reproduction of visually perceived forms. *Perceptual and Motor Skills*, 1957, **7**, Monograph Supplement 2, 171–186.

Hess, R. D., and Shipman, V. Early experience and the socialization of cognitive modes in children. *Child Development*, 1965, **36**, 869–886.

Hill, J. P. (Ed.), *Minnesota symposium on child psychology*. Vol. 2. Minneapolis: University of Minnesota Press, 1969.

Hockett, C. F. Chinese vs. English: An exploration of the Whorfian thesis. In H. Hoijer (Ed.), *Language in culture*. Chicago: University of Chicago Press, 1954.

Holland, V. M., and Palermo, D. S. On learning "less": Language and cognitive development. *Child Development*, 1975, **46**, 437–443.

Ingram, D. Transitivity in child language. *Language*, 1971, **47**, 888–910.

―――. Phonological rules in young children. *Journal of Child Language*, 1974, **1**, 49–64.

―――. If and when transformations are acquired by children. Paper presented to the Georgetown University Round Table, Washington, D.C., March, 1975.

Irwin, O. C., and Chen, H. P. Development of speech during infancy. *Journal of Experimental Psychology*, 1946, **36**, 431–436.

Jacobs, R. A., and Rosenbaum, P. S. *English transformational grammar*. Waltham, Mass.: Blaisdell, 1968.

Jakobson, R. Why "mama" and "papa"? In *Selected writings Roman Jakobson*. The Hague: Mouton, 1962. Pp. 538–545.

―――. *Child language, aphasia, and phonological universals*. Translated by A. Keiler. The Hague: Mouton, 1968.

―――, and Halle, M. *Fundamentals of language*. The Hague: Mouton, 1956.

Jesperson, O. *Language*. New York: Holt, Rinehart and Winston, 1925.

John, V. P. Styles of learning—styles of teaching: Reflections on the education of Navajo children. In C. B. Cazden, V. P. John, and D. Hymes (Eds.), *Functions of Language in the Classroom*. New York: Teachers College Press, 1972. Pp. 331–343.

―――, and Moskovitz, S. Language acquisition and development in early childhood. In A. H. Marckwardt (Ed.), *Linquistics in school programs*. Chicago: National Society for the Study of Education, 1970. Pp. 167–214.

Johnson, D. L. The influences of social class and race on language test performance and spontaneous speech of preschool children. *Child Development*, 1974, **45**, 517–521.

Jones, H. R. The use of visual and verbal memory processes by three-year-old children. *Journal of Experimental Child Psychology*, 1973, **15**, 350–351.

Kaplan, E., and Kaplan, G. The prelinguistic child. In J. Elliot (Ed.), *Human development and cognitive processes*. New York: Holt, Rinehart and Winston, 1971. Pp. 359–381.

Katz, J. J. *The philosophy of language*. New York: Harper & Row, 1966.

————, and Fodor, J. A. The structure of a semantic theory. *Language*, 1963, **39**, 170–210.

Keeney, T. J., Canizzo, S. R., and Flavell, J. H. Spontaneous and induced rehearsal in a recall task. *Child Development*, 1967, **38**, 953–966.

————, and Wolfe, J. The acquisition of agreement in English. *Journal of Verbal Learning and Verbal Behavior*, 1972, **11**, 698–705.

Kelley, K. L. Early syntactic acquisition. Rand Corporation Report No. P–3719, 1967.

Kemp, J. C., and Dale, Philip S. Spontaneous imitation and free speech: A grammatical comparison. Paper presented to the Society for Research in Child Development, Philadelphia, March, 1973.

Kessel, F. S. The role of syntax in children's comprehension from ages six to ten. *Monographs of the Society for Research in Child Development*, 1970, **35**, No. 6 (Serial no. 139).

Kiparsky, P. K. Linguistic universals and linguistic change. In E. Bach and R. T. Harms (Eds.), *Universals in linguistic theory*. New York: Holt, Rinehart and Winston, 1968. Pp. 170–202.

Kirk, S. A., McCarthy, J. J., and Kirk, W. D. *Examiner's manual: Illinois test of psycholinguistic abilities*. (Rev. ed.) Urbana, Ill.: University of Illinois Press, 1968.

Klima, E. S., and Bellugi-Klima, U. Syntactic regularities in the speech of children. In J. Lyons and R. J. Wales (Eds.), *Psycholinguistics papers*. Edinburgh: Edinburgh University Press, 1966. Pp. 183–208.

Koch, H. L. *Twins and Twin Relations*. Chicago: University of Chicago Press, 1966.

Kohl, H. R. *Language and education of the deaf*. New York: Center for Urban Education, 1966.

Kohlberg, L., Yaeger, J., and Hjertholm, E. Private speech: Four studies and a review of theories. *Child Development*, 1968, **39**, 691–736.

Krauss, R. M., and Rotter, G. S. Communication abilities of children as a function of status and age. *Merrill-Palmer Quarterly*, 1968, **14**, 160–173.

Labov, W. *The social stratification of English in New York City*. Washington, D.C.: Center for Applied Linguistics, 1966.

————. *The Study of Nonstandard English*. Urbana, Ill.: National Council of Teachers of English, 1970. (a)

————. The logic of nonstandard English. In J. E. Alatis (Ed.), *20th annual round table*. Washington, D.C.: Georgetown University Press, 1970. Pp. 1–39. (b)

————. *Language in the inner city: Studies in the Black English vernacular*. Philadelphia: University of Pennsylvania Press, 1972.

————, and Robins, C. A note on the relation of reading failure to peer-group status in urban ghettos. *Teachers College Record*, 1969, **70**, 395–405.

LaCivita, A., Kean, J. M., and Yamamoto, K. Socio-economic status of children and acquisition of grammar. *Journal of Educational Research*, 1966, **60,** 71–74.

Ladefoged, P. *Elements of acoustic phonetics.* Chicago: University of Chicago Press, 1962.

Lakoff, R. Language in context. *Language*, 1972, **48,** 907–927.

Lambert, W. E. A social psychology of bilingualism. *Journal of Social Issues,* 1967, **23,** 91–109.

————, and Tucker, G. R. *Bilingual education of children: The St. Lambert experiment.* Rowley, Mass.: Newbury House, 1972.

Langacker, R. W. *Language and its structure,* 2d ed. New York: Harcourt, 1973.

Lantz, D., and Lenneberg, E. H. Verbal communication and color memory in the deaf and hearing. *Child Development*, 1966, **37,** 765–799.

————, and Stefflre, V. Language and cognition revisited. *Journal of Abnormal and Social Psychology*, 1964, **69,** 472–481.

Lee, D. M., and Allen, R. V. *Learning to read through experience.* New York: Appleton, 1963.

Lee, L. *Northwestern syntax screening test.* Evanston, Ill.: Northwestern University Press, 1969.

Lee, L. L., and Canter, S. M. Developmental sentence scoring: a clinical procedure for estimating syntactic development in children's spontaneous speech. *Journal of Speech and Hearing Disorders*, 1971, **36,** 315–338.

Lenneberg, E. H. Understanding language without the ability to speak. *Journal of Abnormal and Social Psychology*, 1962, **65,** 419–425.

————. (Ed.). *New directions in the study of language.* Cambridge, Mass.: M.I.T. Press, 1964.

————. *Biological foundations of language.* New York: Wiley, 1967.

————, and Roberts, J. M. *The language of experience.* Memoir 13, Indiana University Publications in Anthropology and Linguistics, 1956.

Leopold, W. F. *Speech development of a bilingual child: A linguist's record.* Vol. 1, *Vocabulary growth in the first two years.* Vol. 2, *Sound learning in the first two years.* Vol. 3, *Grammar and general problems in the first two years.* Vol. 4, *Diary From age 2.* Evanston, Ill.: Northwestern University Press, 1939, 1947, 1949 (a), 1949 (b).

————. Semantic learning in infant language. *Word*, 1948, **4,** 173–180.

————. Patterning in children's language learning. *Language Learning*, 1953, **5,** 1–14.

Lewis, M., and Freedle, R. Mother-infant dyad: The cradle of meaning. Paper presented to a Symposium on Language and Thought, University of Toronto, March, 1972.

Liberman, A. M. The grammars of speech and language. *Cognitive Psychology*, 1970, **1,** 301–323.

Limber, J. The genesis of complex sentences. In T. E. Moore (Ed.), *Cognition and the acquisition of language,* New York: Academic Press, 1973. Pp. 169–186.

Loban, W. *The language of elementary school children.* Research Report No. 1. Champaign, Ill.: National Council of Teachers of English, 1963.

Loftus, E. F., and Palmer, J. C. Reconstruction of automobile destruction: An example of the interaction between language and memory. *Journal of Verbal Learning and Verbal Behavior,* 1974, **13,** 585–589.

Lovell, K., and Dixon, E. M. The growth of the control of grammar in initiation, comprehension, and production. *Journal of Child Psychology and Psychiatry,* 1967, **8,** 31–39.

Luria, A. R. The directive function of speech in development and dissolution. Part I: Development of the directive function of speech in early childhood. *Word,* 1959, **15,** 341–352.

Lyons, J. (Ed.), *New horizons in linguistics.* Baltimore: Penguin, 1970.

Maccoby, E. E., and Bee, H. L. Some speculations concerning the lag between perceiving and performing. *Child Development,* 1965, **36,** 367–377.

———, and Jacklin, C. N. *The Psychology of Sex Differences.* Stanford, Calif.: Stanford University Press, 1974.

———, Newcomb, T. M., and Hartly, E. L. (Eds.), *Readings in social psychology.* (3d ed.). New York: Holt, Rinehart and Winston, Inc., 1958.

MacDonald, J. W. Review of Sir James Pitman and John St. John, *Alphabets and reading. Harvard Educational Review,* 1970, **40,** 317–325.

Macnamara, J. Cognitive basis of language learning in infants. *Psychological Review,* 1972, **79,** 1–13.

Maratsos, M. P. Decrease in the understanding of the word "big" in preschool children. *Child Development,* 1973, **44,** 747–752. (a)

———. Nonegocentric communication abilities in preschool children. *Child Development,* 1973, **44,** 697–700. (b)

———. Children who get worse at understanding the passive: A replication of Bever. *Journal of Psycholinguistic Research,* 1974, **3,** 65–74. (a)

———. How preschool children understand missing complement sentences. *Child Development,* 1974, **45,** 700–706. (b)

———. Preschool children's use of definite and indefinite articles. *Child Development,* 1974, **45,** 446–455. (c)

McCarthy, D. Language development in children. In L. Carmichael (Ed.), *Manual of child psychology.* New York: Wiley, 1954. Pp. 452–630.

McCarthy, J., and Kirk, S. *Examiner's manual: Illinois Test of Psycholinguistic Abilities* (experimental edition). Champaign, Ill.: University of Illinois Press, 1961.

McCarver, R. B., and Ellis, N. R. Effect of overt verbal labeling on short-term memory in culturally deprived and nondeprived children. *Developmental Psychology,* 1972, **6,** 38–41.

McCawley, J. D. The role of semantics in a grammar. In E. Bach and R. T. Harms (Eds.), *Universals in linguistic theory.* New York: Holt, Rinehart and Winston, 1968. Pp. 124–169.

McNeil, J. D. *The ABC learning activity: Language of instruction.* New York: American Book, 1966.

McNeill, D. The development of language. In P. H. Mussen (Ed.), *Carmichael's manual of child psychology.* Vol. 1. (3d ed.) New York: Wiley, 1970. Pp. 1061–1161. (a)

———. *The acquisition of language: The study of developmental psycholinguistics.* New York: Harper & Row, 1970. (b)

Meadow, K. P. Early manual communication in relation to the deaf child's intellectual, social, and communicative functioning. *American Annals of the Deaf*, 1968, **113**, 29–31.

Menyuk, P. Children's learning and reproduction of grammatical and nongrammatical phonological sequences. *Child Development*, 1968, **39**, 849–859.

————. *Sentences children use.* Cambridge, Mass.: M.I.T. Press, 1969.

————. *The acquisition and development of language.* Englewood Cliffs, N.J.: Prentice-Hall, 1971.

Mervis, C. B., Catlin, J., Rosch, E. Development of the structure of color categories. *Developmental Psychology*, 1975, **11**, 54–60.

Miller, G. A., and Isard, S. Some perceptual consequences of linguistic rules. *Journal of Verbal Learning and Verbal Behavior*, 1963, **2**, 227–228.

Miller, J. F., and Yoder, D. E. Assessing the comprehension of grammatical form in mentally retarded children. Paper presented to the Third Congress of the International Association for the Scientific Study of Mental Deficiency, The Hague, September, 1973.

Miller, S. A., Shelton, J., and Flavell, J. H. A test of Luria's hypotheses concerning the development of verbal self-regulation. *Child Development*, 1970, **41**, 651–665.

Miller, W., and Ervin-Tripp, S. The development of grammar in child language. In R. Brown and U. Bellugi (Eds.), *The acquisition of language.* Monographs of the Society for Research in Child Development, 1964, **29** (Serial No. 92), 9–34.

Moore, C. L., and Retish, P. M. Effect of the examiner's race on Black children's Wechsler preschool and primary scale of intelligence I.Q. *Developmental Psychology*, 1974, **10**, 672–676.

Moore, T. E. (Ed.). *Cognitive development and the acquisition of language.* New York: Academic Press, 1973.

Moores, D. F. Nonvocal systems of verbal behavior. In R. L. Schiefelbusch and L. L. Lloyd (Eds.), *Language perspectives, acquisition, retardation, and intervention.* Baltimore: University Park Press, 1974. Pp. 377–417.

Morse, P. A. The discrimination of speech and nonspeech stimuli in early infancy. *Journal of Experimental Child Psychology*, 1972, **14**, 477–492.

Moskowitz, A. I. The two-year-old stage in the acquisition of English phonology. *Language*, 1970, **46**, 426–441.

Mueller, E. The maintenance of verbal exchanges between young children. *Child Development*, 1972, **43**, 930–938.

Müller, E., Hollien, H., and Murry, T. Perceptual responses to infant crying: Identification of cry types. *Journal of Child Language*, 1974, **1**, 89–95.

Mussen, P. H. (Ed.), *Carmichael's manual of child psychology.* Vol. 1 (3d ed.) New York: Wiley, 1970.

Nelson, K. Pre-syntactic strategies for learning to talk. Paper delivered to the Society for Research in Child Development, Minneapolis, 1971.

————. Structure and strategy in learning to talk. *Monographs of the Society for Research in Child Development*, 1973, **38**, No. 149.

————. Concept, word and sentence: Interrelations in acquisition and development. *Psychological Review*, 1974, **81**, 267–285.

Nelson, K. E., and Bonvillian, J. D. Concepts and words in the 18-month-old:

Acquiring concept names under controlled conditions. *Cognition,* 1973, **2,** 435–450.

————, Carskaddon, G., and Bonvillian, J. D. Syntax acquisition: Impact of experimental variation in adult verbal interaction with the child. *Child Development,* 1973, **44,** 497–504.

New English Bible. Oxford: Oxford University Press, 1970.

Norman, D. A. Rumelhart, D. E., and the LNR Research Group. *Explorations in Cognition.* San Francisco: Freeman, 1975.

O'Connor, N. (Ed.), *Present-day Soviet psychology.* Oxford: Pergamon Press, 1966.

Oller, D. K. Simplification as the goal of phonological processes in child speech. *Language Learning,* 1974, **24,** 299–303.

————, Wieman, L. A., Doyle, W. J., and Ross, C. Infant babbling and speech. *Journal of Child Language,* in press.

Oller, J. W., and Richards, J. C. *Focus on the learner: Pragmatic perspectives for the language teacher.* Rowley, Mass.: Newbury House, 1973.

Olver, R. R., and Horsby, J. R. On equivalences. In J. S. Bruner, R. R. Olver, and P. M. Greenfield (Eds.) *Studies in Cognitive Growth.* New York: Wiley, 1966. Pp. 68–85.

Osborn, L. R. Language, poverty, and the North American Indian. In F. Williams (Ed.), *Language and poverty.* Chicago: Markham, 1970. Pp. 299–247.

Osgood, C. E. Motivational dynamics of language behavior. In M. R. Jones (Ed.), *Nebraska symposium on motivation.* Lincoln: University of Nebraska Press, 1957. Pp. 348–424. (a)

————. A behavioristic analysis. In *Contemporary approaches to cognition.* Cambridge, Mass.: Harvard University Press, 1957. (b)

Osser, H. The syntactic structures of five-year-old culturally deprived children. Paper presented at East Psychological Association Annual Meeting, New York, 1966.

————, Wang, M. D., and Zaid, F. The young child's ability to imitate and comprehend speech: A comparison of two subcultural groups. *Child Development,* 1969, **40,** 1063–1075.

Palermo, D. S. Still more about the comprehension of "less." *Developmental Psychology,* 1974, **10,** 827–829.

Paraskevopoulos, J. N., and Kirk, S. A. *The development and psychometric characteristics of the Revised Illinois Test of Psycholinguistic Abilities.* Urbana: University of Illinois Press, 1969.

Paris, S. G., and Carter, A. Y. Semantic and constructive aspects of sentence memory in children. *Developmental Psychology,* 1973, **9,** 109–113.

Parisi, D. Development of syntactic comprehension in preschool children as a function of socioeconomic level. *Developmental Psychology,* 1971, **5,** 186–189.

Park, T. Z. The acquisition of German syntax. Working Paper, Psychologisches Institut, Univer. Munster, Germany, 1970.

Pavlovitch, M. *Le Langage Enfantin: Acquisition du Serbe et du Francais par un enfant serbe.* Paris: Champion, 1920.

Peisack, E. Relationship between knowledge and use of dimensional language and achievement of conservation. *Developmental Psychology,* 1973, **9,** 189–197.

Peterson, C. L., Danner, F. W., and Flavell, J. H. Developmental changes in children's response to three indications of communicative failure. *Child Development*, 1972, **43**, 1463–1468.

Phillips, J. R. Syntax and vocabulary of mothers' speech to young children: Age and sex comparisons. *Child Development*, 1973, **44**, 182–185.

Philips, S. Acquisition of roles for appropriate speech usage. In R. D. Abrahams and R. C. Troike (Eds.), *Language and cultural diversity in American education.* Englewood Cliffs, N.J.: Prentice-Hall, 1972. Pp. 167–183.

Piaget, J. *Judgment and Reasoning in the Child.* London: Routledge, 1928.

———. *The language and thought of the child.* Translated by M. Gabain. Cleveland: Meridian, 1955.

———. *The language and thought of the child*, 3d ed. London: Routledge, 1959.

———. Development and learning. In R. E. Ripple and V. N. Hardcastle (Eds.), *Piaget rediscovered.* Ithaca, N.Y.: Cornell University Press, 1964.

———. Language and thought from the genetic point of view. In D. Elkind (Ed.), *Six psychological studies.* Translated by A. Tenzer. New York: Random House, 1967.

———. *Six psychological studies.* New York: Vintage Books, 1967.

———. Piaget's theory. In P. H. Mussen (Ed.), *Carmichael's Manual of Child Psychology*, 3d ed., Vol. 1. New York: Wiley, 1970. Pp. 703–732.

———, and Szeminska, A. *The Child's Conception of Number.* Translated by C. Gattegno and F. M. Hodgson. London: Routledge, 1952.

Pitman, Sir J., and St. John, J. *Alphabets and reading.* New York: Pitman, 1969.

Popova, M. I. Grammatical elements of language in the speech of pre-preschool children. In C. A. Ferguson and D. I. Slobin (Ed.), *Studies of child language development.* New York: Holt, Rinehart and Winston, 1973. Pp. 269–280.

Postal, P. *Constituent structure: A study of contemporary models of syntactic description.* Publication 30, Indiana University Research Center in Anthropology, Folklore, and Linguistics. Bloomington: Indiana University Press, 1964.

Pozner, J., and Saltz, E. Social class, conditional communication, and egocentric speech. *Developmental Psychology*, 1974, **10**, 764–771.

Premack, D. Teaching language to an ape. *Scientific American*, 1972, **227**, 92–99.

Prucha, J. Research on child language in East European countries. *Journal of Child Language*, 1974, **1**, 77–88.

Prutting, C. A., Gallagher, T. M., and Mulac, A. The expression portion of the NSST compared to a spontaneous language sample. *Journal of Speech and Hearing Disorders*, 1975, **40**, 40–48.

Quay, L. C. Negro dialect and Binet performance in severely disadvantaged Black four-year-olds. *Child Development*, 1972, **43**, 245–250.

———. Language dialect, age, and intelligence-test performance in disadvantaged Black children. *Child Development*, 1974, **45**, 463–468.

Rasmussen, D., and Goldberg, D. *A pig can jig.* Chicago: Science Research Associates, 1964.

Read, C. Pre-school children's knowledge of English phonology. *Harvard Educational Review*, 1971, **41**, 1–34.

Rebelsky, F., and Hanks, C. Fathers' verbal interaction with infants in the first 3 months of life. *Child Development*, 1971, **42**, 63–68.

Rips, L. J., Shoben, E. J., and Smith, E. E. Semantic distance and the verification of semantic relations. *Journal of Verbal Learning and Verbal Behavior,* 1973, **12,** 1–20.

Rosch, E. H. On the internal structure of perceptual and semantic categories. In T. E. Moore (Ed.), *Cognition and the acquisition of language.* New York: Academic Press, 1973. Pp. 111–144.

Ruddell, R. An investigation of the effect of the similarity of oral and written patterns of language structure on reading comprehension. Unpublished doctoral dissertation, School of Education, University of Indiana, 1965.

Sachs, J. S. Recognition memory for syntactic and semantic aspects of connected discourse. *Perception and Psychophysics,* 1967, **2,** 437–442.

Sapir, E. Language and environment. In D. G. Mandelbaum (Ed.), *Selected Writings of Edward Sapir in Language Culture, and Personality.* Berkeley: University of California Press, 1958. Pp. 89–103.

Sattler, J. M. Racial experimenter effects in experimentation, testing, and psychotherapy. *Psychological Bulletin,* 1970, **73,** 137–160.

Schane, S. A. *Generative Phonology.* Englewood Cliffs, N.J.: Prentice-Hall, 1973.

Schiefelbusch, R. L., and Lloyd, L. L. (Eds.), *Language perspectives—acquisition, retardation, and intervention.* Baltimore: University Park Press, 1974.

Schleicher, A. Some observations made on children. In A. Bar-Adon and W. F. Leopold (Eds.), *Child language: A book of readings.* Englewood Cliffs, N.J.: Prentice-Hall, 1971. Pp. 19–20.

Schlesinger, H. S., and Meadow, K. P. *Sound and Sign.* Berkeley: University of California Press, 1972.

Schlesinger, I. M. Production of utterances and language acquisition. In D. I. Slobin (Ed.), *The ontogenesis of grammar.* New York: Academic Press, 1971. Pp. 63–101.

————. Relational concepts underlying language. In R. L. Schiefelbusch and L. L. Lloyd (Eds.), *Language perspectives: Acquisition, retardation, and intervention.* Baltimore: University Park Press, 1974. Pp. 129–151.

Shantz, C. U., and Wilson, K. E. Training communication skills in young children. *Child Development,* 1972, **43,** 693–698.

Shatz, M., and Gelman, R. The development of communication skills: Modifications in the speech of young children as a function of listener. *Monographs of the Society for Research in Child Development,* 1973, **38,** No. 152.

Shipley, E. F., Smith, C. S., and Gleitman, L. R. A study in the acquisition of language: Free responses to commands. *Language,* 1969, **45,** 322–342.

Shriner, T. H. A review of mean length of response as a measure of expressive language development in children. *Journal of Speech and Hearing Disorders,* 1969, **34,** 61–68.

Shriner, T. H., and Miner, L. Morphological structures in the language of disadvantaged and advantaged children. *Journal of Speech and Hearing Research,* 1968, **11,** 605–610.

Shvachkin, N. Kh. The development of phonemic speech perception in early childhood. In C. Ferguson and D. I. Slobin (Eds.), *Studies of child language development.* New York: Holt, Rinehart and Winston, 1973. Pp. 91–127.

Silverstein, A. (Ed.), *Human communication: Theoretical explorations.* Hillsdale, N.J.: Lawrence Erlbaum Associates, 1974.

Sinclair, H., and Ferreiro, E. Temporal relationships in language. *International Journal of Psychology,* 1971, **6,** 39–47.

Sinclair-de-Zwart, H. Developmental psycholinguistics. In D. Elkind and J. H. Flavell (Eds.), *Studies in Cognitive Development.* New York: Oxford University Press, 1969. Pp. 315–366.

———. Language acquisition and cognitive development. In T. E. Moore (Ed.), *Cognitive development and the acquisition of language.* New York: Academic Press, 1973. Pp. 9–25.

Slobin, D. I. The acquisition of Russian as a native language. In F. Smith and G. A. Miller (Eds.), *The genesis of language: A psycholinguistic approach.* Cambridge, Mass.: M.I.T. Press, 1966. Pp. 129–248. (a)

———. Grammatical transformations and sentence comprehension in childhood and adulthood. *Journal of Verbal Learning and Verbal Behavior,* 1966, **5,** 219–277. (b)

———. Soviet psycholinguistics. In N. O'Connor (Ed.), *Present-day Soviet psychology.* Oxford: Pergamon Press, 1966. (c)

———. Imitation and grammatical development in children. In N. S. Endler, L. R. Boulter, and H. Osser (Eds.), *Contemporary issues in developmental psychology.* New York: Holt, Rinehart and Winston, 1968. Pp. 437–443.

———. Universals of grammatical development in children. In G. B. Flores d'Arcais and W. J. M. Levelt (Eds.), *Advances in psycholinguistics.* New York: American Elsevier, 1970. Pp. 174–184.

———. (Ed.). *The ontogenesis of grammar.* New York: Academic Press, 1971.

———. Cognitive prerequisites for the development of grammar. In C. A. Ferguson and D. I. Slobin, *Studies of child language development.* New York: Holt, Rinehart and Winston, 1973, 183–186.

———, and Welsh, C. A. Elicited imitations as a research tool in developmental psycholinguistics. In C. A. Ferguson and D. I. Slobin, *Studies of child language development.* New York: Holt, Rinehart and Winston, 1973. Pp. 607–619.

Smith, F. *Understanding reading.* New York: Holt, Rinehart and Winston, 1971.

———. *Psycholinguistics and reading.* New York: Holt, Rinehart and Winston.

———, and Miller, G. A. (Eds.), *The Genesis of Language: A Psycholinguistic Approach.* Cambridge, Mass.: M.I.T. Press, 1966.

Smith, M. E. An investigation of the development of the sentence and the extent of vocabulary in young children. *University of Iowa Studies in Child Welfare,* 1926, **3,** No. 5.

Stewart, W. A. On the use of Negro dialect in the teaching of reading. In J. C. Baratz and R. W. Shuy (Eds.), *Teaching Black children to read.* Washington, D.C.: Center for Applied Linguistics, 1969. Pp. 156–219.

———. Toward a history of American Negro dialect. In F. Williamson (Ed.), *Language and poverty.* Chicago: Markham, 1970. Pp. 351–379.

Stodolsky, S. Maternal behavior and language and concept formation in Negro preschool children: An inquiry into process. Unpublished doctoral dissertation, Department of Psychology, University of Chicago, 1965.

————, and Lesser, G. Learning patterns in the disadvantaged. *Harvard Educational Review*, 1967, **37**, 546–593.

Stokoe, W. C. Sign language structure. *Studies in linguistics*, Occasional Papers, 8. Buffalo: Buffalo University Press, 1960.

Strickland, R. The language of elementary school children. *Indiana University School of Education Bulletin*, 1962, **38**, 1–131.

Stuckless, E. R. and Birch, J. W. The influence of early manual communication on the linguistic development of deaf children. *American Annals of the Deaf*, 1966, **111**, 452–462.

Sullivan, M. *Storybook 1A*. (Rev. ed.) New York: McGraw-Hill, 1966.

Tanner, J. M. Growing up. *Scientific American*, **229**, 1973, 34–43.

Snow, C. E. Mothers' speech to children learning language. *Child Development*, 1972, **43**, 549–565. (a)

————. Young children's responses to adult sentences of varying complexity. Paper presented to the 3d International Congress of Applied Linguistics, Copenhagen, August, 1972. (b)

Spence, C. M. An evaluation of the comparison of hearing and deaf subjects to investigate the language-thought question. Unpublished paper, Department of Psychology, University of Washington, 1971.

Spring, D. R. Effects of style of maternal speech on infants' selection of vocal reinforcement. Unpublished paper, University of Washington, 1974.

————. Linguistic stress discrimination in one- to four-month-old infants. Unpublished doctoral dissertation. University of Washington, 1975.

Steinberg, D. D. Phonology, reading, and Chomsky and Halle's optimal orthography. *Journal of Psycholinguistic Research*, 1973, **2**, 239–258.

Stewart, W. A. Urban Negro speech: Sociolinguistic factors affecting English teaching. In R. W. Shuy (Ed.), *Social dialects and language learning*. Champaign, Ill.: National Council of Teachers of English, 1964. Pp. 10–18. (a)

————. (Ed.), *Non-standard speech and the teaching of English*. Washington, D.C.: Center for Applied Linguistics, 1964. (b)

Tatham, S. M. Reading comprehension of materials written with selected oral language patterns: A study at grades two and four. *Reading Research Quarterly*, 1970, **5**, 415–483.

Templin, M. C. *Certain language skills in children: Their development and inter-relationships*. Minneapolis: University of Minnesota Press, 1957.

————, and Darley, F. *The Templin-Darley Tests of Articulation*. Iowa City: University of Iowa Press, 1964.

Trehub, S. E. Infants' sensitivity to vowel and tonal contrasts. *Developmental Psychology*, 1973, **9**, 91–96.

Tucker, G. R. Methods of second-language teaching. *Canadian Modern Language Review*, 1974, **31**, 102–107.

Tulkin, S. R. An analysis of the concept of cultural deprivation. *Developmental Psychology*, 1972, **6**, 326–339.

Turnure, C. Response to voice of mother and stranger by babies in the first year. *Developmental Psychology*, 1971, **4**, 182–190.

Tyack, D., and Gottsleben, R. *Language sampling, analysis, and training*. Palo Alto, Calif.: Consulting Psychologists Press, 1974.

Velten, H. V. The growth of phonemic and lexical patterns in infant language. *Language*, 1943, **19**, 281–292.

Vernon, M., and Koh, S. D. Effects of early manual communication on achievement of deaf children. *American Annals of the Deaf*, 1970, **115**, 527–536.

————, and ————. Effects of oral preschool compared to early manual communication on education and communication in deaf children. *American Annals of the Deaf*, 1971, **116**, 569–574.

Vincent-Smith, L. Bricker, D., and Bricker, W. Acquisition of receptive vocabulary in the toddler-age child. *Child Development*, 1974, **45**, 189–193.

Vorster, J. Mothers' speech to children: Some methodological considerations. Instituut voor Algemene Taalwetenschap, Universiteit van Amsterdam, 1974.

Vygotsky, L. S. *Thought and language*. Translated by E. Hanfmann and C. Vakar. Cambridge, Mass.: M.I.T. Press, 1962.

Wahler, R. G. Infant social development: Some experimental analyses of an infant-mother interaction during the first year of life. *Journal of Experimental Child Psychology*, 1969, **7**, 101–113.

Warren, I. B. The development of the phonological system. Unpublished doctoral dissertation, University of Washington, 1975.

Waterhouse, L. H. Child language acquisition in mother-twin interaction situations. Paper delivered to the Society for Research in Child Development, Philadelphia, March, 1973.

Weinreich, U. Explorations in semantic theory. In D. D. Steinberg and L. A. Jakobovits (Eds.), *Semantics: An interdisciplinary reader in philosophy, linguistics and psychology*. Cambridge: Cambridge University Press, 1971. Pp. 308–328.

Weir, R. *Language in the crib*. The Hague: Mouton, 1962.

Werner, H., and Kaplan, B. *Symbol formation*. New York: Wiley, 1963.

Whorf, B. L. *Language, thought, and reality*. New York: Wiley; and Cambridge, Mass.: M.I.T. Press, 1956.

Wieman, L. A. The stress pattern of early child language. Unpublished doctoral dissertation, University of Washington, 1974.

Williamson, J. V. A look at Black English. *The crisis*, 1972, **78**, 169–185.

Wisland, M. V. (Ed.), *Psychoeducational Diagnosis of Exceptional Children*. Springfield, Ill.: Charles C Thomas, 1974.

Wolff, P. H. The natural history of crying and other vocalizations in early infancy. In B. M. Foss (Ed.), *Determinants of infant behavior*. Vol. IV. London: Methuen, 1966.

Wolfram, W. A., and Fasold, R. W. Toward reading materials for speakers of black English: Three linguistically appropriate passages. In J. C. Baratz and R. W. Shuy (Eds.), *Teaching Black children to read*. Washington, D.C.: Center for Applied Linguistics, 1969. Pp. 138–155.

Yoder, D. E. Evaluation and assessment of children's language and speech behavior. In M. V. Wisland (Ed.), *Psychoeducational diagnosis of exceptional children*. Springfield, Ill.: Charles C Thomas, 1974.

Zakharova, A. V. Acquisition of forms of grammatical case by preschool children. In C. A. Ferguson and D. I. Slobin (Eds.), *Studies of child language development*. New York: Holt, Rinehart and Winston, 1973. Pp. 281–284.

Zigler, E., Abelson, W. D., and Seitz, V. Motivational factors in the performance of economically disadvantaged children on the Peabody Picture Vocabulary Test. *Child Development*, 1973, **44**, 294–303.

———, and Butterfield, E. C. Motivational aspects of changes in IQ test performance of culturally deprived nursery school children. *Child Development*, 1968, **39**, 1–14.

Index